FULL OF LIFE

FULL OF LIFE

A BIOGRAPHY OF JOHN FANTE

STEPHEN COOPER

NORTH POINT PRESS

A DIVISION OF FARRAR, STRAUS AND GIROUX

NEW YORK

North Point Press
A division of Farrar, Straus and Giroux
19 Union Square West, New York 10003

Copyright © 2000 by Stephen Cooper
All rights reserved
Distributed in Canada by Douglas & McIntyre Ltd.
Printed in the United States of America
Designed by Jonathan D. Lippincott
First edition, 2000

Library of Congress Cataloging-in-Publication Data
Cooper, Stephen, 1949–
    Full of life : a biography of John Fante / Stephen Cooper. — 1st ed.
        p.   cm.
    Includes bibliographical references (p.   ) and index.
    ISBN 0-86547-554-7 (alk. paper)
        1. Fante, John, 1909–   2. Authors, American—20th century—Biography.   3.
Screenwriters—United States—Biography.   I. Title.

PS3511.A594 Z62 2000
813'.52—dc21
[B]   99-056197

Grateful acknowledgment is made to Tom Fante for permission to reproduce the photograph on page 53 and to the Regional History Center, Department of Special Collections, University of Southern California, for permission to reproduce the photograph on page 93. All other photographs and art used in this book appear courtesy of Joyce Fante.

For the whole family . . .

CONTENTS

I would rather believe their authority than to believe that of my own eyes.

—Boccaccio, writing of the ancient authors
in *Genealogia deorum gentilium*

"Well, it's not normal. It's like one of them gory stories, it's something that people have quit doing—like boiling in oil or being a saint or walling up cats," she said. "There's no reason for it. People have quit doing it."

"They ain't quit doing it as long as I'm doing it," he said.

—Flannery O'Connor, *Wise Blood*

Oh, the infinitely small in the midst of the infinitely great in this incomparable world. I am glad to be alive again.

—Knut Hamsun, *On Overgrown Paths*

FULL OF LIFE

CHAPTER 1

In the summer of 1960, at the age of fifty-one, John Fante flew from Los Angeles to Rome. The veteran screenwriter had been hired by producer Dino DeLaurentiis to write a story about a modern-day Italian outlaw. Fante knew something about Italian outlaws from his family's history, which had been much on his mind; and since he needed the money— chronically needed the money, the old plight of the artist bringing his talents to market in exchange for one more season's expenses—he came to live in a glorious Renaissance apartment hard by the wall of the Vatican. With a maid who came daily, light from the high windows and keys to a company car, Fante settled into the task of writing.

It was the summer of the Rome Olympics, the year of Fellini's *La Dolce Vita*. As a de facto member of the city's cosmopolitan film colony, Fante divided his days between sieges at the typewriter and the dreaminess of a Roman summer. When he wasn't writing he could be found at a favorite trattoria ignoring doctor's orders about his diabetes, or out at the Capanelle racetrack playing his hunches, or wandering the catacombs that webbed the underside of the city, refining his sense of mortality.

Fante's eldest son, Nick, nineteen and full of piss, came to stay for several weeks. But Nick's visit was soon over, and before long Fante was nearing the end of the script, the conclusion of which was to feature a miracle. In order to write the scene accurately Fante drove south in September to witness the feast of the liquefaction of the blood of San Gennaro, patron saint of Naples, an exhibition of faith which strengthened his own, if only in God's everlasting strangeness. As he motored back to Rome afterward the first tang of fall was in the air. Soon he would be returning home to his wife and three younger children and their sprawling California ranch house on Malibu's Point Dume. First, however, there was another pilgrimage he needed to make; so he headed east toward the mountains of the Abruzzi. With each kilometer of his ascent into the Central Apennines the air grew lighter, the same lightness that for eons had sustained the Abruzzi's inhabitants, the legendary highland people of Fante's ancestry.

The mountains were full of legends. One of the oldest of these told of a *ver sacrum*, literally and in general a spring sacrifice of firstlings, but in this case a sacred vow by the forefathers during an evil time to send their firstborn sons beyond the known territories. And so the tribes had branched out in search of new homelands, Fante's ancestors the Peligni to the rugged peaks and valleys of the Majella Range. There they settled into an austere independence amidst rocky soil, frequent earthquakes and savage winters. Despite the region's harshness, in time the remote reaches of the Abruzzi proved attractive to a breed of outsiders as well. As early as the second century B.C. in the aftermath of the Punic Wars, the defeated forces of Hannibal took to the mountains, where they remade themselves into roving highwaymen. The cutthroat descendants of these brigands were still roaming the high passes early in the new millennium, when the most celebrated poet of the Abruzzi, Ovid of Sulmona, died. In a land filled with stones—"a nightmare of stones," in the words of one traveler— the word sorcerer of *Metamorphoses* had been powerful enough to make the stones speak, to transform men into birds and maids into poplars, but not to rid the land of its bandits. Nor had the notorious *banditti* disappeared by the thirteenth century, when another Abruzzese poet, Francis of Assisi's biographer Blessed Thomas of Celano, gave voice to the sinner's fear on the Last Day in the grave cadences of "Dies Irae," a poem that could have been written only by someone who knew the terrors of earthquake and ambush:

> *Dies irae, dies illa,*
> *Solvet saeclum in favilla . . .*

> That day of wrath, that dreadful day,
> Shall heaven and earth in ashes lay,
> As David and the Sybils say. . . .

> Now death and nature with surprise
> Behold the trembling sinners rise
> To meet the Judge's searching eyes.

Soon a staple of the Latin requiem mass, this dark Catholic vision remained rooted in the region's sensibilities even as modern times dawned. But it did not supplant the pagan taste for magic also favored by the folk of the Abruzzi. Rather, the primitive vigor of superstition intermingled with the primal fears of Christianity. For protection against bandits a right-thinking peasant might as soon make the fork-fingered sign of the evil eye as invoke the saints in heaven. And just in case—for in the Abruzzi the saints could be as fickle as the gods, and a man had to look out for himself—there was always near to hand in a boot top or a pant leg one's favorite short-bladed, razor-sharp dagger.

John Fante's forebears were known as stout peasant workers as far back as the early 1700s, when the name *Fante* first appeared in the parish archives of Torricella Peligna's church of San Giacomo Apostolo. The first Fante to distinguish himself was one Tommaso Fante, long remembered for his excellence in making fireworks. Only one other member of the Fante line would enter Torricellan memory, this one through his participation in the Abruzzi's long and bloody history of brigandage.

Domenico Fante, known as Mingo, served "with valor and honor" in the army of the Spanish Bourbons during the pivotal decade of the 1850s. By that time the House of Bourbon had ruled the Kingdom of Two Sicilies for over a century, maintaining power by pitting the hated middle class, who could read and thus think, against the illiterate peasantry with its twin allegiances to Cross and Crown. To enforce this split, Bourbon strongmen had long exploited the Abruzzese inclination toward brigandage by paying the mountain desperadoes salaries and even pensions for helping to keep the populace in check. So that when the egalitarian Risorgimento, or war of national unification, forced the Bourbon king Francis to flee Naples, the loyalist Mingo Fante took to the highlands. Like men in defeat since the time of the Carthaginians, there he assumed the life of a highwayman-rebel to await the return of his king. In the end, however, his king remained dispossessed; the Risorgimento triumphed; and Mingo Fante, an unwitting peasant royalist who in his way lived up to the name of Bourbon—which to this day denotes an obstinate clinging to the old order—was apprehended, tried for treason, and hanged. Owing to aggressive enforcement of laws enacted after the 1861 unification of Italy, the brigands of the Abruzzi soon came to exist mainly in tales told around the hearthstone at night.

One spinner of such tales was a nephew of the hanged Mingo, an itinerant knife grinder by the name of Giovanni Fante. Inclined to the outdoors because of a shrewish wife and a love of claret, the unlettered Giovanni had about him the sensibility of a poet. To his son Nicola Pietro, born in 1878, Giovanni passed on stories of Uncle Mingo's heroism, and in time a congenital taste for wine. From his mother Maria Andrilli the boy inherited a hot temper, a sharp tongue and a tendency toward braggadocio. Nicola showed little interest in tracing his vagabond father's footsteps, however, displaying instead the far more down-to-earth talents for stonework and masonry. The problem with having such skills in an impoverished village like Torricella Peligna, however, was that little opportunity existed to ply them. By the time he was nearing twenty Nicola Fante was growing restless to improve his chances in life, not least of all for the sake of a girl.

In the late 1890s the whitewashed walls of Italian villages were festooned with broadsides for the steamship lines that were then ferrying waves of emigrants across the Atlantic: North German Lloyd, Guion,

Cunard, Inmon and Hamburg-American, among others. Like millions of others throughout Europe, vast segments of Italy's young and able-bodied peasantry were being drawn to emigrate. Nicola Fante was no exception. In order to make enough money to marry he would try his luck across the ocean.

His first bid to succeed overseas took him to Argentina. But the once thriving economy of the South Río de la Plata had bottomed out, and Nicola managed only to eke out a living for a year or so. Then, inexplicably, his eyesight began to fail and he made arrangements to return home. Halfway across the Atlantic, after a mysterious sailor urged him to bathe his eyes in the waters of the middle passage, his vision was miraculously restored. But the triumph of his homecoming turned into a tragedy when he discovered that the girl he had left behind had been betrothed to another man. Though the girl fell to her knees to plead for Nicola's forgiveness, his heart had been hardened. But that was not the worst of it. In Nicola's absence his father had decamped for the United States, leaving a wife and young daughter to fend for themselves. Nicola looked around him, and what did he see? Infidelity, hysteria, destitution . . .

And yet that was where John Fante was driving now, to his father's birthplace in Torricella Peligna. Over the years he had heard his father Nick tell the story of his Argentine odyssey many times. It was part of the old man's legend of himself, the automythography of a confirmed embellisher of facts. In that respect his father's tale-telling had been one of the earliest models for John Fante's own bent for fiction, a way of remaking the world. This trip to his father's birthplace was, among other things, an effort to see with his own eyes the place that had produced such a specimen of manhood, the redoubtable Nick Fante—*Papa*—the single most important man in John Fante's life. According to the road map he was almost there.

Whatever he might have expected, when John Fante drove into Torricella Peligna in the fall of 1960, he found a poor village perched atop a cold and stony mountain, inhabited by suspicious crones in black shawls and hostile youths idling about the piazza. His father's hometown struck him as a wretched and unlivable place, at once familiar and as foreign as a bad dream. Except for the donkeys straining under their great loads, no one appeared to be employed. Indeed, the donkeys turned out to be the most interesting aspect of the village's life, striking in Fante an unexpected chord of sympathy. There was something about them, a look of timelessness in their eyes, which suggested how little life had changed in the world where his father had been born. The sight was too depressing for words. Having seen his father's birthplace, the stone walls and dusty streets, Fante too wanted out. He turned the car around and headed back down the mountain.

Driving back to his apartment in Rome, Fante was unhappy not for the townsfolk of Torricella Peligna but for their long-suffering beasts of burden. With those dumb animals he felt a bond. He had spent the last two months writing a movie story involving an outlaw's quest for sacred jewels, dagger-point dealings on the Neapolitan black market, and a vulgar miracle of uncoagulating blood, all for the sake of a buck and at the whim of a meddling producer. It was a far cry from the kind of writing he had done in the years when he was young and broke, when he had written straight from the heart. Although he had included a secondary character in the script who was loosely based on the legendary Uncle Mingo, the story had little to do with the truer dramas of family lifelines and artistic desire that compelled him, stories of fathers and mothers and sons and brothers—and the alter-ego writer always at their center—that characterized his life's best work.

In 1960 John Fante had no way of knowing that that work, most of it already behind him and long forgotten by the world, would one day be regarded as deserving a place among the finest achievements of twentieth-century American writing, would even come to be compared favorably to masterpieces of world literature written by the likes of Knut Hamsun and Dostoevsky. Fante's first two novels, *Wait Until Spring, Bandini* and *Ask the Dust*, had been out of print for more than twenty years; he had not published a first-rate short story in over a decade; and the distractions of Hollywood, as always, still beckoned. But although he would not live to hear the praise of a later generation of critics, or to realize that his novels and stories would still be speaking to readers and writers in a dozen languages around the world long after his death in 1983, Fante was not finished yet. Screenwriting was one thing, but his fiction was another, and it was his fiction that as late as 1995 would lead Nathanael West's biographer Jay Martin to name Fante "our major meditative novelist." Strange praise, it might seem, for the chronicler of such sagas of the lower depths as *The Road to Los Angeles* and *Ask the Dust*, but praise befitting the author whose works also defined the exalting strangeness of youthful desire. Before the critics rediscovered him, however, it was this rough aspect of Fante's work that would compel other writers to champion his legacy. As one of the first of many younger authors to acknowledge Fante's influence, renegade street poet Charles Bukowski would be moved to call *Ask the Dust* "the finest novel written in all time," a sentiment echoed by no less an aficionado of Fante's place and era than the screenwriter Robert Towne, who would affirm that "[i]f there's a better piece of fiction written about L.A., I don't know about it." But in late 1960 all such words of praise were still in the distant and unknowable future.

Back in Rome it was full autumn, cold and storm sodden, trattoria weather now more than ever. Having finished the script but still on contract and collecting his salary, Fante was drinking again, and his blood sugar was running high. When his left foot began to bother him he curtailed his long walks about the city and started staying in his room with its high ceilings and classical painter's light. But he was no longer in the mood for things classical much less legendary, neither outlaw tales nor Ovid's changelings nor least of all Blessed Thomas of Celano with his dirge from the Mass for the Dead.

With an effort Fante roused himself. In the last days of his stay in the Eternal City he cut out rich foods and all the good local wines from his diet and set about preparing for the trip home. He missed his wife's bed and the night sounds of the Pacific. As his father had done more than sixty years before him, John Fante was looking west.

Nick Fante sailed into New York Harbor aboard the Red Star Line's S.S. *Friesland* on December 6, 1901. Moving through the inspection lines at Ellis Island, Nick produced a document that had been notarized in Denver one year earlier attesting to Giovanni Fante's financial ability to sponsor his son Nicola's immigration to America. To one inspector after another Nick showed his life's savings of $20, demonstrated an ability to read and write rudimentary English, and displayed the scar over his right eye noted in his passport (*"Segni particolari: Cicatrix in fronten"*). Although possession of a passport exempted him from the shorthand status accorded Italian immigrants arriving without papers—w.o.p.—his deep-set eyes, his accent, even the cut of his mustache branded Nick a wop in the curt American view. And New York City was certainly curt. In the days ahead as he walked the city streets Nick may have been handed a pamphlet like the one widely circulated by the Daughters of the American Revolution urging him to "Give up all 'campanilish' prejudices," "Treat women and children very kindly," and "Throw away all weapons you may have, [especially the] knife with a blade about the length of a man's middle finger which the Italian brings with him from his native land." Such advice could only remind Nick that he was in a strange and foreign place. He wasted no time getting out of New York, and headed by train for Colorado.

With a turn-of-the-century population of 134,000, the mile-high city of Denver boasted 149 churches, 80 schools, 8 hospitals, 9 libraries, 11 banks, and 334 saloons. After a long and exhausting search, it was in one of those saloons in the Italian quarter of North Denver that Nick finally found his father. There have been more touching reunions. It was unclear whether Giovanni had suffered a financial reversal since signing the notarized *Consenso d'espatrio* the previous year, or simply exaggerated his circumstances in the first place. But when Nick tracked him down, the old man was laid out on a bench in the back room of a dingy drinking establishment looking neither prosperous nor sober. *"Figlio mio,"* he said upon seeing his son, *"tiene un scuta?"*—"You gotta buck?" At which Nick pushed him roughly, threw him over his shoulder and carried him out into the Rocky Mountain winter.

For the next several years Nick lived with his father off and on, first in Denver, then in Boulder, working diligently between bouts of fist-fighting drunkenness to shape an American future. In Boulder several of the great buildings of the University of Colorado were under construction—the library was completed in 1903, and the Guggenheim Law Building was begun not long thereafter—making brick- and stoneworkers valued tradesmen. Nick's efforts to bring his mother Maria and sister Giuseppina, known as Pepina, to join him and his father were stymied, however, as immigration rules fluctuated: at least once Maria made it as far as Ellis Island only to be detained for several weeks over some confusion about her passport, then returned to Italy. In Maria's absence Nick's father Giovanni continued his vagrant ways as the tippling walkabout knife grinder. Five years after arriving in Boulder, Nick was living alone at 713 Pearl Street, just off today's modern outdoor mall; but by the following year, 1907, the City Directory listed him and his parents, John and Mary, all by their Americanized first names and all occupying the same second-story flat.

Reunited though they were, theirs was by no means a family free of tension. For one thing, there was no real Italian quarter in Boulder, not like the one in North Denver, and the shrill voice of Nick's mother could often be heard disturbing the peace of Pearl Street as she hurled violent Abruzzese imprecations upon the godforsaken land to which she had reluctantly moved. Despite her name change, the vitriolic Mary Fante never acclimated to life in America. On the contrary, she fought the New World with her every Italian fiber, and when her husband or Nick or, what was worse, when both of them had gotten enough wine in their bellies to fight back, the uproar emanating from their upstairs apartment was enough to test the tolerance of even the most forbearing American neighbors.

None of this improved the family's standing in a community poorly disposed to the Fantes' kind of people in the first place. Of the various immigrant groups that came to labor on the railroad, in the mines or, like Nick, in construction in turn-of-the-century Colorado, Italians were among the least welcome. Many native Coloradans, themselves of largely northern European extraction, held Italians in lower regard than even the Irish because of the melodramatic Italian brand of Catholicism, flamboyant Italian food preferences, and notoriously demonstrative Italian ways—in short, because Italian customs differed from the safely familiar. True, there had been no recent lynchings of Italian nationals in Boulder as there had been in Denver less than a decade earlier, when the mob shouted, "Death to the Dago!" The 1890s had been the decade when Protestant Coloradans by the thousands joined the anti-immigrant, anti-Catholic American Protective Association, a grassroots movement whose popularity prefigured an even darker turn in Colorado politics to come during the 1920s. All the same, even in the years between these two eras, a palpable undercurrent of anti-Italian sentiment was part of the atmosphere Nick Fante breathed, a bad situation made only worse because of the ways in which he and his parents seemed to live down to so many stereotypes.

When it came to making a living, however, Boulder was a good place for a stoneworker to be. Even the town's name suggested the local importance of stone. In contrast to the brooding Majellas, which overshadowed the economic stagnancy of Torricella Peligna, the dramatic Flatirons towering up west of Boulder were reminders of the area's bustling quarries and thus a symbol of the burgeoning economy. On the strength of a $300,000 bequest by Boulder banker Andrew J. Mackey upon his death in 1907, in fact, the University of Colorado's greatest single building project to date was about to commence, and Nick Fante was looking forward to all the advantages of a long and steady job.

When a discontented adoptive stepdaughter of Mackey's contested his will, however, plans for the auditorium's construction were put on hold, and Nick found himself drifting back to North Denver's Italian section, where a man could feel more at home over a flagon of Chianti and a good bitter Toscanelli cigar. In Denver, with time on his hands and no steady attachments, Nick Fante was about to take the next logical step for a man of his age and experience, a step that would lead to the creation of an American-born namesake for that knife-grinding ne'er-do-well, his father.

Bordered roughly by 38th Avenue on the north, the South Platte River on the south, Inca Street on the east and Pecos Street on the west, Denver's Italian quarter was home to a vibrant community of new Americans hailing largely from the lower half of Italy's boot. There, amidst all the other small but well-kept homes along the pleasant tree-lined streets, John Capolungo, a tailor whose family hailed from the province of Potenza in the lower Italian region of Basilicata, had settled with his wife Louise and their eight children at 3104 Osage Avenue.

Before coming to Denver the Capolungos had been parishioners at

Chicago's Church of the Assumption, where in 1899 Mother Frances Xavier Cabrini had opened one of the country's first Italian parochial schools. Later canonized the first American saint, Mother Cabrini was a prime influence on John and Louise Capolungo's fifth child, the Chicago-born Mary Concepta. Even as a young woman the pious Mary could often be seen walking the four blocks from her home to mass at North Denver's Our Lady of Mount Carmel Italian church on Navajo Street.

Like Chicago's Church of the Assumption, Our Lady of Mount Carmel was staffed by Italian priests of the Servite order, whose business it was to know their parishioners so as to serve their needs and ultimately cultivate their eternal salvation. Certainly they knew soft-eyed, soft-spoken Mary Capolungo, who, still unmarried in her mid-twenties, was showing signs of a vocation. Mary's devotion to Saint Teresa, her attachment to the rosary, and the joy she took in adorning the altar with flowers from her own garden all marked her as a promising candidate for the novitiate. The good fathers and sisters of Our Lady of Mount Carmel knew of these things, and they agreed that Mary would make a fine nun, a quiet one, to be sure, perhaps a contemplative to be cloistered in silence. What they didn't know was that Providence had other plans for saintly Mary Capolungo, in the ungodly person of Nick Fante.

In two published stories, an important unpublished manuscript and a screenplay written for Orson Welles, John Fante would repeatedly fictionalize the meeting, courtship and marriage of his parents. In each version of these events the traditional Italian theme of the dominant, aggressive male and the submissive, nonerotic female is treated with Fante's trademark irony, so that the strutting figure of the suitor is comically deflated by his own overbearing ways, while in her passivity the figure of the future wife and mother is revealed to be the wiser and more reliable of the two. Fante had behind him—indeed, inside him in his inherited perspective—the Latin culture of an overwhelming masculine mystique, which cast mothers and wives alike in the strange role of Madonna. Women were to be worshipped for their likeness to Mary, the virgin mother of God—but they were often also walked on. Thrust into the role of *mater dolorosa*, the suffering mother, a woman was likely to respond by repudiating her sexuality and embracing a life of sublimation spent serving the men in her life, sons included. Romantic courtship was a trap door.

It is unknown how Nick Fante met Mary Capolungo. Perhaps, as in Fante's story "A Kidnapping in the Family," their first encounter was at a street parade celebrating the feast of San Rocco, with brass bands, sacred statues and a wine-enamored Nick Fante pursuing the demur but fascinated Mary all the way to her mother's house. Or perhaps they met in a more sober moment, as in "A Nun No More," while Nick laid bricks at the house next door to the Capolungo home on Osage Street. Or then again, maybe they met as Mary passed her uncle Rocco Capolungo's saloon on Navajo Street, a mere block from Our Lady of Mount Carmel. There would have been music in that saloon, and Nick liked to sing, and all three of Mary's brothers were musicians, levelheaded professionals who hoped that their sister would come down from the clouds and find a man to marry, preferably someone with a solid trade.

Speculation aside, it is a fact that on Monday, June 29, 1908, Nick Fante and Mary Capolungo were united in holy matrimony at Our Lady of Mount Carmel Church. Family lore would later have it that the ceremony took place on a Monday rather than on the traditional Saturday because Nick had disappeared on a drunk, showing up two days late. The couple stood before the altar that Mary had often adorned with flowers in the days when her heart had been set on becoming a bride of Christ. As the words were spoken, angels and saints looked on from numerous Italianate statues and paintings: Saint Francis, Saint Anthony, Saint Dominic, Saint Joseph, the Archangel Michael and the virgins Cecilia and Lucy. As if to edify wives-to-be, Saint Lucy held before her a saucer, and on it her eyes, plucked from their sockets in the course of the martyrdom she chose to suffer rather than surrender the treasure of her virginity. Presiding over all in the gilded alcove above was the Blessed Virgin Mary, Mother of God and Queen of Heaven, scepter in one hand, Holy Infant in the other, floating atop an ethereal cumulus cloud.

At the priest's prompting the groom responded, "I do." Chances are that his virgin bride was crying, and that Nick could have used a drink. But having come this far he was determined to live up to his duty. Within days he had seen to the necessary details of his wife's first conception. Immortality was bound to follow.

CHAPTER 2

On April 8, 1909, nine months and nine days after their wedding day, Mary presented Nick with a baby boy. The child was named John after Nick's father Giovanni, and Thomas after the ancestral pyrotechnician. Sharp knives and fireworks: the associations suggested the pride that Nick felt at taking his place in the generation of generations. He now had a family of his own. In time this family would provide John Fante with the warring elements of his temperament and a wealth of conflicted characters, the raw materials he would spend the greater part of his life reconceiving in fictional terms.

John Thomas Fante was baptized on June 13 at Our Lady of Mount Carmel. Acting as godparents were Mary's beloved sister Marie Antonette, known as Nettie, and her husband Nicholas Campiglia, a genial harpist who had once toured the Colorado mining camps in a trio with his two musician brothers. Afterward there was a gathering at the house where the young Fante family lived at 3439 Osage Street, to this day the only house on the block faced in stone. Advertising himself as a contractor in the Denver City Directory, Nick was using both his hands and his head to gain the attention of his community and a share of its bustling trade. Despite his taste for wine and a weakness for bar fights, Nick was becoming a man of substance, in proof of which he could point to the stonework of his house and a firstborn son now duly christened.

Within a year of John's birth Nick moved his family to another rental home at 3510 Pecos Street. According to the United States Census of 1910, the family kept a boarder, a sixteen-year-old hod carrier from Italy who could neither read nor write English, while in the backyard they kept four farm animals, most likely a pair of laying hens, a rooster and a goat. The census also indicated that in the previous year Nick had been out of work for a total of eight weeks. Such slack time was one of the risks of self-employment in a fresh-air trade like masonry, which depended on the extremes of Rocky Mountain weather. Those extremes, and the attendant inconsistencies in subsequent years' income, contributed to Nick's restlessness during this time. In 1912 the Fantes moved back to Osage Street, to 3143, and in 1913 they moved again, across the street to 3116, establishing a pattern of residential instability that would continue through John's earliest years, and resume when he became a young man.

Early photos of John show a round-cheeked alert child with slightly prominent ears and bright, expressive eyes. In one formal portrait he sits propped up in a white lace gown at about the age of one, his fair reddish hair cut in bangs. In another, taken a couple of years later, he is seated with his scuffed button shoes crossed at the ankles, smiling broadly for the camera despite a Sunday-best suit and itchy-looking long wool stockings. A snapshot taken about the same time shows John standing upright, straw hat in hand, in the grip of a friend of his father's. Of the eight men in this photograph, all are wearing serious suits and ties except Nick, whose work clothes and cigar radiate insouciance; but from the tilt of their hats and the glint in their eyes all look to be having an equally high time initiating Nick's boy into the world of men.

Even in dirty work clothes Nick Fante knew how to fit in with men dressed for business. "He was a handsome man for one thing," recalled

Fante's cousin Edward Campiglia. "And secondly he had a golden voice that commanded you to listen." Combined with his boastful bent and artisan's expertise, these gifts benefited Nick during the years he was shuttling between Denver and Boulder on various construction jobs. As early as 1907, for example, while directing the construction of the dressed stone church for Boulder's Sacred Heart of Jesus parish, Nick had impressed the pastor, Father Agatho Strittmatter, a Benedictine priest with friends in high places. Similarly, through his work on Mackey Auditorium, the architectural showpiece of the University of Colorado which was finally being erected, Nick befriended prominent Boulder attorney Mike Rinn, the same man who had held up construction for so long representing the banker Mackey's stepdaughter in her lawsuit contesting his bequest.

In short, despite his rough edges Nick Fante knew how to charm. Decades later surviving relatives would agree in the main that as a cousin, an uncle, a father-in-law and a father, Nick could often be a disgrace to the family. But he was also capable of cultivating people's trust and even affection, and in the years ahead his contacts with men like Father Agatho and Mike Rinn would prove valuable in his effort to rise in the world.

Meanwhile, Nick's father Giovanni was growing old. He still wandered the streets of North Denver crying, "Knives! I sharpen knives!" But increasingly he pined for his grapevines in Torricella Peligna, and his beloved sheep. He was very fond of his grandson Johnnie, and he would often take the boy for long hand-in-hand walks under the roaring 16th Street viaduct and along the muddy banks of the South Platte searching for mushrooms. These excursions usually ended with Mary Fante or Nick's mother, known as Grandma Mamona, chasing after them for fear that the old man would take Johnnie off roaming; for in his last years when Grandpa Giovanni grew nostalgic on wine, he would drift away from Denver's North Side in search of his phantom flock, ending up lost and hungry and at the mercy of the police as far north as Longmont, twenty miles away.

In fact, Grandpa Giovanni had good reason to long for escape. Ever since her admission to the United States in 1904, Grandma Mamona had never ceased vilifying the country that had once turned her away, this stupid, accursed land where the children were animals, where old age was scoffed at, and where the speech emanating from native gullets grated like the grunting of pigs. Under the lash of his wife's abuse for tricking her into coming to this stink hole, America, the old man sought solace in the company of his young and attentive grandson.

Sitting under the corner gas lamp on summer evenings, Grandpa would tell Johnnie stories about the wild mountain outlaws of the Abruzzi, just as he had told Johnnie's father when he was a boy. Then he would take his grandson's hand and point to the sky, saying that the moon was a hole in the floor of heaven, and that after he died he would peer down from there to make sure Johnnie was being good. The old man's stories made a deep impression. Giovanni Fante died when John was seven, and for many years afterward the boy would look to the moon and remember his grandfather's promise.

By this time the young Fante had acquired a brother and a sister, Pete and Josephine, born in Denver in 1911 and 1914. (Tommy, the last of the four Fante children, would be born in Boulder in 1917.) The larger family clan had also expanded, for living near the Fantes in their tight-knit neighborhood were many Capolungo and Campiglia cousins. One of these cousins, Mario Campiglia, was John's age exactly, and the two boys were inseparable. They were also so physically alike that they came to be known as the Twins. But the affinities between John and Mario ran deeper than that, accounting for a serious crisis later on.

John's attachment to his cousin Mario had to do with the wrenching contrast between their respective home lives. It was no secret among the extended families that tensions were often high at the Fante house. Among other things, Nick's reputation as a provider—he made as much as eight dollars a day when working—was blackened by his proclivities for cards and liquor and God only knew what other vices. Many were the evenings when Nick was absent from the house and Mary, wearied from the children and bearing the marks of Nick's abuse, had to rely on her relatives, notably her sister Nettie, to put dinner on the table. Aunt Nettie was Mario's mother, and as John well knew she and Uncle Nicholas didn't fight as his own parents did, and their children always had plenty to eat.

A snapshot of nine Fante, Campiglia, and Capolungo cousins from this time is revealing. While John stands at the rear of the group looking guardedly bemused, his grinning double, Cousin Mario, sits beside Mario's big sister Josephine Campiglia, who cuddles both a dog and a kitten. The worn shoe soles of both brother and sister indicate that theirs was far from an affluent life, but the Campiglia children look openly happy. By contrast, a certain distance is betrayed in the faces and postures of John and his siblings Peter and Josephine, each of whom occupies a space apart from the rest of the group.

Gentle Nick Campiglia the musician made no more money than did gruff Nick Fante the stoneworker, and with ten mouths to feed the Campiglia family's expenses would have been nearly twice those of the Fante household. And yet by dint of sober hard work and goal-oriented frugality, Nick Campiglia would soon manage to move his family away from North Denver's boisterous Italian ghetto to the Park Hill section on the city's East Side, a peaceful neighborhood made desirable in part by the fact that few other Italians lived there. Soul mates John and Mario were thus separated from each other at a highly impressionable age. The separation widened when Nick Fante relocated his family yet again, this time out of Denver to a cheap rental house in Boulder at 1743 Walnut Street, thirty miles distant. And then suddenly the separation was final, for as Mario walked home one day from altar-boy practice at Saint Philomena's in East Denver, he was run over by a car and killed.

In keeping with Italian custom, before the funeral John viewed his cousin's corpse laid out in a coffin in the parlor of his aunt and uncle's house. The image of his double lying dead before him would haunt him for a long time afterward. In the short story "One of Us," written more than ten years later, Fante would dramatize the effects of Mario's death on himself and his family, employing the fictional guise of the family Toscana to explore through this crisis the mysteries of identity and grief.

When a telegram arrives at the Toscanas' Boulder home with word of cousin Clito's death in Denver, Mamma Toscana clasps young Mike to her bosom and refuses to let him go, for Clito was the very likeness of Mike. "But Mamma," Mike protests, "I'm not the one that's dead! See?" As witness to this scene of tearful extravagance Mike's big brother Jimmy is a clear-eyed narrator, but he can't help also witnessing his father's dry-eyed response. Not surprisingly, Papa declines to attend the funeral, but when Uncle Frank, Clito's "gentle and generous" father, is the only one who doesn't cry throughout the long day of mourning, the question of paternal emotion grows only more troubling. Through it all Jimmy watches Mike watching Uncle Frank's impassive face until the younger boy can no longer refrain from asking why he doesn't cry. "I am crying, Mike," Uncle Frank answers, but before Mike can make sense of this answer Mamma sends him outside for his impertinence. Mike is soon joined by Uncle Frank and the two walk away without telling anyone where they are going. Not until Jimmy goes looking for them are the story's contrapuntal tensions of life and death and identity and otherness finally brought together, for he finds Mike in an ice-cream booth at the corner drugstore drinking a malted milk, "sucking it down greedily," while across from him Uncle Frank sits with his face in his hands, "great tears rolling off his cheeks and falling on the table as he watched Mike sucking down the malted milk."

The relation of this fiction to the facts of John Fante's life is compelling. Growing up poor in North Denver, Johnnie and his cousin Mario were virtually identical, inseparable but for the divergent lives laid out for them by their fathers: while one father sacrificed to better his family, the other indulged himself. When the Campiglias moved to East Denver, John must have felt Mario's absence keenly, but at least he had the comfort of knowing that his double still lived with a gentle and generous father in a fine home on the far side of town. When Mario died, however, the young Fante's sense of loss must have been acute, for this was his other half, his Twin. Reimagining the aftermath of his cousin's death in "One of Us," John Fante the man would stand outside himself in order to glimpse the story's vision of an unselfish father, but for an accident of heredity his own. In that respect "One of Us" can be seen, narrowly but legitimately, as artful wish fulfillment. More to the point, transforming wishes and fears and the tangle of memory into shining works of the imagination—that was what fiction was for.

But Fante's wishes had their own way of enduring. More than twenty years after Mario's death the *San Francisco Chronicle* ran a profile of Fante to coincide with the publication of *Dago Red*, his 1941 story collection which included "One of Us." In this profile the up-and-coming young author seems to have been at pains to convey a public persona closer to the undying soul mate whom he carried within than to the real John Fante himself. For as a boy, the article stated matter-of-factly, Fante

> lived for ten years just off Denver's fashionable East Side, ran with the sons of English, Irish, Swedes, rarely saw another Italian boy. Italians in Denver live for the most part on the middle-class North Side, where they used to bicker occasionally over secret imports of "Dago Red" during prohibition. Fante scarcely knew about the bootleggers.

In fact, by the time the Volstead Act was ratified by Congress in 1920 to enforce Prohibition, the Fantes had been living in Boulder for almost five years. There in his father's basement John had opportunities galore to learn all about Dago Red. More to the point, before his family moved to Boulder John lived off Denver's fashionable East Side only in his wishes, and ran with the sons of fathers more emotionally giving than his own only in his dreams. "One of Us" belies these abiding fantasies; moreover, the story's title suggests a nettlesome question: *Which* one of us? Another way of asking which is, Why me?

Nick Fante moved his family to Boulder in 1915, gaining some distance from his disapproving in-laws and increasing his chances for steady work. In the wake of that move Nick did three things that would prove important both to the family and to John's future as a writer: he joined the Elks Club, built the new Sacred Heart of Jesus grammar school, and became an American citizen.

Now designated City of Boulder Landmark L-92-3, the handsome brick building housing the old B.P.O. Elks Lodge at 2045 13th Street was dedicated in 1904, part of the national upsurge in fraternal organizations in the early part of the century. Inside, members gathered to shoot pool, play cards, smoke and imbibe while maintaining their civic good name by observing Flag Day, sponsoring Big Brothers and pursuing other activities designed "to quicken the spirit of American patriotism." All of this appealed to Nick Fante, who was looking for not only an atmosphere of masculine conviviality but also a leg up in the world. As a Catholic and an alien, moreover, Nick was drawn to the Elks because unlike their Masonic and Odd Fellow counterparts the B.P.O.E. discriminated only against blacks. And last but not least, the Exalted Ruler of the Boulder Elks Lodge was none other than Nick's colorful litigator friend, Mike Rinn.

With his own golden voice and silver tongue Nick soon learned to join in the amateur poet Rinn's famous and frequent toasts "To Our Absent Brothers," helping to spread good cheer among his fellow Elks. True, he was away from home almost every night of the week, prompting Mary to worry and youngest son Tommy to imprint in his memory the number 101, which his mother often had him phone in an effort to get Nick to show his face at home. When that effort failed, as it often did, oldest son John would be sent to try to pry his father from the smoky, boozy retreat, the kind of place John would also come to love later in life.

Aside from such unpleasantness for his family, Nick's involvement in the Elks did afford certain advantages. For a new resident of the town, and all the more so for an alien, ties developed with such pillars of the community as Mike Rinn and Boulder businessman Martin Reinert over a standing game of pinochle and a decanter of sipping whiskey could amount to a great deal indeed. Then as now it did not hurt to have as a friend a resourceful and energetic lawyer who shared one's tastes for a good time and who knew how to finesse the enforcement of certain niggling laws. Too, although Nick did not often go to work in a suit and tie, he was more than willing to dress up when the occasion called for it, and the expert haberdashers at Martin Reinert's downtown Hub Clothing House stood ready to oblige.

One such occasion occurred on September 16, 1916, when Nick donned vest and tie to join Father Agatho Strittmatter for the blessing of the site of the new Sacred Heart of Jesus School, on Mapleton Avenue between 13th and 14th Streets. While three priests chanted the sacred invocations, Nick stood by with one hand on a hoist, ready to set the cornerstone in place. The day marked the start of a new era in the lives of Boulder's Catholics, and it was celebrated with both religious solemnity and patriotic cheer, as afterward the parish community posed for a group portrait spangled with American flags. In the center of the front row knelt seven-year-old Johnnie Fante, flag in one hand and his father's hat in the other. Within a year the boards beneath his knees would form the ground floor of a three-story white brick building built by his father and housing the school all four Fante children would attend through their respective eighth-grade graduations. Renamed Saint Catherine's, this school would figure prominently in *Wait Until Spring, Bandini*, the 1938 novel in which Fante would grapple with the problem of a son's feelings for a father much like Nick Fante. Needless to say, those feelings were mixed.

Whatever else he might make of his father later in life, holding his father's hat on that September day in 1916 John must have seen Nick Fante as a big, important man, expertly swinging the great stone into place and then standing up there beside God's holy men. It stands to reason that Nick must have felt much the same way about himself. After all, he could take pride in the fact that he had wasted no time establishing himself in Boulder. Unlike his father, Nick Fante nursed no regrets about leaving the old country behind. Now that he had found his place in America, this was where he would stay.

On July 6, 1918, Nick filed his Declaration of Intention to become an American citizen. Eighteen months later, on January 3, 1920, he took the next step in the process, raising his right hand to take the Oath of Allegiance and swearing to defend the Constitution of the United States against all enemies. Signing his Petition for Naturalization were witnesses Agatho Strittmatter, identified as clergyman, and Martin Reinert, merchant, impressive evidence that Nick Fante was no mere wop bricklayer but a man among men to be reckoned with.

It is unknown what occurred in the ensuing year to necessitate a pair of substitute witnesses on the actual day of Nick's naturalization. But on January 3, 1921, Father Agatho and Martin Reinert were absent from the proceedings at the downtown courthouse, their places taken by one Joe Minici, shoemaker, and another Ralph Perry, shoe shiner. The judge signed the order admitting Nick's petition, and the ceremony was over. Outside, the cold stole your breath away.

Six months later, at the stroke of midnight on June 29, 1921, a torch-waving mob descended on downtown Denver's Rivoli Theater, scattering pamphlets and demanding the reengagement of a certain movie. According to the pamphlets, *The Face at Your Window* showed "the hooded figures of the knights of the Ku Klux Klan riding to the rescue and . . . the final triumph of decent and orderly government . . . over the alien influences now at work in our midst." The mob action worked. Enjoying a successful second run, *The Face at Your Window* helped to usher in the new day then dawning in Colorado. The fear and hatred that had combined to ignite the mob's torches that night were about to take over the Mile High City's municipal government, its police force and the general tenor of public discourse, making a run at the state legislature as well. The young John Fante would be marked indelibly by this poisoned atmosphere, as would the fiction he would later write.

Much of the harm occurred in Fante's encounters with neighborhood bullies like the young Eddie Cox of Fante's story "Hail Mary." In that story Fante dramatized the anti-Catholic animus at the heart of the anti-alien hysteria then sweeping Colorado. Remembering how he used to pass the Protestant Eddie Cox every morning on the way to school at St. Catherine's, the adult narrator of "Hail Mary" recites the gruesome litany of accusations that would pour through Eddie's teeth, of priests eating nuns' babies, drinking the blood of young girls, and performing human sacrifices at mass. For as long as he can contain himself the boy withstands this abuse like a good Christian. But when Eddie calls the Blessed Virgin "a whore like all Catlickers," his young victim makes him pay by knocking his teeth out and smashing his nose.

Colorado's turn-of-the-century cultural politics illuminate the anti-Catholic and anti-Italian themes that permeate so much of Fante's work. As has been mentioned, 1890s Denver had already witnessed the ominous rise of the American Protective Association, with its spearheading efforts to boycott Catholic businesses, blackball Catholic candidates for public office, and railroad the passage of a convent inspection law. In the early years of the 1920s the next generation of reactionary Coloradans was flocking to join the sheeted fold of the Ku Klux Klan. In Colorado, in fact, as in few other regions of the country, the brunt of Klan hatred fell less upon the state's black and Jewish minorities, whose relatively small numbers were concentrated in Denver, than on the quarter million Catholics spread throughout all sixty-three counties. Given a total population of just under one million, this was a sizable minority, dangerously large in the febrile minds of those who were shouting for "100 Per Cent Americanism!"—the rallying cry of the revitalized Ku Klux Klan. As recently as the early years of the century the Klan had been little more than a moribund curiosity of the Deep South. But thanks in large part to a mounting backlash against the great transatlantic migration in which Nick Fante had taken part, membership in the Invisible Empire was mushrooming nationally. The Klan's man in Colorado was Dr. John Galen Locke, a failed physician and rumored abortionist who was also a master recruiter, directing Klan activities statewide from his private offices in Denver. Grand Dragon though he was, the Machiavellian Locke managed to maintain a public image of moderation, avoiding charges of personal bigotry from the very groups whose targeting he oversaw.

Of those groups the Catholic Church was viewed in the most lurid light, all the more so because its largely immigrant constituency was not of the acceptable Anglo-Saxon variety. Depicted as an oily foreign presence bent on subverting the American way of life, the Church was rumored to be engaged in a secret program of infiltration of the country's most cherished institutions—its neighborhoods, its local governments, its schools—all in the cause of ultimate world subjugation. Considered especially vulnerable to the Babylonian Whore's unholy agenda were the children of right-living Americans. In the apocalyptic vision of one Klan drumbeater foreseeing the nightmare of papist takeover, "there would be a string of beads around every Protestant child's neck and a Roman Catholic catechism in its hand. 'Hail Mary, Mother of God,' would be on every child's lips, and the idolatrous worship of dead saints a part of the daily program."

It is in this light that the story "Hail Mary" helps us to understand the years leading up to the resuscitation of the Colorado Klan in the 1920s. These were the years when the impressionable Fante was daily traversing the ten-block-long gauntlet between his house and the Sacred Heart school. During this time he was also learning how easily the rising undercurrent of contempt for all things Catholic could break out in actual anti-Catholic incidents—hate crimes, they would be called today—thanks to the real-life likes of Fante's fictional Eddie Cox. Because of this pervasive prejudice parochial schools were a haven and the first choice of families like the Fantes, who labored under the triple burden of religion, ethnicity and class. That the Fantes' deepening poverty was a direct result of Nick's self-centered improvidence could only confirm the widely held view of the Italian male as a debauched immoralist given over to his lower instincts and thus a drain on, and a danger to, the public weal.

Under the direction of Galen Locke the Klan would achieve its ascendancy in Colorado in the mid-1920s. During John Fante's childhood in the late teens and early twenties, however, the atmosphere in Boulder was already thick enough with suspicions of Romanist atrocities, immigrant intrigue, and Italian outlawry to make an alert first-generation Italian-American boy acutely aware that he was an object of fear and hatred in the eyes of a significant segment of his hometown's population. In a world of Catholics and non-Catholics, wops and real Americans, the poor—like himself—and the monied, Fante was coming to know who he was by the way other people regarded him. More often than not, and too often to be forgotten as he grew older, that knowledge was a grave and painful wound.

John was enrolled as a first-grader at the Sacred Heart school in the fall of 1915. His teachers were Sisters of the Blessed Virgin Mary, no-nonsense midwesterners wearing long, flowing habits and wielding sharp hardwood rulers. His classmates, including a handful of fellow Italians, were mostly the children of teamsters, miners, garagemen, firemen, and laborers both skilled and unskilled. One boy, however, came from a family that had prospered in business, and with this tall blond German the short freckled Italian became friends.

Paul Reinert was the grandson of Nick's fellow Elk Martin Reinert, the prominent store owner who would sponsor, and then skip, Nick's naturalization. A good friend throughout grade school and beyond, Paul grew to know well how sensitive Johnnie could be about his family background. On the few occasions over the years that he saw Fante at home, Paul found himself ill at ease because of a palpable feeling that Nick Fante resented the boys' relationship. As he later described the situation in his office as the President Emeritus of St. Louis University, Father Paul Reinert, S.J., recalled that in those years Nick "was drinking, and I think that was the biggest reason why John never encouraged me to come over.

. . . Home was, in a way, the last place he wanted to go, and he always welcomed the opportunity to . . . get away from the house."

Reinert's sense of Nick Fante's resentment squares with the characterization of Svevo Bandini in *Wait Until Spring, Bandini*. There Arturo's father is described as "highly sensitive to the distinction of class and race, to the suffering it entailed, and he was bitterly against it." Sad to say, Nick Fante often made a difficult social and economic situation worse by the way he comported himself, drinking to excess and getting in fights in public and at home. None of this was lost upon John. As can happen, however, instead of abjuring the example he despised, the young boy was impelled perversely to behave in ways not unlike those of old Nick himself. At an early age Fante took to carrying himself with a certain pigeon-toed swagger, as if daring all comers to put up their dukes and find out why. And according to Paul Reinert, John got in fights, lots of fights. "He was a dogfighter," Father Reinert recalled nearly eight decades later:

> He'd kick and bite and . . . whatever it took. Part of it was he was so small. He probably was never fighting anybody that was his size. He was always a small guy and so he felt that he had to use every trick he could. He had that kind of a temperament. If he was mad at you, boy, he was mad and anything would go. And I think he had just seen so much fighting at home, and just didn't have the sense that most people live peacefully.

Such scenes would appear repeatedly in Fante's later autobiographical fiction. Perhaps the best example is the story "The Odyssey of a Wop," in which Fante traces the passing of a violent temperament from barroom brawler father—who bites the ear off an antagonist—to playground fighter son—who fights so much and so well that he grows to relish the smack of fists against bone as "fun." In this story the violence is directed outward against the racist name-callers of the time, those who made the mistake of using the hated epithets wop and dago. However, in an unpublished story, "My Father and My Brother, Dirty Fighters," Fante made it clear that he was also an authority on the ways violence could turn inward on a family. In either case, the dogfighter's bent that the young John Fante inherited from his father would remain with him throughout the years. Sometimes he would put it to positive use, as when he harnessed its energy to write stories about hot-tempered characters and their hot-blooded families; at other times he would surrender control and the fight that was inside him would be unleashed on others who did not always deserve it; and sometimes he would effectively beat himself up. One way or the other it had to come out: in furious accounts or in fury.

By 1920 Nick had moved the family from Walnut Street to another cheap rental at 959 Arapahoe Road. The house had no indoor toilet or bath and only a coal-burning stove for heat, all the more reason during frigid winter nights for John, Pete and Tommy to let their mutt Rex join them in the one bed they shared. Next door at 957 was a small general store, while across the street stood a truck farm and a private fish hatchery. Out back behind the house, past the coal shed and the outhouse, Boulder Creek tumbled through a broad pasture, freezing in the winter and thawing in the spring. Out there in the summer Fante took the lead among his gang of neighborhood boys, organizing ball games, building tree houses and swimming naked in the creek. Eight decades later a former member of the Creekside Gang, Jack Keeley, would remember Fante for his athletic grace and mischievous nature, which often led him to bait his pious but explosive younger brother Pete into uncontrollable fits of anger. When one of these outbursts occurred within sight of their little dark-eyed sister Josephine, she would run and tattle on John, who would escape with his pals to Boulder's Isis Theater to lose himself in the silent jungle adventures of Tarzan, played by the inimitable Elmo Lincoln, or the Wild West romances of Tom Mix, Buck Jones and Hoot Gibson.

Such all-American boyhood idylls were one thing, but the realities of life at 959 Arapahoe were another. With his father's bad habits regularly draining the family pocketbook—Nick smoked at least five ten-cent cigars a day and played a regular losing hand of poker at the Elks Lodge—household tensions over money remained high. Mary often could not afford the modest two-dollar monthly tuition charged each student at Sacred Heart, so she would send pathetic partial payments of a dollar or two skimped from other necessities. To offset the mounting debt Nick would sometimes grudgingly agree to do work around the parish, laying a concrete floor in the rectory's garage, for example—only then to resent

Father Agatho for not paying him. When Mary dared express her anxiety over the tuition, Nick would bluster and fume about the church's debt to him, threatening to yank the goddamn kids out of Sacred Heart and send them to public school. But to Mary this prospect verged so close on blasphemy that despite her meek and generally ineffective way she always persisted until she had succeeded in convincing Nick that the children must continue at the Sisters' school; and so they did.

Mary's successes in this struggle only ensured that the financial pressures would continue, and it was on her that the burden was heaviest. In two stories, "Bricklayer in the Snow" and "Charge It," both later incorporated into *Wait Until Spring, Bandini*, Fante would give a withering suggestion of how his mother suffered owing to the family's chronic shortage of money. In the fictional version of events lifted from his family's life, Fante depicted the humiliation Mamma endures at the hands of the niggardly Mr. Craik whenever she enters his store to beg for a few potatoes or a cheap cut of beef. But the actual owner of the store next to the Fantes' house was apparently a "friendly, generous" man named Roy Clapp who "was liked by everyone." Although he was angry at Nick for not keeping up with his bills, Clapp was never known to refuse Mary Fante the things she needed. Eventually, Nick was engaged by Clapp to build a brick chimney in order to balance the books, but it was only a matter of time before the grocery debt began to climb again, a festering issue over which Mary, not Nick, paid the long-term emotional price.

Remembering Nick Fante many years later, Jack Keeley tempered his praise with criticism: "He was a good bricklayer and had plenty of work. Too bad that he spent so much on booze." Asked point-blank about his feelings toward the Fante children's father, Keeley was more forthcoming. "I never liked their dad. He was real mean to them [and] he had a terrible temper. [He] was all right to them as long as he was sober. But the man drank quite a lot. [He] was rough with them at times. He used to throw things at them and kick them. . . . He was especially kind of that way with John."

Just as blunt in her assessment of Nick was his niece Della Minici (Friedman), the daughter of Nick's sister Pepina and her husband Joe Minici, the shoemaker. "He was a mean old man," Mrs. Friedman recalled of Nick in 1996. "And my dad didn't care for him at all. He wouldn't let my mother see too much of [the Fante family] because [Nick] was just kind of an abusive fellow."

Nor did John himself mince his words when late in life he described his father. "He was very abusive, cruel and cold," he told an interviewer in 1978. "There were scenes between my mother and father that were just brutal. And I couldn't bear to write them. I toned them down. My father was in many ways a beast."

Seething with resentment at the vicious circle of his father's selfishness, his mother's suffering, and the poverty at the center of it all, Fante vented his anger by staging neighborhood wrestling matches in which he pitted himself against the son of Roy Clapp the grocer. Though tall and athletic, Bob Clapp consistently came out the loser in these contests owing to the ferocity of Johnnie's attack. But the consoling sweetness of such victories was only temporary. Fifteen years later Fante would still be nursing his resentment when he came to write *Wait Until Spring, Bandini*. There in Chapter 4 Arturo refuses to spare his mother the humiliation of going next door to beg for food, hating the grocer Craik as much as his mother fears him, "that skunk, always asking him if his father was drunk or sober, and what did his father *do* with his money, and how do you Wops live without a cent." Turning away from his mother, Arturo rejoins a snowball fight between two teams of neighborhood boys, including Bobby Craik, the grocer's son, on the opposing side. "I'll get you, you dog," Arturo thinks. "Arturo kicked a stone from the frozen earth and shaped it within a snowball. The Craik boy was fifty feet away, behind a tree. He threw with a frenzy that strained his whole body, but it missed—sailing a foot out of line."

In a world where God can be a dog—"*Dio cane*" is Svevo Bandini's blasphemous curse—the dogfighter does not shrink from fighting dirty. But if he misses in one way, he hits home in another, for the writer's words are stones too, stones of another kind thrown backward through the years at the memory of his pain and forward through time as well, to the moment of our reading and further still into the future of readings yet to come.

In the group photo of Sacred Heart altar boys taken when John was close to eighth-grade graduation, his are the only hands not elevated in the sanctioned steeple-to-heaven position. If he was beginning to demur to the more outwardly rigorous forms of Catholic observance, there can be no question that during the crucial era of his earlier childhood he had embraced both the forms and the faith of his church. When later he came to write about the sacramental milestones and ceremonial paces of a well-trained Catholic boyhood—in stories like "First Communion," "Altar Boy," and "The Road to Hell," among others—Fante would be full in the godless thicket of his early twenties. Those boyhood experiences would thus reemerge in his fiction highly ironized, indeed, all but sent up in some cases as the cast-off superstitions of an earlier, more gullible age but not something the writer could be imagined to hold serious truck with anymore. But Fante could never have written those stories had he not at one time known what it was to believe with a child's fully rounded belief. After all, this was the same John Fante who through forty-six years of marriage would insist to his wife that as a boy of nine one night at the foot of his bed he had witnessed an apparition of the Virgin Mary.

Together with his intelligence and potential for leadership—and despite his wild fighting streak—the light of his faith attracted the attention of his teachers, who saw signs of God's holy calling. In "Big Leaguer," Fante would make sad comedy out of the efforts of one such nun, who sees in Jimmy Toscana the raw but moldable material of a priest. The irony turns on Jimmy's romantic misunderstanding of Sister Agnes's attentiveness as she helps him compute his batting average—"Oh, she was keen!"—for what she really wants to do even while flattering him with comparisons to the great St. Louis Cardinal slugger Rogers Hornsby is talk about his vocation to the priesthood.

Nearing the end of his time at Sacred Heart, Johnnie Fante was thinking less of his soul than of certain other verities; as we learn of Arturo in Wait Until Spring, Bandini, "After his twelfth year the only things in life that mattered were baseball and girls." But someone, a nun, probably Sacred Heart's Sister Mary Ethelbert, had noticed the inclination John showed for higher things as well, and she had conveyed her observations to the parish pastor. Father Agatho, in turn, had passed the good word along, until it reached the attention of certain people in Denver on the lookout for Catholic boys of high promise.

In the municipal elections of May 1923, one month before John would graduate from eighth grade, Benjamin F. Stapleton, a Democratic protégé of Dr. John Galen Locke and member No. 1,128 of the Denver Klavern of the KKK, was swept into the mayor's office of the Mile High City. The hateful sentiments expressed by the return appearance of *The Face at Your Window* two years earlier were now being enacted by popular vote. It would not be a good time to be Italian and Catholic and poor in a Colorado public high school. And so when upon graduation from Sacred Heart John was favored with acceptance into Regis High, the pricey Denver prep school run by priests of the Society of Jesus, Nick Fante swallowed his pride and worked out a deal, so much brickwork in lieu of so much tuition. It had been one thing for John to spend his grade-school years under the nuns of the Blessed Virgin Mary, who, no matter how many knuckles they busted, were still known to coddle their charges. It would be something else for him to spend the next four years under the Jesuits.

CHAPTER 3

John arrived at the stately hilltop campus of Regis High School and College on September 4, 1923. For fourteen years he had known only the strife and tension of home. Now all the first-day uncertainties of a boy leaving home were generating new tensions as he and his father made their way across the manicured quad toward the imposing four-story edifice of Main Hall. Over the doors was an inscription, RELIGIONI ET BONIS ARTIBUS. Far from the world of childhood, John would spend much of the next four years inside this building dedicated to the Catholic mysteries and the liberal arts; but first he had to endure the unexpected ordeal of parting from his father. If we can believe the fictional version of this moment written ten years later, it was the first time John cried for any reason but a licking. And then he turned to enter the great double doors and the strange new world beyond.

Fante dramatized this farewell and its aftermath in his short story "The Odyssey of a Wop." Asked during the school registration process to state his parents' birthplaces, the narrator tries to obscure the facts of his heritage by claiming that his father was born in Buenos Aires. John may not have used this particular subterfuge on entering Regis, but he did use another, declaring the year of his birth as 1910 instead of 1909. It was a curious lie, an all but unnoticeable disguise, but one he would maintain well into his adult years; and yet his motive for adopting it remains a mystery. Whatever the reason, it seems that he needed some imaginative distance from the facts of his life, and so he recorded this first instance of fictionalizing himself. It would not be the last, or the boldest.

Try as he might to sidestep his origins, John would soon learn that certain inescapable parallels thereto were reflected in the very history of his new school. After defeating the Bourbon Kingdom of Naples in 1860, the government of national unity seized religious houses throughout southern Italy in retaliation for their support of the monarchy. Banished by the same forces that had executed Nick Fante's great-uncle Mingo, a handful of Neapolitan Jesuits sailed for the United States, their mission to found the first Catholic institution of higher learning in the Rocky Mountain region. For the next half century Sacred Heart College would remain under the jurisdiction of the Jesuits' Dispersed Province of Naples, a Far West outpost of certain Old World traditions and sensibilities. Though it was renamed in 1921 after the French Jesuit Saint Jean Régis—consider the narrator's wish in "The Odyssey of a Wop" to pass off his Italian surname as French—the school to which the naturalized Nick Fante sent his American-born son in 1923 had behind it a foreign past which to John was distinctly, even achingly, familiar.

John would also learn the deeper history of Jesuit schooling as he became familiar with the life of Saint Ignatius Loyola, founder of the Society of Jesus and a significant influence on John's future development. Shot through the legs at the battle of Pamplona in 1521, the pleasure-loving Basque nobleman had come under the spell of a book of saints' lives during his recuperation. So inspired was he by the stories of faith in that book that following his recovery the swaggering aristocrat soldier was reborn a fervent missionary and champion of youth. In time the educational system he founded would span the globe in a network of schools dedicated to the formation of young Catholic men through a code of physical, intellectual and spiritual rigor, all For the Greater Glory of God.

Ad Majorem Gloriam Dei. In its essentials, this code was at the heart of the life into which John was now entering as a freshman at Regis High. From dormitory to washroom to chapel to refectory to classroom to gymnasium to study hall, it was a life lived in common and according to a rule that was not far removed from the monastic. Luxuries were rare, women nonexistent, and the days full of hard work and high expectations. Still, John got off to a good start. He did well enough in his classes and he made new friends, glory to God or not. Viewed as "a scrappy little fellow but . . . a guy you liked to be around," John wasted no time in impressing his classmates with his double-edged tongue—he fast earned the reputation of having a word for everything—and his anything-goes athleticism.

John was one of the fastest runners in his class, but he was not fast enough to catch up with the carload of hooded figures who stole onto campus the night of November 10, 1923. With Paul Reinert and a group of other outraged boarders John helped chase the intruders off, but not before a wooden cross had been erected and set ablaze. In fact, the flames John watched reddening the sky came from but one of eleven crosses ignited throughout greater Denver that night in a synchronized exhibition of the Klan's new claw hold on power. Ominously, this brazen act of terror elicited not one word of protest from City Hall.

The incident was an exception to the norm of Regis's peaceful self-containment, and a reminder of why that quiet was so closely guarded. Isolated from the mainstream of secular Denver, John and his classmates were being taught to live up to the Ignatian ideal of *contemplatio in actione*, contemplation in action, a way of being in but not of the world. Undergirding this ideal was the school's curriculum, built on the three pillars of Christian Doctrine, Latin and English. Four years' immersion in this course of study was meant to give every Regis graduate a lifelong grounding in matters of moral, historical and scientific substance, as well as aesthetic style. But given the energies of boys in the roil of adolescence—John first among equals in many ways—a measure of discipline was needed to ensure compliance to the high-minded Jesuit program.

This discipline was established in the school's guiding principle that

Regis teachers stood *in loco parentis*, where by parent was meant authoritarian father. In short, the school's faculty had license to inflict so much "corrective" corporal punishment. Most of this work was left by faculty priests to the scholastics, young Jesuits in training who did much of the teaching, coaching and mentoring. Clad like priests in cassock and collar and addressed by the boys as "Father," each scholastic was entitled by Jesuit tradition to the same respect as were his priestly superiors; but in some cases respect shaded into fear. Typical was one scholastic by the name of Benson, remembered by a classmate of John's as especially "hard-nosed." This Benson was "a big, tough guy, and he used a lot of physical violence. Slapped the hell out of us and knocked us down. I remember John ran afoul of him on several occasions. Talking in chapel, or being late for study hall . . . The guy always seemed like he was around."

In this respect Regis was Fante's home away from home, as resonant with the smack of paternal authority as was the house on Arapahoe. Not surprisingly, in later years Fante would remain unsentimental about his years at Regis. Most of the time he would remember being miserable there, chafing at the discipline and the regimentation, and longing, oddly enough, to be home. At least at home the knocks were all in the family, and he could risk defying his father, up to a point. At Regis, by contrast, Fante learned to take what he had to take at the hands of this or that "father," so that when the bell rang at the end of the school day he was primed to release his pent-up frustrations in the organized violence of sports.

One of the smallest in his class—as a grown man he would list his height as five feet four, or five feet three when he was being honest— Fante made up for his size with his natural athleticism and ferocious competitive streak. At Regis he played all three major seasonal sports, excelling in football and baseball. In basketball his height kept him from advancing beyond the B team, but in football he eventually started at quarterback. His gridiron exploits were regularly lauded in the campus newspaper, *The Red Jug*, which noted his flair for the dramatic forward pass and head-butting plunges through the line. Fante was the team leader, and his controlled explosiveness "presented many thrills to the spectators." But he could also lose control of himself. In an intramural baseball game one day Fante, a cagey left-handed pitcher who could also hit and run well, flew into second sliding hard. The baseman had words for Fante, "dago" among them; and suddenly, as team captain Paul Reinert later recalled, "John went after this guy, and we all had to pull them apart. He had a quick temper, just a flash. And so you didn't cross him and walk away, because he'd be after you."

In addition to team sports, Fante found two other ways to focus his energies at Regis, both relatively individual pursuits. The first was in the campus gym, where a senior student of the college, Pedro Quintana, had started a boxing society. There John came to train under the popular featherweight, who, fighting under the professional name of Eddie Mack, was earning a reputation by winning Saturday-night club fights against larger, heavily favored opponents. Like Fante a small man and cocky but self-conscious enough about his foreign-sounding name to maintain an alternate public identity, Quintana-Mack helped John refine his mauler's style, teaching him the value of timing his punches, and showing him how by overcoming others a man could transcend himself.

The second way Fante discovered to focus his energies was considerably less violent and more inward: he took to keeping a scrapbook. Later in life Fante would write often and well about sports and the sporting passions in stories such as "Big Leaguer," "The Odyssey of a Wop," "The Road to Hell," "One-Play Oscar" and "In the Spring," as well as in several novels. Long before he began to write, however, he was filling page after page of his high-school scrapbook with news accounts of football games, baseball races, basketball championships and boxing matches, interspersed with action shots of his many heroes: Ty Cobb, Tris Speaker, Grover C. Alexander, George Sisler, Walter Johnson, Ernie Shore, Carl Mays, Babe Ruth and Christy Mathewson from baseball; Red Grange and a gallery of collegiate All-American footballers; and others from the worlds of basketball, boxing and the martial arts.

Physical immersion in athletics was one important way Fante sought to prove himself. In the long run, however, the attention he focused on his scrapbook would prove equally important, if not even more so, for in cutting and pasting and putting it all together he was learning something vital about how raw experiences could be reimagined and arranged on the pages of a book into stories that moved him and thus mattered. Significantly, this first effort to put key elements of himself into a book was not limited to his enthusiasm for sports. Keepsakes of other interests and activities were also included, two of which in particular—a commemorative holy card and a reserved-seat ticket stub—reveal much about Fante's development while at Regis.

Illustrated with a silhouette of radiant chalice and communion host, the autographed holy card Fante saved in his scrapbook memorialized the ordination and first mass of Father Bernard J. Murray, S.J. Father Murray was Regis's popular young principal and moderator of athletics, and as such an important influence on Fante in both his sporting and spiritual development. It was Father Murray who named Fante during his junior year Captain of the Guard of Honor, an athletic achievement society. More to the point, during his sophomore and junior years Fante increasingly felt called to serve God in the priesthood, a direction in which the affable Murray certainly encouraged him, if only by example. Like the sports-minded Sister Agnes of "Big Leaguer," Father Murray was living proof that the religious life could also be a vigorous life, as full of baseball and football as it was of benedictions and vespers. Soon John was planning to continue his studies after graduation at the Jesuit novitiate in Florissant, Missouri, filled with a sense of vocation which only the life of writing could ever replace.

Another sign of the spiritual direction John's life was taking at this time was the ticket stub preserved in his scrapbook. John had used this ticket to attend a three-day retreat at Denver's City Auditorium Theater in the spring of his junior year. Devoted to the theme of "Youth," the retreat was conducted by the Reverend Daniel A. Lord, S.J., a prolific author and charismatic retreat master whose appearances before sodalities across the country in the 1920s and 1930s attracted droves of young Catholics eager to hear his optimistic message of faith in their ability to live up to Christ's example. More than simply an inspiring speaker, Lord was also a trail-blazing film critic who had traveled to Hollywood the year before to work as a consultant on Cecil B. DeMille's *The King of Kings*, then filming on Catalina Island. Such diverse experiences made Lord a living example of the Jesuit ideal of detached engagement, in the world but not of it; and with his gift for words and warm sense of humor, he conveyed to Fante something of lasting value.

In short, Lord offered his audiences a simplified version of the Ignatian method of active contemplation. While his eerie opposite on the religious lecture circuit of the mid-1920s—the Klan-sponsored "ex-nun" Mary Angel—was horrifying the gullible at Protestant revival tent meetings with lurid tales of papist abominations, Father Lord was reminding his listeners of that still inner place each of them could achieve in the midst of a chaotic world. Like dreaming, he assured them, meditation was a natural impulse—and who knew more about dreaming than young people? Neither education nor long training was needed to reach a point where it became easy to keep God in mind, and thus "to walk with mind and heart in the company of the world's savior."

Unlikely as it may seem given Fante's pugnacious temperament and frequent need for the corrective rod of discipline, this was an attractive message for a dreamer like Fante. In fact, the intensity of this young man's inner creative life would soon match the intensity of his pulses, his nerve life of muscle and bone. The importance of Jesuit meditation practices in John Fante's life and future art must thus not be underestimated. As critic Jay Martin has recently observed, in grammar school Fante learned "something simple about devotional practices; but during four years at Regis . . . he would have absorbed the formal habits of mind that are encompassed by [Ignatius of Loyola's] *Spiritual Exercises.*"

Published in 1522, this little book formalized an approach to meditation which would not only underpin the Jesuit way of living but also influence an important literary tradition. Emulated in hundreds of other meditation manuals following its appearance, the *Exercises* inaugurated a widespread upsurge in the practice of meditation, so much so that the effects were felt far beyond strictly religious contexts, and nowhere more so than in certain forms of literature. The dramatic structure of such literature, whether a sonnet by a seventeenth-century metaphysical poet such as Donne or Herbert or Crashaw, or a novel or short story by John Fante, is essentially the same as the structure of the traditional Ignatian meditation. Typically initiated by the so-called composition of place, a remembered mental drama is conjured up, turned under the imagination's critical focus, and concluded with a moment of enlightenment. Moreover, the focused memory need not be explicitly religious in nature, but may be "about" anything, baseball or bricklaying or dinner-table bickering just as well as confession or first Holy Communion. Foregrounding

Fante's debt to this Catholic tradition of meditation, Martin highlights what other critics have failed to see, namely, Fante's place within a discernible literary tradition. Martin's conclusion is a strong, even startling one: "If Eliot and Stevens are our major meditative poets, Fante is our major meditative novelist."

Martin correctly surmises that Fante would have "absorbed" certain Jesuit habits of mind rather than learned them outright, for in fact there was no formal instruction in the Spiritual Exercises for high-school students at Regis, such instruction traditionally being reserved for committed aspirants in the so-called Long Retreat of thirty days. There was, however, the memorable three-day retreat which John attended, led by the great American popularizer of the Ignatian method. Father Daniel A. Lord helped validate John's impulse to dream, knowing that in such openness to waking states of intentional dreaminess lay the foundations of the disciplined ability to shape the contents of one's mind according to a plan. That plan might be marked out by Saint Ignatius—for the Greater Glory of God—or by the constructive consciousness of a fiction writer with an eye on other glories. In either case the mind was free to create after its own needs and aspirations; and in some cases the two could overlap.

It would be a mistake to overlook this wellspring of Fante's later achievements as a writer; but as yet he was not writing. Tellingly, when John was invited to join the staff of *The Red Jug* as a contributing editor, he declined. Only his scrapbook suggested that his mind was turning toward the remaking of his life into so many readable pages—and not simply in terms of sports and religion. Into the scrapbook he also pasted pictures of saucy Roaring Twenties flapper girls with bare arms and legs; a series of cutout pouting bee-stung lips; and the fragment of a love letter in a girl's florid hand: ". . . most of all I want your love, your sweet caresses, and the haven of rest in your arms." Before he graduated from Regis both his mind and his heart were turning away from the godlier aspects of his parochial education and in a worldlier, indeed, an increasingly godless direction.

This shift resulted from a combination of factors both intellectual and personal. By the time Fante was a senior, the strong sense of vocation that had held him for two years was beginning to fade. Paradoxically, he could lay partial blame for this loss at the doors of a system meant to bolster the life of the spirit. Immersion in the liberal arts had given Fante the intellectual tools to question the religious tenets he was learning side by side with so much logic and science. The dilemma was neither original nor unique: thoughtful young Catholics have long been visited by doubts about their childhood beliefs in what often amounts to a rite of spiritual passage. In John's case, moreover, a budding literary discernment, the result of immersion in so much classical literature, was leading him to suspect certain other aspects of his Catholic formation. Not least among these was the endless series of "genuine American boy" novels he was forced to read while at Regis, all from the pen of the insufferable Francis J. Finn.

Finn, another Jesuit, was the leading author of Benziger Brothers, a New York publishing empire identified on the title pages of its products as "Printers to the Holy Apostolic See." Nearly a thousand titles long, the Benziger list featured works in the categories of Doctrine, Instruction, Devotion, Theology, Liturgy, Sermons, Philosophy, Lives, Novels, Stories and Juveniles. To the latter line belonged Father Finn's Famous Stories, edifiers every one of them, with such unsubtle titles as *Candle Beams*, *Lord Bountiful*, and *Tom Playfair*. Standard reading at Regis, these fictional attempts to inflame the reader's religious ardor backfired on John, who grew to resent their predictably pious plots and their haloed characterizations. This resentment would resurface a few years later when, in one of his earliest attempts to write fiction—and in one of the few times he ever wrote about Regis—Fante took revenge on Father Finn's fictional homilies with a parable of his own.

"The Poet" featured Pat Scott, a Jekyll-and-Hyde creation described as both "the best poet" in his class at an unnamed Denver Jesuit high school and "a brawling animal" outside the classroom. While Pat fills his speech on the football field with a flood of barnyard obscenities, he also wins his English teacher's praise for a prayerful sequence of poems dedicated to the Virgin Mary. On graduation night Pat is called upon to recite his masterpiece, "O Virgin Queen, I Bow to Thee," for which he is awarded the annual Hibernian Award. The next day Pat departs abruptly, traveling west by train, but not without leaving in his locker the evidence to incriminate himself, a smutty volume entitled *Parisian Nights*, which had triggered his lofty-seeming cynicism. Several poems in the book have been worked over in pencil, with handwritten words substituting for the originals to preserve the original metric inflection. One of the many doctored titles reads, "O Harlot Queen, O Come to Me," while above it, in pencil, is written, "O Virgin Queen, I Bow to Thee."

In constructing the character of Pat Scott, Fante may have had in mind his classmate James Vincent Cunningham, who was indeed the best poet in their class of 1927 and who would go on to a distinguished career as a poet and professor of English at Brandeis University. (Many of J. V. Cunningham's poems, published beginning in 1931 and continuing through the 1970s, would be explicitly religious, and Catholic, in nature.) Since no sign points to Cunningham's involvement in such callow and blasphemous plagiarism as the fictional Pat Scott revels in, however, it seems likely that for the model of Scott's violent and cynical side John looked to himself. But from where was this cynicism emerging?

During his last year at Regis, Fante may not have been as embittered as Pat Scott nor as alienated from his Catholic faith as he would be a few years later when he came to write "The Poet," but it does appear that he was drifting—and not only in reaction to Father Finn's stories. In addition to his growing intellectual reservations about so many dogmatic mysteries, it seems that Fante had a strong personal reason to begin distancing himself from at least one representative of the Church, and by extension from the Church's teachings and devotions as well. If Fante's thinly disguised fiction can be taken at face value, that person was none other than his spiritual and athletic advisor, the much-admired Father Bernard Murray.

The story is again "The Odyssey of a Wop," one of Fante's richest. Among several humiliating memories Fante's narrator here invokes, he recalls the pain of being called a wop by the Jesuit principal of his high school. In Fante's fiction being called a wop always hurts, even when no harm is meant; but this time the pain is unendurable, for until this juncture in his senior year our narrator has considered the priest in question a trusted friend, as John had considered Father Murray. What is notable about the way Fante's alter ego responds to the hurt is that he does so in writing, sending the offender a heated note threatening "trouble" if an apology is not forthcoming. But when next they meet on graduation day, the priest merely freezes him with a look, and the narrator retreats into the cold of his own silence, refusing to thank the priest when he hands him his high-school diploma: "I look squarely at him, just stand there and look, and I don't say anything, and from that day we never speak to each other again."

Fante graduated without distinction from Regis. According to school transcripts, in the four years he was there he had failed Algebra II, Plane Geometry and Latin III. Most of his other classes he had passed with low to middling grades, and though he had started off earning 90s in his first year of English, by the time he finished as a senior his grade had dropped to an 80. Most telling of all was the plunge in his marks for Christian Doctrine, from a cumulative high of 91 in his junior year, when he still felt the pull of the priesthood, down to a 75 as a senior, when evidently he suffered the permanent estrangement from his former friend and mentor. Having recently played out his final season of baseball with the other guys on the Clover Club, John was ready to leave Regis behind him. He was ready, or so he thought, to go home.

John had spent the summers in Boulder working with his father, mixing mortar, carrying hod, cleaning up job sites and so forth, brute mind-numbing labor but temporary. After graduating he was home to stay. The transition was hard, for while he had begun to grow up and out of himself at Regis, everything at home was the same. Although Nick had managed to buy the house and had even installed rudimentary plumbing, with its unkempt lawn and peeling paint 959 Arapahoe was as dreary as ever. John's mother still cooked and scrimped and worried and prayed, rarely leaving the house, while his father stayed away as much as possible, laying brick, playing cards and drinking. True, Grandma Mamona was gone. Unmellowed with age, Grandma was said to have tried breaking up a violent fight between Nick and Mary, only to have her own son turn on her with his fists. Only when Father Agatho came and spirited Grandma away to the J. K. Mullins Home for the Aged had peace, such as it was, been restored. So much for the older generations. As for John's younger siblings, Pete especially got on his nerves, so pious and dense and short-tempered. At thirteen Josephine was starting to attract the attention of neighborhood boys but she was too much her mother's daughter, growing soft already and hoarding her anxieties. Little Tommy was the one bright spot, smart and articulate, but the eight-year difference between him and John limited the reach of their simpatico. In all, Fante felt like a stranger in his own family.

To regain some sense of independence Fante registered for the fall 1927 term at the University of Colorado. Again he committed the fiction of his postdated birthday, but if he was hoping to impress the registrar by appearing to have graduated high school a year early, the impression fizzled when his Regis transcripts arrived indicating that he had finished "in the lowest third of his class." Nor would his scholarship improve. After the rigid structure of his high-school years, simply walking onto the university campus could be a disorienting experience for him. For one thing, his father's presence loomed everywhere in the cut sandstone of the major new buildings; and after womanless Regis the fragrant swirl of coeds kept Fante's mind far from his studies. Gone was the mental regimentation of the Jesuits, but gone too was the balancing physical release of regular organized sports. The freedom could be exhilarating, but without a program to follow, much less any spiritual direction, there was nothing to help shape his future track. The results were prompt and predictable. By term's end he had failed two of three classes, and on December 12 he withdrew from the university. Six months after finishing one of the West's finest prep schools, he had not so much as a plan for the following day.

He drifted through the early days of winter. When the mortar-freezing snows came, masonry jobs dwindled, so that both Fante and his father had plenty of time on their hands to see how things were with each other. John increasingly resented the way his father treated his mother, always coldly and at times with the back of his hand. Oddly enough, Nick responded by contriving to buy John a car, perhaps to deflect his simmering filial resentment with a not-so-shiny distraction. The car was an old heap of a Plymouth, and John took to driving aimlessly around town and up the roads above Boulder, coasting downhill, burning gas, going nowhere.

It was during this time that Fante took up boxing again. Always his father's son despite abiding ambivalences, he began training under Nick at the Elks Lodge gym for the so-called Demolay smoker bouts held there, doing rope work, shadowboxing and hammering away at the heavy bag with Nick hanging on from behind. John's sparring partner was a student at the university, Herman Hansten, who years later would recall Fante's ferocity in the ring. One bout in particular stuck in Hansten's memory. Fante was slated to meet a local Protestant boy by the name of Dutch Schaefer, a crowd pleaser who fought in the 150-pound class. Fante lacked twenty pounds, but according to Hansten he

> had complete confidence. In the two months of training John never really hit me, although he could have killed if he wanted to. He said, "I'll get him in the second"—and he did. What a release! I had doubts. Schaefer had a wry-neck, and was completely unpredictable. Boxers telegraph movements with their heads and shoulders, but with a permanent twist to the neck, there was no message. Schaefer lay on his stomach in the ring, unable to rise. I felt sorry for him. He was the favorite, and some anti-Catholicism was obvious [but] John's unjustified optimism was a delight.

For a time John and Nick cut quite a figure in Boulder's cigar and straw hat society, a father-and-son fighting machine. For once Nick was crowing about his son. For his own part, with each opponent he destroyed John grew increasingly proud of himself. Thus paired up against other fighters, John and his father had found some small common ground, a way to avoid their own brewing confrontation for a little while longer.

This confrontation would be dramatized in "Home Sweet Home," one of Fante's earliest published stories. Amidst a series of heartwarming memories all centered on the family dinner table, the narrator suddenly recalls the awful night when he and his father

> got very drunk, and yet remained brutally sober, and I began to curse him for neglecting my mother, and he cursed me for the misery I had flung upon her, and we grew angrier and angrier, and my mother tried to make peace, and presently my father lost himself in an insane passion to make me suffer for the things I had said, and at that same second I too saw scarlet before my eyes, and the two of us leaped upon each other, and we were like two ani-

mals, and I knocked my father to the floor, and he fell with a thud, and, lying on the floor, began to cry like a little child.

It is an appalling scene, all the uglier when father and mother lunge "for each other's guilty throat in the way of fanatics, . . . whining and snarling" like beasts. To be sure, it is not known how precisely modeled on the scarred life of the Fante family this scene may have been, but in terms of John's need to write it in the first place, the emotional truth was unequivocal. John and his father were locked in a fighters' embrace which the Elks Lodge smokers helped disentangle only in part, by redirecting the murderous father-son antagonism onto the poor guy in the other corner.

John was eighteen when he dropped out of the university and started breaking his mother's heart. Instead of going to mass with Mary on Sundays, he would sleep in late nursing his bruised ribs, then spend the whole day poring over strange books and magazines. He may not have lived up to the academic ideals of Regis, but the Jesuits had primed John's natural intelligence; and now, superbly conditioned in body but out of kilter in his soul, he longed for the mental stimulation—if not exactly the spiritual exercise—to which they had accustomed him. Much to his mother's dismay, he found that stimulation not in good Catholic books but in the Greek-style public library at 1125 Pine Street, where he now went regularly to browse and read, and where while browsing he discovered a substitute savior in the writings of H. L. Mencken.

Editor of *The American Mercury* as well as a prolific author and critic, Mencken was arguably the most influential man of letters in the country. With his raffish all-American voice of outrage, the so-called Sage of Baltimore spoke as if directly to the vacancy in John's breast. John responded by soaking up the *Mercury*'s ironic attitude and its editor's barbed bemusement at all manner of human foible. Here was Mencken leveling at every shade and fashion of bunk, quackery, moonshine and wind music, saving some of his fondest shots for theology, the professional practitioners of which he branded "less men than intellectual machines." (Mencken's translation of Nietzsche's *The Antichrist* had appeared in 1918.) To a young man lately cut off from the Jesuit worldview, reading Mencken was like a lifeline, and John followed the great man's editorial guidance by roaming further among his myriad works as well as among those of his *Mercury* contributors.

It was at this time that John also began to explore the possibilities of writing. In the fall of 1928 he was readmitted to the university, where he enrolled in a full schedule of five classes, including Introductory English. Once again he left a lasting impression on his sparring partner and fellow student Herman Hansten, who found in John's earliest literary efforts some of the same qualities that distinguished his boxing style. "I was delighted with his freshman English themes," Hansten would later say, recalling that in these writings John "assumed the infantile capacity of Gargantua in coping with immense odds with phenomenal success. Pure, delightful fantasy. I knew then that he had the gift, and that it would not be recognized by the turkeys who teach freshman English."

The final grade of 78 John received for this class would seem to have borne out his friend's premonition, but at least he had completed the course. He had also squeaked through Modern European History with a 71, but not so his other three classes, College Algebra, American Ideas in Literature and Freshman Gym, all of which he failed outright. In the winter term of 1929 John raised his English grade to an 86, but he barely passed the second parts of Modern European History and American Ideas in Literature, and again he flunked Algebra, Gym and, this time by exam, part one of American Ideas in Literature. His interest in writing was gaining focus but on March 25, 1929, he was dropped by the registrar for failing to maintain the required minimum units.

John was preoccupied with other things. For one, he had fallen in love with a girl named Nina, who worked in a shop in town. Little is known of this affair but like both his literary adventuring and his emancipation from the church, it must have provided a modicum of escape from the grinding atmosphere of lovelessness between his mother and father at the house on Arapahoe. John would later explain his lapse of faith as the result of several factors, including "skepticism and too much Voltaire and his counterparts, and a sense of injustice over the ruination of my mother's life." The cruel irony, however, was that in flying from the Church into the arms of foreign philosophers, John was ensuring his mother's ruination just as surely as was his father. First an unloving husband, and now an apostate son: little wonder that Mary Fante venerated the Mater Dolorosa, the virgin Mother of Sorrows with her heart eternally pierced by the seven swords of tribulation.

One day John's cousin Stella Campiglia, then a student at the university, was out walking with several girlfriends when she saw a woman trudging toward them in the gutter. From the frazzled nest of the woman's hair and the incoherence of her muttering, Stella judged the poor thing to be crazy. It was only when they drew close that Stella recognized her Aunt Mary, obviously beside herself and completely distraught. One of the girls made a smart remark, at which the others suppressed a laugh; but Stella could only bite her tongue and keep silent, so afraid was she of exposing herself to her aunt, and her aunt to her giggling friends.

Edward Campiglia would long recall how hard his big sister Stella cried when she got home to East Denver and poured out this story to their mother, John's beloved Aunt Nettie. "It nearly broke her heart," Edward Campiglia later said, adding what had to be known for the situation to be appreciated: "Of course Nick beat [Mary] up all the time. And sometimes my mother would get a call in the middle of the night to go up to Boulder right away, Mary was hurt, stuff like that. And [my mother] had to catch the next Interurban [commuter train]."

Such extremity was too often the norm in the Fante household, which was now a home on the verge of dissolution. The precise chronology of this time has been lost in the blur of events. Indeed, that blur may be the surest indicator of how traumatic those events were: Tom Fante, who at age eleven or even twelve was old enough to know that bad things were happening, believably reports being unable to remember key developments in the collapse of his family. One fact is clear, however. As the frantic decade of the twenties drew to a close, Nick Fante left his wife and four children and ran away with another woman.

In artful testimony to this fact we have *Wait Until Spring, Bandini,* Fante's fictional treatment of the bricklayer Svevo Bandini's affair with the rich widow Hildegarde, and the shattering effects on Svevo's wife and their children. Without equating fictional events with actual occurrences, again we can trust Fante's creative reworking of the facts to convey a core emotional truth. Central to that truth is the ambivalence John felt in the face of his father's desertion. Like the novel's Arturo, John hated his father for hurting his mother even as he admired him for his deviltry. "I'm for you, old boy," Arturo muses at one point. "Some day I'll be doing it too, I'll be right in there some day with a honey like her"—as if every cad's son should have a sex-starved widow of his own. But admiration was only one of the many warring emotions John felt for his father throughout his life, and not the strongest or the most profound by far. From the time of John's childhood to the time of Nick's death and beyond, the strongest feeling was love. Any account of their embattlement that overlooks this point misses something essential about John Fante's character. John hated and loved with equal intensity, and often simultaneously, and no one was better at provoking such damned-if-you-do-damned-if-you-don't binds than his damnable—and deeply loved—father.

These emotional contradictions now threatened to destroy what remained of the Fante family. With his father gone and his mother breaking down, Fante found himself the head of the household. He was twenty years old, with little experience of leadership under fire beyond his high-school football play. As quarterback he had relied less on long-range strategy than on explosive tactics like the long bomb—the Hail Mary!—and the frantic lunge across the line of scrimmage. Now, before he could confront the far graver responsibilities suddenly facing him, he first made an effort to flee.

Nina, the town shop girl with whom he had fallen in love, had moved to North Platte, Nebraska. On impulse Fante left his mother and younger siblings and hitchhiked 250 miles across the state line, arriving dusty and broke at the girl's rooming house. Sitting her down on the porch swing, he proposed marriage: he would get a job laying brick and they would raise a family of their own. Nina listened patiently but needed no time to consider. She did not want to marry him. She did not want to see him. That was why she had moved away.

As Fante made his way home in defeat it may have dawned on him that in leaving Mary and the children to take up with a woman he had acted eerily like his father, right down to the bright idea of laying brick for his life's work. Somewhere along the road he made a manic stopover, perhaps to drown his sorrows, but certainly to put a seal of sorts on a time in his life that was crashing to a close; for when he arrived back in Boulder he was bearing a still raw tattoo on his left shoulder, the numerals 5237. He never explained the enigma of those numbers except to say that they had to do with a telegram he had once sent a girl. But before the scabs on his shoulder had blackened and sloughed off, that telegram was far in the past. Now that he was home again he had other things to do besides look back. Now that he was man of the house.

By late 1929 the stock market had crashed and the country was teetering on the brink of economic disaster. Other changes, less cataclysmic but still of great consequence, had also occurred in the six years since John had left home for boarding school. For one, the movies, long silent, had begun to talk, signaling to writers a new era of opportunity out on the West Coast. For another, the Ku Klux Klan had seen its official Colorado heyday pass into dust. Undone by internal dissension, revelations of malfeasance and ultimate defeat at the polls, the Klan had retreated to its 100 percent American hole in the ground, and light-of-day reason, such as it was, again prevailed.

To Fante, who was now paying keen attention to the world about him, it must have seemed a weird time, a homegrown bit of the apocalyptic promise about the lion lying down with the lamb. For example, the pastor of Sacred Heart, Father Agatho Strittmatter, had become fast friends with the goateed Doctor John Galen Locke, would in fact be named an honorary pallbearer at the former Grand Dragon's 1935 funeral. It is uncertain if these two community leaders were ever seen together tootling about in Father Agatho's gleaming new Chrysler, a gift from another of the popular priest's friends, automobile magnate Walter P. Chrysler, or if yet another friend, chairman of the board of Bethlehem Steel Charles M. Schwab, ever joined the father for a spin around town. But it would have been in that car that Father Agatho pulled up in front of the sad house on Arapahoe if as was his duty he came to console his devoted parishioner Mary Fante in her time of abandonment and desolation.

If John happened to be home at the time of the priest's assumed visit, there would have been a strangeness between the two men, a mutual awareness of John's recent slipping away from Mother Church. With his own jalopy no longer running, it is possible to imagine John trying to alleviate the strangeness by remarking on the shiny new Chrysler at the curb. If it was noontime they would have paused to take in the ringing of the Angelus, and John would have again felt the strangeness, knowing that Walter P. Chrysler had also donated to Sacred Heart what came to be known as the Chrysler chimes, said to be worth more than $13,000. Hanging in the steeple of the dressed stone church Nick Fante had helped build, these were the same chimes that, when John came to write *Wait Until Spring, Bandini*, would beckon to the guilt-ridden Svevo Bandini lying in bed beside the widow Hildegarde: "From afar he heard the tolling of bells, the call for midnight mass at the Church of the Sacred Heart."

Again the blur of events obtrudes, and only hypothetical questions can be posed. Did Mary appear in the doorway of her bedroom looking vacant and disheveled, or did Father Agatho have to enter to see her? And if the latter, did John step outside, faintly nauseated, to gaze with longing at the priest's automobile? Assuming that he did, assuming this whole fabrication, it is possible to imagine what went through his mind: If only he had the keys to a machine like that, his mother could let the wind blow in her beautiful destroyed face all the way to their new life in California.

But John had no such keys. What he had was an address in Wilmington, California, where three of his mother's brothers had moved several years before. Wilmington was on the coast, close by Los Angeles Harbor, where word had it the winters were like spring and Hollywood a mere streetcar ride away. John had heard that his uncles Mike and Ralph Capolungo, professional musicians and identical twins, took turns leading the ballroom band on board the S.S. *Catalina*, the Great White Steamship which ferried pleasure-seekers twenty-two miles across the San Pedro Channel to the idyllic town of Avalon on Santa Catalina Island. John knew that Zane Grey, the most popular writer of pulp fiction in the world, lived in Avalon in romantically rugged splendor. He also knew that the whole legendary island was owned by Chicago chewing-gum baron William F. Wrigley. One of the wealthiest men in the country, Wrigley also owned the Chicago Cubs, one of John's favorite major league teams, and each spring the players traveled to their preseason training facilities at Catalina, where junketing baseball scribes discovered the inspiration to wax poetic against the backdrop of swaying palms, azure seas and tropical breezes. Nothing like that ever happened in Boulder, where the snow on the red-rock Flatirons looming over the town often lingered well into summer. The pull in John's solar plexus was palpable.

Colorado was finished for Fante, a dead place of grimy slush and frozen mortar and the gaping hole of his father's absence. After what his old man had done to his mother and to all of them, Fante wasn't about to lay brick for a living, or ever pick up a trowel again. He was leaving this place, the latest firstborn son in the long line of his father's people to risk crossing the known boundaries of their native lands during seasons of want. It was a season of want again all right, and if he wasn't leaving to fulfill a sacred vow exactly, there was for all that nothing less venturesome about his departure. He was making his way west ahead of the shambles of his family to find a new life for all of them, and he was going to start with himself. He was going to become a writer.

"Poverty drove me out to California," Fante would later recall, "and I hitchhiked my way. I thought it might take me two weeks, but it was two months later when I got to Wilmington, California, and got a job in a fish cannery."

In the end Colorado was easy to leave. Fante had a friend in Boulder, a fellow baseball fanatic named Ralph Burdick who vaguely fancied the idea of California. Ralph's sister Peggy, a dancer who dreamed of landing a spot in a New York City chorus line, had struck sparks with John's sparring partner Herman Hansten, who was also itching to go somewhere new. But nobody wanted to leave Boulder more than John did. Knowing how things stood with Herman and Peggy, John persuaded Ralph that their fortunes were awaiting them out on the coast, and the two hitched out of town, riding a series of open trucks and westward-bound freight trains from Colorado into Utah and on through Nevada, across the great hungry landscape of the depression.

Frigid nights, empty bellies and sap-wielding railroad bulls made travel by thumb and boxcar as much an adventure as an ordeal for the displaced masses who hit the road in search of better lives in the America of the 1930s. Little is known of Fante's tramp west, but whether two weeks or two months, the journey burned itself deeply enough into his memory to reckon in several stories he would later write.

Two of these stories, "In the Spring" and *1933 Was a Bad Year*, would be written from the safe vantage of Fante's middle years in the 1950s and 1960s, when he could soften the edges of his youthful desperation into something winsome and thus, he hoped, marketable. The novel *1933 Was a Bad Year* would remain unpublished until after Fante's death; but in March of 1952 "In the Spring" would appear in *Collier's*, a slick-paper confection of adolescent daydream and paternal bigheartedness aimed at an audience eager to settle into the Cold War evasions of the fifties. As such, the plot traces a circle: trying to escape the confines of family, young baseball fans Jake Crane and Ralph Burton freight out of Boulder dreaming of walk-on tryouts at the Giants' Arizona training camp, only to be intercepted by kindly police who return them to their fathers and the realization that the best place after all is home.

Had Fante written about his trip to California only in this vein we would have known little about the wrenching emotional extremities he had to endure once he was beyond the city limits of his Boulder childhood. But there is an earlier version of Fante's California trek, a far more raw story written within weeks of his arrival in Wilmington, which sheds valuable light on the turmoil of this time. Entitled "Circumstances," this unpublished manuscript survives in four handwritten pages which pitch us headlong into the violence of his narrator's flight:

The whistle blew, the wheels screeched, and the train clanged to an abrupt stop. I was thrown face forward into the corner of the freight car. My forehead thudded against a steel rivet; I lay half-stupid in a pool of warm blood. Trembling, I clawed the sides of the car and attained my feet again. I felt my twitching face, it was drenched in blood that spurted from a gash over my left eye and streamed into both eyes, almost blinding me. . . . Stumbling forward, whimpering that I might suppress the screams twisting my sanguine lips, I reached the door of the car, pushed it open, and leaped into the darkness.

Disregard the overwriting, for what matters here is how the young John Fante, all but still in the grip of the experience he was fictionalizing, hurled his narrator straight into danger and strangeness. That gash over the narrator's left eye, for example, seems a mirror image of the scar over the right eye of John's father noted in his Italian passport. Strange too is the leap into darkness, which unlike Jake Crane's cozy night *inside* the boxcar leads not to a happy father-son reunion but to a torturous sequence of events. By story's end the narrator is left at even graver hazard in a hostile world than when we first met him: a victim of mistaken identity and a suspect in the murder of a woman whose plea for help he has failed to heed. The story closes with the terrified youth in flight from the police, gazing out at "the somber water" of the Great Salt Lake on a freight roaring through the desert at midnight.

Unlike the sentimental plot of "In the Spring," the overwrought melodrama of "Circumstances" cannot mask the authentic urgency in the writing throughout. If, as seems likely, John knew that his father had absconded to California with his lover after leaving Mary all but a walking dead woman—see Arturo's boyish sleuthing after his unfaithful Papa in *Wait Until Spring, Bandini*—then poverty was not the only urgency that drove the scarred man's son, the one with the self-inflicted tattoo, to take off hitchhiking and hopping freights in the same general direction. This father and this son were too much alike to trace anything but hauntingly similar paths. John's path, however, was leading not to an early, much less happy, reunion but toward a time of testing and tempering of mettle, a time of separation and aloneness and reinvented identity: a hard time, and a necessity.

Wilmington was paranoid, a seaport town in the midst of war. It did not seem to have been laid out so much as dumped out. Big trucks hogged the streets, roaring through crowded intersections where soldiers, sailors and civilians ignored traffic signals in the middle of honking claxons and cursing drivers. I moved with the flow of people, aimlessly following a surge down Avalon Boulevard. I was tired, dirty and dazed, tumbled like a cork along a street of oil derricks, factories, lumberyards, piles of girders and steel pipe, row upon row of army tanks and trucks, poolhalls, poker palaces, used-car lots, and even an amusement park with a merry-go-round and a Ferris wheel. The laughter of women in bars flooded the streets. Hustlers leaned in doorways, drunks sat on the curb, smiling cops cruised in bemused attention. Where was I? Liverpool? Singapore? Marseilles? I thought of my father, how he would have loved this singular place—the gambling, the bars, the buildings shooting up on every piece of land.

When more than forty years later John came to write this passage of *The Brotherhood of the Grape*, he saw fit to reimagine his arrival in Wilmington in the midst of World War II. To be sure, the only war to be fought when John actually did arrive there in 1930 was the war to survive—physically, emotionally and, now that he was going to be a writer, artistically as well. But when John straggled into the Heart of the Harbor after his long tramp across the American desert, his nerves would have been jangled enough to twist his perceptions of the city into an emotional register that mimicked wartime. Not all that he saw and felt as he wandered about would have been merely projected, however, for his state of mind would have been fairly well met and matched by a salty and even phantasmagoric port city, certain parts of which to this day retain an aura of at-limits strangeness unlike that of any other part of greater Los Angeles. The reek of copra and electricity and fishmeal and tar mixed with damp breaths of ocean air; the incessant rumbling of produce- and livestock- and garbage-conveyances; the rescue mission soup lines filled with the shuffling down-and-out; the swaying ranks of palm trees—palm trees!—along Avalon Boulevard; the lifting seaplanes bound for romantic Catalina Island; the rusting hulks, the steaming slag heaps, the fog-shrouded scrap yards: to avoid arrest for loitering he kept walking to stay awake; yet as he walked it was as if he were dreaming.

Soon after his arrival in Wilmington John contacted his mother's brothers. He apprised them of the ghastly state of family affairs back in Colorado, and they treated him to a few meals and a rudimentary introduction to the ins and outs of their adopted city. Working for the Wrigley Corporation like so many other locals, John's musician uncles were doing well. Two of them, Uncle Paul and Uncle Mike Capolungo, lived with their families in homes they owned in the Wrigley Development, three handsome residential blocks east of Avalon Boulevard, the line of demarcation between Wilmington's small but relatively affluent side and the proletarian-industrialized rest of town. His uncles told John that things were tight just then but that if a fellow could get on working for Mr. Wrigley's "Chewing Gum Navy" his troubles would be all but over. Mr. Wrigley treated his people right, and all of Wilmington owed him thanks. It was Mr. Wrigley who had ordered all those palm trees planted along either side of Canal Street, which he had then had renamed Avalon Boulevard so that folks coming from Los Angeles to Wilmington on their way to Catalina would get the feel of the tropics just by looking out the window of the Pacific Line Red Car. But right now things at the corporation were tight. His uncles would keep their ears open and let John know what they heard about prospects for work. In the meantime Fante was on his own in Mr. Wrigley's Wilmington.

In a city built to serve the interests of big money—oil, shipbuilding, and international commerce, among others—Wrigley was not the only absentee landlord famous among the townspeople. There were also the Van Camps, the Doles, the Dohenys and the Fords, among others, respective owners of so many canneries, oil refineries and auto plants. Wilmington's first tycoon, however, had not been an absentee at all, but an active citizen and city builder, General Phineas Banning.

Born on a farm near Wilmington, Delaware, in 1830, Banning had set out in 1851 on a ship bound for Panama, traversed the jungles of the isthmus on foot and by burro, and continued sailing north three thousand miles farther before disembarking at shallow San Pedro Bay. Like Richard Henry Dana before him, Banning noted the unprotected nature of the bay, observing that deepwater traders had to unload their cargoes far offshore onto so many flat-bottomed barges. Banning made his first fortune in the overland freight business, hauling goods and travelers from San Pedro to Los Angeles. In 1858 Banning was instrumental in founding New

San Pedro, the name of which was changed five years later to Wilmington in memory of his Delaware youth. An enthusiastic supporter of the Union cause during the Civil War, Banning built his own antebellum-like mansion in 1864. Set amidst twenty acres of lush gardens and orchards, the twenty-three-room Banning Residence became a magnet for the region's most prominent business leaders and politicians. Before he died at the age of fifty-four in 1885, Banning would found an oil company, launch a ship, build a telegraph, and accept a commission as brigadier general in the state militia. He would also win election to the California senate, from the floor of which he would lead the fight for a Los Angeles–San Pedro railroad, and champion federal funding for a bay breakwater and the dredging of a deepwater port. From these and many other achievements would emerge Banning's reputation as a founding pioneer of modern mass communications in southern California and in particular as the father of the Los Angeles Harbor.

The presiding spirit of Wilmington's founding father would not have been lost on the now fatherless John Fante. Wherever he walked in the days after his arrival, searching for work or just wandering the streets, lining up for a meal and a Holy Ghost sermon and then searching for another unlocked car to spend the next night in, Fante would have encountered memorials to the legendary Banning: Banning Park, Banning Boulevard, Banning High School, Banning Landing and the fabulous Banning Residence, that gleaming white dream house on M Street. But hadn't Banning, like Fante himself, ventured out into the great world at the age of twenty-one, ready to overcome high seas, fetid jungles and every other challenge in search of his fortune? And hadn't he made something of himself? Something special?

No doubt Fante grew lightheaded more than once in these vagrant days, from hunger and walking and exhaustion and longing. No doubt in this state he also indulged his Jesuit-approved talent for dreaming, so that as he trudged the endless sidewalks he was both himself and someone else, at one moment a world-famous author not unlike Zane Grey with his globe-circling yacht, at the next the storied Banning, and now a fabulous combination of both, author and Banning, the great author Banning, changing places in his imagination from one fantasy to the other as he struggled to resist the spiraling suck of the depression, worse off than if he had remained at home. But he had no home anymore. This was it all around him, this city and its strangeness, and inside him a clawing hunger.

As Fante walked he kept seeing knots of young foreign-looking men milling around on downtown corners. These men were trying to flag down work it seemed, any work, work for pennies, work for food. They were dark complected, Mexicans or Filipinos, he couldn't tell the difference, but he could see they were watching him coming, watching him approach in the way their eyes narrowed and cut away when they grazed his own, as if refusing to recognize the kinship that Fante too sensed and rejected. As he crossed the street and stepped up on the curb he found himself slipping in among their numbers. Most of them were short too. A few of them moved over. They were making room for him.

Day jobs tided Fante over during his early time in Wilmington, menial pick-and-shovel, heavy-lifting labor that paid in pitiful sums of cash at the end of the working day. Of all the jobs Fante worked during this time, however, none marked him more deeply than the job he landed at the California Packing Company on Terminal Island. In the fish stench of that canning plant he learned not only the harsh realities of unregulated factory work but also the reciprocal harshness of spirit such work could unleash in its victims—and in no one more susceptible than himself.

The scarifying cannery scenes of *The Road to Los Angeles* testify to this harshness. In that novel, written and rewritten through the mid-1930s, eighteen-year-old Arturo Bandini has already succumbed to the terrible defensiveness of racism, spewing forth epithets such as "Chink" and "greaser" at his Filipino and Mexican coworkers in an effort to maintain a misguided sense of his own Americanness. Fante's boyhood exposure to such assaults explains how he could go on to write stories in which his fictional alter ego underwent much the same painful experiences. But *The Road to Los Angeles* does not answer the question of how Fante came to see his fictional alter ego as the willful *perpetrator* of such assaults. A possible answer to this question is strongly suggested, however, in an unpublished short story Fante wrote well before *The Road to Los Angeles* and entitled simply "Fish Cannery."

If anything, "Fish Cannery" offers a harsher, less ironic and more personally revealing treatment of the racial themes of the novel, for in the story Fante dramatized a failed effort to resist the brutalization of racist thinking and behavior rather than, as in the novel, the net failure of *not* resisting either. In the short story, Fante's unnamed narrator initially quashes the impulse to lash out at his coworkers for what he perceives to be their contempt at his not being a Mexican like them. Valiantly he tries to summon a "pure altruism" and thus to rise above the rancor. But his insecurities soon win out. Remembering how much it hurt as a boy to hear his father called a wop, the narrator perversely imagines that one of the Mexicans in the cannery, Big Joe, is now calling him a wop, and he launches a preemptive attack, first raining down torrents of verbal abuse and then pounding Joe with his fists. Joe's friends turn on the narrator and beat him up mercilessly, stopping only when Henry, the cannery foreman, intervenes. But this Henry is no peacemaker; rather, as an experienced enforcer of crude but effective open-shop labor practices, he pits race against race. Before the blood has congealed on the face of the narrator, Henry takes him under his arm. "I like you boy," Henry says ominously, "because we're both Americans. "

There follows a grotesque deal. In exchange for the favor of not being fired, the narrator must agree to attack Big Joe again, this time under the secret protection of Henry, who promises to break up the fight after the narrator has landed the first punch. Sick of fighting but dizzy with thoughts of losing his job, of his mother in a hot kitchen in a small Colorado town, of himself as a little boy going to holy communion, the narrator leans in to his grim task. To brew courage for an act of revenge that is not his but rather the draconian Henry's, he forces himself mentally to replay his earlier humiliation; and then, re-enraged, he slams his powerful left fist into the Mexican's belly, a savage sucker punch that staggers the man, bringing him to his knees in agony. When one of the Mexican's friends yells, "Kill him, Joe!" the narrator can find it within himself only to sneer, "Blah. Kill me." It is as if he is already as good as dead to his own desire for a better life, for any life, as the story concludes with the narrator filled with as much contempt for himself as fear of Big Joe, reduced to wishing that he had never left his mother and the Colorado town where he had grown up. The hideous game has been won by Henry, who ends it all by making the two antagonists shake hands in an even more hideous charade of making up. Whatever his actual experiences may have been while working in the cannery, Fante knew how it all felt: the day laborer's helplessness in the face of a heartless middle management, his shredded and swollen knuckles, and deep inside the pit of his stomach the inching worm of guilt.

Despite the authenticity of its setting and the knowing descriptions of a certain kind of industrialized labor, "Fish Cannery" is far too lumpen in its sensibility, and far too pessimistic in its conclusion to qualify as en-lightened proletarian writing. Indeed, during his time in Wilmington Fante worked and he worked hard, but he worked only sporadically and always with a deep-seated reluctance, never keeping any one job long enough to uphold his part of his forefathers' reputation as steady and reli-able workers. Fante did not last long at the California Packing Company, where he gained the experience to write "Fish Cannery," nor did he last long at the ice company, or digging ditches, or on the docks, or aboard the glamorous S.S. *Catalina*, where his uncles managed to get him only occasional day work as a "peanut butcher," one of the concession-stand sales clerks who walked the decks with a tray suspended from his shoul-ders selling snacks to passengers.

Later in life Fante would claim more than once to have worked as an oiler on a ship. But there is no indication of his having done so in the vo-luminous employment records of the Wilmington Transportation Com-pany, which operated the Catalina steamers. Perhaps he managed to talk his way down into the engine room at some point and, once there, per-haps he did assist or at least observe one of the regular oilers in the job of swabbing the giant piston rods with cylinder oil. But it seems just as likely that he enjoyed the sound of saying he had worked as an oiler, what with the heroic associations that job would have had for him thanks to Stephen Crane's great tale of survival "The Open Boat." If John did not manage to gain a regular position as an oiler on the *Catalina*, however, it was not owing to any fault of his own, for he did pass the test required of all prospective male shipboard workers, demonstrating the ability to oper-ate a lifeboat. Issued by the Steamboat Inspection Service of the U.S. De-partment of Commerce, Fante's Certificate of Efficiency affirmed that he had been "trained in all the operations connected with launching lifeboats and the use of oars; that he is acquainted with the practical handling of the boats themselves; and, further, that he is capable of understanding and answering the orders relative to lifeboat service." Nonetheless, Fante would have known that it was not the oiler in Crane's story but the correspondent—the writer—who survives to tell the story of the wreck of their ship and the subsequent ordeal at sea in the open boat. And in the wake of the wreck of his family in Colorado, Fante was fiercely determined to survive.

One way he managed to do so without benefit of a steady job was by hiring himself out as a casual laborer on the docks and in the warehouses of the harbor. Before dawn he would go down to the hiring hall of the Waterfront Employers Association (WEA) at the corner of 1st Street and Harbor Boulevard in San Pedro, known significantly as the Slave Market among the men who congregated outside blowing into their hands and talking low. And when the employers' rep appeared in the doorway with bullhorn in hand to divvy out the various low-end jobs going that day, John would shoulder his way to the front of the crowd in order not to be overlooked. Although a poorly organized dockworkers' union of sorts existed at the beginning of the 1930s, it exerted little real power, and the dawn-hour jostle for work at the WEA was strictly a free-market affair. If you impressed the man with the bullhorn as looking strong enough to lift your own weight in oranges or bananas or untreated steer hides still dripping lymph and bound in scabby quarters freighted straight from the L.A. slaughterhouses; or quick enough to work the steel boats, to leap out of the way of snapping cables when the winch operator overdid it and a sprung load of steel rods went whipping about the hold; and if you knew how to talk right to the foreman, who might not be above exacting some slight commission for the favor of taking you on, then you might be hired for a full day's work at a lean day's hourly wage.

Working the steel boats is what the unnamed narrator of another remarkable short story dating from this time has to look forward to, even though his heart is in something else: "I've got to write, write, write. I ought to get to bed early. The steel boats tomorrow. I hate the damn steel. It cuts my hands to ribbons. What the hell. I should be lucky I have a job. Lucky? What the hell?" Entitled "To Be a Monstrous Clever Fellow," and as yet unpublished, this story offers a penetrating view into the strained existence John Fante was leading once his mother, younger sister

Josephine and brother Tom joined him in Wilmington. Their arrival forced John to undertake the obligations of providing for a family at the same time that he was grappling with the complexities of independence, not the least of which was the independence of mind he was coming to prize no matter how dependent on menial physical labor he was forced to be.

With the house on Arapahoe in foreclosure, John's mother, his sister Josephine and his youngest brother Tommy had been transported by car the thousand miles to California—Tommy sat in the rumble seat all the way—by a Good Samaritan acquaintance of the family. Pete, having undertaken his studies for the priesthood at the Dominican seminary in Canon City, had remained behind in Colorado; and so it was the four of them who now set up housekeeping in the shabby second-story apartment John rented at 729 Marine Avenue, a furnished one-bedroom with a view of the corner gas station in a largely Filipino neighborhood. When his family arrived John was working as a night desk clerk at the Anchor Hotel in south Wilmington, but in the short story "To Be a Monstrous Clever Fellow" his anonymous alter-ego narrator still works on the docks unloading the steel boats even as he toils by night to make himself into a writer.

The dock work and the writing are essential parts of the back-story of "To Be a Monstrous Clever Fellow," the foreground events of which are confined to one highly charged night in the life of the narrator. Sitting on the beach as the story opens, the nameless young man considers his friend Eddie Aiken's proposal that they go "stag some dances" at the Majestic, a waterside pavilion featuring live jazz. Initially the prospect fails to enthuse the narrator, for he is a clumsy dancer and plagued by self-awareness, and he needs to be on the docks early the next morning. Most important, he wants to be home in time to write his nightly allotment of one thousand words and read his self-imposed quota of fifty pages. But it is one of those nights when the lights are "carelessly bright," "reflecting the moods of people hurrying nowhere in particular." Halfheartedly the narrator agrees to Eddie's proposal, and off they go to the Majestic.

There they survey the packed dance floor amidst the tawdry prettiness of lights flashing against wall mirrors and crepe-paper streamers looping from the rafters. Sailors, stevedores, laborers and tourists clomp past with their women while the orchestra blazes away at "Tiger Rag." Even as he watches, the narrator's mind is in two places at once, for his constant impulse is to find words to describe his experiences.

I tried to think of a suitable descriptive adjective; instead, my thought supplied me with a feeling of uselessness for descriptive adjectives, and I began to wish I had stayed at home and done my thousand words. A girl in black satin, flaunting sleek hips, raced down the floor, pulling her sweating partner after her. I followed her with my eyes, wondering what she did for a living, if she had read Nietzsche; and with such hips, I rambled, she had certainly had no children, but I would bet she was no virgin.

Cursed by this double consciousness to stand outside himself as both critical and creative observer, the narrator spins words into sentences which he appraises for their comeliness even as he joins Eddie in the hunt for a couple of girls. When they meet such a pair, the narrator is "too aware of my size, my smallness, to be suave" but he asks for a dance anyway. The girl refuses then reverses herself, saying, "I guess you can have this one with me." Ever ready to take offense, the narrator retorts that "since this is a guessing game, I guess you can go to hell," then thinks in rapid succession of Voltaire, James Gibbons Huneker and George Jean Nathan, masters all of the cutting comeback. But it is to Nietzsche that his mind keeps returning.

I thought of Nietzsche, reminding myself that I was not sure I was pronouncing his name rightly, even though I respected it as much as my own. I recalled Zarathustra: Bitter is the sweetest woman, and, Thou goest to woman? Do not forget thy whip. I wondered if Nietzsche wrote such acidy words as platitudes. I must forget Nietzsche if I want to have a decent evening; I vigorously told myself that at thirty-three, Nietzsche would still influence me. "But," I thought, "suppose Nietzsche should step off the floor and say, 'Hi there, lad. Go outside and blow out your brains.'" I wondered how badly I would take it. The girl in black satin glided by, and I forgot him, and my mind spurted into a soliloquy on loving her. Sherwood Anderson, I remembered, had written that often to see a woman walk across the floor was a spectacle of pure beauty. He must have meant a woman in black satin; he must have meant something a little off the mark of beauty, the sheer aesthetic quality.

Such galloping inwardness does not distract the narrator's eye from the waist of the dancing woman, though when the waltz is over he upbraids himself for having the thought that he has committed a sin. He reacts by mentally cursing all priests, launching in on a perverse reverie about his fourth-grade teacher, Sister Mary Ethelbert, musing that, even though at this moment she is probably praying for his soul, "every time I think of her, I think of going to bed with her."

The mental leap here from dancing woman to praying nun makes sense, for one of John's teachers at Sacred Heart was a Sister Mary Ethelbert, remembered by one former student as always with a clove in her mouth to sweeten her breath. Like all nuns of the order of the Blessed Virgin Mary, Sister Mary Ethelbert wore the severely wimpled habit the nuns called, half in jest but also wholly in earnest, their "coffin on the back," a memento mori quite literally to be inhabited and consisting of a shiny black garment shrouded about the avowed's person like an old-fashioned coffin that bulged out around the middle and narrowed at the top and bottom. In short, as he wrote this story Fante's mind was veering between associational opposites—slim black satin waist, bulging black shrouded middle, one a virgin, the other not—which merged in his narrator's fantasy of having sex with his fourth-grade teacher, a nun praying for his eternal soul. All of Nietzsche's anti-God jeremiads notwithstanding, the pull of the narrator's Catholicism is so strong that right there in the swarming dance hall his mind teems with unfictionalized figures from John Fante's Catholic boyhood, their abiding faith a reproach to his apostasy. "But that's kind of vicious," he thinks guiltily about his fantasy of having sex with Sister Ethelbert, because, after all, "she prays for me. And my mother's home right now praying for me. And so is Father Benson in St. Louis, and so is Paul Reinert and Dan Campbell. Why should they be priests?"

To counter the line of this thought Fante has his narrator invoke a cohort of literary figures, effective comrades-in-arms in his campaign for imaginative license. The names of such now forgotten authors as E. Boyd Barrett and Everett Dean Martin take their place alongside those of Anderson, Emerson, and Sinclair Lewis, as well as, recurrently, that of Nietzsche. Along with Nietzsche, the author who plays the most central role in this story's pitched inner battle is James Branch Cabell. Seldom read today, Cabell was at one time hailed in the same breath with Hemingway, Faulkner, Dreiser, and O'Neill as one of the prospective immortals of early-twentieth-century literature. His romance *Jurgen: A Comedy of Justice* (1919), against which Fante's dance-hall story begs to be read, has been compared to James Joyce's *Ulysses* and Thomas Mann's *The Magic Mountain*. Indeed, Fante took the title for his story from Cabell's *Jurgen*, the eponymous hero of which is fond of referring to himself as "a monstrous clever fellow."

Much of Jurgen's romance occurs on Walpurgis Night, 1277, that is, on the eve of Saint Walpurga's Day, or May Day, the night of the year when witches were once held to ride to their appointed rendezvous. Jurgen, a poet, encounters a foul-mouthed monk who is damning the Devil for causing him to trip over a stone. Chronically impudent, Jurgen mounts a poetic defense of evil, only to find when he returns home that his wife Dame Lisa has vanished. The plot traces Jurgen's search for Lisa through a picaresque series of adventures which take him among other places to the fantastic realm of Cocaigne, and which do not end before he has visited both Hell and Heaven. During his quest Jurgen samples a ravishing sequence of beauties, buzzing from one conquest to the next and cowing each with his pretended erudition and his ascendant mountebankery, as in escalating order of self-exaltation he pretends to be duke, prince, king, emperor and finally—in Heaven—Pope. The point of Cabell's farcical treatment of the themes of mountebankery and libertine sexuality is to demonstrate Jurgen's evolution from an unsatisfied poet into a paragon of gallantry, for having had his fill of sensuous adventures Jurgen chooses his wife in the end.

All this is not as far removed from the steel boats and the jazz of "To Be a Monstrous Clever Fellow" as it might seem. For rather than admit to his next dance partner, a junior-college student, that he is a mere longshoreman, the narrator of "To Be a Monstrous Clever Fellow" introduces himself as Professor Cabell of Stanford University. When to his amazement the girl swallows that lie he goes on to amaze her further by explaining that his area of expertise is communism! From the dance floor they proceed to a darkened corner of the hall where she lets him kiss her "many, many times. It was great sport to kiss her. . . . She tossed her body carelessly and quite willingly." But when he asks her to take a stroll along the beach she refuses to go along, and he snaps her garter in frustration. Feeling the calluses on his palm, the girl exposes him as a fraud, a mere worker, and then slaps him across the face, at which he jumps to his feet, wanting to knock her down. "Instead, I scribbled mentally, 'Her hand shot out, and he felt a sharp pain under his eyes, and he leaped to his feet.'" Abandoned, the mental scribbler reconvenes his company of writer-heroes for a battle royal of mental hero-trouncing:

> Suddenly, I thought of Nietzsche and Cabell and Nathan and Lewis and Anderson and many more. God damn Nietzsche. God damn the great Mencken. God damn Cabell. God damn the whole God damn outfit. I should have torn the virago to shreds. What's wrong with my hands. God damn my father. God damn my mother. God damn myself. Why didn't I hit her? Why didn't I knock her for a roll? Be hard—Oh Nietzsche, get away, will you? For Christ sake, leave me alone for a minute.

All he wants to do now is go home and write. But home is where his mother is, waiting up for him with her disapproving pieties. When Eddie reappears with the news that he has two girls waiting for them, the narrator sees that the girl who has been lined up for him is the same one he earlier told to go to hell. The moment of recognition is thus also a moment of mutual repulsion, during which he smells the girl's breath, a far cry from the clove aroma of Sister Mary Ethelbert's, for it is "putrid, smelling of garlic and wine." To test the limits of her repulsion he shows her his hands, but unlike the college coed before her, Elsie does not recoil from his calluses, but rather presses a stinking kiss in each shredded palm. Differences thus settled and mutual aims agreed upon, Eddie drives them to a dark part of the harbor where they pool their money for a case of bootleg beer, and then on to a hotel. Although like the narrator this hotel remains unnamed, the temptation is strong to identify it as the Anchor, where Fante worked as night clerk. As the party makers pass the front desk the clerk is looking the other way, but he "allowed us to transport the beer through the lounge room, so we gave him a dollar and two bottles of the liquor."

The tip here is also a tip of his own hat to the writer himself, John Fante, the artist's signature writ small in a story which, without ever naming his name, signs its author-narrator large, this Monstrous Clever Fellow both inside and outside the margins of the story, reinventing himself as he wrote. As Fante himself did on numerous occasions, the would-be writer who narrates the story gets home at five in the morning, debauched but now sobered by the fog-whitened air and redetermined to write until it is time to go down to the docks. But as he had feared, his mother is waiting up for him with her own ideas.

"Why can't you be a good boy like Paul Reinert?" she asks. "He's studying to be a priest, and there's God in his heart. He never done the things you do. He don't get drunk or read books against God."

Neither Emerson nor Jurgen can protect him from his mother's interrogation, nor from her accusation that, "Like father, like son. You're worse than your father. Oh why . . . didn't God strike me dead at the altar?" Peeling off his sweaty socks the narrator endures her litany of tribulations, responding with anger only within: "God damn Paul Reinert and all God damn priests in the world." But the effort to contain himself costs. It has been a long night, and he finally admits he is too tired to try to write after all. With his mother threatening to burn his books, and his brother and his sister shouting for quiet, he decides to read a passage from his revered Nietzsche and ponder it in bed before sleep. He goes to his desk and finds *Thus Spake Zarathustra*, the book that has usurped his Bible.

> At random I opened it, reading "They called God that which opposed and afflicted them: and verily, there was much hero-spirit in their worship!"
>
> Kissing mother, I rolled into bed.
>
> She went into her room. I heard her knees crackle as she knelt down; then the rattling of rosary beads.

Nietzsche's philosophical severities could hardly have consoled John in these days of his embattlement. But consolation softens, and what he needed was hardness, a hero spirit of his own. From here on it was going to be a forced march. "Damn all religion," he thinks through his narrator at one point in "A Monstrous Clever Fellow," "I must strengthen my irreligion."

As a bridge between the losses of the past and all the unknowns of the future, Wilmington was serving its purpose. Among other things, John was learning how to distinguish what he would need for the journey from what he could leave behind. Even as he reinvented himself as a writer, Fante was reconstructing a system of beliefs and values to take the place of all that had been lost, a system which, for better or for worse, was centering on himself. No wonder then that he was now spending so much time practicing his signature, *John Fante, John Fante, John Fante, John Fante*, filling page after page with its looping curves and double crossings. Somebody new was being born inside him.

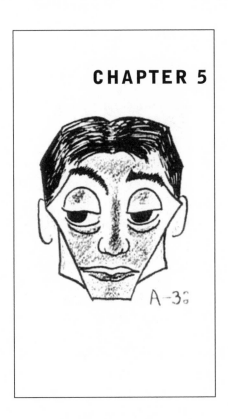

CHAPTER 5

It wasn't a very pretty sight, the John Fante that he was becoming. In Colorado he had left behind an image of himself among certain relatives and acquaintances as a cocky little hothead. Now that he was in California that image did not improve. At their most charitable, those who remember John from this time recall a volatile young Turk who was "very aggressive in conversation, very opinionated," and "willing to sacrifice everything to become a writer." According to his cousin Louise Capolungo McLean, he was

> angry, very angry. He was mad at the world, at the church, filled with venom. I knew him as a kid when he didn't have any friends, and I think what made him so sarcastic and everything, he was embarrassed by [his family's] predicament. So he turned bitter. He

tried to fight it off by being superior. He was so superior to his mother and his sister. He wasn't any nicer to his sister than his father was to his mother. He sort of had that superior male Italian attitude.

Well after Nick's desertion and the subsequent move to Wilmington, John's mother continued in her traumatized state, complicated by both her utter destitution and her permanent physical debilities. Of her three brothers, Paul was the most generous in helping Mary get by, but he could not afford to support her completely. Nor was there in Wilmington the equivalent of a begrudging Mr. Clapp to let her run up an unlimited grocery bill. John was in and out of work, able to provide for the family only inconsistently, and days came when there was nothing in the apartment to eat. More than once, on days when Tommy should have been in class at Banning High School, the youngest Fante found himself sneaking onto the docks where the tuna boats tied up, waiting for a moment when nobody was looking. Small though he was, he would snatch the tail of the biggest fish he could throw over his shoulder and then run like hell with it all the way home, where his mother would cook and serve it, reheat and serve it, days on end of tuna and more tuna for breakfast, lunch and dinner.

As for her physical problems, not only was Mary hard of hearing, but from years of hauling coal from the backyard shed into the house on Arapahoe she had also suffered more than one hernia. In the face of Nick's unconcern, her family had helped to pay for an operation, which was only a partial success; she wore an ungainly support belt for the rest of her life. To her niece Louise Capolungo, Mary Fante appeared a "very pathetic character . . . beaten and bedraggled. . . . I think that [Nick] just beat her until she was stupid and insensible practically." And now, in the Italian tradition of the eldest son's assuming responsibility for the family in the absence of the father, John was taking up where Nick had left off, not, to be sure, by dealing out actual blows but with a manner of thinking and speaking that could be just as hurtful to both his mother and his sister Josephine. Before he had left Colorado, Fante had told Herman Hansten that Josephine was no longer a virgin, a spiteful remark which left Hansten wondering. Only favorite brother Tommy, with whom John shared the davenport on those nights when he slept in the apartment, escaped the teeth of Fante's sarcasm and the occasional eruptions of his temper.

An episode that occurred while Fante was working at the California Packing Company in the summer of 1930 illustrates how ready he was to unleash his cruel and vindictive side. Because of the danger of a major wharf-side fire, smoking was prohibited in the cannery's tinderbox facilities. True to its divide-and-conquer philosophy in dealing with employees, the cannery's management paid workers to snitch on each other when this or any other regulation was violated. A Filipino coworker, one Julio Sal—whose name Fante would later appropriate for his fiction—saw the chance to make a few extra dollars when he caught Fante smoking with his friend Bob Aiken, and he turned them both in. As a result the two were nearly fired. After work that night Fante and Aiken jumped Sal, stripped him naked and pitched his clothes into the harbor, then poured stencil ink over his penis. With its crude writerly implications, the inked exclamation point to this act of payback was an aggressively literary touch by the resident literatus of the cannery's labeling crew, the self-proclaimed writer who, as such, was often the butt of his coworkers' disdain.

To his credit, Fante was not oblivious to his faults, but he was a long way from apologizing for any of them. "Though I'm young," he boasted to a new and important correspondent,

> I've done a lot of harm. I'm revengeful, and I shall never reach a maximum of tranquility until the injuries and humiliations I've suffered have been compensated. Maybe that is conceited rationalization, but who of human flesh and blood can prove beyond adjectives that I'm right or wrong?

Right and wrong were much on John's mind in these days, albeit in decidedly different ways from the teachings of his childhood catechism. In this respect the importance of his newly inaugurated correspondence with H. L. Mencken cannot be overstated. In the summer of 1930, flush with excitement over Mencken's broadside assault on organized religion in *Treatise on the Gods*, the former altar boy had initiated a lopsided exchange of letters. In missive after missive fired off from Wilmington, and indifferent to his own self-contradiction, Fante idolized the idol smasher. "Futilely," he blurted in one of the first of these letters, "a man must have a god. You're still mine." Several months later the hosanna was still echoing: "I've got to have a god, and you're he." In return, Mencken—"the man who replaced God Almighty in my heart"—responded courteously and with interest, if in brief: "I can imagine no reason whatever why you shouldn't make a success of authorship. You write very clearly, and your experiences have given you plenty of material." With such words of encouragement Mencken had assumed in Fante's mind the crucial role of literary mentor, and in his heart that of surrogate father. "I would have done anything to get the praise of H. L. Mencken," Fante would recall late in life. "I adored the guy."

Hand in hand with his conversion to Menckenism came Fante's autodidactic encounter with philosophy, and in particular the philosophy of Friedrich Nietzsche. *The Philosophy of Friedrich Nietzsche* (1908) was in fact the title of H. L. Mencken's lionizing critical assessment of the German philosopher's life and works. Through Mencken's book Fante passed into a thoroughgoing if unsystematic immersion in several of Nietzsche's principal works, including *Thus Spake Zarathustra, The Antichrist* and *Beyond Good and Evil,* branching out into a survey of the works of Nietzsche's predecessor Schopenhauer and extending to the philosophies of Bergson, Spengler, Kant and Marx. The philological appeal to language as the court of last resort ("Who can prove beyond adjectives that I'm right or wrong?") was an idea Fante had gleaned from his readings in Nietzsche. As such it was also an idea that was deconstructing itself generations before the word *deconstruction* ever came into currency. For where the river run of language is relied upon as final arbiter of reality, of experience, of the difference between right and wrong, a radical and mercurial ambivalence sets in, an uncertainty about where one stands. And so did it set in for Fante, manifesting itself not only in his daily life as manic mood swings but also in the life that he was increasingly leading in and through his writing. To wit, there occurred during this time of reading and rereading Nietzsche and writing and rewriting his earliest fictions the instant of John Fante's transmogrifying split into the alter-ego protagonist of *his* life's principal works, the character who would live with and through him for much of the rest of his life.

This instant can be pinpointed if not exactly in time then in the nine wrinkled and yellowing onionskin pages of an untitled, unfinished and unpublished manuscript found among John Fante's papers. Written sometime before 1935, when Fante started work on *The Road to Los Angeles* with that novel's eighteen-year-old narrator Arturo Bandini living fatherless in Wilmington, these pages appear to be the beginning of a novel that would have followed the younger Arturo from his home in Boulder to Denver's "Loyola High." Although merely a fragment of an unwritten novel, these pages are noteworthy because they contain the first appearance of Arturo Bandini, and doubly so because here as nowhere else Arturo has an older brother, named—but what else?—Johnny. This proto-Arturo is for the most part a passive observer, a set of eyes and ears to take in the family drama swirling around Johnny, who is a freshman at the University of Colorado. This Johnny is also in the grip of a rebelliousness inspired by his reading of Nietzsche, a rebelliousness that hurls him into confrontation with the rest of his family, and most directly with his father. In a variation of the dinner-scene motif so familiar to Fante's readers, Arturo observes as Johnny sits eating with a copy of *The Antichrist* propped up in front of him, a self-conscious demonstration of his "rights" that has sent Mama to her bedroom in anguish.

"I'll give you a kick in the pants if you don't cut out reading that stuff," Papa said.

That was a mistake. It gave Johnny another chance to defend his rights.

"Now listen, Sir," he said. "You may be my father, and the nominal head of this household. You may be an older man. Presumably you are entitled to the respect that goes with old age. But let me say in no uncertain terms, Sir, that your stinking bigotry offends me. Your intolerance nauseates me. Your hypocrisy offends me. And your idiotic Christianity bores me."

My father was so surprised that a slice of tomato fell from his mouth and landed in his plate. He pushed back his chair, hitched up his suspenders, and walked around the table to Johnny. With one hand he lifted Johnny clear out of the chair, and with the other he slapped Johnny's face. Johnny jerked himself loose and they stood nose to nose.

"Go ahead," Johnny sneered. "Strike me again. Revert to type. Persecute me as your forebears persecuted the innocent during the Inquisition. Club me down. Boil me in oil. Tear out my eyes. Go ahead, Sir. But you can't blind me from the truth. You can't quench the torch of liberty. Go ahead. Strike me."

Papa thought about this a moment and then he hit Johnny again with the back of his hand. Johnny held his mouth and sat down.

"And shut up," Papa said.

Blaming the dark swerve in Johnny's personality on the godlessness of his public schooling, Mama persuades Papa that Arturo will not go to Boulder Prep, as Johnny did, but rather to Loyola High in Denver. Johnny recoils at the prospect of his younger brother being subjected to such a plan, which he considers nothing less than a spiritual death sentence, and he demands to know how much his mother knows about the infamous history of the Jesuit order. But as for Arturo, he still looks up to his big brother.

I wanted to talk to him about Loyola, but every day it was getting harder to say anything to Johnny. He sure was changed. He had taught me all I knew about football and baseball and fighting, but now that he was a Frosh at Colorado he didn't care anymore. Anything I said, he used it to make some crack against God or our church. He had been an altar boy at St. Vincent's, just like me. He had been a super student, and the president of our Holy Name Society. When he graduated from St. Vincent's, the class prophet had said he would be a priest. That's what Mama had prayed for too. But it was too late now. If there was anybody on earth who was a sure-fire cinch for hell, it was my brother Johnny. What made it worse was, he knew it, and didn't care. Sometimes I said a prayer for him, but not often. It was hard to pray for a guy who would laugh if he knew about it. . . .

"Is Loyola that bad, Johnny? How bad is it?"

"You're in for a sad awakening."

He lit a cigarette and took a couple of puffs.

"You're moving into a strange world," he went on.

While Fante strove to write this story he was also striving to break decisively from his past in Boulder, using Nietzsche's anti-Christian doctrines of the will to power and the Superman to fill the gap left when he abandoned his Christian youth with a new and independent identity. (As for the present in Wilmington, only John was changing, for Mary, Josephine and Tommy were now regular churchgoers at Saints Peter and Paul Church on Opp Street.) John had assigned no name to his narrator in either "Fish Cannery" or "To Be a Monstrous Clever Fellow," transitional fictions that took for their raw material experiences that Fante was currently living in Wilmington. But now when he looked back to Boulder for material he suddenly did have a name—Arturo Bandini—and not just one name but two, for Arturo had a brother named Johnny. In a word, Johnny was John, or a close enough fictional approximation to himself as to render moot the indefinable differences. But what about Arturo Bandini, the younger version of himself who had suddenly appeared as if for the express purpose of observing and reporting on Johnny? Where did he—and his enduring name—come from?

There are at least three possible explanations. The first and oldest theory, really no more than an assumption, is that Fante took "Bandini" from the California brand of a well-advertised fertilizer. Even if Arturo's surname did not come by that route directly, Fante would certainly have been aware of, and appreciated, the ironic juxtaposition of the word *art* in Arturo and the implied shit in the Bandini bag. The second possibility, suggested in the previous chapter, is that Fante created the name Arturo Bandini by mock-Italicizing "author" and "Banning" in a self-ironizing sort of portmanteau nomination, again juxtaposing the unproven artist in Arturo—his vaulting artistic ambitions, his fabulous poverty and grinding failures—with the grand fortunes and successes of Phineas Banning.

The third possibility is somewhat more historically grounded. In his desire to make over his new southern California surroundings into a landscape of his own, Fante was devouring works of local history at both the Wilmington branch of the Los Angeles Public Library and, somewhat later, the Long Beach Public Library. In these researches he may well have come across the figure of Don Arturo Bandini, whose forebears, like the Picos, the Sepulvedas and other landed family dynasties, had been prominent in early southern California. Approaching old age at the close of the nineteenth century, Don Arturo could still remember many of his

Bandini forebears, a vigorous line of *rancheros* renowned for their revolutionary passions and physical beauty. But compared to his ancestors, Don Arturo Bandini seemed a mutant. Unremarkable in his appearance, retiring in his manner, he grew up in old Los Angeles surrounded by books, leading the quiet life of a scholar of early California Christmas pageants. In all, if Fante was in fact aware of his existence, Don Arturo Bandini was the most ironic possible historical original for the fictional Arturo Bandini.

Whatever the particulars of Arturo's naming, Fante was beginning to establish the aesthetic distance necessary in order truly to individuate his protagonist. But that individuation would require a face-off as it were, a recognition scene in which fact and fiction could meet and coalesce; and thus the defining moment of these nine onionskin pages, as Arturo and Johnny briefly coexist in the same story before Arturo moves off in the direction of a strange new world indeed, not as it turns out to "Loyola High" but to the world of John Fante's imagination: and the fictional "Johnny" ceases to exist. In this context "One of Us" again comes to mind, that haunting tale in which the young narrator faces his double lying dead before him yet must insist, "It ain't me!" Likewise, Arturo was not Johnny, not exactly anyway; nor would the two come to seem interchangeable until twenty years later when in writing *Full of Life* Fante would unabashedly substitute his own name, "John Fante," for that of Arturo Bandini. Now, however, in the early 1930s, it was a different matter as Arturo began to materialize, a matter of (fictional) truth in telling, for this was the time when Fante was first making his bid to enter the tradition of the kind of writing that Northrup Frye has helpfully called the confession.

Partly fictitious autobiography and partly autobiographical fiction, the confession tends to emphasize the inner life and development of a central character, making proportionally less of surrounding social reality and external nature alike. As such the form can be traced back as far as St. Augustine's *Confessions* and forward through Sir Thomas Browne's *Religio Medici*, John Bunyan's *Grace Abounding to the Chief of Sinners*, Goethe's *The Sorrows of Young Werther* and Joyce's *A Portrait of the Artist as a Young Man*, to name the leading exemplars. Heady company, to be sure, to be shouldering one's way into, but the John Fante of this era in his personal and artistic development was nothing if not headstrong. And now he had experienced the first stirrings of Arturo Bandini, who eventually would help him butt his way in.

Around the time that he abandoned his effort to write the story of Arturo and Johnny Bandini, high-school and university students, respectively, Fante enrolled for the fall 1931 semester at Long Beach Junior College. Despite his dismal experience at the University of Colorado, he was not yet finished with his formal education. While still at Colorado—that is, before the fiasco in Nebraska with Nina—he had fallen in love with one of his English teachers. It had been an entirely one-sided affair, with Fante writing several anonymous love letters, which the teacher in question ignored, even though she knew who was sending them. Undeterred, one night John went up to her apartment equipped with a copy of Sherwood Anderson's "I Want to Know Why" and the intent to "spill her chastity." As Fante recounted the episode two years later for the amusement of H. L. Mencken, his "Jesuitical" approach to seducing the poor woman entailed asking for her interpretation of Anderson's story, which treats an adolescent boy's curiosity about sex. But the teacher was not so literary in her romantic preferences and the result, as Fante put it, was that he "was sure a flop with her." Now he was going to have another go at his self-styled rake's progress as a matriculated student of not only English but also Elementary Spanish, Social Institutions, Physical Education, and Citizenship.

John's cousin Louise Capolungo happened also to be attending classes at Long Beach Junior College during this time. Although she and John "were not buddies," she saw enough of him on campus to retain a vivid image, if not any very warm memories. In her view the John she observed at LBJC "was a character, sort of a beatnik before beatniks. I was almost ashamed to say he was my cousin. He wore his pants low on his hips, tied up with a rope. He had quite a vocabulary and he created quite a furor."

The loud-mouthed bohemian survived the fall semester of 1931, but only after withdrawing from Spanish and one of the two English classes he had started, the first half of a two-part survey of English literature. As for the other English class, a composition course devoted to the "study of the technique of narrative and descriptive exposition, analytical reading of the informal essay and of selected novels, training in the writing of narrative and descriptive sketches, and the preparation of the critical essay," he received a grade of C, the same grade he received for both Social Institutions and Citizenship, while in P.E. the athletically gifted returning student had to content himself with the tepid endorsement of a mere gentleman's B.

Again he was underachieving. But something was drawing him back to school, and if it was neither the visible evidence of academic achievement—high grades—nor the disinterested love of learning—pure scholarship—then it had to be the hunger to prove his growing sense that he was destined to be a great writer. What he needed was someone to prove it to. After disappointing a long line of teachers, and in turn being disappointed by them, in the spring semester of 1932, when he was nearly twenty-three, John finally met the one teacher in his life who would exert a powerfully positive influence.

Florence Carpenter had studied English at Cornell and earned her M.A. at Berkeley before joining the original faculty of Long Beach Junior College in 1927, the year of the school's founding. Buxom, maternal and only slightly less passionate about the English language than she was about her students, the thirty-something Miss Carpenter conducted her section of English C5, Public Speaking, more or less along the lines of what today is called a writing workshop, with students reading aloud from works in progress and then engaging with classmates in discussion, all under her broad-minded and lively direction. Early in the term she asked the class to write a theme on campus love. Sad to say, John's response to this assignment has been lost, but as he explained many years later whatever it amounted to left Florence Carpenter "ecstatic":

> From the time of that theme onward I was her favorite, her pet, her genius. Whenever we met on the campus, in the hallways, in the classroom, her face brightened with an endearing smile. She loved me—no, not an emotional love or anything like that; rather a deep affection and a respect for a talent I did not even know I had. But it worked like magic.

The magic lay in Miss Carpenter's impassioned embrace of John's writing, the first such face-to-face acceptance he had ever received and a far cry from the cold shoulders of his English teachers at Colorado. By this time he had been assailing Mencken with letters and stories for nearly two years, and the great man had been reservedly encouraging. But the encouragement of Mencken's neatly typed rejections, no matter how they might be cushioned by requests to see more, was of a different order from the flesh-and-blood inspiration of Miss Carpenter's smile. Soon John was spending all his waking hours writing short stories, essays and critiques for his newfound fan. He also joined Skalds, the campus literary society which met monthly under Miss Carpenter's sponsorship. This step was unusual for the maverick Fante, who in later life would join only one other literary group, the Screen Writers Guild, subsequently known as the Writers Guild of America, and virtually no other organizations at all. Insofar as joining Skalds would help substantiate his confidence, it was a step in the right direction.

John was on average three or four years older than his fellow Skalds. Unlike the club's other members, who hailed mostly from lower-middle- to middle-class backgrounds, John was obviously blue-collar. He had been out in the world earning a living, moreover, and now he was writing about that world. (One story, no longer extant, which he read at a Skalds meeting involved a worker in a fish cannery who watches a girl undress through a peephole, only to have his eye gouged out by a hatpin.) These facts were enough to set John apart. Further, while John exuded an unmistakable if not always fulfilled heterosexuality, at least five of the dozen or so other male members of Skalds were or would eventually discover themselves to be gay. All in all then John was a loner—in the group though not really of it—and it was as a loner that he was perceived. What really distinguished him in the eyes of all the others, however, was the level of sheer talent exhibited in his stories.

In two years he had gone from writing such labored juvenilia as "The Blind Girl," heavy with last-minute but-look-I'm-blind-too irony; the aforementioned "Circumstances"; and "Eleven-Thirty," a melodramatic tearjerker of failed romance and suicide which would be printed in the 1932 edition of the campus literary journal *Edda*; to short-story gems in the making like "First Communion," "Home Sweet Home" and "Altar Boy." Between February and April of 1932 he presented drafts of all three of these latter stories at Skalds meetings. In the words of one person who was present at these readings, "With Fante we were aware from the start that we were in the presence of a unique talent."

Though Fante controlled himself while the maternal Miss Carpenter was presiding, his classmates were also in the presence of an angry young man still in the throes of personal turmoil. One person who knew this side of Fante was Ellenore Boggegian. A fellow student in Florence Carpenter's English class, Boggegian became a sounding board for the numerous furies and frustrations then possessing John. The two would pace the campus together while Ellenore indulged her childhood habit of "interviewing people." Whether because as a member of one of the only Armenian families in Long Beach she was, like John, obviously an ethnic minority and thus an outsider in the midst of the city's midwestern WASP mainstream, or because she was, even more so than John, exceedingly small, even birdlike, Ellenore presented the right combination of qualities to enable him to open up.

> He really let his feelings be known. I mean, he was wretched. So here is this ugly little loner, and he could afford to have something to do with me, you know. He hated his father. Just hated him. It was as though his father was the source of all his problems, every one of them. That's what I remember about him so vividly. That he just hated him. He also was fixated on sex [and] he was always mad. If he just said like, "Hello," it would be like, "Hello you bastard," you know. . . . He talked a lot about sex. And he bragged, bragged like everything. One really funny story he told me, he was like yelling at me. Now, why he was yelling at me I don't know, unless of course it was because he was so miserable, I don't know. He said, "And you know what I used to do? I used to catch a chicken and I used to screw it!" That was the level of his thing. And I never heard anybody say that before or since.

An entry in John Fante's writer's notebook dated February 2, 1934, mentions by name two boyhood friends respectively "fucking a chicken" and "masturbating a horse." Notwithstanding such experiences, indirect or otherwise, the shock value of such ranting is obvious. As vulnerable as he must have been during this time, John was not about to let just anyone get close to him. But he clearly needed to vent, and the open-eared Ellenore Boggegian was willing to take it all in, fang and venom, as fascinated as she was repulsed. Sixty-five years after their last strolling talk, she would maintain that Fante felt a true antipathy toward her, and that despite or perhaps because of this feeling he would routinely subject her to self-incriminating braggadocio in the course of his steady stream of invective against his father. Evidently Florence Carpenter was not the only audience John needed at this point in his life, nor her praise the only response. But as Ellenore Boggegian saw it, Miss Carpenter also served John in another way.

"He was living with Miss Carpenter," she recalled, "and we used to make jokes of it." If Fante was indeed living with his teacher, or even if he was seen simply to be an occasional visitor, overnight or otherwise, in Florence Carpenter's quarters at the rear of 2505 East 1st Street in Long Beach, the joking would help explain the care Fante seems to have taken later to dispel any lingering notions other people might retain of a romantic attachment between himself and the passionate older woman. Perhaps he was telling the truth, and then again perhaps he was protesting a little too much when he stated, "She loved me—no, not an emotional love or anything like that [but] rather a deep affection and a respect for a talent I did not even know I had."

Be that as it may, there came the night when John arrived at the monthly Skalds meeting with a new short story which so enthralled Miss Carpenter that she stood up and read it herself. The story was "Altar Boy," and when she was finished reading, John's fellow members rose to congratulate him with pats on the back and the unanimous exhortation that he send the story out to be published. And so he did, straight to his god, H. L. Mencken. The manuscript was written in longhand, and when a week later a bulky envelope appeared in the mail Fante assumed it was his story and yet another rejection letter to add to his collection. But the note attached to the manuscript's front page was not a rejection at all:

Dear Mr. Fante:
    What do you have against a typewriter? If you will transcribe this manuscript in type I'll be glad to buy it.
                                        Sincerely yours,
                                        H. L. Mencken

In *Ask the Dust*, written seven years later, there is a scene based on this moment that gives us Arturo's joy at receiving such an unexpected acceptance from the revered editor J. C. Hackmuth. Having thus paid homage to his literary father H. L. Mencken, Fante neglected to include a fictional counterpart to the maternal Florence Carpenter, who was as responsible as anyone for his first success. Absent though such a figure was from his fiction, Fante would never forget the real Florence Carpenter, and how he raced to her office with Mencken's acceptance. When he burst in she was at her desk grading papers. She smiled up at him over her glasses.

Fante's attachment to Florence Carpenter ended not long after this time of flurried developments. In a strangely unexplained coming-of-age gesture, John announced that he was going to have himself circumcised. Then, midway through the semester, he stopped attending his classes and Skalds meetings alike. On April 18 his enrollment at Long Beach Junior College was officially canceled, four grades of "Fdr" (Failed/dropped) being recorded on his permanent record. He was "staying with friends, here there and everywhere," and, with only "a few cents" to his name, "looking hard for work." For the second time in less than two years, John's world was being turned upside down.

Once again the precise order of events has been blurred in the tumble of years. In talking about this time in his family's life, Tom Fante would later cite the "depressive state" he was in because of his father's disappearance as a possible reason for his failure to remember key details and their chronology. But at some point before the spring of 1932 the prodigal father had returned. Drawing upon her faith, Mary had forgiven her wayward husband, and she and Nick were reconciled. Together with Tommy and Josephine, Nick moved Mary far from Wilmington to the California town of Roseville, twenty miles north of Sacramento. There Nick went to work laying brick and doing odd jobs less for proper wages than in barter for groceries, doctor's care and other necessities. In the wake of his adulterous adventure, the formerly overbearing Nick now struck Tommy as greatly "humbled by the whole experience. He'd gone down. Because of the depression and his contact with the other woman, he had really been beaten down." Still, Tommy was happy about both the reunion and the move, for now he would no longer have to sell newspapers on the corner of Anaheim and Avalon Boulevards, where street-savvy Communists would bully him into scaling the fence at the Ford plant and leafleting as many cars as he could before blackjack-wielding security goons came chasing after him.

Nick's chastening helps explain in part why John elected to stay behind in southern California, for there he would not have to gaze upon his own father brought so pathetically low. Too, for Fante things were beginning to look up right where he was in terms of the one thing that now mattered, his writing. Once again he might be homeless, broke and on the verge of starvation, but he had lived to write a story that the mighty Mencken had accepted, and he was going to live to write more.

Hard upon Mencken's acceptance of "Altar Boy," Fante received a letter from the publisher of *The American Mercury*, Alfred A. Knopf, inquiring if the young author had "a book in process or in mind," and, if so, requesting the first opportunity to read or discuss it. John could only have been buoyed further when the August 1932 issue of *The American Mercury* appeared, with his name topping the list of that month's contributors on the magazine's handsome green cover. The confessional nature of Fante's writing was clear in this his first national publication. At the most obvious level of subject matter, the story dealt with a number of ironically "sinful" episodes in the life of a young Catholic boy and the subsequent confessions thus necessitated. Adding further to the confessional implications of "Altar Boy" was the fact that the narrator-protagonist's name was John, as if Fante was writing directly about himself. (When the story was reprinted in *Dago Red* eight years later, the character's name was changed to Jimmy in order to help unify the collection by having the various stories narrated by the same Jimmy Toscana.) But the John who had written this story was far from an altar boy any longer, and nowhere is it recorded that he breathed a prayer of thanks when his story hit the newsstands in mid-July. On the contrary, his response was distinctly secular: "Pretty hot stuff," he wrote to Mencken about seeing himself in print. But now that he had broken into the national spotlight—he reported receiving some seventy-five letters about the story, including several from Jesuits in Denver and St. Louis, and one from a fellow *Mercury* contributor, the proletarian writer Albert Halper—there were going to be those readers who were less impressed with his work than the writer himself happened to be. In fact, he did not have to wait long to receive his first critical drubbing, an event that took place, appropriately enough, on the front page of the *Denver Catholic Register*.

> John Fante, who studied in Catholic schools of this diocese, has an amazing article in the August *American Mercury*, entitled "Altar Boy." He gives supposed experiences of himself in youth, telling how one time he put red ink into a cruet and thus caused a priest to go through an invalid Mass, and of another when a tough comrade, to test what a nun had told him about a miracle, desecrated the Blessed Sacrament. Fante writes as if he has faith. The article is not really blasphemous. But it is in horrible taste even if it is partly true, and it is in worse if, as we strongly suspect, the major part of it is fiction.

Fante did not see this review immediately, but he did get word of it, and feel its slap, as is made evident by his request to his Denver cousin Jo Campiglia that she go to the offices of the *Register* and get her hands on a copy for him. No doubt the article's charge of "horrible taste" made Fante laugh, for the only tastes that now mattered to him were those that he was indulging, not least among them his ripening taste for women. "I never have and never shall be interested in anything but beautiful women," he wrote to Jo, not without, it is true, a certain half-winking suggestion that he might be laying it on somewhat thick. Not too many years earlier, a younger, less experienced John would turn often and eagerly to favorite cousins Grace and Jo Campiglia for inside information about girls and their mysterious ways. Now, riding the crest of his "present little success as an author," he held forth to Jo on his latest string of conquests, waxing poetic on one lover in particular, yet another older woman under whose tutelary "influence" he had been basking for some while.

The woman's name was Helen Purcell. After bouncing around from address to address for several months, including a raucous two-week stay in the home of a man who worked with Ralph Burdick at a tango joint on the Long Beach Pike, by the summer of 1932 Fante had settled in a Long Beach hotel to write. "I would rather write than anything else," he affirmed to Mencken; but even a writer as obsessed with writing as the young John Fante had other needs, and Helen Purcell was there to satisfy them. For a couple of years John was a frequent and sometimes long-term visitor at her Long Beach home, first at 212 Quincy Street and later in unit 15 of the Patrician Apartments at 926 East 4th Street. Nine years John's senior at thirty-three, twice married, once divorced and once widowed, Helen was a music teacher at Hamilton Junior High School in Long Beach, and a woman of both cultured tastes and extreme beauty: slavically severe cheekbones, sensual lips, and raven black hair parted down the middle after the siren style of the movies.

He had been driving himself mercilessly for the last year, a self-imposed apprenticeship of harrowing extremities during which he was often "crazy with poverty and worry" and "practically starving." By his own account he had lost a pound a day in one thirty-day period while writing 150,000 words, a period in which he had devoted ten hours of each twenty-four to writing and reading—"all of Hemingway, Dos Passos and DeMaupassant, besides great stacks of H. G. Wells and a chronic dose of Mencken," not to mention rashers of Krafft-Ebing's abnormal psychology as well, for the variety if not the edification of it. Now, with his efforts beginning to pay off in terms of making both a name for himself and some money—"Altar Boy" had earned for him the not inconsiderable sum of $125, though of that he had sent $115 to help his mother pay off a grocery bill—he would not deny himself the luxury of indulging Helen in her appetites for "the immense music" of Wagner and his own professedly formidable "bedding talents." With her he cultivated the fine art of his "cocksmanship" while amusing her with a diversion over which he dallied on and off, his *Pimp's Anthology: A Collection of Pornography Gathered from Lavatories and Behind the Barns of the United States.* And if she was in love with him but not quite the other way around, well, who could blame him for succumbing to such a useful arrangement?

Useful too was the acquaintance Fante had made while at Long Beach Junior College with fellow Skald and *Edda* contributor Richard Emery, who had recently begun working at the *Long Beach Press-Telegram.* When Fante received the letter from Alfred A. Knopf inquiring about the possibility of a book, Emery had slipped a puff piece into the paper touting the interest John's work was eliciting from a top New York publisher. Thanks to Emery, Fante gained access to a desk and a typewriter in the basement of the paper's offices at 604 Pine Avenue. It was a favor, not a job, but the basement was a good place to write, and as *Press-*

Telegram columnist Malcolm Epley would later recall, Fante took to going there to "write all night. Fighting for what he wanted, he scattered papers far and wide over the floor as he yanked unsatisfactory bits from his typewriter and discarded them. The janitors used to get pretty sore about that." Another writer then at the paper, sports columnist Art Cohn, later of the *Oakland Tribune*, recalled that it was his Underwood that John liked using, and that Fante's nocturnal writer's residence at the *Press-Telegram* lasted over a period of several months. Fante would later send an astonishing four-page letter to Cohn which the newsman considered worthy to be called literature, even though what it boiled down to was a desperate plea for journalistic work, "anything . . . for $5 a week."

Despite the generosity of friends like these, Fante continued to endure the severest of circumstances. It was "a bad season" in Long Beach, "the worst in the town's history" as those who knew local history told him, with droves of aimless people drawn to the lurid attractions of the Pike day and night "simply walking around and not spending a dime." And when he wasn't writing or reading or enjoying himself with Helen, the penniless Fante turned into one of the aimless ones himself.

Fante had already made one trip to Roseville at the beginning of the summer, a brief and soul-taxing stay which he set about transforming into a new story when he returned to Long Beach the second week of June. He was also working hard on "Big Leaguer," draft after draft of which he kept submitting to Mencken, only to have each returned. On July 26 he sent Mencken the story about his recent trip to Roseville, "a last fling before I take a freight for home." Enclosed with the manuscript was a letter describing not only the rigors of his writing schedule but also, if perhaps inadvertently, the fears that were creeping into his hopes: "barring death or blindness a man can get whole warehouses of work done." Then John dashed off a note to his mother: "I am coming home. Leaving tomorrow, Wednesday. I'm forced to hitch-hike. Consequently I don't know when I'll arrive. No need to worry tho, for I'll make it somehow." Suppressing whatever apprehensions he may have felt about being under the same roof with his family again, Fante thumbed his way north through California's sweltering Central Valley. It was no cooler in Roseville.

Soon after Fante arrived at the house at 423 Lincoln Street, Mencken's letter of August 3 reached him with the welcome news that "Home Sweet
Home" was already on its way to the printer and that payment would follow within the week. Responding in this letter to Fante's description of his
death-march rate of production, Mencken opined that 150,000 words in
thirty days was "absurd," suggesting instead that a sensible limit for a
young author was three hours of writing per day, with proportionally more
time allotted to reading and recreation. Because Fante had earlier pointed
out an error in his author's note that had appeared in the August issue of
the *Mercury*—"I never did study for the priesthood, nor did I say so in the
note I submitted"—Mencken closed by requesting a more accurate note.

Perhaps he should have known better. Fante began his amended author's note by shaving off another year from the date of his birth, which
he now claimed had occurred in 1911. He then went on to state that he
had been born in a macaroni factory. By contrast, he was evidently more
sincere in promising to follow Mencken's advice concerning working
hours and writing output, for in the next two weeks he wrote only one
short story of some 3,500 words, an unpublished sequel to "Home Sweet
Home" but just as revealing.

"I have been among my people for a week now," the narrator of this
story tells us, "and again I go to the library." Into this sentence are com-
pressed the key elements contributing to the central tensions of the three-
part story, each part involving the writer-narrator's respective conflicts
with different members of his family. In the first part, the narrator struggles to read the books he has brought home from the library, one about
World War I, another about the human body, while his mother sits across
the living room from him playing solitaire. Books are strange, even dangerous things to the mother, and as the narrator tries to read he can feel
her eyes on his forehead and her fears for the immortal soul which he no
longer believes to be his. Soon "the prose is hard to read. The room fills
up with a million eyes of the relatives and friends of my mother, the nuns
and priests of my boyhood. They tell me I am a thief who steals the sweetness of my mother, for the book I read is saddening her." Overcome with
guilt, he promises her he will have done with books, then steals out the
back door and into the space beneath the porch, where, "feeling truly like
a thief," he continues reading.

In the story's second part the narrator invites his pious younger brother Victor to go for a walk. It is a warm summer evening, and as the brothers walk through the town two girls appear strolling in the same direction, each dressed in sleek black satin. Try as he might, the narrator cannot interest Victor in making a play for the girls, for Victor is an upright young man who works hard for their father when there is work to be had and cherishes the hope of becoming a priest. (With his parents reunited, Peter Fante had left the monastery in Colorado and come to live in Roseville.) The brothers settle on a movie instead, but the love scenes are spoiled for the narrator with Victor sitting beside him, and they walk home afterward without speaking. In the bedroom they share the narrator watches Victor change into his pajamas and then get down on his knees to pray, "and my own knees sing a prayer, asking me to get down at my brother's side, but my mind yells derisively, 'Don't be a goddam jackass!' So I go on with the reading of my book."

In the third part of the story the narrator is walking home from the store when he sees his out-of-work father idling along the sidewalk half a block in front of him. The two are strangers to each other, unable to communicate, so that even when they make eye contact each keeps to his own pace in order to avoid the other. "It is all a feeling," the narrator thinks, keeping the distance constant between himself and his father:

We smother the music of kinship under brazen skins while we avoid each other's eyes and speak not in soft terms lest the beauty of affinity burst forth and make stuttering fools of us. My father's life is a big scab of kicks and tears and frustrations. He builds a steel wall around himself. There are little slits in the steel through which I may crawl, but to crawl is to crawl, and he nor I would have me down on four legs.

At the railroad tracks a train approaches and the pedestrian blockades descend, forcing the two to stand side by side. It is a long, noisy train and a long, uncomfortable silence. Finally the narrator finds something innocuous to say to his father, but the awkward overture leads only to angry words and frustrated feelings, which are all either man knows in the other's presence. Although they are greeted at home by the delicious aromas of dinner, the narrator refuses to join the family at table, going instead to his room to "fight the words in the book, coaxing them, furious," and remembering a time not so long before when "a rosary would have assuaged" his pain. But when he touches the crucifix on his brother's rosary, all he feels is brass. And yet he cannot deny the charge in a letter he has recently received from an old school friend, now a Jesuit, a letter that haunts him with his friend's sure knowledge: "It's in the blood. It's in the blood of all you Latins. 'Anima naturaliter Catholica,' and once you guys forswear your birthright, it's wandering you will be through the arid wasteplaces of the spirit, sick with the unappeasable longing of a nostalgia of the soul."

This is the story that Fante submitted to Mencken on August 25, along with a long letter explaining the impossible conditions of life with his family in Roseville. He had endured those conditions for nearly a month, but he could not find it within himself to endure them any longer. "I'm forced to freight out of here," he told Mencken in that letter, and again the line between himself and his fictional speaker was all but invisible, if not nonexistent. "I had better begin running away again," the narrator of the submitted story thinks at one point, "for someone has poured acid into home sweet home."

It was a devil's choice between the acid of home and the arid waste places awaiting him, but like the "Johnny" of that other fiction who "was a sure-fire cinch for hell," Fante knew where he was going. He was going to switch freights in Stockton and catch a train heading south down the coast, all the way down to Los Angeles.

In 1933 Frank Lloyd Wright envisioned a city. Broadacre City, as he named his dream, would follow a decentralized pattern of development based on the liberating mobility of the automobile, thus integrating the best of both urban and rural advantages. In exercising their freedom of movement in and through repeating swaths of nature, agriculture and suburb, citizens of Broadacre would daily enact in their lives not only the Jeffersonian principle of individual self-fulfillment but also Thoreau's ideal of right relation to the earth. Wright's scale model was the size of a small ballroom.

Two years later a man by the name of Harry Carr published his vision of the city the world was ending up with instead of Wright's Broadacre, a fabulous place which it pleased Carr to call the Wonder City:

Los Angeles is an epic — one of the greatest and most significant migrations in the long saga of the Aryan race. . . .

The Aryan tribes took to boats and crossed the sea. The last trek was across the American prairies in covered wagons to the Pacific Coast—to California.

Whether we were sun worshipers coming here to thaw out, real estate subdividers seeking to coax the innocent into our clutches, is a detail without significance. The point is, Los Angeles was a milepost of destiny. It happened here because it could not help itself.

Images of movement—migrations, treks, mileposts—were as central to Carr's vision of his so-called Wonder City as they were to Wright's vision of Broadacre, with the latter's everyman at the wheel of his sedan, the mobile measurement of enlightened democracy. But at the core of Carr's vision was an end to movement, a terminus at no mere geographical destination but rather at a millennial racial destiny. As such, Los Angeles as *Wunderstad* seemed no less inevitable than such epics of progress perennially appear to the profiteers who merchandise them, and just as grasping and exclusionary as any taker might like, so long as the taker happened to be one of the anointed white.

Carr's vision can be found in his 1935 book *Los Angeles: City of Dreams*, written to help boost the reputation of a city that had been built up on boosterism but that like cities across the nation was now suffering the letdown of the depression. It was no coincidence that Carr was a close associate of *Los Angeles Times* publisher Harry Chandler, "the man most responsible for molding the distinctive character of Southern California." If that character, as promulgated by the newsmaking–public relations combine of Chandler and company, seemed strangely devoid of complexion and accent, who was going to object? Frank Lloyd Wright would design and build some of the city's most truthful and enduring and humane self-expressions. But scale models aside, on his own he could not an entire city contrive. Times were tough and business was business and in Los Angeles of all places visions were a drug on the market. If you had a vision of your own it had better be a sharp one, especially if it was to compete with the received wisdom that *It happened here because it could not help itself.*

"A wonderful city," Fante wrote to his mother from Los Angeles in early October of 1932, "but it takes money to really enjoy it." With another week's experience of the city under his belt but little in the way of eats, he wrote her again to report that "this is a better town to loaf in than anywhere in the United States. However, every person in this town is a crook and a liar, all trying to make easy money, and doing their best to make something for nothing." As for himself, he needed money, "and damned badly," not to mention a haircut, clothes, a new pair of shoes and a decent meal. He had hopes for a new story which was now with Mencken, who had returned the sequel to "Home Sweet Home" with the admonition that Fante stop writing about his family. "The subject seems to obsess you," Mencken said. "Why don't you do some stories about other people? Certainly life in California should suggest a great many ideas." In fact, Fante was already at work on not one but two things, a story about a Filipino, and a humorous piece ("now that I'm actually experiencing it") called "How to Go Hungry."

He had been looking for work for several weeks but so far he had found none, neither a job at the *Los Angeles Record*, where he had gained an interview with the editor, Gilbert Brown, nor even work for room and board at a county cooperative in Compton that served the masses of unemployed. At first he stayed with his aunt Dorothy in her apartment at 2820 West 8th Street. But Dorothy, whose marriage to John's uncle Ralph Capolungo had recently collapsed, was as destitute as John was. Nephew and aunt liked one another well enough, and to while away the hours the two played game after game of Chinese checkers. But their dead-broke situations, with each of them close to living on the street, were too similar for comfort, and after a week John moved in with Dorothy's next-door neighbors, good churchgoing Catholics who Fante claimed got him to accompany them to mass. Humoring his mother as he often did in his letters—in contrast to his attitude when with her in person—Fante wrote that though he was "a hell of a poor Catholic . . . it wasn't so bad last Sunday. . . . It was peaceful in that Church. My mind went to sleep for an hour, and who knows? I might turn out to be a monk yet, or even a nun."

Evidently this sense of humor had been lacking when John met with Jim Tully in mid-September. Known as the Hobo Novelist of Hollywood, Tully had lived the rough-and-tumble life of a tramp, prizefighter and jailbird before finding international success as a writer. Starting in 1922 he turned out a steady stream of books and articles about the hobo life which soon landed him in Los Angeles. There he became the broad-shouldered intimate of everyone from Charlie Chaplin to Jack Dempsey. Even when he was pulling in as much as $80,000 a year, however, Tully did not forget his beginnings, and his mansion, Tall Timbers, on the shore of then-remote Toluca Lake opposite that of W. C. Fields, was always open to aspiring writers. Tully had long been a favorite of H. L. Mencken, so when Fante telephoned, Tully returned the first-time *Mercury* contributor's call and invited him to pay a visit.

Afterward, Fante reported to Mencken that he had met Tully, and liked him, and that Tully had tried to help, but that the older author had found him "too young and too serious and too dramatic and too humorless." None of this prevented the generous Tully from dashing off a realistic but encouraging letter before he left town the next week for New York's Algonquin Hotel. Tully had read the story Fante had given him, an unidentified work which had been rejected by *Atlantic Monthly* editor Ellery Sedgwick. "It will be hard to sell an anti-Catholic bitter yarn to magazines," Tully wrote.

> It is not a question of bravery. . . . You'll find that editors are generally right—if not always as to literature, at least as to what they can use, and get away with. I think the tale would be better without bitterness. You might try it on others. That's the way to learn, but you'll save yourself a lot of grief by knowing your markets. The Atlantic Monthly would no more use the article than it would run Joyce serially.

Tully's clear-eyed advice helped guide Fante in revising the next story which he soon sent to the *Mercury*, a draft of which he had presented several months before during one of his last appearances at Skalds; for late in November he received another one of those letters from Mencken that never failed to make him giddy with joy. "Thanks very much for 'First Sacraments,'" Mencken wrote. "It seems to me that it is the best thing you have done so far, and I'll be delighted to print it in The American Mercury." Again the check was in the mail and the story would appear (as "First Communion") in the February issue. But for the time being John was still fighting the wolf of immediate need.

Fante was now living in unit 15 of the Carol Arms Apartments at

345 South Rampart. He had a roommate, Charles Green, another struggling writer but generous enough to share with Fante "a bit of a job downtown." The job, such as it was, involved Fante's permitting his name to appear on the letterhead stationery of the Jean C. de Kolty Manuscript Service as the entire "Editorial and Sales Dept." Since de Kolty, a selfstyled authors' agent, was rarely burdened by any kind of business, Fante was free to come and go at the service's F. P. Fay Building office. Seven stories above the traffic at the downtown intersection of 3rd and Hill, Fante could peer out his office window and see the arched entrance to the picturesque funicular railway known as Angel's Flight. In addition to the view he had access to a typewriter, paper and postage stamps, and though the "job" paid a mere $1 per day, it was enough to fund John's way around town on the city's extensive network of nickel-per-ride Red Cars in his push to meet people who might help him jump-start his career as a writer.

One of these people was film scenarist Ernest Pagano, like Fante an Italian-American with mutual friends in Denver. John visited Pagano at his office on the Burbank lot of Universal Studios, and the two hit if off over drinks. John was amazed to learn from Pagano the kind of money a man could make writing film stories—$500 a pop for starters—and he set to work studying the form. Soon afterward Fante contacted Pagano's younger brother Jo, also a writer, and the two became instant pals, going out together nearly every night for the next week, presumably on Jo's dime. With his pockets still empty, Thanksgiving of 1932 could have been a bleak holiday for Fante, but it turned out to be a real feast day because he was the guest of the Paganos at a huge dinner of turkey, spaghetti, Denver celery and "all the good things which I like so well." As hungry as he had often been in recent weeks, the meal must have been all the tastier.

Fante suddenly had contacts in Hollywood, a reputable New York agent by the name of Maxim Lieber, and hopes that the lean days would soon be a memory. But mere contacts paid nothing, and hopes were uncertain. By early December Fante was feeling restless again. Maybe he would light out for a cottage on Catalina Island, or maybe he would go back to the haven of Helen Purcell's apartment in Long Beach. "I want to settle down and do some serious writing," Fante told his mother, but "I don't know my exact destination." What he did know was that his suit "was pretty near worn out. I have been wearing it every day for the last six months, and it's time I made a change." Mary's heart must have melted at John's catalogue of missing buttons, loose linings, and frayed spots on his trousers, all the more so when he confided his plan for cutting costs on new clothes, if he could ever afford them: "I can get my suit in the boys' size." Christmas was approaching, and no doubt John was feeling small when he told his mother he wanted to be home with his family for the holidays.

Instead, when he received payment from Mencken for "Altar Boy" he and Charlie Green rented a bigger apartment with good light and ventilation at 932 South Lake. Winter had come to southern California, bringing with it the rains and the winds, fine weather for gallery-hopping along Wilshire Boulevard and elsewhere. John was sharpening his eye on Japanese art and dismissing the attempts of certain local artists to paint Los Angeles as if it were New York with the curt declaration, "I have no love for bad artists." Fortunately for Fante, when he came home from these outings the new apartment was gas heated, and his bed had plenty of extra blankets. He was writing stories again, including one about the death of his cousin Mario, the doppelgänger of his vanished childhood. As he worked through his memories of that time, arranging the story's deeply felt life-and-death pairings, John fell ill with the flu. The penniless life of "vagrant bohemians" was taking its toll on John's digestion, which he had been fearing might "go to pieces soon unless I get decent, dietetic foods." As he happened to be in Long Beach at the onset of his illness, he stayed with the solicitous Helen Purcell, who for five days took care of him in her own bed.

Before the year was over John was back on his feet, buoyed by Mencken's acceptance of the much rewritten "Big Leaguer"—"the boy is myself, anxious to become a great writer"—and again sound enough in his stomach to go to lunch as the guest of a new acquaintance. Once again it was Mencken who facilitated the meeting between Fante and another Los Angeles–based contributor to the *Mercury*, an energetic lawyer and prolific writer who, like Fante, was also from Colorado. "He seems to be a very fine man," Fante wrote his mother the day following the lunch, going on to express a certain guarded optimism: "I think he likes me." Nor did Fante stop with that little confidence, for the feeling he came away with in the wake of this lunch was in reality also a hope: "I have a feeling something good may come of this." The feeling was mutual:

> One day I got a letter from Mencken saying that a promising young writer whose first story had just been published in *The American Mercury* wanted to meet me. His name was John Fante. So I asked him to have lunch—the first of countless meetings, at all hours, in every conceivable setting and circumstance. The visitor was a young Italian-American, quite short, with wicked rolling black Italian eyes and a glorious sense of humor. . . . He once dedicated a book to me as a "good friend but evil companion." I can say the same of him, in spades: he was, indeed, a more deplorable influence on me than I ever was on him.

Although Fante and his new friend both hailed from Colorado, their backgrounds could hardly have been more different; yet there were striking parallels as well. Born in 1905, Carey McWilliams had been raised on his father's cattle ranch in Steamboat Springs, Colorado. Jerry McWilliams was one of the wealthiest men in northwestern Colorado when he was elected to the Colorado state senate, and the young Carey attended an exclusive military academy in Denver. But the postwar slump caused the collapse of the big cattle empires and caught the senator by surprise. When he died in 1921 he was virtually a pauper. The reversal of fortune and sudden death of his father no doubt helped trigger Carey's excessive acting out the next year, his first at the University of Colorado in Denver, culminating with his expulsion after a disastrous Saint Patrick's Day celebration. His mother had gone to live in Los Angeles, so Carey came west to join her and to make a fresh start. Although he was without contacts in the strange new mushrooming city then flush in the boom of the 1920s, McWilliams did know how to type, and with that skill he landed a job in the business office of the *Los Angeles Times*. He spent the rest of the decade drinking up an education in the remorseless ways of laissez-faire capitalism, an interested witness to the Wonder City's mad scramble to outstrip itself in terms of every known human excess, and then some; so that by the time he completed his law degree at the University of Southern California in 1927, he was radicalized for life.

Brilliant, voluble, and a fiend for both work and play, as a student

McWilliams had edited *The Wooden Horse*, the literary journal of USC's Pen and Quill Club. An astute appreciation of H. L. Mencken which McWilliams contributed to the journal in 1925 had elicited an appreciative two-page response from his subject, and led in turn to the addition of McWilliams's name to Mencken's life list of significant young discoveries. In 1930 at the age of twenty-five McWilliams published his first major book, a magnanimous biography of that most misanthropic American, Ambrose Bierce. By the time he met John Fante for the first time over lunch in December of 1932, McWilliams had established a significant law practice devoted largely to social issues, a rising reputation as a writer and public speaker, and what amounted to a whirlwind presence at the ever-shifting centers of Los Angeles political and cultural life. When lunch was finished and McWilliams picked up the bill, Fante had good reason to be happy that his new acquaintance seemed to like him, because Carey, like John first and foremost a man's man, was also clearly a man who knew how to make things happen.

One of the first things Carey made happen for John was a meeting on the Culver City lot of Metro-Goldwyn-Mayer Studios with the head of the Story Department, Ross Wills. Wills had helped his friend Carey help other friends before, notably the literary critic Wilson Follett, who through Wills's good offices had gotten into MGM's Reading Department and then risen rapidly to writing scenes for Greta Garbo. Now Wills was taking John's breath away with talk of the princely sums commanded by adequate scenarios and the suggestion that John might have the inside track on a sophisticated drama Wills had in mind for Joan Crawford, or, failing that, a rather more trifling comedy drama. Talk with Ross Wills was always an adventure involving much expressive gesticulation and the telegraphic passing of notes, for he was stone deaf, a condition resulting from a near-fatal bout with spinal meningitis contracted when he was in the Navy. But John was a quick study, and he immediately began picking up from Ross the rudiments of sign language, soon mastering the system completely.

In addition to Wills, during this visit to the MGM lot Fante met screenwriter Donald Ogden Stewart, gossip columnist Hedda Hopper, and the lovely Maureen O'Sullivan, fresh from her role as Jane opposite Johnny Weissmuller in the studio's *Tarzan, the Ape Man*. It must have seemed to Fante a lifetime ago when he had played Tarzan back in Boulder with his creekside gang, inspired by the first film version in 1918 of Edgar Rice Burroughs's classic adventure yarn *Tarzan of the Apes*. Now that he was face to face with the people who made the dream factory work, and with the prospect of real money to be had once he started cooking up the right stories, playacting had never looked so good.

But he was not banking entirely on Hollywood. In January he wrote to Alfred A. Knopf asking for advance royalties on a novel. Knopf's response was prompt and encouraging, promising another quick response as soon as Fante sent him a synopsis. Pausing only to consult with McWilliams about possible legal ramifications, Fante fired off to Knopf a proposal for a novel to be called *Mater Dolorosa*. As he had told his cousin Jo Campiglia, brimming with self-confidence, "I am greedy to begin my novel. . . . I will write a great first novel, of this I'm positive."

Set in Denver, the proposed novel would focus on characters and themes that would concern Fante for years to come, centered on a colorful Italian-American family and the not always comical vicissitudes of poverty. Central to Fante's conception of the novel was an emphasis on the issue of birth control and the tensions sparked by the deeply Catholic mother's ambivalence regarding her husband's carnal propensities. "The idea is that she, being a religious woman, can't see her way to using contraceptives, while he, being a he-man feller, has simply to wave his prong in the air and the poor gal screams helplessly." Fante might joke about his novel with fellow writer Albert Halper, but he also confided that "I am putting myself in the book all I possibly can in the way of emotional reaction."

While he waited to hear back from Knopf regarding his proposal, as well as from the higher-ups at MGM about a scenario he had submitted, Fante took off with his new friend Ross Wills on a two-day, thousand-mile road trip to Death Valley. Snapshots show a rock-jawed Wills grinning from the driver's seat of a convertible roadster, and an implike Fante squatting behind a tumbleweed beside a rough unpaved road, careless of the desert immensity all about him. Once again John had fallen into likeminded and generous company, for although he was still always broke— the January sale of the story "Washed in the Rain" to *Touring Topics*, the monthly magazine of the Automobile Club soon to be renamed

Westways, had brought only $40—Wills never stinted on treating him: to meals, to drinks, and to the sporting events on which they both thrived, including football, both professional and collegiate clashes, and Pacific Coast Conference basketball matchups, especially Stanford games.

Like Carey McWilliams, Ross Wills was a graduate of USC, but the school that held the most symbolic weight for Fante was Stanford. Fante had already put the school to ironic use in "To Be a Monstrous Clever Fellow," in which the story's narrator claims absurdly to be a Stanford professor of communism. In the story he had sold to *Touring Topics*, Stanford assumed yet further significance, again absurd but now also tragic.

"Washed in the Rain" takes us back to Wilmington. The narrator, Frank, a poor cannery worker with a penchant for big dreams, falls in love with a picture of his boss's sister. Hazel is a popular student at USC and the steady girl of star Trojan quarterback Phil Mannix; as such she is not only oblivious to Frank's existence but also entirely out of his wishful reach. In order to compete with Mannix in the only way he knows how, that is, in his imagination, Frank lies about his past, concocting an elaborate fantasy in which he was recruited to play quarterback for Stanford by the legendary football coach Pop Warner. Then, as if to seal the fantasy with a sort of unintended death wish, he bets a whole month's wages on underdog Stanford in its upcoming game against USC. When the odds are upset and the bet pays off, Frank yields to an even more self-destructive impulse, ordering a custom-made Stanford letterman's sweater. The night that his sweater arrives he reads in the local paper that Hazel is returning to Wilmington with Phil Mannix, presumably to announce marriage plans. It is storming outside, but Frank is so angry at the inequities of his existence that he puts on the Stanford sweater and stalks out into the blinding downpour. He walks on and on, without aim or direction, until a bright yellow sports car pulling up at a stop sign splashes mud all over him. He recognizes the car's occupants to be Hazel and Mannix, but before he can blurt out anything the car speeds away, and Frank is left to stand there soaking in his despair.

> I didn't care anymore. I didn't give a damn for anything. When I thought of how Hazel was sitting so close to Phil Mannix, with both her arms around his right arm, and her head on his shoulder,

I didn't care. I was through. I was all washed up. And I didn't care about the black splotch across my sweater. I didn't care at all. And while I was walking through the rain toward home, I took out my jack-knife, and I cut and hacked that sweater off me. I ripped it off in hunks and strips, and tossed them into the gutter.

It is a startling conclusion, the narrator all but attacking himself with his own knife in order to be rid of the emblem of his undoing. Into the image of the false letterman's sweater is compacted all that is dangerous about Frank's inordinate ambition in wanting Hazel, and the self-destructive delusions that ensue. At Regis Fante would have learned all about inordinate ambition, one of the so-called Capital Sins forever pitted against the Cardinal Virtues. The Stanford cardinal, in fact, lends its hue to the sweater's false letter S, a scarlet letter of another kind, for it proclaims Frank's ensnarement in the web of his own lies, a web he can escape only by violently cutting and ripping and hacking himself out of it and thus exposing himself to the world's hostile elements. In doing so, of course, Frank also reveals not only what he has been, a liar and a self-deceiver, but also what he may be coming to be, namely, and paradoxically, a teller of truth in his (frank) confession of lies.

The paradox is as essential to "Washed in the Rain" as it is to so many other Fante stories. Not the least of these paradoxes is the story of John Fante's life as a storyteller, in which he strove to create something truthful by making things up, often deliberately blurring the line between the life that he lived and the fictional lives that he imagined in his writings. Speaking of the "truth" he pursued in his serious work, Fante would say, "I don't mean autobiographical fact. I mean something else. I don't know what you would call it, but it's different from autobiography, yet it's very much like it." The closest Fante could come to clarifying what he meant was to call that elusive something a "feeling." Fante knew how it felt to tell the truth, and he knew how it felt to lie. To say that these opposing activities often amounted to one and the same thing for Fante is to observe that he was able to contradict himself without qualm or compunction in his pursuit of that more rarefied feeling. The story was the thing. And in a most important way the story was John Fante, hacking away at the fictions in which he wrapped himself until his emotional guts were hanging out and he was beside himself with joy, it felt so good.

Hand in hand with his developing artistry, Fante's professional savvy was also coming along. "Washed in the Rain" had already been rejected once by *Touring Topics* when Fante learned that the magazine's editor was in love with his secretary, the sister of one of Fante's friends. Fante promptly talked his friend into talking her sister into interceding with the editor, and the story was accepted.

The editor's name was Phil Townsend Hanna, and he poured his boundless enthusiasm for Californiana—the state's history, literature and human esoterica—into each issue of *Touring Topics*. In addition to studying the marketplace potential of Hanna's magazine, Fante learned much from its regular columns and special features about his new home state and city. He would also have been aware of Hanna's *Libros Californianos: Or, Five Feet of California Books*, a list of essential readings on the Golden State published by Los Angeles bookdealer Jake Zeitlin and printed by Ward Ritchie in 1931. True, the deepest part of Fante's imagination was still in Colorado, to which he thought occasionally of returning. "I know that I could write a better book in Denver," he wrote to his mother in February, "due to the fact that the scene of the story is laid in Colorado." But the part of his imagination that was now in Los Angeles was also steadily deepening. For this he was indebted in no small way to Hanna, who in June hired Carey McWilliams as Wilson Follett's replacement on a monthly column, "Californiana Curiosa," featuring colorful and offbeat items about the state. (When *Touring Topics* became *Westways* in January 1934 the column was renamed "Tides West.") As much an outsider as Fante may have been when he arrived in the city, within a matter of months he was vitally connected, via McWilliams, Wills and now Hanna, to the very heartbeat of Los Angeles. But the problem was still how to survive.

When a new story, "My Mother's Goofy Song," was accepted by Whit Burnett and Martha Foley for publication in the first American edition (April 1933) of *Story*, until then published in Vienna, Fante's ego was lifted but not his finances, for the sale resulted in a nominal payment of only $15. His situation was again acute, though not as desperate as the situations of those hundreds of drifters who were being rounded up every day and jailed for being homeless. John had been "bumming around the very cheap and poverty-stricken sections of town and in the police stations," gathering material for an article he planned to write. Nothing came of this plan, but he was able to write his mother of the shock he felt at seeing other mothers, "[e]ven mothers with infants at their breasts," among the jailed. "God help those people," he wrote.

In February of 1933 Fante received a contract for a novel from Alfred A. Knopf. Instead of the $75 he had hoped for he would receive $50 each month until November, when the 150,000-word manuscript would be due to Knopf's offices in New York. It was by no means a fortune; he would be unable to have his brother Pete come join him in Los Angeles, for example, as he had been promising to do. But the money would keep him fed, clothed, sheltered and above all writing for the best part of a year. On February 18 the up-and-coming author was feeling flush enough to have a downtown artist trace his silhouette, which with its outline of the crisp knot in his necktie and a cigarette tucked jauntily between his lips made him look for all the world like a million bucks. The next day he sent the silhouette to his mother, asking her in the accompanying letter, "Say Mother. What do you think about me going back to Denver?" Also on that day, his mind obviously going in more than one direction at once, he wrote a letter to the American Consulate in Buenos Aires requesting assistance in contacting long-lost relatives on the Andrilli side of his family, as if to begin making for himself some kind of international reputation. In all it was a heady time.

After moving briefly to a hotel on Temple Street near the Mexican quarter downtown—his roommate Charlie Green had left L.A. for New York—by late February Fante was back in Long Beach and staying again with Helen Purcell. (One of the confounding lies confessed by the narrator of "Washed in the Rain" goes like this: "When I told you I took a girl named Helen Purcell to the Santa Barbara Biltmore, it was the truth, but there isn't any Helen Purcell that I know about.") There he attempted briefly to settle into a life of good works, but his efforts were at best contradictory, involving rash assurances that he was going to get his brother Pete either back into the seminary in Colorado or, alternately, into a job at the Tango Hall on the Long Beach Pike. But his real attention was on his writing, or for now at least on the publicity that his new status as an author under contract was generating. His name was mentioned favorably in an article by William Soskin in the *New York Evening Post* of March 1, and on March 3 the *Los Angeles Examiner* ran a breathless blurb evidently inspired by Fante's own self-promotion: "No one can boost an author but himself, so it is startlingly hopeful to learn that John Fante, who has been in the employ of Jean de Kolty, has landed on a rich lode." For its part, the *Long Beach Press-Telegram* used the occasion of Fante's contract to tout itself as a supporter of the arts by claiming not that the youthful novelist-to-be had merely borrowed a desk and a typewriter but rather that he had been "employed part-time by the Press-Telegram last Fall." What with all this and more—back-to-back stories in the February and March issues of *The American Mercury*, letters from far-flung fans, not to mention the appreciative attentions of Helen Purcell—it was enough to turn the head of an excitable twenty-one-year-old, especially if the head in question belonged to a shameless yarn spinner not a day younger than twenty-three. The tyro author had much to celebrate.

In the days ahead Fante extended his celebration, carrying the Knopf contract with him wherever he went. At some point he turned his attention back to the contract's final page, where he had signed his name. Again he uncapped his pen. Beneath Knopf's signature, which was directly beneath his own, he scrawled the following addendum: "very drunk and eating soft-boiled eggs at the Newhouse Café on March 6, 1933 at 11:53 A.M. and God bless the lord, even tho the banks are closed and god bless Mencken."

In vino veritas, quoth the Romans, who knew the truth serum that was wine. But wine was not the only thing moving Fante to write those words. Hunkered down in the Newhouse trying to settle his stomach, the once-faithful young scribe took up his pen to call down heaven's blessings in the face of what lay ahead.

Accounts of Fante's whereabouts and actions on the subsequent Friday afternoon, evening and night vary. But this much is clear: at 5:55 p.m. on March 10, 1933, a massive earthquake measuring 6.3 on the Richter scale struck downtown Long Beach. Buildings collapsed, fires broke out, and more than a hundred people were killed.

Fante's experience on this day would prove crucial six years later when he came to write *Ask the Dust*, for it is during that novel's pivotal earthquake scene, a postcoital moment like no other, that the freshly deflowered Arturo Bandini is shaken to the depths of his soul. In a novel with no shortage of memorable scenes, the earthquake scene is perhaps the most memorable of all, a tour de force rendering of interior tumult amidst external calamity which does justice to both extremes. Arturo has just left the apartment of the scarred and haunted Vera Rivken and is walking along the beach in an agony of guilt.

There was something breathless about the sky, a strange tension. Far to the south sea gulls in a black mass roved the coast. I stopped to pour sand from my shoes, balanced on one leg as I leaned against a stone bench.

Suddenly I felt a rumble, then a roar.

The stone bench fell away from me and thumped into the sand. I looked at the row of concessions: they were shaking and cracking. I looked beyond to the Long Beach skyline; the tall buildings were swaying. Under me the sand gave way; I staggered, found safer footing. It happened again.

It was an earthquake.

Now there were screams. Then dust. Then crumbling and roaring. I turned round and round in a circle. I had done this. I had done this. I stood with my mouth open, paralyzed, looking about me. I ran a few steps toward the sea. Then I ran back.

You did it, Arturo. This is the wrath of God. You did it.

The nightscape that follows is reminiscent of Brueghel's *The Triumph of Death*, as Arturo wanders through a desolation of broken bodies, smashed buildings and mad panic. Fante likewise mixes elements of physical and spiritual extremity in "The Wrath of God," a short story about grace and the restoration of faith set against the backdrop of the Long Beach earthquake. Here Jimmy Toscana is in the apartment of his lover, the Helen Purcell–inspired Claudia, moments before the quake.

All is banal—Claudia boiling marmalade on the stove as Jimmy thinks idly about having left the church for "a sinful woman" who has since begun to bore him—when the first temblor hits. In the ensuing chaos the lovers are separated, and Jimmy finds himself thinking of Augustine, Aquinas and St. Ignatius Loyola, then praying a prayer he did not know he remembered. Amazed, he realizes that his faith "was still there, strong as ever, right there in my blood, fighting off my fear of the quake, beating it down with a forgotten Latin and making me laugh for joy that it should guard me so selfishly, protecting me in a film of blood-prayer." Not for nothing was Fante a descendant of that race of poets who gave the world Blessed Thomas of Celano and his earthquake-inspired "Dies Irae": that day of wrath, indeed.

So much for Fante's fictional treatments of the earthquake. As for Fante's actions on the night of the quake, reports differ. Carey McWilliams claimed that at the time of the quake Fante "was spending a flirtatious evening with one of the more attractive instructresses" from Long Beach Junior College. Tom Cullen, one of the gay members of Skalds, remembered Fante handing out oranges from the back of a truck in Bixby Park, where survivors were camped out: "and I believe that [Fante] and I shared a pup tent there on one occasion." For his own part, calling upon his nascent gift for self-publicity, Fante saw to it that his experiences were duly embellished in at least two newspaper accounts. In one we read that real

> drama interrupted fiction when the Long Beach earthquake hurled John Fante, 21, Hollywood writer, from his typewriter to the floor unconscious.
>
> The young writer had written 15,000 words on his new novel when the temblors struck the beach city and wrecked the Patrician Apartments on East Fourth St. where Mr. Fante was domiciled. His prized manuscript was burned when the two-story building collapsed and later caught fire.

The tale he fed to a local Roseville paper was even taller, by two stories in fact: "A four-story apartment house in which he was residing . . . was completely destroyed, its walls crumbling to the force of the two major tremors. Despite the fact that he fell 60 feet amidst the tumbling debris, Fante was uninjured."

Blithely reporting him to be unconscious on the one hand and uninjured on the other, these self-serving concoctions would have fit right in to the humorous piece Carey McWilliams wrote for the June 1933 issue of *The American Mercury*, a compilation of myths, rumors and popular fancies occasioned by the Long Beach earthquake in the manner of his *Westways* column. One wonders, in fact, if Fante might not have contributed a morsel or two to his friend's comical stew, perhaps the one about the naked lady and the legionnaires, or the other one about the Beginning of the End. Though the earthquake had terrified him, he could still manage a laugh. But he was getting out of Long Beach for good.

A week after the earthquake Fante went back to Roseville. There he stayed with his family through the first week of July, or long enough to undergo a crisis in his writing. In a remarkable letter to Carey McWilliams written early in the summer, Fante told of how he had torn up all he had written of *Mater Dolorosa* to date, three months of work amounting to some sixty thousand words. What he had written was mere smartaleckry produced by the "wise guy" Fante knew how to impersonate and "not my real self." "The result horrifies me," Fante wrote, raking himself over the coals. And why?—"because there is no truth in it." Although the tensions at home were more than he could bear—among other things, his father was still without steady work, and in John's eyes Nick was more pitiful than ever—Fante had had it too easy for the past several months, living off his advance and merely playing at being a " 'novelist' Hey! Hey!" Now that he had realized his mistake it was time to get serious. He would return to Los Angeles, get some kind of a menial job, and make a new start on the book.

It suited him, life with a typewriter in a room downtown and a mindless job to help keep his head clear. Before the year was over Fante had found the room that would serve as the model of Arturo's room in *Ask the Dust*, "a man's room" as he called it, with leather chairs and good lamps, apartment 23 in the Alta Vista Hotel at 255 South Bunker Hill, in an area of dilapidated mansions dating back to L.A.'s heyday of the 1880s but long since converted into so many subdivided rooming houses. In July he had found a job as a busboy at the Marcus Barbecue Lunchroom at 328 West Third Street, where in August he was photographed for a flattering article in the *Los Angeles Examiner* headlined "Bus Boy During Day, By Night He's An Author"; and in October he had been let go. He had spent an August night in jail with Jo Pagano for disturbing the peace at a bar on Hollywood Boulevard, and in November at Santa Monica Beach he had swum naked in the ocean at two a.m. with a beautiful Mexican girl, an edgy skid-row *loca* named Audrey who waitressed at the Liberty Bar on L.A.'s Main Street and who liked to shock pedestrians by dangling her bare leg out the window of moving cars. By December he was being hailed as part of the "advance guard" of new American writers. He was living with his pores open, making Los Angeles his own, this city which could dizzy him with hope in one second and disaster in the next, this city with its swarming possibilities. He was doing what he had come there to do.

CHAPTER 7

Fante rang in 1934 at a New Year's Eve party with Ross Wills. The party was a Hollywood affair, and before the last guest staggered out Fante had met the screen siren Dolores Del Rio, consumed quantities of top-shelf liquor, and for several hours disported himself with equal parts abandon and cunning in a setting of industrialized glamor that he found both fascinating and repulsive. He might be living in squalor on Bunker Hill but in a crowd like this he knew better than to be self-effacing. After all, he had nothing to lose. By the end of the night he had wangled a dinner date with Del Rio's secretary, and not solely, if at all, for romantic purposes. "She has plenty of influence," he explained when sober the next day, "and I want to know her for that reason."

From the start Fante's attitude toward Hollywood was utilitarian and cynical. As young as he was, he did not have a starstruck bone in his body.

Rather, he had a ferocious desire to advance himself, by turns intuitive and calculating, which he was willing to put to work in order to make things fall his way. It would be months before he saw a nickel for all his efforts to crack the Hollywood system, but he was ready to play by the rules. And if a dinner date with the "snooty" secretary of a second-rate movie queen was part of the deal, well, that was a deal he was prepared to make.

His deeper emotional investments were reserved for the novel, which was showing signs of bogging down again. Though he was nearing the end of the manuscript, he was worried about losing control of the story he had contracted to write for Knopf—a story based largely on his father. Adding to these worries was Fante's concern about what he saw as his father's inexplicable deterioration. In January Fante unburdened himself to his surrogate father, Mencken, explaining the torment of witnessing the great Nick Fante's slide from brawling animal vitality to Sunday-mass-going helplessness. Mencken reassured Fante that "the ancient fact" of a father's aging was nothing to be upset about, but less than a month later Nick was involved in a horrible automobile crash in Roseville. Tossed from the car unconscious, he landed facedown in the creek that skirted the road, and he would have drowned had he not been pulled to safety by fast-acting witnesses. The accident's other victim had not been so lucky; the left side of his face was almost completely sheared off and he died. Though Nick recovered—his worst injury a broken wrist—it was not the sort of news to set a first-time novelist's mind at rest as he agonized his way toward the end of a project that had come to bedevil him with unforeseen difficulties.

Still, he finished it. By early April the manuscript—then called *In My Time*—was on its way to New York and Fante, nervous about a Knopf rejection, was again turning his attention to Hollywood. He and Ross Wills, the erstwhile Death Valley road trippers, were concocting "a nasty piece of hypocrisy" in the form of a scenario about the murderer John Dillinger, nasty because of its cynical portrayal of "the triumph of good over evil."

My partner and I have forced John Dillinger and his pals into Death Valley, California, and little by little the Lord is killing them off. The fiends die one by one of rattlesnake bites, lizard bites, tarantula bites, poison water, and hunger. It's all very terrible, and only goes to show what happens to sinners who break the law.

Fante's bête noire in all of this — "the obscene wails of the stinking, rotting modern Catholic church in the papers every day" — was the Catholic Legion of Decency. Beginning in November of the previous year, the Catholic Legion had mounted an increasingly successful crusade to pressure producers into abiding by the newly invigorated Motion Picture Production Code. The moralizing excesses of the Fante-Wills Death Valley treatment were thus contrived to pander to producers' fears.

Ironically, the man responsible for the anonymous writing of the Production Code was none other than Daniel A. Lord, S.J., the same Jesuit film consultant and inspirational retreat master who had regaled a younger John Fante with the liberating wonders of the imagination. Because of industry concerns about a ticket-buyers' backlash should the Jesuit authorship of the Production Code be revealed, the document was allowed to appear as if it had been spontaneously generated by the collective goodwill of the industry, and Lord's name went largely unmentioned in connection with it. (In a further twist of irony, Lord's Production Code — the single most effective force in ensuring studio self-censorship for the next quarter century — eventually came to be known as the Hays Code, after Will Hays, whose office had originally been established in an effort to weld the wildcat film industry into a socially responsible business and thus render censorship *un*necessary.) A decade after being urged during the three-day "Youth" retreat to soar on the wings of his imagination, Fante was putting his undeniably buoyant creativity to far lowlier, even grubbing uses, unaware that in doing so he was going up against a formidable opponent the likes of the uncredited Father Lord.

To make matters worse, scenario writing was in no way fulfilling. "The hell of it is," Fante complained to Mencken, "I'm writing for the studios, and it's the most disgusting job in Christ's kingdom." He found this way of writing to be treacherously different from the writing of literary prose, for you always had "to think of the motion picture machine."

Without even a paycheck to compensate for the mechanical drudge work—Fante and Wills were writing on speculation, gambling on the chance that they might lure a studio into purchasing the story and developing it into a film—Fante turned back to Nietzsche for sustenance. Forced by the censors to write with one hand tied behind him while trying to claw his way into the newly buttoned-up demimonde of filmdom, Fante found it necessary for his sanity to keep nightly vigil with the bristling antichrist himself—who before dying in 1900, hopelessly insane, had taken to signing himself "the Crucified One." Fante likened his need for the philosopher at this time to that of a sick man for medicine, "heavy doses" of it; but the image of an embattled Fante supplicating the unlikely Saint Friedrich in his time of need is an apt enough emblem of the inner life of contradictions on which Fante was now embarked.

When he heard back from Knopf the news was bad. Refusing so much as to recognize the manuscript of *In My Time* as a novel, Knopf insisted that Fante start work immediately on another book in order to fulfill his contractual obligations. Fante made a game effort not to show that he was crushed. After all, he had felt the warning of his doubts about the novel, and now he had to agree that it was "truly . . . bad." But he did not let the setback keep him down.

Soon he was revisiting Los Angeles Harbor in order to view for himself the scene of the bloody longshoremen's strike. In mid-June of 1934 several hundred strikes were in progress all over the country, most of them, like the action that was paralyzing docks from San Diego to Seattle, aimed at forcing owner-management recognition of newly formed labor unions. In the week that Fante came to witness the conflict, one striker died of police gunshot wounds, another was stabbed in the face with a pitchfork, a number of scabs were beaten up, and homemade mortars were used to lob bombs on Terminal Island. With Los Angeles Police Chief James Edgar Davis's notorious Red Squad all too ready to use both billy clubs and guns, Fante's sympathies leaned toward the strikers. But he was not about to subordinate his own artistic ambitions or individual desires to the escalating economic-political struggle then spreading throughout the land. If anything, this visit to old haunts from his days as a stevedore was a way of reframing his personal struggles as a writer vis-à-vis a mass labor struggle that he perceived to be external to, and apart from, his own. Men were being clubbed and gunned down in their battle for

the right to organize, and some of Fante's most-admired fellow writers were taking up positions in the thick of the political fray, men like
Carey McWilliams and the Yugoslav-American author and editor Louis
Adamic, whom Fante met about this time. But Fante remained unrecep-
tive to the "parlor Marxism" suddenly on the lips of "every bohemian and
lesbian and fairy," not to mention all the "schoolteachers and literary
hostesses and smelly slovenly radicals" holding their breaths for "the New
Day of Upton Sinclair." After seeing what he saw at the L.A. Harbor that
day, Fante knew where he stood, and that was squarely by the side of John
Fante. "My business in life," he proclaimed to Mencken, "is to save myself. That's a tremendous job. I shall not dirty my hands trying to save the
masses."

In order to save himself, however—at least insofar as he now understood the mechanics of salvation—he would not hesitate to dirty his
hands writing more "movie hokum." In July, even as *The Atlantic
Monthly* was accepting the beautifully executed if lugubriously titled
"One of Us Dies" (published in the October 1934 issue as "One of Us"),
Fante was back at work on another speculative collaboration. This time
he was working with a new partner named Frank Fenton, an English-
born graduate of Ohio State University who had come to Hollywood in
pursuit of a writing career. Undaunted by the failure of his Death Valley
collaboration with Ross Wills, Fante was now setting his sights on family
fare with a heart-warmer about a fatherless boy who, when his mother is
unjustly sent to prison, finds himself in an orphanage. Once again the
motive force in the choice and treatment of material was the invisible
hand of Father Lord. To his mother Fante wrote that "in view of the great
pressure and censorship brought upon the movies by the Catholic
Church," producers lately had been forced to scrap practically all of their
planned productions and were thus "now on the lookout for stuff that
won't arouse Mother Church." In a ploy to appeal to the producers' insecurity, Fante had "shrewdly inserted a Jesuit priest into the yarn." He had
the whole racket figured out. "The Catholic church is playing straight
into my hands with their absurd censorship. Joe Breen and Cardinal
O'Connell will glory at the sight of a Jebbie in the movies."

On July 26 Fante and Fenton submitted their scenario to Sam
Bischoff, a producer at Warner Bros. Leaving nothing to chance, Fante
didn't shrink from lying to Bischoff about his failed Knopf novel, telling

him that it was being seriously considered by the Catholic Book Club. Bischoff was evidently eager to be persuaded that he was hiring the right man, for he swallowed the bait whole; and on August 3 a Warner Bros. interoffice memo was circulated to studio chief Jack Warner indicating that the original unpublished story "Dinky" was being purchased from John Fante and Frank Fenton for $1,500. Later that day Fante and Fenton appeared on the studio's Burbank lot to close the deal, but only Fante was offered a contract, based on his relatively greater success as a published writer. Agreeing informally to subcontract half the work at half the salary to Fenton, Fante was suddenly a man of means, one of the lowest men on the Hollywood totem pole, it was true, but for all of that gainfully employed at the rate of $250 per week (minus Fenton's share), with a desk in the Writer's Building, a typewriter, a secretary—and all the anxieties that came with the turf.

In lying about his novel, Fante had exploited Bischoff's executive anxiety, and now he was to learn all about the razor's-edge discomforts of studio contract employment. In a letter to his mother announcing that he had signed the contract, Fante hastened to dampen whatever hopes Mary might have had for her son's long-term welfare by emphasizing that the "movies are very uncertain." "I'm not going to last long here," he wrote in another letter from this time; and in yet another, "I may be out of a job tomorrow. They are very strange about such things. You never know where you are, and at any moment you can expect to be fired." It would be the refrain of his long and checkered career as a Hollywood screenwriter, and one of the themes to which he would return in his novels more than once, notably in *My Dog Stupid* and *Dreams from Bunker Hill*. But for now he was situated, even cushily so, and there came over him at times in waves of merriment a sense of the far-fetched nature—the absurdity—of it all. Since Mencken had preapproved this detour into cinematic hack work, encouraging Fante to "get something from the movie magnates in order to finance the work you want to do," Fante now wrote to share his incredulity.

Dear Mr. Mencken:
Here I sit, laughing and laughing. I have a secretary and a great big office and a lot of people bow low when I pass, all of them hating my Dago guts.

I not only made these folks swallow that bilgewater but I did it to the tune of $1500, plus $250 a week for an indefinite period. Whoops! I never had so much money in the offing in my life; moreover, if my luck holds good I shall certainly bed Del Rio inside of four weeks.

But even capering for Mencken, Fante could not restrain the real writer within him. Before this letter was finished Fante was all but levitating on the poetry to be found even in the fabricated stage name of "the world's worst actress," and on the destiny he felt was his:

all I do is write and laugh and laugh and think of Dolores Del Rio: the sorrows of the river. Sweet river. My river. I'm going swimming in that river. I'm going to navigate that river. I think maybe I shall buy that river. I am like Columbus. I stand at the water's edge and dream. And like my countryman, they shall bring me back in irons. But I love it.

The rhapsody continued in a seagoing vein as Fante quoted from Oliver Wendell Holmes's "Old Ironsides"—"And the harpies of the shore shall pluck the eagle of the sea!"—before moving on to *Childe Harold's Pilgrimage*—"Roll on, thou dark and deep blue ocean, roll!"—claiming for himself a genius equal to that of Byron's. For someone who had published a grand total of five short stories, that was a claim that remained to be proven. But this being Hollywood, whatever genius he might possess would have to be put on hold for a time, while Fante attended to the business at hand.

Over the next two months that business included finishing up work on "Dinky" and then plunging immediately into two subsequent projects. The surprise is that the first of these latter two turned out to be a story entitled "Bandini," a fifty-five-page treatment about Svevo Bandini, described as an artful stonecutter in New York's Little Italy who specializes in carving gravestones. A widower whose wife died in giving birth to their only son, Bandini is a rough, swashbuckling braggart who nevertheless concentrates his whole existence in the passionate love of ten-year-old Gino. In contrast to his father, Gino is quiet and sensitive but he is also a chip off the paternal block in being artistically gifted (he plays the violin), physically compact and, when angry, unable to control his temper.

Now that he had successfully marketed himself as a writer to Hollywood, Fante would try to have it both ways. Far from home and cut off by "the motion picture machine" from the kind of writing that he knew and loved best, he was going back to the well of personal memory even as he strove to satisfy the story needs of his bosses. "Most of the ideas in the story," as Fante wrote to his mother, were "borrowed from my recollections of Papa." Moreover, operating under the constraints of B-movie melodrama, he managed to use this treatment to experiment with story elements that four years later would reemerge transformed in *Wait Until Spring, Bandini.* For example, against all common cultural sense the passionate paisano Svevo Bandini allows himself to be seduced by the icy blond widow Inger Tremaine, a crude but unmistakable prototype for the novel's Mrs. Hildegarde. And like Arturo in the novel, the Gino of "Bandini" is thrown deeply out of sorts by the rupture in his family life caused by the interloping widow. But at its core "Bandini" is merely more movie hokum, replete with a gangland slaying, a hidden treasure and a prison sequence featuring none other than Svevo Bandini behind bars. Whether or not Fante was already beginning to feel in some way a prisoner of his own first success, he was learning that the constraints of the business, if not completely inflexible, could be suffocating enough.

Despite the recommendation of one Warner executive that Fante's story "could be whipped into an excellent picture," the project was ultimately shelved, although not before producer Hal Wallis had put Fante back in his writer's stall with a memo forbidding him to infringe any further on producer Bischoff's domain by trying to talk up the project on the lot with various actors, among them Edward G. Robinson. But there was little time to begrudge the scolding. By October Fante and Fenton had been assigned to develop another original story, again with a distinctly Italian flavor. "Dago Mike Cantello" had its hero Dago Mike working his way up from carrying hod to becoming the richest, most important builder of skyscrapers in New York City, only to lose everything in the stock market crash of 1929. Unlike "Bandini," however, which showed flashes of life in the writing, the fifteen pages of this treatment are a deadening labor to read, pure potboiling bunk, evidence, it would appear, that even as he was writing it, Fante's interests, not to mention his heart, were elsewhere.

Specifically, he wanted to refocus and take another shot at the novel. The October appearance of "Washed in the Rain" in *Westways* and "One of Us" in *The Atlantic Monthly* must have amounted to some kind of self-reproach, for although earlier he had been hoping for a long-term Warner contract, Fante now expressed no disappointment when on October 10 he was released. On the contrary, he hastened to put a full thousand miles between himself and Burbank, boarding a train "on impulse" the next night for his first trip back to Colorado since he had left nearly five years before. For the first time in his life he had made some money. He had hated most aspects of the wage-earning process, it was true, but now that the cash was his he was putting it to the kind of use that only a certain kind of citizen—a novelist in the making, for example—would consider a sound investment. He was going back to confront his "bitter memories of a devilish boyhood."

In two of the three extant versions of this Denver trip—a 1941 caricature by Ross Wills that had Fante boarding the train in a clownish suit, and Chapter 25 of *Dreams from Bunker Hill*—the returning native makes a fool of himself by bragging of his exploits in Hollywood. The fictional nature of both these accounts notwithstanding, it is possible that while in Denver Fante did stoop to something of the kind. Back among people who in the past had had reasons to doubt him, he may well have succumbed to his weakness for self-aggrandizement and been stung by his own overdoing. This is conjecture, of course. What we know for sure from the terse third version of the trip—less colorful than the fictions but in its simplicity more convincing—is what he later reported to Mencken, namely, that while in Denver he had "felt very lost and sad."

On November 2 Fante left Denver by train. Two days later he arrived in Roseville, where he stayed long enough to report on his trip and eat a few home-cooked meals before training out again for Los Angeles. He had spent the first part of 1934 in a beachside Venice apartment at 40 Westminster Avenue, a period seared in his memory by an encounter with a tubercular young Jewess whose desperation and mysteriously scarred loins would reappear in *Ask the Dust*'s characterization of Vera Rivken. After that he had moved to Culver City to room with Ross Wills at 2316 Clyde Avenue, but even though it was a house, the quarters were too close for comfort and the move did not prove conducive to writing. Wanting badly to get back to his novel, Fante returned to his beloved rooming house on Bunker Hill. There he had two windows, one of which looked out on a deep green grassy hillside, the lights of the city and in the distance the San Gabriel mountains. "It is a fine room," Fante wrote in describing it, "a room I know I shall always like and one where I hope to work hard and pleasantly."

Situated at last, Fante felt virtuous enough to report going to Christmas Eve midnight mass, most likely at the venerable chapel of Our Lady in the Plaza downtown, or perhaps at the grander cathedral at 2nd and Main, where he would have been able to see atop the altar encased in a glass coffin the wax effigy containing the relics of third-century Roman virgin and martyr St. Vibiana. If indeed he did go to midnight mass, we can wonder if he prayed, in spite of himself, for the success of his new novel, and for the Guggenheim fellowship he dreamed of winning. If so, then perhaps as an afterthought he also prayed for world peace—or if not for world peace then for his own precious hide—in view of the coming world war. Like everyone else with a sense of the darkening world situation, he could feel the war coming. But as with the longshoremen's strike, he wasn't about to sacrifice himself. His notions of obligation were far too self-centered for that, as is suggested by his reflexive response to the possibility of a second global cataclysm: "I often ask myself what the war will do to me when it comes." As worldviews go, Fante's could be as narrow and shallow as that, revolving entirely about himself; or as deep as he could see looking inside.

CHAPTER 8

What he saw when he looked into the mirror in January 1935 was that he had grown to look startlingly like his father, Old Nick himself, and "[not] such a bad looking devil after all." But he was also putting on a lot of weight. Even though he knew better, he would binge at times on greasy fried meats and dairy products by the gallon—behavior that suggests a sharp level of unhappiness. If such was indeed the case we may have to look for explanation no further than his writing and how it was coming along.

Rather than settling into his room and getting back to the novel— "That novel," he professed, "means everything"—by the tenth of January Fante had abandoned Bunker Hill and was again living in studio-convenient Culver City with Ross Wills. He was nearly broke and back to toiling on speculative movie possibilities, once more harnessed up with

Frank Fenton, whom he candidly considered "a competent hack-writer." On February 8 he signed on as a client of theatrical literary agent Minna Wallis, president of International Play Company, the better to get studio writing jobs. By February 15 he was back on the Warner Bros. payroll, teamed up now with New York writer Joel Sayre under producer Robert Lord on a project entitled *Stiletto*.

The material this time was not new, having passed through the Underwoods of various writers since at least 1933. Recently arrived in New York's Little Italy, the story's cousins Joe and Luigi Toscana take different life paths, Joe entering law enforcement while Luigi falls into the Mafia. With Prohibition repealed and liquor no longer illegal, Sayre and Fante strained to make olive oil the focal point of a gangland extortion scheme. The presiding tone of the story is thus one of ethnic burlesque, featuring a mustachioed hurdy-gurdy man with a dancing monkey and other such "Italian" touches. But when the building in which Luigi's parents live is dynamited by the Mafia, the tone turns abruptly ponderous. Joe vows single-handedly to hunt down the murderers, one by one, and while doing so he captures the heart of the beautiful young Stella. Wedding bells ring out. The End.

Though he had never set foot east of North Platte, Nebraska, Fante had fast become in studio eyes the screenwriting equivalent of a native guide to New York's Mulberry Street and environs. It was a charade he did not enjoy but he was willing to play along for what it was worth, in this case his old salary of $250 per week. As for the thoroughly pedestrian story he was being paid to rehash, there could have been no enjoyment in that either. But he liked Joel Sayre, a generous and easygoing man who taught him much about the business—too much, perhaps, for while Fante came to the job "on fire . . . to make good," Sayre, who would rather play poker than write, urged him to take it easy. Fante could not bring himself simply to sit there and collect his paycheck—he would later claim to have written most of *Stiletto* on his own—but as long as he was going to be on the lot upstairs in the two-story Writers' Building he would heed Sayre's advice to the extent that he would take his pleasures where he found them. Among other things, he got to play a little baseball again, pitching on a Warner Bros. pickup team that included comedian Joe E. Brown at second base and a number of other writers as "slow and fat and lazy" as John himself.

It was a life he was discovering he could live; so that before he and Sayre were both fired in April because of Sayre's nonchalant working habits, Fante applied for and was granted membership as an Associate in the newly formed Screen Writers Guild, at this early point in its history still a branch of the Authors' League of America. In joining the Guild Fante was signaling a professional interest in sticking around what could be a highly unprofessional industry, one in which writers in particular were regarded as so many interchangeable parts in its vast and relentless scheme of production. But, lest we forget, Fante brought with him to the job a wealth of factory-hand experience gained from working at the California Packing Company, canning fish. If his genius didn't pan out, he had a skill to fall back on. Just in case.

In April *Dinky* was released to the secondary movie houses for which it was intended, and to uniformly unenthusiastic reviews. Typical was the one in *The Hollywood Reporter*, which called the picture "mildly entertaining," commending the efforts of its child actors but flatly declaring, "The story is no great shakes." As Fante shared the credit line for Original Story (with Frank Fenton and Samuel Gilson Brown, with Screen Play credit going to Harry Sauber), he could now say with more conviction than ever, "I don't like the movies, I have never liked them, and I shall never like them. But," the problem was, "I *do* like the salaries they pay."

Now, however, he was off salary again, living "in constant anticipation of a telephone call which will send me to work at one of the studios." But the phone was not ringing, so he was finally taking the first uncertain steps in starting the new book, which he was calling a "personal novel." He had spent the last year writing nothing but letters and movies—his mind was stale, and he found himself starting over and over again. He was ripe for another head-clearing road trip with the ever-ready Ross Wills, who was flush with cash and a new car from the recent sale of a scenario. Again the pair headed for the desert, but instead of Death Valley this time they found themselves in the little upstart town of Las Vegas, Nevada, where they gambled themselves down to Ross's last dollar. When he got home Fante was exhausted, hung over and fed up: with Los Angeles and Hollywood and people and talk, and with being fat and not feeling well. Here in the city there were too many temptations, and he was weak in both flesh and spirit. He longed for the old days when he might have been hungry but when he had done so much good solid work. If he could not put the devil behind him in the desert, he would flee in the opposite direction, to land's end at Terminal Island, where he would "rest and read and let the sun burn all the impurities out of my heart."

Today Terminal Island is the center of the planet's busiest port, an otherworldly landscape east of the Vincent Thomas Bridge featuring giant heaps of smoking asphalt, a dry-dock boneyard for the dismantling of scrapped ships, a sewage treatment plant, a pet food cannery, a stock-car drag strip and a maximum security federal prison. By contrast, when Fante moved there seeking refuge in late May 1935, he found a quietly thriving fishing community of mostly Japanese and Filipinos, as far removed in spirit and pace from the desperation of depression-era Hollywood as he could have hoped for. There he settled into a comfortable room in an old house at 153 Seaside Avenue and, as he had promised, he began getting back into shape. He swam, fished and grew brown under the sun, all the while observing with particular attention the island's Filipinos, who fascinated him. He also got down to work on the novel, which was going to be "autobiographical, of course." But try as he might he could not separate himself entirely from the other half of his writing self, for during this time he continued to keep careful tabs on the progress of a story he and Fenton had circulating among the studios. Nor was this the only connection to Hollywood from which Fante found it hard to shake free. When his Denver cousin Eddie Campiglia, in California to spend the summer with his Capolungo relations, came to the island to visit late one day, he had to step out on the porch and amuse himself for the entire evening while inside Fante entertained a visitor from Hollywood, the Warner Bros. contract starlet Ann Dvorak.

All his good intentions notwithstanding, by mid-July the Terminal Island experiment in self-purification was finished, and John was back in town living in a tiny Hollywood garden bungalow. Days were spent working on his fiction—both the new novel and the failed Knopf manuscript, which like a quarry worker he was breaking up into individual stories— while nights were given over to yet another get-rich-quick script collaboration with Ross Wills. Increasingly split between these two modes of writing, Fante found himself holing up alone for days on end, and then making a spectacle of himself when he emerged, snarling and yapping like a hurt dog in frustration at his inability to satisfy his desire for success. It was a maddening shuttle, tearing himself away from the book he was working hard to make "honest to the point of ghastliness" in order to show up for glad-handing job interviews at Warner Bros., at RKO, at Paramount and at MGM. It was all the more maddening when not a single interview amounted to anything.

By mid-August he was again without a cent, living on what Ross Wills would loan him. With no novel on submission he could look forward to no news from his New York literary agent, while closer to home he was hearing nothing from the Hollywood film studios. Then, the things of heaven never being far from his hell-bent train of mind, Fante made the mistake of getting into "a religious talk" with his landlady, who, taking offense at certain caustic remarks he made about Los Angeles evangelist Aimee Semple McPherson, promptly evicted him from his bungalow. He managed to stay off the streets by accepting the shamefully low salary of $100 a week to work "like a dog," six days a week, at the aptly named Mascot Studio, and by moving into the Hotel Mark Twain on North Wilcox Avenue, then as today a squalid but centrally located operations base for Hollywood newcomers, outsiders and passers-through. He hated the hotel, his job was pure misery, and again he felt the omens of coming war. But whenever the war might arrive he would have nothing to do with it: "The only war I care to fight is the one I start myself." Trouble was, he was already fighting just such a war, and the battlefield was himself. By November he was a casualty. Struggling to write an impossible Foreign Legion story at Republic Studios ominously entitled "The Legion of the Lost," he fell victim to all the pressures.

I nearly collapsed last Wednesday. The blood left my head and knees and everything began to whirl. I had to grab a chair to keep from falling down. My heart was pounding furiously, the sweat broke out in my face, and all at once I had a terrible fever. The siege hit me so suddenly and so unexpectedly that I got a real scare. For a moment I thought I had been poisoned and that I was about to die.

For three days he endured shooting pains in his stomach and chest, difficulty in breathing, ringing in his ears, and insufferable anxieties bordering on an extended panic attack caused by the terror of impending death. When he was finally able to move about, he went for medical assistance. But the doctor was unable to make any conclusive diagnosis, placing him by default on a strict vegetable diet and sending him on his way to deal as best he could with the aftereffects of what must strike us at least in part as something perilously close to a breakdown.

Fortunately he now had a helpmeet. She was Marie Baray, a beautiful bronze-skinned Mexican girl with high-cheeked Indian features who swayed when she walked, and who made enough money to get by working as an artist's model around town, notably at the Otis Art Institute and the Chouinard Art Institute, both located near MacArthur Park. For the past several months Marie had been like a wife to John, washing his clothes, darning his socks and sharing what little money she had with him. Throughout his recent ordeal she had been indispensable, helping him to get through the worst part of it, the nights. As 1935 drew to a close, she had nursed John back to a reasonable state of health. True, he had lost an alarming amount of weight and his gums were still bleeding, but when he was strong enough he joined the Hollywood YMCA, where he would go "every afternoon for exercise and nude sun baths" on the canvas-fenced roof of the building. Having his health back was good for he could be with Marie almost constantly, and when they were together they had a lot of fun.

They liked doing things differently. In order to celebrate Christmas they pooled their money, all nine dollars of it, and rode a Pacific Electric Red Car to a romantically isolated beach town, most likely Seal Beach. There they took a hotel room, waking up early enough on Christmas morning to have breakfast and attend mass in the town's little church. In John's view Marie was "a highly excitable girl, easily frightened," and she needed John as much as he needed her. So when she gave him to understand that she wanted him to be her husband, John promised that they would soon marry. Perhaps in his charity, such as it was, he did not want to excite her unduly, or perhaps he had other reasons; but the fact was that they needed each other in distinctly different ways. Marie did not know John well enough to understand that when he wanted to tell the truth, he put it in his fiction, which could be "honest to the point of ghastliness." But the truth did not always coincide with the facts. And the fact was that Fante needed Marie just enough to tell her what she wanted to hear, which was not in this case the truth. He had no intention of marrying her.

Another woman entered John's life at this time who understood the young writer far better than did Marie, and with whom he had a far deeper if ultimately unconsummated relationship. For much of 1936 theirs was a passionate, indeed, tumultuous affair and yet, strange to say, the two never met face to face.

Elizabeth Nowell was an independent New York literary agent whose clients included Thomas Wolfe, Alvah Bessie, Vardis Fisher and Nancy Hale. Before striking out on her own she had worked at Scribner's for five years, where she had lobbied editor Maxwell Perkins to accept Fante's "My Mother's Goofy Song" for *Scribner's Magazine*, only to have Perkins finally refuse the story on the grounds that it was "too cruel." Later she had been associated briefly with Fante's agent Maxim Lieber, who in February, incensed at what he considered Fante's badgering inquiries about the nonsale of his stories, was calling Fante "a spoiled little baby with a bit of a talent," and throwing in for good measure that he, Lieber, "would just as soon have someone else be a nurse-maid to you." (Relations between the two men had been strained ever since mid-1934, when, according to Fante, Lieber had refused to handle one of his stories because it was ironically pro-Catholic.) Doubtless aware in the small world of New York publishing that a break was imminent, Nowell wrote Fante the first of a remarkable series of letters, professing authentic enthusiasm for both his work and the promise of his career, and proposing herself as his agent. With Lieber out of the picture Fante accepted the proposal, and thus ensued a crucial era in his development as a writer—and, as we might say, thanks to Nowell's passion for her new client, in the development of the writing genius that he had long assumed to be his but that he had not yet resoundingly demonstrated.

Fante's half of the correspondence has been lost, but Nowell's alone, covering the period from January to August 1936, would fill a small and very interesting volume. In ardent single-spaced missives as long as six typed pages, Nowell alternately sweet-talked and harangued Fante on the subject of his writing and how best to ensure its placement not only in the hands of the best publishers but also in the annals of lasting literature. Taking up her cudgel she railed against the cheap trick Knopf was playing on Fante by pretending his first book didn't exist simply because, in Knopf's eyes, it "wasn't a novel," and then demanding a second novel to fulfill the original contract. She entered Fante's application for a prestigious Houghton Mifflin fellowship for first-time novelists, and she kept a steady stream of his stories on submission at the most prestigious magazines and journals, always accompanied by her heartfelt endorsement. After three years of dealing with an increasingly testy Lieber, Fante found Nowell's full-service enthusiasm a welcome change. But where she did the most to further Fante's advancement as a writer was in her relentlessly refining criticism of the novel with which he continued to struggle, the book that would become *The Road to Los Angeles*.

The first thing Nowell did was to steer Fante away from the "Hollywood ending" of his first outline, which called for the plot-heavy descent of a mere deus ex machina in the form of some "murder-insanity-melodrama business." What this business consisted of specifically is unknown, but Nowell was convinced that the story of eighteen-year-old Arturo Bandini in Wilmington, California, had less in common with run-of-the-mill studio pap than with a certain international literary classic. In fact the book's hardest selling point—it was yet another first novel based on the notorious first-novel cliché of a young misfit who justifies himself by becoming a writer—was precisely what put the discriminating Nowell in mind of Knut Hamsun's great novel *Hunger*.

Published in 1890, *Hunger* was the first of a four-novel cycle—including *Mysteries* (1892), *Pan* (1894) and *Victoria* (1898)—which, thanks to Nowell, Fante would come to prize as highly as if not more than any other works of literature. In *Hunger* Hamsun told the story of a destitute youth in the city of Christiania (now Oslo) who, under the twin pressures of hunger and a spiraling obsession to become a great writer, grows increasingly delusional. The plot of the novel is vagrant, even negligible, but the uncanny power of Hamsun's writing to evoke the tick and whir of another consciousness is nothing short of dazzling, and no less so in

George Egerton's 1921 English translation for Knopf, which Nowell and Fante were now closely discussing in their letters.

Even absent Fante's half of the correspondence, Nowell's provides a record of Fante's crucial immersion in the model that, more than any other, would influence his style at its most idiosyncratic, which is also to say its most characteristic: a style of deceptive simplicity, emotional immediacy and tremendous psychological point, all delivered in a seemingly improvised first-person voice which by turns addresses itself in the second person and narrates itself in the third. In arguing mightily that *Hunger* was the right model for the work he had set out to do, Elizabeth Nowell helped John Fante overstep the charming limitations of his early stories—the emotional ingrowth and homebound narrowness Mencken had pointed out—in order to become John Fante the novelist, whose quartet of Arturo Bandini novels would eventually become his own self-defining monument.

But back to Nowell and Fante's mighty arguing:

Dear Fante:

Well, at least my letter did some good. . . . You sound plain outraged and insulted and I don't blame you. Probably I ought to say: my dear, you're completely right, forget anything I wrote you but I'm too convinced of the ruin that I might be responsible for by such a laissez-faire policy. Because after all it's far better for you to have fifteen fits of rage at me than for you to go ahead and do another book half-cocked and then let it put you into another period of despondency and mistrust of yourself and all that cycle you've just been through. I guess you're the kind of guy who's bound to get himself in for as much punishment as anybody in the world, but if you'd only take things more easily.

What Nowell was trying to persuade Fante of by ripping into his manuscript so ruthlessly was that his was a talent, and this was a story, of potentially lasting value—as long as he didn't blow his chances for success on tricked-up Hollywood effects. When it came to understanding how to get a rise out of Fante, Nowell had his number down cold. But she also knew how to gentle him once she had gotten his hyped-up attention. (An extended comparison she draws at one point between her concern to keep Fante "steered right" and the sensitivity required in "riding a colt who's too highly bred and green and excitable" suggests that Nowell was a seasoned horsewoman.) In short, she understood Fante in a way no one else had yet understood him:

> Now you, John Fante, are a sort of split personality for the purposes of this argument. On the one side you're Arturo with all his petty weaknesses. . . . On the OTHER side you're a really fine and talented writer . . . with a sort of understanding of the world in some queer intuitive way, a tremendous sympathy and pity and tenderness for the people in the world, and an almost indescribable power of being a character and still seeing that character from the god-the-author angle. . . . I think you'll learn as you go on to control the two sides of yourself and to feed the god-the-author side with material from the Arturo-the-worm side. It's a kind of psychological perpetual motion scheme which writers have evolved and patented. Arturo uses John Fante as a safety valve and John Fante uses Arturo as a subject for study and a means of livelihood, and if you keep the balance right you'll get along smoothly and successfully and be both happy and a great writer.

Considered in the retrospective light of Fante's four Bandini novels and indeed of his oeuvre as a whole, these are acute observations. But they were much more acute and even prescient in 1936, when not one of those novels had yet been completed and John Fante was still feeling his way toward an ending, a novel, a career. Through much of their correspondence Nowell pressed hard for Fante to recognize the wholeness of his vision: "The more I think of it the more I'm convinced that both your books and most of your stories are all segments from this one big subject." Similarly, she pressed just as hard for a recognition of how central to that vision was the religious and specifically Catholic basis of Fante's sensibility. (The "constant struggle between religion and reason," which Nowell saw permeating Fante's work, inspired her to exhort Fante toward "a sort of DeQuincey's 'Confessions of a Catholic Opium Eater,' " and for a time the novel was called *Good Morning God!*) But Fante resisted this recognition, disavowing the very part of his earliest outline that Nowell found most compelling. In goading him to reconsider, Nowell quoted back to him this part of that outline:

> "Arturo's hatred for the Church is superficial. . . . Having been taught by nuns, the result is a Catholic intuitively but a renegade intellectually, and Arturo is at all times a renegade. But in completing the circle of his renegade adolescence, he finally returns to the values of his birth: his home, his mother and sister, his Church. Once a Catholic always a Catholic is the adage, and it holds good here."

Never mind, as Nowell was convinced, that such an approach would "have bearing on all the muddled Catholics in the wide world over." As she saw it, this essentially religious appreciation for the cyclical nature of things—and not the Hollywood sharper's angle—was the deep human theme that gave resonance to Arturo's story, and that would catapult it, strangely enough, into the same universal realm as Hamsun's areligious (or pantheistic) *Hunger*. The dispute was a sticking point in their dialogue, but more than anything Nowell wanted Fante to see it her way. And once they could reach some kind of agreement she promised she would "stop fighting you like a tiger and fight *with* you instead, against the rest of the world, editors, book buyers, critics, and what not." In so many words Elizabeth Nowell was a fierce and uncompromising partisan, the kind of rival Fante needed on his side.

Before Fante could be convinced of her point about the religious theme, however, he went and mucked everything up. In an ill-conceived effort to impress James W. Poling, an editor at Doubleday, Doran and Company, Fante dared to say in a letter that Louis Adamic had read and liked the novel in progress—before Adamic had ever laid eyes on it. It was another case of Fante lying to promote himself, only this time it backfired, for when Elizabeth Nowell got wind of the deception, she laid it on the line for Fante: "[I]f I find I can't trust you [then] I can't represent you so it seems only fair to give you warning." She continued pushing the Fante cause, touting his prospects with William Soskin of Stackpole Sons and coaching him through a third and then a fourth set of revisions. But on July 29, after delivering the novel to Knopf, she sent him an unexpected bombshell: she could no longer in good conscience be his agent. "I guess it'll hurt your feelings," she wrote, sounding herself like the injured party, "but I realized in the midst of this worrying that I really didn't trust you and never could." Seizing the advantage of the higher moral ground, she said she didn't expect him to pay her any commission, even if he could afford to. And at the risk of sounding "too damn noble and generous for words," she reiterated her admiration. "You really are one of the most talented writers I've seen," she said sincerely. But she had come to her decision, which "under the circumstances I honestly think [is] the best and only way for both of us. . . . I do hope you'll understand." In tone and content it was all very much like a wised-up lover's regretful but determined kiss-off.

Thus forsaken, Fante sent letter after letter—"all those roses," Nowell called them—in an effort to win her back. But all to no avail. He was free as a bird. Or any worm in the dirt. We can be sure he was chewing his liver.

A month before being dumped by Elizabeth Nowell, Fante had extricated himself from his duplicitous and increasingly stormy relationship with Marie Baray. As late as 1980 Fante would recall Marie as "a beautiful Mexican model" and the "cruel memory" of the time they spent together "fighting like tigers, ending our sojourn together in a bitter quarrel from which we never recovered." Although his announced intentions had remained the same, it had become clear that he did not want to marry. At most, as he admitted to his mother, he wanted a wife who could "dress well and increase my own prestige." According to Yetive Moss, a close friend of Marie's at the time, Fante made no end of promising that he and Marie were meant for each other, but in the end he treated her shabbiliy. How exactly he ended up treating her remains a secret, for to this day Moss refuses to break her friend's confidence, which she swore more than sixty years ago. But a close reading of Fante's June 24 letter to Carey McWilliams suggests that Marie tried to institute some sort of civil action against Fante. Having washed his hands of all involvement with Marie, he told McWilliams, "I bequeath her to you. However, I hope she has not come with further trivia in the way of penny ante law suits. That last one was very embarrassing to me, and it was nice of you to dismiss it so easily." One wonders if it could have been a paternity suit that McWilliams had brushed aside. If so, all the sadder for Marie Baray, for it is plain from Fante's cavalier attitude about the whole affair that he was in no way ready to look out for, much less take care of, anybody other than himself.

With the wifely Marie now gone from his life and Hollywood's teat sucked dry for the time being, Fante was in the mood to be mothered. In May he moved back to Roseville, intending to stay for the next six months or so. Quarters were close at the house his family now occupied at 211 Pleasant Street—as in his Colorado childhood he again shared a bed with both Tommy and Pete—so he arranged to work in a basement room of the Carnegie Library at 557 Lincoln Street, today the site of the Roseville Historical Society. There he finished revisions of *The Road to Los Angeles*, which, though it might "be too strong, i.e., lacking in 'good taste,'" nevertheless pleased him with all its "blood and pain." He was also delving into the library's relatively well-stocked holdings, devouring among other things Hubert Howe Bancroft's multivolume *California Pastoral* and Plato's *Dialogues*, the *Apologia* of Socrates striking him in particular as "the finest thing ever written." For diversion he took up golf.

Early in August his novel was rejected by Knopf as "unworthy of publication," and, in the words of the editor writing on Alfred A. Knopf's behalf, it was being rejected with "particularly great disappointment." Then again late in the month the book failed at Vanguard Press, whose president found Fante's manuscript "extremely provocative . . . but, I fear, not for us." By mid-September the book had suffered its third rejection, this time from Story Press editor Martha Foley, who praised Fante's "marvelous writing" throughout but found fault with what she felt was the narrative's "boring . . . effect of repetitiousness." Fante was ready to burn the manuscript as soon as it was returned. Fortunately he restrained himself, and *The Road to Los Angeles* was finally published, albeit only after Fante had died. As it stands today, *The Road to Los Angeles* is an entrancing tour de force of manic energy and youthful bravado, with its self-obsessed no-gooder Arturo Bandini enduring a ghastly comedy of existential torment, and dishing out much of the same thing to anyone unlucky enough to cross paths with him. *Hunger* certainly must come to mind as we follow Arturo's demented peregrinations through the pitiless streets of Wilmington and witness him spouting Nietzsche, scribbling nonsense, and shadowing women who terrify him, all in the name of his own self-proclaimed genius. Under *Hunger's* influence, *The Road to Los Angeles* captures the tensile grip of a consciousness pushed to extremes by poverty, ambition and failure.

The novel opens with an unsentimental declaration: "I had a lot of jobs in Los Angeles Harbor because our family was poor and my father was dead." The struggle to survive in the face of what Bandini's father has bequeathed him—by all appearances little more than a monstrous narcissism—is thus announced in the first breath of a novel that lives on the acrid fumes of its own black humor. There follows the chronicle, as appalling as it is hilarious, of Bandini's disastrous experiences in a series of humiliating menial jobs: ditch digger, dishwasher, warehouse truck flunky, grocery clerk, and, final insult of all, labeling crew worker on a cannery assembly line.

What makes Arturo's passage through this punishing gauntlet of jobs comical is Fante's ironic development of Bandini's character. No longer a child though not yet a man, the Bandini who stalks through the pages of this novel is a walking, talking buzz saw of megalomaniacal blab, forever railing in ersatz Zarathustranisms against the perceived foibles of his prayerful mother and sister, his unsympathetic bosses, and his hapless fellow workers, not to mention the generalized everyman whom he brands Boobus Americanus, claiming one of Mencken's pet epithets as his own. Beset by insecurities, Bandini lashes out not only at the boobs and bounders he takes most everyone else for, but also at lower forms of life as well, at sea crabs and ants and half-dead fish, which he engages in crazed mock-heroic battles, slaughtering them, smashing them, biting off their heads, then proclaiming himself "Dictator," "Superman," "Fuhrer Bandini"—"What guts! God, I was mad."

As portrait of the artist as a young man this is hardly the stuff of aesthetic restraint. What it is, besides being ironic, is an aggressively strange vision of a germinating artistic sensibility at war with the world at large. But if we laugh when Bandini demands of a flopping hundred-pound tuna that it spell *Weltanschauung* or die—the outcome of the ultimatum yet one more outrage—we must not think we have seen quite everything. For Bandini is also one of literature's great slaves to the libido, so surpassingly overheated that even his own sister is not immune to his frustrations. When he is not wasting away at the exigencies of his dead-end employment, he is devoting his evenings to closeted raptures with favorite pinups from *Artists and Models,* or wandering the city in the fragrant wakes of anonymous women, clueless as to how to comport himself in their presence yet driven to betray his cluelessness.

At least as deep as the mysteries of sex for Bandini are the bottomless mysteries of writing. Like the hero of *Hunger,* he launches into one over-ambitious undertaking after another, "A Psychological Interpretation of the Stevedore Today and Yesterday," "A Moral and Philosophical Dissertation on Man and Woman," in reality nothing more than grandiose titles for never-to-be-written masterpieces. When Bandini does finally buckle down to write, however, he writes like a man possessed, an entire novel in one week, the madcap adventures of the filthy rich Arthur Banning, circling the globe in his yacht in order to seduce women of every race from every country in the world.

Try as he might, Bandini cannot bring himself to write in the approved vein of 1930s social realism, and in any case he has no feeling for proletarian solidarity. On the contrary, when his Mexican and Filipino coworkers at the cannery ridicule their fellow labeler for his literary pretensions, Bandini wishes he could kill them off like so many flies. Realizing the impracticality of this notion—Bandini does surface occasionally from his solipsistic bubble to note the limitations of reality—he decides to fight back in the one way that he knows from experience will exact the greatest toll: he resorts to the openly brass-knuckle tactics of racist name-calling.

It is an ugly scene, painful to read, and it goes on for several pages, with Bandini shrieking "nigger" and "Spick" and "slimy Oriental," until an exhausted silence overcomes him. The words having done their dirty work, the other workers back off, thinking him crazy, and Bandini is left "alone for sure, with plenty of freedom. Nobody spoke. I felt alone indeed. I felt like a corpse."

Were it only for the deathlike effect this assault has on its perpetrator, it would be clear that what Fante was depicting was the simultaneously murderous and suicidal toll of racism. But to make sure that his readers understood the etiology of alienation at work here, Fante had Bandini recall his own pain as a child when "the kids used to hurt me by calling me Dago or Wop. It had hurt every time. It was a miserable feeling. It used to make me feel so pitiful, so unworthy." From bitter experience Fante understood the power of race-baiting, and he unleashed that power to chilling fictional effect. In making the scene real Fante ensured the reader's discomfort, just as he made it clear that his hero's actions are deplorable.

Such behavioral extremities are only exacerbated by the thematic superaddition of Bandini's one-man crusade against the Church. Here again the novel draws liberally on Nietzsche and Mencken for Bandini's virulent outbursts, which at their worst have much the same boomerang effect as does his race-baiting. When after one especially vivid attack on "the decadence of a fraudulent Christianity" Arturo's mother comes after him with a broom, the unholy son invites his own anti-Christian martyrdom: "Persecute me! Put me on the rack! . . . Gibbet me! Stick hot pokers in my eyes. Burn me at the stake, you Christian dogs!" As suggestive as such mirror imagery is of yet more reversal to come, however, the novel ultimately does not end with Bandini's return to the faith of his mother, as Elizabeth Nowell had argued it should. If hindsight enables us to see that it was too early in Fante's development for any such return to be truthfully rendered, then all the better for us today, for Fante was thus left with a crucially unfinished arc in his protagonist's development, one to which he would return again and again in treating his "one big subject."

From early September to early October Fante distracted himself by penning a column for the *Roseville Tribune and Register*. Appearing a total of six times at roughly one-week intervals, "Swords and Roses" gave the failed novelist a local platform to hold forth on topics ranging from the fanciful to the heartfelt. In his self-appointed role of town gadfly he declaimed among other things about "radio today" ("wheezy twaddle"); chewing peanuts at the movies ("a crime really unforgivable"); and the women of Roseville (mostly "hard on the eye"). In a more civic-minded mood he called for the public library to enrich its "storehouse of enchantment" with an extensive wish list of books, including works by

Voltaire, Schopenhauer, Spengler, Nietzsche, Fielding, Shaw, Mencken, Dostoevsky, Gogol, Marx, Engels, Dreiser, Caldwell, Faulkner, Odets, Hecht, Joyce, Lawrence, Spinoza, Lucretius, Aristotle, Bergson, Russell and Santayana. And at perhaps his most uncharacteristically high-minded, if also his most candid, he asked,

What has become of that magnificent vitality we call Faith? How many men of genuine Faith do you know? I do not mean faith in the sense of devout Catholicism, or sincere Protestantism. I mean much more than that. I mean Faith over and above ritual. I mean a great man who breathes God, speaks God, smiles God—a man of God-inspired laughter whom we envy because of his purity, his freshness, his tireless joy in the business of living. That man, whether he know it or not, is blessed with Faith. Nay, he is even God-like. I have never seen him, but I feel he exists somewhere.

The same week that he wrote these words he sent a letter to a New York agent, August Lenniger, expressing interest in the so-called smooth-paper market, that is, the mass circulation magazines such as *Woman's Home Companion* and *McCall's*, which catered to the nation's house-wives. Lenniger responded with a no-nonsense checklist of ingredients Fante would have to incorporate into a story if he wanted to crack the market. First among these were "characters who are one hundred percent American, the type . . . with whom the smug readers of these magazines want to identify themselves." Whether or not he heard the echo of Col-orado race supremacists in the call for something that was one hundred percent American, Fante cranked himself up and churned out just such a story. But he could generate little enthusiasm for the task, and was soon proclaiming himself "almost cured of the prostitution of the modern short story."

As if thumbing his nose at the call for pure American types, Fante be-gan reworking his perennial Italian-American material. Again he was fo-cusing on a family novel and the *Mater Dolorosa* theme of birth control. Now, however, he was writing the story from the perspective of fourteen-year-old Arturo Bandini, who had three things on his mind: his parents, baseball and sex. Sex was clearly on Fante's mind as he wrote in the library basement, and not only there but also on the public links where he played golf, the game to which he was turning more and more frequently in an effort among other things to work off the frustrations of enforced celibacy. Sex even crept into his political discussions, as when he condemned poverty not in the parlance of any conventional party line but rather because, being poor, "I can't fuck enough." Indeed, he would have his own parlance. Thumping the bully pulpit of his correspondence with Carey McWilliams, Fante fulminated, "I am not in favor of Capitalism or Communism, but Clitorism." If only he could write to his heart's content, anarchy would suit him just fine.

For his part McWilliams was busy organizing. Among his myriad commitments, McWilliams served on the Board of Editors of *Pacific Weekly*, a radical journal based in Carmel, California. Through its pages he was promoting the Western Writers' Congress, set to convene in San Francisco for three days in mid-November. In the same November 2 issue that featured the Writers' Congress program, including such sessions as "Censorship, Suppression and Fascist Trends," and "Writing and Propaganda," there appeared a short story that Fante had sent to McWilliams. Cowritten as a lark with Frank Fenton, the enigmatically titled "We Snatch a Frail" was a trifling parody of the Caldwell-Hemingway-O'Hara school of hardboiled writing, and notable if only for the absurdity of its narrator's continuing to narrate even after he has been killed with a bullet through the heart. In the thoroughly engaged *Pacific Weekly* the Fante-Fenton contribution stood out for its ironic detachment, an indication of Fante's skepticism toward all things political, both of the Left and the Right.

Fante felt himself moving in different directions. On the one hand, as he wrote Carey McWilliams on October 31, "[i]f America went Soviet tomorrow I'd still read Nietzsche, long for beauty, seek the turmoil of women, and dream of the greatest novel ever written." On the other hand, as he reported to no less an iconoclast than Mencken less than two weeks later, he felt himself gravitating "toward marriage and a return to Catholicism. Augustine and Thomas More knew the answers a long time ago. Aristotle would have spat in Mussolini's face and sneered at Marx." Still, when Ross Wills appeared in Roseville with a full tank of gas, Fante climbed in beside him and off they rumbled to San Francisco to witness the proceedings of the Writers' Congress.

The list of the conference's 250 participants included an impressive number of West Coast novelists, poets, playwrights, screenwriters, journalists, academicians and humorists, all gathered to wrestle with a wide range of political, economic and aesthetic challenges facing writers in a time of globally charged tensions. Among those assembling at San Francisco's Scottish Rite Auditorium and California Club were Upton Sinclair, William Saroyan, Kenneth Rexroth, Elsa Gidlow, Lawrence Clark Powell, Manchester Boddy, Oliver Thornton, Irwin Shaw, Louis Adamic, Michael Gold, Ella Winter, Hildegarde Flanner, Humphrey Cobb, John Bright, Robert Tasker, Donald Ogden Stewart, Dorothy Parker, Budd Schulberg, and Nathanael West. Greetings were read from Andre Malraux, Thomas Mann and John Steinbeck, who was ill and could not attend. Even pulp writers were well represented.

Afterward, depending on whom he was addressing, Fante's response to this historic gathering was either reservedly supportive or devilishly sardonic. To Carey McWilliams he sent his qualified congratulations for mounting a successful conference, despite all the "frauds and soapboxers." Not altogether in jest he suggested that if the energies of the Writers' Congress were to be parlayed into a successful permanent organization, people like himself would have to be excluded. But he did not hide his scorn for either the confirmed ideologues or the tatterdemalion fringe the gathering attracted in its concerted effort to do battle on so many fronts. In writing to Mencken he was nastier. Though he indicated he had appreciated the chance to talk with Australian-born Harry Bridges, the avowedly Marxist leader of the Longshoreman's and Warehouseman's Union, he skewered a number of the other participants at the Writers' Congress with wicked ad hominem attacks, calling even McWilliams a "sucker."

In Fante's eyes the only answer to all the large questions and looming crises addressed in San Francisco was money. So too was it the answer to all of his. Even if Hollywood was "a bad place," even if writers died "young and violently down there," he was going back to "make a lot of money, barrels of it." But by Christmas he was still stuck in Roseville, "very low and broke," hoping against hope for a job with the Federal Writers' Project of the Work Projects Administration, and reduced to a long-distance collaboration with an old acquaintance in Denver on a doomed pulp novelette about football. The correspondents went back

and forth haplessly on possible titles, each more ridiculous than the last—
"Coffin Corner," "Fate Is a Football," "Pigskin Is a Woman"—before settling on the serviceable "Ringer." But nothing would come of their effort.

And then, just like that, Fante received back-to-back acceptances from
Scribner's Magazine and *The American Mercury*, for the short stories
"Charge It" and "The Postman Rings and Rings," respectively. He did not
receive a third acceptance at this time from *The Atlantic Monthly*, nor
did he receive three acceptances all on one day, Christmas Eve to be exact, as he would falsely brag to Mencken; but it made a better story to say
that he had. On both Christmas and New Year's Eve Fante got "loop-
eyed" on scotch, claiming in each case no ill aftereffects. But what kind
of a writer wouldn't make such a claim? And what kind of a writer was he,
after all?

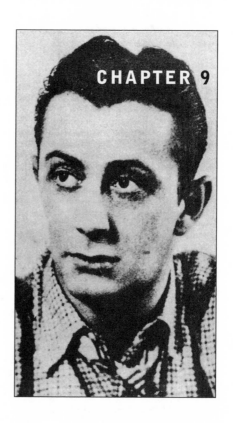

CHAPTER 9

One day as he worked downstairs in the Roseville library Fante was approached by Miss Willetts, the sympathetic librarian who had helped arrange the use of the basement office where he now spent so much of his time. Beside her stood an elderly gray-haired lady obviously eager to meet an Actual Author. Allowing the flattery of the old lady's approach to overcome his impatience at the interruption, Fante extended a hand. But when Miss Willetts withdrew he was surprised to discover that his visitor, for all her unprepossessing appearance, was intelligent, articulate and well-read. They fell into a lively chat about contemporary American writers.

On the short walk home—home being only two doors away from the library—Addie Smart Thomas may well have thought of her brother Joe Smart's daughter, not the snobby older one, Justine, a graduate of exclu-

sive Mills College in Oakland and already married to one of the Vander-
bilts' inner circle, but the younger one, her favorite, Joyce. Joseph Smart
had died when Joyce was only seventeen but the successful lumber merchant, landowner and leading citizen of Roseville had left his wife Louise
and two daughters well provided for. Golden-haired, blue-eyed and beautiful, Joyce Smart had been the first girl from Placer County to be admitted to Stanford, where she pledged Chi Omega, majored in English and
distinguished herself as both a poet and an editor, working on the *Stanford Yearbook of Writing* and serving as night editor of the *Stanford Daily*.
Upon graduating in 1935, she had moved to San Francisco to work on
the staff of *The Peninsulan*, an ambitious attempt at a West Coast *New
Yorker*–style magazine and a promising place for a talented young writer-
editor to begin her literary career. Because of the stranglehold of the depression, the magazine did not survive, and Joyce eventually found her
way back to Roseville, where she set to concentrating again on her poetry.
Visiting her kindred soul Aunt Addie one day she happened to mention
the author of that strangely charming newspaper column "Swords and
Roses."

"Oh, I know him," Aunt Addie said. "Why don't I ask him over for tea
so you can meet?"

And so it was that on January 30, 1937, Joyce Smart, dressed as if for
business in her favorite tweed suit and lace-up granny shoes, first met
John Fante. John had arrived first in Aunt Addie's dollhouse Victorian
parlor, and when he turned to make his greeting—Joyce's first impression
was of his eyes—the teacup he had been balancing fell to the floor and
shattered. They both got down on hands and knees to pick up the pieces.
Aunt Addie didn't seem to mind. In fact, when after a long and animated
conversation John and Joyce agreed to meet again later that evening to
take in a movie, Aunt Addie was beaming.

But Joyce's mother was not pleased. From the moment Louise Runkel
Smart learned of Joyce's interest in an unemployed writer from a family
of impoverished outsiders she was tight-lipped and ominously silent. And
after meeting John for the first time, when she finally broke her silence, it
was only to voice her strongest, her unhappiest disapproval.

"He looks so *Italian*," she told Joyce, thrusting straight to the heart of
the problem. "I can't even pretend he isn't."

Not for the first time, however, did a willful mother's disapproval have an unintended opposite effect on the behavior of an equally self-willed daughter. Soon John was a frequent visitor at the Smart house on Lincoln Street, where down on the red carpet of her mother's living room Joyce joined him in writing a play. By the standards of the day their theatrical effort might have been considered daring, even risqué, that is, had anyone besides themselves ever read it. But the coauthors' hilarity while tossing dialogue back and forth was suggestive enough for Louise Smart; so when John left *The Road to Los Angeles* for Joyce to read, Mrs. Smart sprang at the chance to scrutinize the manuscript, and was duly scandalized. So much filth and depravity: that crazy crab massacre! those closeted sex raptures! The offending author was promptly banished from the Smart house; Joyce was told what would happen if she tried to circumvent the interdiction; and a clandestine affair was born.

Soon unsigned letters began appearing in the daily mail addressed to Mrs. Smart. Some reported sightings of Joyce and John together—swimming at the Lincoln plunge, holding hands in front of the bank on Vernon Street—while others confined themselves to colorful vilifications of John. In writing these letters various Roseville busybodies were taking it upon themselves to protect poor Louise Smart from the catastrophe of social disgrace. Strange to say, however, the town busybodies were not responsible for writing all of these letters; for John, consumed with mischief and heedless of the consequences, had joined in the anonymous poison pen campaign against himself. At first it was all in fun, an epistolary lark, like drawing horns on his own head in a self-caricature. But when Mrs. Smart persisted in not getting the joke, John's mischief darkened and the letters turned scurrilous. As Joyce would remember, her

mother was alarmed. She had been brought up in a small town where disapproval was death. She recalled tales she had heard about the Black Hand, and Italians who were said to beat their wives. She was badly frightened and anxious to protect her daughter. John Fante looked dangerous. He was dangerous. I became more attracted.

Since he was forbidden to enter the house, he took to writing me letters, signed letters. Every day I went to the post office to get the mail, and there was a letter from him. At first they were just shocking. Then they became passionate love letters. I would open the letter coming down the post office steps, and there he would be waiting for me. We would get into my car and drive out into the country.

Joyce owned a spiffy little Plymouth coupe, a gift from her mother on her twenty-first birthday, and on one of these country-road getaways from the town's prying eyes John and Joyce became secret lovers. Few would have called it a match made in heaven, but it did seem to be as inevitable as it was unlikely, the Stanford-bred daughter of one of Roseville's first families and the dropout son of so much abject Italian peasantry. Unlike Fante's family, the Smarts had been in the New World steadily improving themselves since arriving from England in the early seventeenth century, and they had lived in the Dutch Flat–Roseville area for nearly one hundred years. They could boast among their numbers prominent pioneers and prosperous men of business, while Joyce's mother's side, the Runkels, also had its list of enterprising German antecedents. And even though Placer County, California, did not have behind it the same ugly shadow of racist electoral history as did Boulder County, Colorado, the sight of John and Joyce together abroad in largely lily-white Roseville was enough to fire fears in many of the town's solidest citizens of miscegenation and all its horrors. To Joyce, still fresh from Stanford, where "the winds of freedom blow," the whole dilemma smacked of another century. As she put it while reminiscing some fifty years later, "Nathaniel Hawthorne could have invented my situation."

Nathaniel Hawthorne, indeed—or, come to think of it, John Fante. For hadn't Fante already imagined the exquisite impossibility of such a dreamer as himself ever gaining access to the world of beautiful blond college girls in up-to-date clothes and sporty cars? And hadn't Stanford University epitomized that dream? In his short story "Washed in the Rain," published three years earlier, his protagonist had tried to pass himself off in the custom-made sweater with the false letter S stitched over his breast. Now here he was, a wop of the deepest dye, making love to the epitome of a Stanford alumna, a rich and promising poet at that, and be-deviling her mother with narcissistic hate mail aimed at demonizing none other than himself. For Joyce's amusement Fante would sometimes slip completely into stage-dago character, twisting nonexistent mustaches and cursing in sulfuric Italian, as if to resurrect the swaggering Nick Fante of old. It was all flagrant playacting but it was also true to life, a masquerade that revealed as much as it hid.

On July 31, 1937, John and Joyce drove over the state line to Reno, Nevada, where they were secretly married. The secret was for good reason. Louise Smart had threatened her daughter with disinheritance if she continued carrying on with Fante, and neither Joyce, who was used to the nice things in life, nor John, who thought he might like to get used to them, was willing to take that risk. Other risks they did not shrink from, such as making love wherever and whenever they could, if but rarely in the privacy of a bedroom. Placer County in the spring and summer is a beautiful place, comparable to the South of France, with apple orchards and great oak-studded meadows for a picnicking couple to lose themselves in; and whenever they could slip away John and Joyce lost themselves in each other and the poetry of Rupert Brooke, whose sonnets they recited together:

> Breathless, we flung us on the windy hill,
> Laughed in the sun, and kissed the lovely grass.

The outward secrecy to which they were holding themselves added to the adventure of their newlywed life, which at times could be dizzying. Adding to the swirl was the gathering sense that they actually did have a future to share. In June Mencken's successor Louis Untermeyer had accepted a poem by Joyce for publication in *The American Mercury*. Joyce was elated to be joining the *Mercury*'s select company of writers, among them her secret husband, who was doing his part for the cause by touting her talents as a poet to his friends and publishing contacts. "A Poet to Her Tangled Verses" appeared in the August issue.

> Bright Pegasus eludes the verbal rope,
> That I, with trembling fingers, and with hope,
> Knotted, to fling about his restless head—
> The rope lies tangled at my feet instead.

Concise in its formal elegance, the poem lent itself to republication on the poetry pages of newspapers from coast to coast, adding to Joyce's satisfaction. Not too many years earlier, under the forthright heading "What I Want," Joyce had spelled out in her diary the ambitions she cherished, and the means by which she planned to achieve them. "I want," she had written, "a marvelous, fascinating man to fall in love with me. I must be: 1. attractive, 2. well-bred, 3. poised, sophisticated, 4. well-dressed. I want to be famous, glamorous, exciting." If we count the small but indisputable literary fame that accompanied the publication of her poem in *The American Mercury*, Joyce was all of these things to Fante, just as he was both marvelous and fascinating to her. But he was also a man who rarely let well enough alone, least of all when there was trouble to be made. At this time Fante's pride in his wife's accomplishment came to be tinged by a certain simmering resentment at all her upper-middle-class advantages, and no doubt at her ambitions as well. One night Joyce got a glimpse of his darker side.

She had been looking forward to a dinner date at an out-of-the-way restaurant, a rare chance to be removed from her mother's stiff-necked prohibitions, a chance for her and John to be themselves, two responsible adults enjoying each other's company in a discreetly public place. It was a big enough occasion that Joyce chose to wear her favorite black velvet dinner dress, the one with the beautiful handstitched white lace collar. Ominously, however, when Fante arrived it was clear he had already been drinking. Joyce did her best to ignore his dishevelment but he continued to drink throughout dinner, ordering more wine and growing strangely belligerent. Soon there came into his eyes something she had never seen before, a disapproving, even contemptuous look. Finally he reached across the table and caught the lace collar at her throat with the tines of his dinner fork. "Look at you," he said, pulling her toward him across the table. "Little Miss Sorority Girl going out on a date, all dressed up. Who do you think you are?" He continued to pull, looking at her with those eyes, until the fork tore through the delicate openwork.

As frightening as this scene was for Joyce, she was not about to end what she had begun. On the contrary, the frisson of fear that shot through her at times in the face of Fante's brutality only helped make their forbidden love all the more exciting to her. And on top of that there was something delicious in secretly defying her mother's wishes. Kept unaware that

Joyce and John were married but increasingly fearful that they might elope, Mrs. Smart finally insisted that Joyce accompany her to Detroit for an extended visit with her other daughter, Joyce's older sister Justine. But Joyce refused to fall into that trap. Instead, she elected to go stay with sympathetic relatives in Berkeley, a freer base of operations from which she and Fante could continue their clandestine life together, even if they had to be temporarily apart. John would stay behind in Roseville figuring out the best course of action, and when the time was right they would be reunited. It gave Joyce hope to think of their eventual reunion, and of the sweet satisfaction of finally announcing their marriage, after which they would make nothing less than a "triumphant departure" from Roseville, shaking the town's puritanical dust from their heels.

As for Fante, he suddenly found himself both a married man and on his own again, another paradox to get under his skin. With Joyce gone and the Smart house closed up, Roseville had never seemed smaller. Nor had his writing ever felt less focused. In the last several months he had made calculated attempts at writing for the women's magazines, the Catholic press, radio and the movies, but for the most part his efforts might as well have been blind lunges. His late stab at returning to the Italian family–birth control material had grown into a disjointed set of scenes running to eight thousand words plus an equally disjointed synopsis retitled "The Man from Rome." Like virtually everything else he tried during this period, almost as soon as he sent it out "The Man from Rome" was returned, accompanied by a none-too-flattering list of descriptors: "monotonous," "wearing," "stark," "bald" and "limited." Even his golf game, his one release from frustration with Joyce out of reach, was making him suffer as only golfers can suffer when they lose their balance, their touch, their grip. One of the few successes he had during this time appeared in the October issue of *The American Mercury*, and it was called, aptly enough, "The Road to Hell." But all the failures aside, the strangest part of his day-to-day existence was that Fante still felt the ache of destiny. He had a great novel inside him twisting to get out. Mysterious gears were meshing, he knew not how or why. Once again he betook himself to Los Angeles.

Around the world in early 1938 insecurities were spiking as power-hungry madmen stoked the fires of global war fever. From Europe and the Far

East came news of escalating tensions and rumors of the inevitable blood-bath. With its innovative application of aerial strafing and saturation bombing of civilian targets, the Fascist side of the Spanish Civil War was offering a ghastly preview of horrors soon to come on a far wider scale as Germany, Italy and Japan massed for imperial assaults against sovereign neighbors. Stateside, meanwhile, the depression was still grinding on, from the Dust Bowl states to the teeming cities. In its own removed way Los Angeles could be just as jumpy as any city in the world under siege.

By late January Fante was staying at Frank Fenton's apartment at 1851 North Argyle in Hollywood, casting about for a situation. Neither the studios nor the WPA were tripping over themselves to hire him, however, and once again he was completely broke. The last hope he had held out for a quality New York house to pick up *The Road to Los Angeles* died when David Zablodowsky of Viking Press returned the manuscript, dryly advising Fante to abandon "this vicious little satire on adolescence" and concentrate instead on something less offensive to readers. It's hard to tell whether sarcasm or despair prompted all the bowing and scraping of Fante's response to Zablodowsky, but in either case his modifiers were excessive. "I am very grateful for your delightful and excellent letter concerning my novel," Fante wrote. "[It] is wonderfully sympathetic, and for that I am completely grateful."

In a seemingly self-defeating move Fante asked that the manuscript be sent back to William Soskin of Stackpole Sons. The unlikeliest of firms, this eclectic little house specialized in political and military subjects with a distinctly democratic and antifascist slant, though it also published works of humor, travel, and outdoorsmanship. Moreover, Soskin had already made it clear that, no matter how much he liked Fante's other writings, he particularly detested this novel. But Fante was undeterred. On the contrary, as if to multiply the possibilities for failure he made haste to send Soskin forty-three new pages of story-cum-synopsis dashed off in a white heat, something he was calling "Pater Doloroso." He covered the submission with a surpassingly Fante-esque letter, then sat back to await Soskin's response.

"The letter may give you the impression that Fante is slightly mad, which he is," Soskin noted in a memo to General Edward J. Stackpole, Jr., president of the company, "but I have been following his work for a number of years . . . and I have been convinced that he is a great writer, and a sure-fire coming man." Miraculous to say, on the strength of that cover letter and the forty-three new pages, Soskin was urging Stackpole to sign Fante immediately to a contract. If Fante delivered, as Soskin was certain that he would, *Pater Doloroso* could lead Stackpole's short fall fiction list.

Negotiations were harmonious and swift. Stackpole accepted Fante's proposal for an advance of $150 and four monthly installments of $150. "My darling you are wonderful," Joyce wired John on March 2 from Berkeley, "everything is wonderful I am so happy leaving for Roseville Thursday morning at 9 will meet you there love." Before departing from Los Angeles to retrieve his bride Fante took the precaution of registering with the United States Employment Service, listing his height as five feet three inches and his profession as Novelist with a capital N. It might not be from Knopf or Viking or Doubleday, but the Stackpole contract still provided the kind of real-world validation of Fante's talent—and of Joyce's belief in that talent—with which even Mrs. Smart could not argue. No matter what anyone thought of it, they were a married couple, now a public fact in which Joyce took great pleasure even though it meant a painful estrangement from her mother. In spite of this sorrow, the air of triumphant expectation for which Joyce had dared hope did indeed accompany the couple's southbond departure from Roseville in her perky little Plymouth. They were no longer the only ones betting on themselves. Assurances had been given and money was changing hands. "Best of luck to you," General Stackpole wrote Fante after wiring him an emergency $75 to cover the rent on the couple's new Los Angeles home in the Berkeley Terrace Apartments at 206 North New Hampshire Avenue, "and let's see you produce a book that will knock their eyes out."

He is short, darkly handsome, street smart, tough. His hair is in need of cutting, his clothes do not quite fit his stocky frame, he looks poor, there is an almost visible chip on his shoulder—and yet somehow all these negatives add up to a man of vitality and presence. His shirt, under an ancient sports jacket, is open two buttons, revealing part of a barrel chest, and a gold cross on a chain. His trousers are rolled up, exposing a stretch of argyle socks. All this seems to say to the world, "This is me. Take it or leave it. I don't give a damn!"

So did Joyce view her new husband, with both fascination and excitement. Fante's view of Joyce was terser. "I was recently married to Joyce Smart," John was soon boasting to Mencken, "a Stanford girl who writes wonderful poetry and is also very remarkable in a kitchen apron." While Fante certainly assumed that this was a fair and even generous assessment, the patronizing equation of his wife's poetic and domestic abilities soon came to rankle Joyce. In her own mind she was a serious writer, not some magazine housewife and certainly nobody's drudge. Without knowing the details, Mencken could surmise enough from Fante's announcement to sympathize with Joyce, if only indirectly, offering his condolences through John and expressing the hope that, once she discovered "that living with a literary gent is a dreadful experience . . . she is never tempted to load your victuals with roach powder." Once the honeymoon was over, as it would be before long, Fante would find more than a little truth in Mencken's ironic forewarning.

Settled in Los Angeles, the newlyweds fell to quarreling frequently, among other things over money. Even with the publisher's advance their budget was extremely tight and Joyce found herself forced to skimp on items she had been raised to consider necessities. Whereas in the past, for example, she had made seasonal trips to San Francisco in order to replenish her wardrobe at Ransohoff's, now she could not even afford to keep up the heels of her shoes. Visits to the beauty salon were out of the question. The tires on her car went bald. She began to understand what her mother had in mind when she used to warn her about the horrors of poverty.

For his part Fante could hardly have cared less about his wife's deprivations, or so at least it seemed. Raised in a home where money troubles were as endemic and perpetual as the fighting they provoked, he not only took his arguments with Joyce for granted but also added to the tensions by routinely removing cash from Joyce's purse without permission or explanation. The fiction was that Joyce oversaw the household finances, balancing the checkbook, paying the bills and so forth, but the fact was

Cousins Fante, Capolungo, and Campiglia. John is standing, hands in pockets, behind his look-alike cousin, Mario Campiglia (seated, right), whose accidental death led to the short story "One of Us." John's sister Josephine stands at far left behind their brother Pete (Courtesy Edward Campiglia)

The young John Fante with his father, Nick (in shirtsleeves, at left), and friends; Denver

The Fante family home at 959 Arapahoe Street, Boulder, now the site of the Boulder Public Library (Courtesy Carnegie Branch Library for Local History, Boulder Historical Society Collection)

Nick Fante, on the doorstep of the house on Arapahoe Street, 1926 (Courtesy Tom Fante)

Nick Fante, in vest, at the cornerstone-laying ceremony for the Sacred Heart of Jesus Elementary School, Boulder. Nick helped build the school, as well as the Sacred Heart of Jesus Church eight years earlier (Photo by Ed Tangen)

September 16, 1916, again at the school's cornerstone-laying ceremony. John Fante, age seven, is kneeling at center front in a white shirt, holding a flag and his father's hat. At left center of grouping, Fr. Agatho Strittmatter stands holding a crucifix. To Strittmatter's right, Nick Fante's face is visible over the right shoulder of a gray-haired man in a dark suit (Photo by Ed Tangen)

Altar boys, Sacred Heart of Jesus Church, Boulder, c. 1922. John Fante is in the third row from the top, third from right

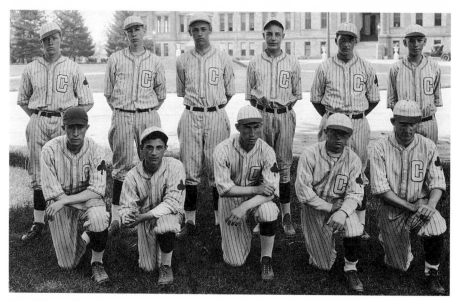

The Clover Club, Regis High School varsity baseball team, 1926. John Fante kneels, second from right. Paul Reinert, team captain and later a Jesuit priest, stands third from left (Courtesy Paul C. Reinert, S.J.)

(*above left*) Cherished little brother, Tommy Fante, 1929 (Courtesy Tom Fante)

(*above right*) Pete and John Fante (Courtesy Tom Fante)

(*below left*) Florence Carpenter, the Long Beach City College English teacher who inspired Fante

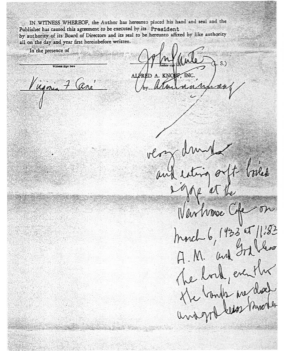

IN WITNESS WHEREOF, the Author has hereunto placed his hand and seal and the Publisher has caused this agreement to be executed by its President by authority of its Board of Directors and its seal to be hereunto affixed by like authority all on the day and year first hereinbefore written.

In the presence of

Carey McWilliams, c. 1938

Fante's book contract with Alfred A. Knopf, with author's addendum

Ross Wills, c. 1933

Los Angeles Examiner article and photo, August 7, 1933

From the *Los Angeles Examiner*, August 7, 1933

WRITER MEETS ACTUAL DRAMA

Real drama interrupted fiction when the Long Beach earthquake hurled John Fante, 21, Hollywood writer, from his typewriter to the floor unconscious.

The young writer had written 15,-000 words on his new novel, when the temblors struck the beach city and wrecked the Patrician Apartments on East Fourth St. where Mr. Fante was domiciled. His prized manuscript was burned when the two-story building collapsed and later caught fire.

Hollywood friends know Mr. Fante as an associate to Jean C. de Kolty, authors' agent, and as the author of a number of short stories in the American Mercury. Alfred A. Knopf is sponsoring the writer during the production of the novel.

Author to Visit at Home of Parents

John Fante, of 423 Lincoln street, short story writer and contributor to The American Mercury and the magazine Story, arrived in Roseville yesterday morning from Long Beach. He is under contract with Alfred A. Knopf, Inc., for a hundred thousand word novel to be completed in the next seven months, and will remain in Roseville to complete his manuscript. He is residing with his parents, Mr. and Mrs. N. Fante.

Fante returned unhurt from the quake-stricken Long Beach. A four-story apartment house in which he was residing, was completely destroyed, its walls crumbling to the force of the two major tremors. Despite the fact that he fell 60 feet amidst the tumbling debris, Fante was uninjured.

Variant news accounts, neither completely factual, of Fante's experience during the Long Beach earthquake of 1933

Marie Baray, c. 1936. They fought "like tigers," Fante would recall of his lover, who served as a key model for the character of Camilla Lopez in *Ask the Dust*

The Alta Vista Hotel, 255 South Bunker Hill Avenue, where Fante lived in late 1933. His room at the Alta Vista became the model for Arturo Bandini's in *Ask the Dust*

Joyce Smart, 1931

that Fante maintained effective control over her by refusing to report his expenditures. The insult such behavior added to Joyce's sense of injury was that Fante was using the money not for anything they needed as man and wife but rather for his own guiltless pleasure as one of the boys, nights of drinking and gambling but mostly serious hard-liquor bar-hopping with Carey McWilliams, Ross Wills and Frank Fenton. Anyone seeking a title for this era in Fante's life could do worse than "How to Write a Novel and Poison a Marriage."

Oddly enough he was doing both. A key reason that the marriage survived this initial period of adjustment, and that Fante continued stacking up the pages of *Pater Doloroso* through the hell of it, was that oldest strategy of conflict resolution between the otherwise incompatibly mated, namely, sex. "Every week or so," Joyce later remembered,

> the tension would mount to the point that one or the other of us would pack, and prepare to leave. When we were not quarreling we were making mad and enthusiastic love—in the shower, on the kitchen floor, anywhere we happened to be when the mood struck us, as many as five times a day. We were truly obsessed. There was something about John. I couldn't stay angry with him. When I looked at his face I melted.

In fact *sex* is too limited a word, too boxlike and unmodulated, to convey the shuddering range of intensities, body and soul, of these insatiable encounters. Aware of the power of nuance, Joyce Fante still resorts to the French for an accurate description of those days: "une grande passion" is the phrase she uses.

In order to help alleviate some of the financial pressures, Joyce applied for a job with the WPA Federal Writers' Project. Try as he had, importuning friends and strangers alike, Fante had been unable to secure such a job for himself, but Joyce's efforts proved successful and she went to work for $94 a month, treadless tires, home-styled hair and all. A significant element of Roosevelt's New Deal, the Writers' Project had been launched in 1935 as part of the government's broadscale attempt to assist unemployed writers and artists and thus to democratize American culture. As in many other regions around the country, in Los Angeles the

Writers' Project was compiling an extensive guide to the city and its environs, and toward this end Joyce joined poet Kenneth Patchen, screenwriter Carl Foreman, political writer Robert Brownell and others at the WPA offices downtown at 8th Street and Figueroa. She was proud of herself, and rightly so, both for the work she was doing and for the money she was bringing home as a writer in the midst of an unyielding depression. She was all the prouder when one day in an informal office poll she was chosen the fourth best writer among a very gifted group. She came home that evening brimming with news of the honor. But Fante's response was like an icicle in her heart. "How can it make you happy," he scowled, "to be fourth best at *anything?*" In Fante's all-or-nothing way of thinking, if you weren't first—in fighting or drinking or golf or writing— you might as well be dead last.

Joyce found it within herself to overlook slights like this in view of the admiration, verging at times on awe, she felt for Fante's writing. Except for a brief period of jitters soon after signing the Stackpole contract, when Fante struck Carey McWilliams one night as "frightened [and] worried" about his book, work on the novel went smoothly. When Joyce got home in the evening from the WPA office, Fante would show her the pages he had written that day, and except for a misspelling here and there which she helped to correct she would be amazed at how finished they were. In May, at Soskin's request, Fante came up with a replacement title for the novel, something more promising to the prospective reader than the dirgelike *Pater Doloroso*. "The new title has a lilt to it that possesses strong appeal," Edward J. Stackpole wrote to Fante. "We are hoping for great things." By midsummer the entire manuscript of the novel was in New York, and both editor Soskin and publisher Stackpole were delighted to find that their confidence in Fante's talent had been well placed. They would indeed lead off their fall list with *Wait Until Spring, Bandini*.

Living in the palmy heart of Los Angeles with his alluring non-Catholic wife, Fante had returned in his imagination to the wintry Colorado of his Catholic youth to write the story of Svevo Bandini's infidelity with the waspish widow Hildegarde, and of the shattering, ultimately reintegrating effects this affair comes to have on the entire Bandini family. For the past five years Fante had struggled to master this material in one false start after another, and now he finally felt he had succeeded. "I have done an immortal work of art," Fante bragged, laying it on thick for new friend and fellow West Coast writer-braggart William Saroyan. All at once, if only at last, Fante had managed to coordinate for the full duration of a novel and to the satisfaction of all involved his fundamental themes of poverty, Italian-American Catholicism, mismatched love, and imaginative untruth, the latter being the one way Arturo Bandini learns early to remake the world when the world's reality becomes too much to bear. Now that he had finally succeeded, Fante would dedicate the book not as he had long promised to his surrogate parent H. L. Mencken but to his mother, "Mary Fante, with love and devotion," and to his father, "Nick Fante, with love and admiration." It was "a more fitting gesture," Fante said in explaining the change to Mencken, adding somewhat disingenuously, "although such things really don't matter."

While he awaited the publication date Fante behaved like any expectant first-time novelist, frittering away the days by playing marathon games of pinball at the Imperial Drug Store on the corner of 3rd and Vermont and the nights by drinking himself brick-headed. Sometimes the days shaded into the nights. On September 4, for example, he spent a long afternoon drinking at the bar of the Hotel Savoy in Hollywood with Carey McWilliams, and on the afternoon of September 14 he and McWilliams drank in Carey's car all the way up to Santa Barbara, where they rendezvoused with Louis Adamic and continued drinking until, as McWilliams put it of himself, his muscles ached the next day. Then again at about five p.m. on October 1, Fante and Wills, both broke and thirsty, descended on McWilliams in his Spring Street office announcing the end of the lawyer's workday. The three made their way to a bar on Los Angeles's old Olvera Street in the downtown Mexican quarter where Carey proceeded to stand them round after round of Bacardi cocktails. Although he could not have known it at the time, what with his dedication of *Dago Red* still three years in the future, Fante was seeing to it on excursions like this one, and on countless others besides, that McWilliams and Wills earned the distinction of being called "good friends, evil companions." Next to an understanding wife, after all, what more did a young man need?

Though Fante seemed to go out of his way to make her role of understanding wife all but impossible, Joyce did her best, even when she was being most sorely tested. One day in the late summer of 1938, for example, at Stanley Rose's bookshop on Hollywood Boulevard, Fante met A. I. Bezzerides, the Fresno-reared Greek-Armenian truck-driver-turned-author whose novel *The Long Haul* had just been published. As Bezzerides has related the episode, before they parted company that day the silver-tongued Fante had talked Bezzerides into loaning him his publisher's advance, then still unspent, which Fante wasted no time in losing at cards. It was only by keeping polite but firm pressure on Joyce over the next several months that Bezzerides ever saw the loan repaid, and then only thanks to Joyce's newfound genius for living beneath her drastically reduced means.

Stanley Rose was a red-faced Texan who sounded illiterate when he talked but who was in fact a canny dealer in literature, art and pornography. A good friend of Carey McWilliams, who owned half interest in his Hollywood Boulevard store after it moved from its earlier Vine Street address, Rose was a favorite among Los Angeles writers for his generosity and good humor, all the more so because of the rumors that swirled about him of a shady past, a stretch in prison and connections to the underworld. Ably staffed by Larry Edmunds, Yetive Moss, Milton Luboviski and Herman Cherry, Rose's shop attracted writers such as John O'Hara, Dashiell Hammett, Erskine Caldwell, Daniel Fuchs, Guy Endore, Aben Kandel, Horace McCoy, George Milburn, Owen Francis, William Faulkner, W. R. Burnett, Jim Tully, Budd Schulberg, John Sanford, F. Scott Fitzgerald, Nathanael West, Daniel Mainwaring, William Saroyan and Jo Pagano. These writers and others would often wander in to browse after dinner in the fabled back room at Musso Frank's Grill, which was only a few steps away. The small gallery in the back of the store featured not only works by local artists but also some of the first appearances in Los Angeles of paintings by Renoir and Picasso, including *The Card Players*. As for the less legitimate merchandise, Joyce Fante would recall Rose presenting her and John with a titillating novel from under the counter in the store's balcony section, a book called *Grushenka* which delighted her because she had never seen anything like it.

With Rose's famous orange wine to help keep the back room conversation flowing—talk ranged freely from Malraux to Mussolini to Louis B. Mayer, returning always it seemed to girls and the future greatness of the talkers—the bookshop was the "nearest thing to a Left Bank" Hollywood had. Listen to Fante's description of breakfast next door at Musso Frank's and you get much that same sense:

> [I]t was a glorious beginning to the new day, a rekindling of the will to survive, a renewal of one's faith in mankind. A great charcoal fire roared in the grill, and a high-hatted chef tended bacon, sausages and small steaks, the fetching aroma hitting your nostrils the moment you entered the room. You sat at the counter, in a comfortable swivel chair, as close to the fire as you could get. The waiter brought coffee as soon as you sat down and French bread, but gave you a couple of minutes to pull down some hot coffee and smoke your first cigarette, before he asked what you wanted. He put the morning paper before you. . . . You were content. . . . You lingered on, watching the charcoal flames slowly falling into a profound lethargy. No doubt it was bad for you, all that coffee, all that cholesterol, all those cigarettes, all that time consumed. But it was beautiful and unforgettable.

Just as unforgettable but far from beautiful was the night at Musso Frank's when Fante subjected Joyce to one of her severest tests. Joyce had just begun to enjoy a rare evening out with her husband when at another of the restaurant's upholstered booths Fante spotted Marie Baray, the sultry Mexican model whom he had once promised to marry. Pointing Marie out to Joyce, Fante watched as the two women locked eyes, and when he saw the expressions on their faces—rage on Marie's, disbelief on Joyce's—he insisted on introducing them. For both women the meeting was unbearable, so much so for Marie when she heard Fante utter the words "my wife" that she tried to escape, twisting from the booth and wrenching out of his way until he ran after her and grabbed her by the arm. Joyce saw the former lovers talking quietly for a moment, and when Fante returned it was to announce that he was taking Joyce home and then meeting Marie for the purpose, as he put it, of explaining everything.

It was nearly dawn when he finally came home. After a long silence he claimed not to have slept with Marie. Rather, he said, he had spent the night at her apartment only to prevent her from following through on the threat of ending it all by slashing her wrists. Joyce refused to believe this story, but when she told him to go back to Marie if he was truly worried about her well-being, Fante again became silent, as if weighing an actual set of alternatives. In the end he remained with Joyce, who filed the whole night away as but one of the many dreadful experiences that were part of living with Fante. But for all of his "devious and treacherous ways," Joyce reasoned, anyone who could write as angelically as John Fante "should be forgiven much."

Wait Until Spring, Bandini was published on October 10, 1938. With the exception of one ambivalent assessment in *The Saturday Review of Literature*, the reviews were strongly positive and in many cases enthusiastic. Fante's prose, at once simple and rich, was compared favorably by one reviewer to Ignazio Silone's, while his imagery struck another as "clear as a Grant Wood painting." The communist *New Masses* paired *Bandini* in its review with a new novel by James T. Farrell, preferring *Bandini* because of Fante's fuller absorption in the lives of his characters, while Farrell himself, writing in *The Atlantic Monthly* and comparing Fante's novel with the latest by Saroyan, also gave the nod to Fante. One of the book's strongest endorsements came from San Francisco's leading critic Joseph Henry Jackson, who found in it "the same qualities of humor, of tenderness, of sympathy [and] understanding" as he found in Steinbeck's *Tortilla Flat*. When best-of-the-year lists were drawn up in newspapers for December gift-giving, *Wait Until Spring, Bandini* was consistently named, along with such other notable novels as *The Yearling* by Marjorie Kinnan Rawlings, *Man's Hope* by André Malraux, *Rebecca* by Daphne du Maurier, and Steinbeck's *The Long Valley*. At least two reviewers, Jackson of the *San Francisco Chronicle* and Sterling North of the *Chicago Daily News*, selected *Bandini* as the finest novel of 1938.

After years of toiling in near anonymity Fante woke to find himself suddenly a literary celebrity. He gave talks at the May Company auditorium and before the Santa Monica Women's Club, and he appeared as a guest on *Meet the Author*, a program produced by the Beverly Hills Library on radio station KMPC, "the Station of the Stars." He was also a featured writer at the Los Angeles Public Library on Hope Street downtown, where in the great muraled Fiction Room he had once spent so many hungry hours reading and longing to join "the big boys in the shelves," as Arturo Bandini puts it in *Ask the Dust*.

The book sold moderately well, climbing as high as number four on the *San Francisco Chronicle*'s "Best Sellers of the Week" list for the week of January 15, 1939. George Routledge & Sons of London brought out a British edition, and within the year Italian and Norwegian translations would be in the works, understandable given the book's emphasis on Italian-American themes on the one hand and its central stylistic influence, via Knut Hamsun, on the other. To celebrate all this newfound recognition and to render it more palpable, more visible, John moved with Joyce from the apartment on North New Hampshire to a mansion on Temple Street. True, it was an old mansion and long ago broken down into separate rental units, none spacious, but it was a mansion nonetheless, situated on the brow of a hill with a superb view of the city, over which Fante could now cast the eye of a successful novelist.

CHAPTER 10

In the November 1938 issue of *The American Mercury* Frank Fenton published a bitterly knowing article entitled "The Hollywood Literary Life." Aimed at pricking the notion of the Hollywood studio system as "a hack's utopia," the article went into painfully funny detail explicating the indignities of a writing life devoted to the production of what today is still called, and with no more irony than in 1938, "an original story," actually "a bastard type of fiction, with no discoverable rules for its composition." Ulcers, ingratitude, frustration and bankruptcy—these were a few of the rewards that the B-movie writer could anticipate in his endless quest for a new line, a new twist, a new gag in a marketplace so unsentimental that it would gladly "throw the Crucifixion out of the New Testament for a laugh."

Coming as it did from Fante's closest screenwriting crony, Fenton's wicked satire sounded a timely cautionary note. Despite all the accolades, the wages of book writing were lowly and slow in coming for Fante, and by late November his coffers—not to mention Joyce's pocketbook—were once again all but empty. To his credit, however, Fante was for once resisting the temptation to backslide into the Hollywood morass of "original story" writing. He was encouraged in this resistance by the voice of experience of his Armenian paisano Wild Bill Saroyan (or Wildcat Willie, or Willie the Wow, as Fante also liked calling him), who on November 20 wrote to admonish Fante not to wait too long between books because the book-buying public had such a fickle memory. The question for Fante was how to tide himself over. His options were few; but for a creative writer in a bind there would always be Western Union. "In reply to a frantic telegram from John Fante," E. J. Stackpole, Jr., noted in an in-house memo dated November 29, "I have wired him $100.00."

On the same day of his telegram, no doubt after signing for the hundred dollars, Fante wrote in a more composed mood to his favorite Colorado cousin, Jo Campiglia. In the past he had trusted Jo to listen to his boyhood secrets, and now he wanted to tell her a new one, about the outline he was working on for his next novel. Using a quotation from his favorite Knut Hamsun novel, *Pan*, he was going to call the new book "Ask the Dust on the Road," and he was going to set it against a Los Angeles, not a Hollywood, background. The book would tell the story

> of a girl I once loved who loved someone else, who in turn despised her. Strange story of a beautiful Mexican girl who somehow didn't fit into modern life, took to marijuana, lost her mind, and wandered into the Mojave desert with a little Pekinese dog. It [will be] a book like Human Bondage, but with humor and wistfulness.

Impressionistic and elliptical as this description might be, it was also a remarkably clear view of the story that would become *Ask the Dust*, and Jo Campiglia was the first to hear of it. When Fante had applied for a Guggenheim fellowship one month earlier (still maintaining on his application the fictitious 1911 birth date), he had proposed no such love story but rather a sprawling 100,000-word saga far closer in spirit to the recently dead and buried synopsis for "The Man from Rome." If honored with a grant, he had promised to write an "absolutely necessary novel," one that would deal with "the problems of orientation and adjustment to the American scene by first-generation Italian-Americans. A work which follows out the lives of four children of Italian parents." Nevertheless, despite recommendations from Louis Adamic, William Soskin, Joseph Henry Jackson, Carey McWilliams and Pascal Covici, Fante's Guggenheim proposal did not make the final cut.

Pascal Covici—not an Italian, as his name might suggest, but a Jew of Eastern European extraction—was a gifted editor at Viking Press then working with John Steinbeck on the manuscript of *The Grapes of Wrath*. Although he had concurred with his colleague David Zablodowsky's rejection of *The Road to Los Angeles*, Covici saw in Fante a writer of enormous talent and promise. Fante's application for a Guggenheim had thus afforded Covici an opportunity to voice his support, and to begin building bridges to the future. "I would not hesitate to give him a contract on his projected novel," Covici had said in his letter of recommendation. While visiting Los Angeles a few weeks earlier, Covici had made a point of meeting Fante for the first time, and found him to be a compellingly "tense, imaginative and creative young man." Although Fante was still flat broke despite the critical success of *Wait Until Spring, Bandini*, Covici's interest in his prospects was a sure sign that the young author's star was on the ascendant. Over the next couple of years Covici would patiently cultivate the acquaintance, ultimately transforming it into a professional relationship after Fante and Stackpole Sons parted ways.

For the time being, however, the rising star was also a sitting duck for the potshots of sportswriter Westbrook Pegler. Always on the lookout for material for his nationally syndicated column, Pegler could not resist the big fat target inadvertently (or was it shrewdly?) held up by Stackpole's publicity department, which had asked Joyce to contribute something to the campaign from her perspective as the author's wife. Joyce had chimed in with an ironically bent note about "the litter of papers, cigarette butts and discarded garments that always surround my husband, who always begins work fully dressed and ends entirely naked." Along with a glib self-description from the author himself ("We live in an apartment house in Los Angeles, where I apply myself somewhat lackadaisically to the dull monotony of becoming an immortal"), Joyce's wisecrack

was sent to reviewers across the country. The great majority of these people were serious enough about books to get past the promotion to the
novel itself, but sports scribe Pegler had been included in Stackpole's
mass mailing because baseball figured prominently in the novel. Admitting that he had not even read the book, Pegler nevertheless seized the
occasion to poke fun at Fante's alleged literary striptease. He wondered
about the distractions of mosquitoes and the hazards of cane chairs before
meandering on to reminisce about a baseball novel he once witnessed being banged out by a fellow sportswriter who had had the minimum good
sense to keep his shirt on while banging. It was good, frivolous copy for a
day's column.

Alive to the chance for more free publicity, Fante fired off a response
to the *Los Angeles Evening News* bristling with mock indignation. In his
column-length letter he accused Pegler of being a Peeping Tom gullible
enough to fall for the "obvious guano" of the press kit, which had been
"contrived strictly for the consumption of women's clubs." He promised
that if Pegler could find it within himself to "lay off such shuddering delights as *Silk Stocking* and *Police Gazette* and cast his eyes upon the lascivious virtues of *Wait Until Spring, Bandini*, he [would] be converted to
sound American literature." The retort wound up on an arresting note:

Put it this way: If instead of a handsome Italian, I had been a ravishing blond authoress with all the succulent attributes of a movie
queen, would Pegler have complained in print? And if the jacket
of my book explained that this gorgeous blonde began her literary
chore fully clothed and ended entirely naked, is it possible that
Westbrook Pegler would have objected in his column? I doubt it.

This was one way of drumming up sales, imagining himself as someone who looked seductively like his own wife, and who in his imagination did as his wife imagined him to do in hers. Tamer but no less
eye-catching was an article detailing the "legend" of Fante's all-night
writing marathons in the basement of the *Long Beach Press-Telegram*
which Fante's old friend Dick Emery wrote for that newspaper to help
boost *Wait Until Spring, Bandini*. One eye this article caught belonged to
the poor wife of a Spanish-American War pensioner whose daughter

Fante had known years before. Reading of the book's success, Mrs. W. R. Feiring of Long Beach wrote Fante a letter congratulating him and entreating him to return the $30 her daughter Evelyn had long ago loaned him "when you were in need." Evelyn's grandmother had given her the money for clothes, Mrs. Feiring explained, but with her husband's meager pension of only $60 a month, they had been unable to buy her anything new for years. "[I]f you can pay just part of it at a time it will help," she pleaded. Unlike Westbrook Pegler, there is no indication that Mrs. Feiring ever received the favor of a John Fante reply.

During this time there were serious undertones to other frivolities as well. The November evening Fante spent in the Stevens Nik-a-Bob at 9th and Western celebrating with Carey and Ross, for example, was devoted at least in part to the election of Culbert L. Olson as Governor of California. Olson was the first Democrat to gain the office in forty years, and after the defeat of Upton Sinclair in 1934, Olson's election indicated that California was at last ready for its own New Deal administration. Fante may have been personally uninvolved in the political fray of his time, but he was neither uninformed regarding the issues nor indifferent to their developments. Indeed, as one of Carey McWilliams's closest friends, he was intimately connected to the innermost workings of liberal political life in Los Angeles. It was not unusual for Fante to accompany Carey on speaking engagements around the city—on the rights of the foreign born, or the plight of migrant workers, or the rising dangers of home-grown fascism—or to join Carey for lunch or dinner or after-dinner drinking sessions at which one or more prospective political candidates, elected officials or political appointees might be present. And when Fante and McWilliams drank as a twosome, as they did on the November night when Fante appeared at Carey's door to borrow two dollars and stayed to demolish a whole bottle of rum, they were certain to speak about the political scene, local, national and international, in which Carey was so thoroughly immersed.

One subject sure to have come up was the early stirring of the so-called Dies Committee. Called to order in Washington for the first time in August 1938 under the chairmanship of Martin Dies, a conservative

Republican member of the House of Representatives from Texas, the Special Committee on Un-American Activities was the forerunner of the notorious House Un-American Activities Committee of the witch-hunting 1940s and 1950s. As such, the Dies Committee was empowered to conduct hearings that welcomed the testimony of volunteer witnesses who held forth, often with gusto, regarding individuals and organizations suspected of being subversive. To no one's surprise, given the rightward bent of the committee's seven members, suspicions gravitated to left-of-center activists and enterprises. In fact, as early as October 1938 Carey McWilliams was named during one of the committee's hearings as part of the "group of liberal and communistic writers" who had organized the Western Writers' Congress of 1936.

Fante may have considered McWilliams a "sucker" for breaking his back over that conference, but he had nothing good to say about the people on this committee who were asking the questions, much less about those lining up to answer. The political climate was becoming increasingly polarized, of that he was well aware. Following *Kristallnacht*, the widely reported orgy of attacks upon German Jews and their businesses on November 7, 1938, for example, swastikas had been appearing with alarming frequency in Los Angeles cemeteries, on synagogues, and across the doors of private residences. But with war now all but a foregone conclusion, Fante was more determined than ever to keep his head down and write the novel about the girl he had once loved.

On January 9, 1939, Fante signed a contract with Stackpole Sons for that novel. This time he would receive an advance of $800 spread out in biweekly payments through the middle of April; the completed manuscript of approximately 85,000 words would be due on May 1, less than four months away. As close as his deadline was, Fante remained blithe enough to tag along for the ride a few days later when Carey had business in Riverside. Then on January 19 Governor Culbert L. Olson appointed Carey Chief of the Division of Immigration and Housing for all of California. Fante immediately wrote to his friend Saroyan exhorting him to join Fante and Joyce and Carey "and a whole slew of people" at San Francisco's Empire Hotel, where they all planned to meet the next week to celebrate Carey's new job. Interestingly, though Fante had often traded literary boasts with Saroyan since the two had first met in Stanley Rose's Bookshop a couple of years earlier, in this letter he was strangely silent about both his contract and the novel he was planning to write. It was as if he was keeping it all inside, conjuring up one last festive extravagance before submersing himself in the work.

The choice of McWilliams to head California's Division of Immigration and Housing was important, for it signaled Governor Olson's intent to check the exploitation of migrant farm laborers throughout the state. McWilliams had been tapped for the job because of his indefatigable activism as an attorney, a writer and a public speaker in behalf of the mostly Mexican, Filipino and Japanese laborers who made up one of the state's most important, if least visible, workforces. His extensive investigations into the pickers' squalid living conditions throughout the agricultural regions of both southern and northern California and in particular the rich Central Valley had equipped McWilliams with a vast and unique archive of facts, figures and human case histories revealing systemic injustice on a tragic scale, and he was now at work on a book that would expose the depth and extent of the problem. What makes McWilliams's passion for social justice notable for us is that his companion on these forays into the misery-shack depths of the Golden State's migrant labor camps was often none other than the supposedly apolitical novelist John Fante, whose interest in matters of race and class was fermenting in other, more artistic ways.

The celebration of Carey's appointment came off as planned. According to McWilliams's diary, Ross Wills and John arrived in Sacramento together to collect Carey at his State Building office before hooking up with Saroyan in San Francisco. Sallying forth from their base of operations at the Empire Hotel—scene-to-be of the famous kiss between James Stewart and Kim Novak in Alfred Hitchcock's *Vertigo*—the merrymakers beat a path from nightspot to nightspot, staying out until four a.m. and in the process wearing down to the point of physical exhaustion even the prodigiously energetic McWilliams. The foursome's muscles may well have been aching the next day when they met for a farewell lunch at the hotel. And then, John's latest exercise in frivolity a success, it was back to Los Angeles and his serious job as a contracted novelist with a deadline.

Fante was superstitious about writing, and whenever he started a major new project he had to have new tables on which to work—secondhand tables, to be sure, but different ones from those he had effectively used up on the previous project. Joyce's suggestion that he purchase one good desk and have done with the bother went ignored as John scoured used-furniture stores for the magical set of tables that would stand just the right height and radiate just the right feeling. When he had finally found what he was looking for, he positioned the chosen tables at right angles in his upstairs studio—he and Joyce had moved back to the Wilshire District in search of more elbow room, this time to a two-story apartment at 826½ South Berendo—neatly arranging his typewriter, pencils, paper and dictionary. And then he plunged into *Ask the Dust.*

The earliest extant fragment of Fante's work on *Ask the Dust*, predating even the bare-bones summary he had shared with his cousin Jo Campiglia, indicates that Fante originally saw this novel in very close relation to *The Road to Los Angeles*:

The kid comes to Los Angeles on a stolen three hundred dollars. He tells everyone he is a writer for the Sat. Eve. Post. He has a lousy affair with a woman like the T.B. case in Venice, then goes back home in disgust. The story closes with the kid getting back to work at the cannery and seriously trying to write because now he has a story.

Now that he had decided to hone his primary focus on Arturo's doomed love for the beautiful Mexican waitress Camilla, however, the "lousy affair" would be relegated to a subplot involving the haunted Vera Rivken, and the bracketing cannery background would be eliminated. For maximum incantational effect Fante now started with Hamsun's words from *Pan*, verbatim—"Ask the dust on the road!"—before taking Hamsun's syntax and making it over into his own: "Ask the Joshua trees standing alone where the Mojave begins. Ask them about Camilla Lopez, and they will whisper her name." Writing fast, he produced a dense and lyrical seventeen-page preamble previewing the novel's main incidents. This summary was delivered in the elegiac voice of Arturo Bandini, who lets on at the outset how the novel will conclude, namely, with Camilla disappearing into the desert never to be seen again. In seventeen pages

Fante encapsulated the entire novel: Arturo's pathetic dreams of becoming a famous writer; his racially charged affair with Camilla; Bunker Hill and its denizens; Angel's Flight; the episode of the murdered calf; Camilla's self-destructive love for the tubercular Sammy and her eventual slide into drugs and madness; Arturo's ambivalent feelings for the Church; and finally the return to the desert and Camilla's climactic disappearance. As he had done before, Fante allowed his fictional alter-ego narrator to claim for his story autobiographical veracity: "It's good. It's myself." Throughout the writing there was a unique and electric charge of urgency.

There was also a problem, one that escaped Fante's notice until he showed the pages to a neighbor who also wrote for a living. Daniel Mainwaring had knocked on the door one day when the Fantes were still living in the Temple Street mansion in order to introduce himself to the author of *Wait Until Spring, Bandini*. Mainwaring was a veteran newspaperman, having worked as a crime reporter for several New York and Los Angeles dailies before trading in his press badge to work as a publicist for Warner Bros. and RKO. From flacking Mainwaring had switched back to writing full-time when the detective novels he penned under the name Geoffrey Homes began to find a market. Before he died in 1977 at the age of seventy-four, Mainwaring would write more than a dozen novels and some forty screenplays, several of them adaptations of his own books, including the film noir classic *Out of the Past* and the early sci-fi hit *Invasion of the Body Snatchers*. In short, though his literary tastes were unabashedly popular, Mainwaring was the kind of neighbor with professional wits and experience enough to have something constructive to say about a work in progress like the preliminary seventeen pages of *Ask the Dust*. Here is how Fante remembered Mainwaring's response:

He said, "You can't mean it. This is terrible. How could you possibly do this?" And he berated me and ridiculed me until he actually talked me out of the whole goddamn thing. And I dismissed the thing from my mind for about two weeks. And then I went back to it and in one fell swoop I wrote it. It took me, oh, I don't know, about a week, and it was all done. And I couldn't tell you what Dan said to me, but he got me awful mad.

Unlike her husband's, Joyce Fante's recollection of this incident is in no way so histrionic. (She ascribes Fante's lasting anger at Mainwaring to a mutual attraction, never acted on, between herself and Mainwaring.) But she agrees that Mainwaring's response proved crucial to Fante's conception of *Ask the Dust*. She also recalls what Mainwaring said. Puffing on his pipe he first praised the writing of those seventeen pages, then politely suggested that Fante consider a new structure, starting not at the end with Camilla's disappearance but at the beginning with the appearance of Arturo. It would take Fante longer than one week to finish writing the novel, but after he had realized that Mainwaring was correct, the writing did in fact begin to flow, starting with the now-famous opening: "One night I was sitting in my hotel room on Bunker Hill, down in the very middle of Los Angeles. It was an important night in my life, because I had to make a decision about the hotel." No longer would the story give itself away in advance. To hook the reader Fante would trust the deceptively simple eloquence of his prose and the elemental power of a forward-moving narrative—what will Arturo do or think or remember *now?*—without allowing him to dip into the future of his own story and thus undermine the reader's experience of wonder at discovering the novel page by page. Readers who consider *Ask the Dust* one of those rare works so rightly formed that it refuses to submit to imaginative alternatives have Mainwaring to thank for his contribution to its creation, a most generous if unwitting gift to the ages.

Fante easily beat his deadline, sending the manuscript to Soskin in New York not long before the Random House publication in May of Nathanael West's *The Day of the Locust*. Fante had written the book fast and with virtually no need to revise, in a state of pure writerly abstraction. "It was an easy book to write," he later recalled. "It just poured out of me."

Tellingly, during the time he was writing *Ask the Dust*, that is, the three months after the January celebration in San Francisco, Fante did not figure once in Carey McWilliams's diary. Then, with the manuscript in others' hands and lots of time on his hands once again, Fante resurfaced to join Carey McWilliams and Ross Wills on a club-hopping tour of Negro nightspots on Main Street, including one featuring marathon sex-act entertainments too sordid even for McWilliams to describe. After the incandescent time of writing, Fante was back in his element, the dingy half-world of downtown bars, taxi dance halls and smoky nightclubs.

By the third week in June Fante was also back in circulation as a B-film scenarist, selling to Warner Bros. for $1,100 the rights to "Mama Ravioli," another highly derivative "original" based in New York's Little Italy and cowritten with Ross Wills. From Warner Bros. Fante migrated to MGM, where in October he was put to work with Frank Fenton and Lynn Root on a wan comedy called "The Golden Fleecing" which in turn would be reassigned to Nathanael West's brother-in-law and sister, S. J. and Laura Perelman. After the concentrated intensity of those three months earlier in the year, Fante could not have been expected to turn around and write yet another novel right away, much less a novel as good as *Ask the Dust*. But in the drastic transition from writing the book that Charles Bukowski would much later call the finest novel ever written to churning out so much cynical twin-biller drivel, Fante was indeed moving from the sublime to the ridiculous.

But then again the tenor of the times ranged from the ridiculous to the tragic. In March a recklessly prolific informer named Rena Vale—a struggling screenwriter, former member of the Communist Party and organizer of the League of Women Shoppers, soon to become a favorite of the Dies Committee—had filed an affidavit with the office of Governor Culbert L. Olson charging Carey McWilliams, John Fante and others with being members of the Communist Party. In May, Italy and Germany signed a formal military alliance, and in August Fante and Ross Wills were at the Unitarian Church on 8th Street to hear Carey speak before the Youth Anti-Nazi League—and, just as important, to go drinking with him afterward until closing time at the Mona Lisa on Wilshire Boulevard.

Carey's meticulously researched *Factories in the Fields* had just been published to serious acclaim, but also to a building backlash. The nonfiction counterpart to Steinbeck's *The Grapes of Wrath*, Carey's book exposed the appalling conditions endured by California's migrant farmworkers. By August both books had been banned in largely agricultural Kern County, and because of mounting protests from conservative readers who were alarmed by what they saw as the creeping Red Menace,

McWilliams was asked by longtime friend Phil Townsend Hanna to step down from his position as contributing editor of *Westways*. In September, England and France declared war on Germany. By October, just before "The Golden Fleecing" came through for him at MGM, Fante was again dead broke. He prevailed upon Joyce to mortgage her Plymouth for a stopgap $138.96. Then, two days later, in an odd departure for someone as seemingly inattentive to his nightly dream life as Fante had always been, he began noting dreams on stray pieces of paper. In one dream he received a letter from Evelyn Feiring, the Long Beach girl to whom he still owed thirty dollars. In another Marie Baray was puckering her lips.

But what mattered most now was the book. *Ask the Dust* was published on November 8, 1939, and Stackpole Sons had done a handsome job. The dust-jacket watercolor depicted the figures of a man and a woman, obviously together but tensely apart, beside a convertible roadster parked beneath the scant shade of a yucca, all under a sky streaked in burnt shades of desert rose. The back cover featured blurbs from William Saroyan, James T. Farrell and John Chamberlain of *Scribner's Magazine*. The book sold for two dollars, a fifty-cent reduction from the price charged for *Wait Until Spring, Bandini*, intended as a sales boost for an author whose publisher believed in him. The rest of the world might be going merrily to hell, but before it wound up there Fante had the satisfaction of holding his second published novel in his hands. Now it was time for him to begin celebrating.

And celebrate he did, first by taking in the USC–Stanford game at the Los Angeles Coliseum with Carey and Ross on the eleventh of November. During the game the three fans matched each other drink for drink, so that afterward Carey felt "none too fit" for his scheduled evening appearance on radio station KFWB to discuss the immigrant problem. A few nights later Fante was again carousing with his good friends and evil companions, this time at Lucy's on Melrose Avenue across from Paramount Studios, where they were joined by Louis Adamic and the wealthy arts patron Mrs. Caroline Keck of Coronado. In Carey's view it turned out to be nothing short of "an amazing evening, with Fante most entertaining." Clearly Fante was feeling on top of a very topsy-turvy world, anticipating with confidence the success of his book and sharing his ebullience with one and all.

As he would soon learn, however, the critical response to *Ask the Dust* did not bear out all his hopes. While reviewers were consistent in praising Fante's ability to write, more often than not their comparisons of the novel with *Wait Until Spring, Bandini* found *Ask the Dust*'s more outre themes lacking in warmth and simple human interest. Even more irksome to Fante must have been the wrongheaded charge that Arturo Bandini was "a character cut wholly out of Saroyan's cloth." Still, the bright spots were very bright. "[N]ow that he has written his Werther," said *The Atlantic Monthly*'s reviewer, "let us hope fervently he can go on to another Faust." In the *New York Herald Tribune* Iris Barry overcame her own preference for *Wait Until Spring, Bandini* to find Fante's "particular vision of a modern inferno" compellingly original, shot through as it was with "flashes of tender poetry, . . . gentleness and vision." And *Commonweal*, while cautioning squeamish readers to approach the novel at their own peril, declared it "quite an extraordinary piece of work, and a very Catholic piece of work at that."

Time has been kind to *Ask the Dust*, which today is widely regarded as Fante's masterpiece. Like *The Road to Los Angeles*, the story of aspiring writer Arturo Bandini at age twenty, living in a squalid Bunker Hill hotel, reverberates with the twin vicissitudes of writing and sex. Here, however, in unexpected ways and with unhoped-for results, Bandini's literary and romantic dreams come to be realized, if not strictly fulfilled. Before the book opens he has already published one story, "The Little Dog Laughed," of which he is inordinately proud; before the book closes he will have written and published his first novel. But having finished it he can find nothing better to do than to throw the thing out into the desert night and leave its pages to blow in the wind. Likewise, having outgrown his passion for solitary encounters with so many magazine pinups, the maturing Bandini of *Ask the Dust* makes contact with several flesh-and-blood women. But with these women—an anonymous prostitute, the fiery Mexican waitress Camilla Lopez, and the mysteriously scarred Jewess Vera Rivken—he can only play out the comedy of his sexual initiation and the tragedy, alternately vicious and sad, of his racial and religious insecurities.

These insecurities manifest themselves on the one hand as Arturo's weakness for ethnic baiting in his dealings with Camilla and on the other as his tendency to revert to Catholic type when faced with the reality of his own inadequacies. Even as he considers Camilla his Mayan princess, his queen, Bandini can turn around and belittle her as a "Spick" and a "Greaser," stooping even to ridicule her Mexican huaraches. (By significant contrast, he never speaks against Vera Rivken's Jewishness, as if her hungrier, more exalted otherness is somehow unassailable.) It is clear, however, that this inexcusable behavior is prompted largely by Bandini's own sense of ethnic alienation. After all, this is the Bandini who, when informed by his landlady that Mexicans and Jews are not allowed in her low-rent hotel, effectively denies his own ethnicity by proclaiming, "I'm an American." And yet it is a Mexican woman and then a Jew whom Bandini comes to embrace—though not before suffering the agonies of remorse for both his cruelty to Camilla, and, by implication, the cowardice of his own self-denial. Lying in bed at night unable to sleep, he recalls "the folks back home,"

> and I was miserable, for tonight I had acted like them. Smith and Parker and Jones, I had never been one of them. Ah, Camilla! When I was a kid back home in Colorado it was Smith and Parker and Jones who hurt me with their hideous names, called me Wop and Dago and Greaser, and their children hurt me, just as I hurt you tonight. They hurt me so much I could never become one of them, drove me to books, drove me within myself, drove me to run away from that Colorado town, and sometimes, Camilla, when I see their faces I feel the hurt all over again, the old ache there, and sometimes I am glad they are here, dying in the sun, uprooted, tricked by their heartlessness, the same faces, the same set, hard mouths, faces from my home town, fulfilling the emptiness of their lives under a blazing sun.

In his misery and guilt Bandini turns to recrimination before finding the inner strength to own up to his shame:

> I have seen them stagger out of their movie palaces and blink their empty eyes in the face of reality once more, and stagger home, to read the *Times*, to find out what's going on in the world. I have vomited at their newspapers, read their literature, observed their customs, eaten their food, desired their women, gaped at their art.

But I am poor, and my name ends with a soft vowel, and they hate me and my father, and my father's father, and they would have my blood and put me down, but they are old now, dying in the sun and in the hot dust of the road, and I am young and full of hope and love for my country and my times, and when I say Greaser to you it is not my heart that speaks, but the quivering of an old wound, and I am ashamed of the terrible thing I have done.

This scene suggests the depth of development that Bandini undergoes between *The Road to Los Angeles* and *Ask the Dust*. The year before *Ask the Dust* was published, while he was writing *Wait Until Spring, Bandini*, Fante had mentioned in a letter to Mencken that he had recently reread all of Nietzsche's works, and that he now found in them considerable "hodgepodge." This discovery marked a significant development from the days when the fire-breathing philosopher of *Thus Spake Zarathustra, Beyond Good and Evil* and *The Antichrist* had been, along with Mencken, one of Fante's gods. Writing under Nietzsche's sway, albeit with his own brand of irony, Fante had produced in *The Road to Los Angeles* an Arturo Bandini who fully subscribed to the gamier aspects of the *Übermensch* program. Thus the shameless "Fuhrer Bandini" raves against not only those mirrorlike others whom he misprizes—his fellow Mexican and Filipino cannery workers—but also against the Church. As the quoted passages make clear, however, the Arturo Bandini of *Ask the Dust* comes to recognize the validity of, and even the need for shame in the wake of shameful behavior. Moreover, while he remains unreconciled in any orthodox sense to Mother Church, he can no longer bring himself to defame the institution that in so many ways has helped to form his way of thinking, his character and his sensibility. On the contrary, in moments of duress, for example in the guilt-ridden aftermath of his first sexual experience, he resorts to the forms of prayer imprinted within him since his earliest youth: "*Mea culpa, mea culpa, mea maxima culpa.*" Automatic lip service, we might surmise; but it is also something else. The simple enactment of ritual evinces Arturo's blood faith in the forms as means to higher ends, for although by reason's light faith may be unreasonable it can also be—and notwithstanding the combined rationalism of Nietzsche and Voltaire—in its own absurd way redeeming.

Compared to *The Road to Los Angeles* and *Wait Until Spring, Bandini,* *Ask the Dust* is thus a more studied achievement in terms of both its protagonist's evolution and the novel's aesthetics. By the time he came to write *Ask the Dust* Fante had learned to layer into his writing conscious thematic substructures and allusions which lent palpable depth to his own novel while simultaneously honoring and in some cases improving upon his sources. Thus, for example, in one of his self-absorbed moods Arturo Bandini can think in passing "about a few other Italians, Casanova and Cellini," leaving it to us to appreciate Fante's ironic skill in counterpointing his own failed lover with two of the most notorious womanizers in all of literature. (Consider especially in this light the violent correspondences between Cellini and his lover-model Caterina on the one hand and Bandini and Camilla on the other.) Two other models, closer to home, will suffice to demonstrate that Fante was now purposefully infusing his novel with allusional depth. We have already considered the good example Fante absorbed from his reading of Knut Hamsun. Less obvious but no less essential to *Ask the Dust* are the examples Fante took from his readings of Helen Hunt Jackson and Don Ryan, the authors, respectively, of two seminal southern California novels, *Ramona* (1884) and *Angel's Flight* (1927).

From his explorations in California history Fante was well aware of the power that *Ramona's* interracial love theme, involving a white heroine and her Indian lover, had exerted on readers for over fifty years, despite Jackson's mawkish treatment. ("This is Ramona in reverse," Fante had written in the discarded prologue to his novel.) So too did Fante recognize the fundamental promise of a story about a struggling young Los Angeles writer who subsists on oranges, wanders the city in search of its soul, rides the little Bunker Hill railway known as Angel's Flight, breaks out in poetic praise of the great god Pan, and falls in love with a dark-skinned Mexican beauty whom he thinks of as his princess, and who in turn abandons him in favor of her own self-destructive obsessions. All of these ingredients and more can be found in Don Ryan's impassioned, diffuse *Angel's Flight,* which Fante used less as a template for *Ask the Dust* than as a selective foil. In writing the novel that no one besides himself could ever write, Fante did not merely imitate these models; he appropriated their strengths while letting what was left over go, remaking them in his own image.

In this light Fante's comparison of *Wait Until Spring, Bandini* and *Ask the Dust* in a letter to Jo Campiglia is revealing: "The first book came from my heart; the second from my head and my—(it starts with p and ends with k)." What Fante was speaking of here was craft, a sexy thing really inasmuch as craft amounts to nothing if not the cultivated discipline to control a performance while retaining the pulse and thrust of artistic spontaneity. In that respect *Ask the Dust* was shot through with craft. For one thing, the novel's plot and prose are both deceptive, for in each case the simplicity that meets the eye belies a rare elegance and depth. Moreover, the poetic flights to which Arturo's voice rises in recollecting his youth counterbalances his youthful despair, and nowhere more so than in his hymn to the joys of writing:

> Six weeks, a few sweet hours every day, three and four and sometimes five delicious hours, with the pages piling up and all other desires asleep. I felt like a ghost walking the earth, a lover of man and beast alike, and wonderful waves of tenderness flooded me when I talked to people and mingled with them in the streets. God Almighty, dear God, good to me, gave me a sweet tongue, and these sad and lonely folk will hear me and they shall be happy. Thus the days passed. Dreamy, luminous days, and sometimes such great quiet joy came to me that I would turn out my lights and cry, and a strange desire to die would come to me.
>
> Thus Bandini, writing a novel.

Considered on its own, *Ask the Dust* stands as a marvel of realistic urgency and poetic power. Considered in relation to the other three novels of the Bandini saga, as indeed it demands to be considered—and for that matter to virtually all of the fiction bearing the name John Fante—it radiates outward its aura of timeless precision in recording the story of one young man's desires: the desire to write first and foremost, and the wayward desire, self-defeating in the end, to love and be loved in return. If it is about anything, in fact, *Ask the Dust* is about desire, and if any single entity is large enough to comprehend the overreaching scope of that desire, it can only be the whole city of Los Angeles:

> Los Angeles, give me some of you! Los Angeles come to me the way I came to you, my feet over your streets, you pretty town I loved you so much, you sad flower in the sand, you pretty town.

Despite decent reviews, however, and notwithstanding the fact that in critical assessment today this work is considered to be his masterpiece, *Ask the Dust* was not the breakthrough novel that Fante had hoped it would be. Perhaps we do well to remind ourselves that 1939 was a tough year for a small story from an obscure publishing house to stand out in. Justly called an annus mirabilis for its outpouring of cultural touchstones, this was the year that also saw the appearance of *The Grapes of Wrath*, *The Day of the Locust* and Raymond Chandler's *The Big Sleep*, among others, not to mention such quintessential American film classics as *Gone with the Wind*, *The Wizard of Oz* and *Stagecoach*. In short, it was a year of stiff competition.

In writing the love story that was *Ask the Dust*, Fante had managed to abstract himself from the world's pressing political exigencies. For the duration of the writing he had reinhabited that magical time when he was young, poor and bursting with desire on Bunker Hill. With equal measures of poetry and guile he had combined Marie Baray's smoldering beauty with the edgy borderline instability of Audrey, the flamboyant waitress from Main Street's Liberty Bar, in order to match the matchless Arturo with his Camilla. Of course, in the end Camilla Lopez would not be Arturo's to possess but rather an infinitely regressing personification of the unattainable, a timeless feature in the landscape of human longing, ragged huaraches and all. Among others, these are the reasons that *Ask the Dust* retains such a strongly contemporary feel more than sixty years after it was written.

But as early as the late fall of 1939, with the publication of his novel already a thing of the past, Fante had long since come out from under the spell of its writing to jostle elbows with the workaday world. He optioned the film rights of *Wait Until Spring, Bandini* to the husband of actress Gladys George in the hope that the book might be made into a movie, and when MGM and Paramount both passed on *Ask the Dust* he hired a fast-talking Hollywood agent for the sole purpose of flogging that novel to the movies as well. Indicative of his mercenary attitude at this time is the joke he told the boys at Stanley Rose's one day, the one about the writer who comes home late from work to find his wife half-dead from some kind of sexual assault. "For God's sake, honey," the writer says, "who did this to you?" "Who did it?" his wife screams. "Your fucking agent, that's who." Upon hearing which the writer asks, "What else did Eddie have to say?"

Distracted by an expensive lawsuit over their unauthorized publication of *Mein Kampf*—Judge Learned Hand's ruling in February 1940 held that the copyright law's protection of entitled aliens included not only homeless war refugees but also Adolf Hitler—Stackpole Sons was investing virtually no thought or money in the promotion of *Ask the Dust*. In order to survive the financial blow of the courtroom reversal, the firm had to reduce the scope of its operations drastically, and one of the first areas to suffer was publicity. So that when Fante drew his $2,000 share of the $6,000 he and Ross Wills and Lynn Root were paid for "The Golden Fleecing," he made haste to take Joyce up to the Bay Area for the Cal-Stanford game, a small gesture in the direction of success. During this trip they discussed John's most recent meeting with Pascal Covici, who on his latest author-scouting swing through Los Angeles had offered Fante a tempting advance on his next book. Problem was, Fante was contractually obligated to Stackpole for his next two books. It was a frustrating situation, but what could he do about it?

In lieu of moving to a new publisher, in December John moved with Joyce from their Los Angeles apartment to a comfortable five-room house at 2904 Manhattan Avenue in Manhattan Beach. Here, with a fine view of the sea and the broad winter sky, Fante planned to regather focus for his next assault on—what? As yet he had no ideas for a new novel. He decided to begin keeping a diary, a habit he had never developed. His first entry was tentative and contradictory, claiming in one breath "No worry" and in the next confessing a "Guilty feeling about my laziness," compounded by worry and fear that Joyce might be pregnant, even though they both wanted a child. The emotional seesaw was typical. Given his ongoing financial insecurity, he saw little chance that he would be able to write anything enduring so long as his deepest motivation was the mere need for money. And yet it could happen. One big full book could put him "smacko among writers like Faulkner, Lewis and Wolfe," as he put it when he had last written Jo Campiglia. Or then again maybe he would try to make a quick killing with a solo script for a big star like Clark

Gable, something original, as they said, with maybe a fish cannery as background. Whatever he finally decided on, he would have to proceed without the "solacing conceit of immortality," because the fact was he had run clean out of that. Even though he was only thirty, like some aging boxer or ballplayer whose inspired playing days were behind him he would have to reach down inside and rely on his pride and his sense of duty in order to get the job done.

Fante's spirits were briefly lifted when early in January *Esquire* accepted a new story. "Man and Wife, Etc." (purchased for $150 but not published until April 1941, and then as "The Taming of Valenti") was a violent comedy about married life in which all the flung bottles and scratched cheeks and blackened eyes and bruised knuckles, interspersed with so many coyly drawn bedroom reconciliations, accrue to a creepy sort of laughing nightmare feeling. "It was either murder and death, or life and love," says the narrator, a novelist who compares writing on the "home stretch of a novel" to going to "China, or Africa, or the moon. You're far away from everything, the days tumble by and you lose track of them."

In Manhattan Beach in early 1940, however, Fante was far from the home stretch of anything, and the only reason he had for losing track of the days was all the drinking he was now doing, night after night of it, stolid, humorless hangover drinking which often left him useless the following day. Although he had removed himself from the distracting thrum of Los Angeles, down here at the beach he was often more distracted than ever. Talkative Al Bezzerides was living just around the corner, as were the convivial Robert Brownell and his wife Kay, and there always seemed to be a crowd of visitors streaming through the Fante house— McWilliams, Wills, Mainwaring and Fenton, to name a few among the many who came and went—playing Ping-Pong, laughing too loudly and drinking too much. Besides this constant superficial annoyance there was the deeper disturbance of coming global disaster. America would not enter the war for almost two more years, and Little Bavaria, the romantic Manhattan Beach *Ratskeller* where Joyce loved to dine when John was behaving, had not yet been forced to close its doors despite rising anti-German sentiment. But still the war seemed to be everywhere, all the time, in the newspapers and on the radio, contributing to a general darkening of people's outlooks and humors, and exacerbating John's volatile moodiness.

Punctuating Fante's slide into outright despair during January 1940 were periodic rushes of enthusiasm for new writing ideas. Chief among these was an idea that Fante credited Carey McWilliams for inspiring, a "magnificent idea for [a] sociological novel" based on the life of Filipino migrant laborers in California. Though "sick as hell" from nights of drinking, Fante would regale himself with thoughts of a novel about a "swashbuckling farmer-fighter" based on Ceferino Garcia, the charismatic California-based Filipino middleweight champion of the world popularly known as the Bolo Puncher. But then the impending reality of war would steal into John's thoughts, and he would veer wildly between the blackest pessimism and the highest hopes. "I am against death, but I think the world would be better if the patient were killed," he could confide to his journal, only to continue in the same entry with equal conviction, "A sort of highly refined Christianity is the only way out, as I see it. Man has never given Christ a break."

The heavy drinking continued, often at after-hours blues joints in central Los Angeles. After one such night in the Negro Quarter, Fante got in a bloody fight with the much larger Oliver Thornton, publisher of the radical *United Progressive News* and the lover of Fante's former Long Beach Junior College classmate Ellenore Boggegian. When the fight was over Thornton had a cracked rib, a black eye and two broken fingers. The next day Fante was drinking again and experiencing "recurrent spells of weakness and depression." Increasingly obsessed with the dream of the Filipino novel and its theme of "sexual maladjustment," Fante was still capable of pulling off an occasional "inspired love affair" with Joyce which left him feeling "warm and lascivious" for hours afterward. But it was not a feeling he could count on to last. More typical were the persistent feelings of futility and disgust he experienced while attending with Carey on several occasions the Los Angeles hearings of the LaFollette Committee, the Democratic counterpart of the Dies Committee aimed at fingering the enemies of labor. To overcome these feelings in the one way most likely to reinforce them, Fante would stay out late drinking night after night, and in the morning when he faced Joyce there would be nothing but hell to catch.

It was a wicked, manic mix, the liquor, the fighting, the politics, the sex, all the more so as it was all bound up in Fante's deep emotional reliance on the anchorage of his writing. During this time he was working on a short story, "Woman Is Fickle," which he felt was one of the best he had ever done. He was also gathering material for the Filipino novel, but he did not want to start the writing on that project until he was truly ready. To prepare himself, on January 19 he left off with the short story uncompleted and accompanied Carey on a research trip through the migrant labor camps of the San Joaquin Valley. Fante was amazed by the degradation he witnessed there, entire families surviving in shanties built of tinder, or in ratty, windblown tents; and then he was even more stunned by the numb detachment of his indifference. "I feel nothing," he wrote in his journal on January 20, troubled enough by his lack of emotion at least to record it. The Conference for Democratic Action which he attended with Carey in Fresno later that same day only depressed him further with its atmosphere of smug, cold-blooded intellectualism, and he retreated to the bar of the conference hotel to mount a misguided counterattack against his depression.

The binge continued all the way back to Los Angeles on the train, so that by the time he arrived home he was suffering from a "bitter hangover depression, suicidal thoughts, degenerate concepts [and] fantastically horrible hallucinations." He made a desperate pledge to stop drinking, but in the next several days the house was overrun with visitors, including the incorrigible Ross Wills with a couple of floozies in tow. While Joyce raged quietly at the impertinence of these people, Fante tried to get back to "Woman Is Fickle," but he found that he was now stuck. For five days he had been trying to shake "a terrific attack of melancholia, much morbid brooding on death, my own, and the general futility of man." And now this. Still, he managed to console himself thinly with the thought that the problem was biological rather than mental, something to do with a glandular deficiency perhaps. If only he could strike just the right note of hopelessness, something short of suicidal, he told himself he would be able to go on.

And then, all at once, the ugly streak seemed to be over. Sunday January 28 dawned a glorious day. John and Joyce loafed at the beach for several hours under the brilliant winter sun. A hundred times Fante had to stop and marvel at the beauty all around him, the clear sky, the sea, his wife. Then that evening, as if to celebrate his victory over the black depression and to prove that luck was again on his side, Fante drove down to Redondo Beach. Anchored out in the bay just beyond the statutory boundary was a ship, the *Rex*, where you could go gambling without fear of the law. That night Fante did not board a water taxi out to the *Rex*, however, for right on the strand he knew of a storefront roulette parlor that circumvented city antigambling ordinances by making payoffs in cartons of cigarettes, redeemable for cash a couple of doors away. Playing with three dollars, which he had practically had to chisel out of Joyce, he quickly went nine dollars ahead. He was feeling good, playing his hunches, enjoying himself for the first time in too long; and though he didn't quite manage to quit before he had lost all he had won, and Joyce's three dollars to boot, he still felt good enough to think he should go back the next night and win it all back again.

The next day he was still stuck on "Woman Is Fickle." He didn't know what the problem was. By contrast, he claimed to know exactly what ailed Joyce as a poet. "She could develop into a splendid poet if she set herself to it," he wrote in the last entry he would make in his journal. "But she won't. Once in a while she gets very conscience-stricken and works like a fiend. But that is not enough."

Not too many months earlier, in his published retort to Westbrook Pegler's ridicule of his supposed habit of writing naked, Fante had imagined himself as a beautiful blond authoress. Now he was presuming to subject the beautiful blond poet in his life to an analysis that might apply even more pointedly to himself. True, he had already developed into a splendid writer, but in the literature racket you were only as good as your latest success, and lately he had been feeling altogether unequipped to deal with the burden of the moment, and with his increasingly restive demons. Let his conscience strike him hammer blows, let him work like the Fiend himself; none of it seemed to be enough. Could it be that he was finished as a writer?

It is not certain where Fante was driving at around eleven o'clock on the night of January 29. Perhaps he was coming home from Bob Brownell's house in Hermosa Beach, as he later told Joyce, or perhaps he was on his way back to the roulette parlor in Redondo Beach, the gambler in him certain which way the wheel was going to spin. Wherever he was headed, he was hurtling through the narrow intersection of 35th Street and Palm Drive in Hermosa Beach at about fifty miles an hour when, as he would later put it in a letter to his parents, he "lost control" of Joyce's Plymouth and slammed into a telephone pole. His right arm crashed through the windshield, the muscles torn to the bone, and when he opened his eyes blood was gushing from his head and face. The car had been totaled but he had regained consciousness. When he climbed out of the wreck he was shaking badly.

The police eventually took him to the emergency room of a nearby hospital. Joyce arrived as he was receiving seventy-five stitches under local anesthetic, sixty of them on his arm and the rest on his face and his legs. The next day he was transported by ambulance to the Hospital of the Good Samaritan in Los Angeles for X rays, which revealed a serious fracture to his right cheek. He underwent surgery to set the bone, then remained hospitalized for more than a week.

When he crashed into that telephone pole Fante had been traveling alone, but his main injuries—to the side of his face and to his arm—bore an eerie resemblance to the injuries suffered in the two-person accident several years earlier involving John's father Nick. Bizarrely enough, we recall, Nick had nearly drowned in the aftermath of that accident; and the other victim had died. Given Fante's deteriorating state of mind over the previous several weeks, the important but unanswerable question that arises is whether he truly lost control of the car—or if perhaps he steered into the pole in a deliberate suicide attempt, desperate with fear that he would never write well again.

Of greater importance was the way he would come through the ordeal of this extended turning point in his life, the post–*Ask the Dust* period of trash writing, audacious dreaming and hell-bent behavior which culminated in the solo car crash. He was thirty years old, more than ever his father's son inasmuch as each seemed to embody some preternatural life force bigger than the individual man. "Some people simply refuse to die," Fante would soon write in reference to his father: "he is one of them." With his head barely out of the self-destructive swirl of this period, he might have been writing of himself once again.

CHAPTER 11

"**I** love war, chaos, gloomy predictions about the end of this civilization. It is always at times like these that I can sock it to my machine. And when in my forties they offer me the Nobel Award you can be sure I will gladly accept it."

His German shepherd had distemper. He was in deeper debt than ever before from the hospital bills occasioned by his car accident. And unlike Bill Saroyan, who in a self-aggrandizing gesture toward "democratic" art had just *refused* the Pulitzer Prize in drama for *The Time of Your Life*, Fante was winning no awards. But by spring 1940 Fante had rebounded far enough from his depression and his injuries to be bragging again about his prospects to Viking's Pascal Covici. In fact, he was not merely bragging. He might have been fiddling on a quickie film idea with Al Bezzerides, but he had also just written one of his strongest stories, "A Wife for Dino Rossi." After a black and fallow period he was again "chafing to write, mad with the desire." Once more, with the world skidding hellward, he was able to believe in himself.

In early 1940 there was no dearth of awfulness on the global scene to help perversely inspire the rebirth of Fante's manic self-confidence. By April Nazi forces had marched into Denmark and Norway, by May into Holland and Belgium, and by the middle of June into Paris, goosestepping through the Arc de Triomphe. A few months earlier the spiral of world events had only deepened Fante's desolation. Now he seemed exhilarated by the spreading catastrophe, which he took as a sort of transcendent permission to dissociate himself from humanity's galloping worldwide insanity. "They can tear this over-rated civilization apart," he went on to Covici, "they can have their fascism and nazism and bolshevism and democracy. I shall type with one hand, the fingers of the other pinching my nostrils. It will be slower, less convenient, but it will be great writing anyway."

Nudged on by Covici's continued support—in February the Viking editor had sent Fante a check for $300 to help with his medical debts—Fante had written in March to General Stackpole requesting release from his contract. Still feeling the sting of the *Mein Kampf* imbroglio, Stackpole had agreed, and again Fante's ego was asserting itself. In turn, Covici's confidence in Fante was strengthened by his pronouncements of artistic sovereignty. When Fante proposed a book of stories, Covici went him one better and offered a two-book contract. Fante accepted the offer along with the $200 more Covici sent him to add to the earlier $300 as an advance on the collection and a novel. After nurturing his relationship with Fante for two years, Covici had secured for Viking one of the most promising young authors on the American literary scene.

In June Joyce left John in Manhattan Beach to be in Roseville with her mother, who had suffered a stroke. With eviction imminent because of unpaid rent, on July 7 Fante drove up the coast with Carey McWilliams on one of Carey's frequent shuttles. Throughout the day—they stopped for a lunch of Pismo Beach clams—and well into a night on the town in San Francisco, Fante was in high form. "Fante is an owlish, demoralizing, and utterly irresponsible wit," Carey wrote in his diary that night, "extremely amusing and very refreshing."

The next day Fante left Carey in San Francisco to rejoin Joyce in Roseville. At her mother's house on Lincoln Street he found that Joyce had set up the screened porch for their bedroom while Mrs. Smart recuperated. The arrangement was free but far from ideal, for although Louise Smart had resolved to bury the hatchet of disapproval over Joyce's marriage to John, Fante could still feel the tension. Soon he was using his parents' home on Pleasant Street to receive his mail and as a retreat, still more son in some ways than husband.

On the day he arrived in Roseville, Fante wrote H. L. Mencken for the first time in two years. As if to reestablish his evolving identity with his former mentor, Fante brought Mencken up to date with a brief history of his career, including thumbnail assessments of his first two books. A month later Viking announced Fante's third book, the story collection *Dago Red*. Shrewdly, the firm's publicity campaign linked Fante with house thoroughbred John Steinbeck, whose Dust Bowl epic *The Grapes of Wrath* John Ford was already filming. The Fante-Steinbeck linkage was a natural, for Fante still intended to write his own California epic about Filipino migrant agricultural workers.

Toward that end he spent the entire day of August 20 with Division of Housing and Immigration chief McWilliams in the sweltering heat of Stockton inspecting Japanese and Filipino farm-laborer camps. Fante was still gathering material on what he considered "the most vicious system of race and class taboo that ever existed." But he knew better than to tell it that way in the novel. Rather than beat his readers' skulls in with so much bare-knuckled polemic, he promised to "break their goddamn hearts. . . . I'll make the little Filipino a hero." Hoping for a boost from his Viking stable mate, Fante was pleased to hear from Covici that Steinbeck was enjoying an advance copy of *Dago Red*. But he was also wary of tipping off the competition. "DON'T tell Steinbeck!" Fante enjoined Covici about his plans for the Filipino book, like a gambler protecting his hand.

Dago Red was published on September 23, with handsome woodcut illustrations by Valenti Angelo. After the mixed reviews of *Ask the Dust*, the critics were again enthusiastic. *The New York Times* found Fante's talent lying "over each page bright as sunlight on fresh green grass." Steinbeck himself, impressed enough to break his rule against publicizing other writers, allowed himself to be quoted: "This is a warm good book

which has in it forgotten things which should not have been forgotten."
And *Time* called *Dago Red* "perhaps 1940's best book of short stories."

Of the thirteen stories, nine had appeared before, most of them in *The American Mercury*. Of the four others—"A Kidnapping in the Family," "My Mother's Goofy Song," "A Wife for Dino Rossi" and "The Wrath of God"—only "A Wife for Dino Rossi" had been written recently, in April of 1940. In that story, however, Fante had broken new ground even as he returned to the world of his North Denver boyhood.

Told through the eyes of young Jimmy Toscana—who is by turns enraged and enthralled as he watches his churlish bricklayer father humiliate his mother and their friend the sensitive barber Dino Rossi by carrying on with the perfumed bombshell Coletta Drigo—the story explores the precarious sliding scales of gender, of so many received ideas about masculinity and femininity. What does it mean to be a man? In answering that question, "A Wife for Dino Rossi" proves less conventional than might be expected given Fante's own often cavemannish behavior. Writing the story may not have signaled any radical change in his behavior, but in the aftermath of his collapse it was an important breakthrough. Besides helping to restore Fante's self-confidence, the story showed that levels of meaning remained to be plumbed in his earliest autobiographical wellspring. All he had to do was keep writing.

In twenty-four months Fante had published three critically acclaimed works. By the time *Dago Red* appeared in September, he was working on two novels simultaneously, the Filipino project and also, once again, the Italian opus, now called *Ah, Poor America!* As if writing two novels at once were not enough, when he addressed the Roseville Rotary Club soon after *Dago Red's* appearance, Fante announced that he was also writing a play for the dramatics class at Lassen Union High School in Susanville, a hundred and fifty miles north of Roseville. The class's teacher, Iris Dornfeld, had been a friend of Joyce's since childhood, and when Fante met her he agreed that she was both smart and sexy enough for Carey McWilliams, whose first marriage had long since foundered. The match had succeeded, and now the two couples got together whenever they could to eat and drink and talk and laugh in the face of ever more appalling world developments. Among other things, the play Fante was writing for Iris's class was an attempt to cement the four-way relationship in an increasingly cockeyed world.

It was also a dangerous way of overextending himself. Despite his assertions of self-confidence, Fante's concentration was wearing thin. He was broke again, and Joyce's mother was now well enough to make known her displeasure about an unemployed son-in-law who stayed up late making noise with his typewriter and stinking up the house with his cigarettes. Nor was Mrs. Smart swayed by *San Francisco Chronicle* columnist Herb Caen's frequent references to Fante as "one of America's most brilliant young writers," and "the great young California writer." Such puffery paid nothing; so that when the chance arose to catch a free ride south, Fante headed back to Hollywood to look for movie work.

Joyce had her own thoughts on this move. "I think you and I both agree that John should confine himself only to his books," Joyce wrote to Pascal Covici. "Movie writing, so far as I am concerned, is a waste of his talent and time. Though we could appreciate a movie salary now, in the long run I am sure that fiction is John's field. I do my best to encourage John to stay with his book, and confidentially I wish you would do the same."

When the Hollywood job search hit a dead end, Covici took Joyce's hint, offering $50 every other week for the next six months to fund Fante's real writing, in this case *Ah, Poor America!* Fante accepted and came back to Roseville. In the next month, however, he focused less on that project than on the Filipino book, reapplying for a Guggenheim grant "to go to the Philippine Islands and study first hand the conditions there." Again he claimed on his application to have been born in 1911, and again he assembled an impressive chorus of supporters: Louis Adamic, syndicated columnist Lewis Gannett, H. L. Mencken, Carey McWilliams, Rachel Field, Sue Barry of *The People's World*, Iris Barry of the *New York Herald Tribune*, Pascal Covici, novelist Gene Fowler, Marianne Hauser of *The New York Times Book Review* and Faith Baldwin.

Missing was the recommendation Fante had solicited from John Steinbeck. In its stead Fante had received a long comical letter verging on the sarcastic in which Steinbeck declined to write in Fante's behalf. Rather, he advised Fante to seek the support of more dignified people, cautious people with robes and degrees from accredited universities; and he urged him to find a topic of greater interest to the Guggenheim people than mere Filipinos—termites, for example, or the wildflowers of North Dakota. Having poked his supplicant with the sharp stick of his wit, Steinbeck closed on a serious note: he didn't know enough about Filipinos to write a recommendation and neither did Fante to write a novel. Still, he wished him good luck.

By the end of November the contrary Fante had abandoned not the Filipino novel but the vaunted Italian project. His attention, however, was mostly on his play, an adaptation of "A Wife for Dino Rossi," which he was calling *Dago Red* "so that, should it succeed, sales of the book will be improved." If that plan of action sounds scattered, it is because in late 1940 Fante's concentration was shot and his energies overspilling. Out drinking in Roseville's Old Town one night with his brother Tom and their wives, Joyce and Dale, Fante got in a fight with not one but two barroom brawlers. When Tom tried to intervene he was knocked unconscious, leaving Fante single-handedly to beat the hell out of the two unfortunates.

Once again he was "very broke" as he put it in a letter begging Covici for more money to stave off a joyless Christmas. His doctors were suing him for outstanding medical bills. Even his veterinarian was after him to settle the long overdue fee of $10.75 for his dog's distemper shots. Drama critic George Jean Nathan wrote from New York to call Fante's play, "in all critical truth, pretty bad." And now people were dying, not only in Europe by the droves, but also closer to home, individuals, writers whom Fante had known. On December 21 in Hollywood F. Scott Fitzgerald had succumbed to a heart attack at the age of forty-four. The next day, on the outskirts of the Imperial County town of El Centro, Nathanael West, only thirty-eight, had been killed with his wife Eileen in a freak automobile collision.

All of these distractions must have been roiling Fante's mind when he met Carey McWilliams and Bill Saroyan for dinner at Solari's in San Francisco two days after Christmas. As McWilliams would describe the evening, Saroyan was in "a wilder-than-usual mood," abetted by Fante in a peculiarly mixed mood of his own. Fante had just sold to *The Saturday Evening Post* his first effort at writing in a Filipino vein, the fine story "Helen, Thy Beauty Is to Me—." Selling a story to the ultramainstream *Post* about such marginal characters as a love-smitten Filipino cannery worker and a gold-digging bleach-blond taxi dancer was a coup for Fante, all the more so for the story's lack of any slick-paper uplift; and the windfall sale price of $600 could not have been more timely. What no one seemed to notice was that Fante had been reading Edgar Allan Poe, for the story's title had been lifted verbatim, though without attribution, from the first line of Poe's poem, "To Helen."

After Solari's, Fante and Saroyan took off to spend a "bibulous night" playing poker with Herb Caen and Paul Jordan Smith, literary editor of the *Los Angeles Times*. A few weeks earlier a drunken Fante had lost $25 to Saroyan, money he did not then have. But an empty wallet had never stopped Fante on all those other nights in the recent months when he had traveled from staid Roseville to Baghdad-by-the-Bay to carouse with Carey, screenwriter Budd Schulberg, RKO story editor Collier Young and others at such watering holes as Murio's, Izzy Gomez's, the Hurricane and the Black Cat. Nor had mere penury ever prevented him, when every legitimate place had closed and most other carousers had gone home, from falling into a "horrible dump" of an after-hours joint in an un-marked basement downtown, where only the most resolute drinkers and death-wish gamblers ended up. But on the night in question he wasn't broke, he was flush, and in a mood.

It is unrecorded how much of his $600 bankroll changed hands on this night, or how the night came to a close. If he was celebrating the sale of "Helen, Thy Beauty Is to Me—," however, perhaps Fante reflected on the end of the author of "To Helen"—Poe mumbling incoherently in a seedy Baltimore malt house, locked in the throes of his own brain's fever as he stumbled out to collapse in the gutter. But Fante wasn't that kind of a suicide, "On desperate seas" and all that. Fante liked to have fun, even when he was suffering; and even, perhaps, vice versa.

In a speech at Charlottesville, Virginia, the previous June, President Franklin D. Roosevelt had responded to Italy's support of the German in-vasion of France by condemning the Italian Duce, Benito Mussolini: "the hand that held the dagger," Roosevelt said, "has stuck it into the back of its neighbor." Forty years after the hot-blooded Nick Fante had ar-rived on Ellis Island, the image of the stiletto-wielding greaser which he had been exhorted to shed was still widely dreaded. No longer young in the winter of 1941, Nick had mellowed considerably. Yet his instincts re-

mained Italian enough that John could accurately describe him as "a pro-
Mussolini man but a mighty democrat and an unquenchable American."

On the night of Friday, January 31, this paradox would assert itself,
with bloody results. In a bar near the switching yards of Roseville's Old
Town, Nick Fante fell to talking about the European war with an Irishman named Kelly Farrell, at thirty-five Nick's junior by twenty-seven
years. Accounts differed afterward but it was generally agreed that as the
drink and the talk flowed the talk turned heated, and that when Farrell
called Nick a "fifth columnist" a fight broke out. When it was over, Farrell was writhing on the floor with multiple stab wounds in his stomach,
and Nick was breathing heavily, clutching a blood-smeared knife. Farrell
was rushed to Sacramento's Sutter County Hospital, and Nick to the
county jail in Auburn. For the next several days he was held on open
charges in the jail's basement cellblock while the unlucky Irishman hov-
ered between life and death.

When it was clear that Farrell's wounds would not prove fatal, Joyce's
mother placed a call to the district attorney, a longtime friend of the family, meaning less to save Nick than to protect her daughter from the
disgrace of having a convicted felon for a father-in-law. As a result no
charges were filed. John and Joyce drove up to Auburn and Nick was released to begin putting the old ways behind him once again.

As they drove back to Roseville, Nick seemed as apt as ever to break
out in off-key arias, oblivious to his narrow escape. But John knew better
than to expect too much. For John it was a comfort to have a father who
in the strict legal sense could not be called an attempted murderer. Even
more comforting in its unreconstructed way was John's sense that his father still had it in him when push came to shove to damn the consequences and let fly. What else did it mean to be a man?

When Mrs. Smart had recovered from her stroke, John and Joyce returned to Los Angeles in March, renting an apartment at 830½ Berendo,
two doors from where John had written Ask the Dust. The hope was that
being close to the site of that novel's creation would translate into luck for
the new phase of work now beginning. But for Fante luck was always the
ficklest of patrons, now as much as ever before.

The appearance of "Helen, Thy Beauty Is to Me—" in *The Saturday Evening Post* had gained for Fante his largest audience yet, as well as widespread acclaim from readers who found the portrayal of Julio Sal and his fellow Pinoy immigrants extraordinarily vivid, sympathetic and moving. Within the small but ardent Filipino literary community, however, the story created a controversy that spilled over into at least one mainstream Los Angeles newspaper. Writing in the *Daily News*, leftist Roman Catholic columnist Ted LeBerthon reported—and agreed with—the Filipino writer Manuel Buaken's charge that Fante felt pity but not solidarity for Filipinos caught in a heartless capitalist system. While criticizing Fante for his political and religious shortcomings, LeBerthon said relatively little about "Helen, Thy Beauty Is to Me—," the piece that had occasioned the flap. Still, Fante stood accused of insensitivity at best and at worst of exploitation in his use of condescending racial stereotypes.

One Filipino writer who did not share this view was Carlos Bulosan, the roustabout farmhand, cannery worker and poet whose lyrical 1943 autobiography *America Is in the Heart* would give voice to the tragic experience of his people. Romantic, impulsive and driven to write by some of the same demons that had driven Fante—grinding poverty, ethnic marginalization—Bulosan now became one of Fante's familiars and a primary source in his researches into the world of the California Filipino. Much of this research took place in the downtown dance halls, bars and boxing clubs favored by Filipinos, where Fante intended to situate his novel. "We had an unexpected dinner last night at the University Cafe on Second Street," Bulosan wrote about one such foray with Fante, "then we had some drinks at the Montezuma on Temple. . . . I got so drunk . . . that I did not know what I was doing."

Carey McWilliams and Joyce Fante certainly remembered such a night, although their respective recollections would indicate the thin line between playfulness and cruelty in John's behavior during this time. First McWilliams:

Once Carlos threw a party for Fante in a night club near Temple and Figueroa streets in Los Angeles, on the edge of Bunker Hill, a place much frequented by Filipinos. I was invited. On this memorable evening, at the height of the festivities, Carlos presented

John with a gift: a glossy white rat. Fante, like Carlos a lover of all living things including snakes, was instantly enchanted with the rat. But his wife Joyce, while amazingly tolerant of highly sexed, ferocious dogs, cats, lascivious king snakes, and other strange pets, drew the line at the thought of a rat in the house and stalked out of the place in high dudgeon. I drove her home and, en route, managed as tactfully as possible to get in a few kind words for John and the white rat. Later, much later, when John returned, the rat promptly escaped into the stuffing of a divan and it was a day or more before the Fantes could extricate him. In the end, of course, Joyce prevailed: the white rat went and John was left desolate, briefly.

Joyce's version of the same evening is darker. While still at the club, she recalls, John demanded that she put the rat in her purse, and when she refused he insisted. Knowing her terror of rats he yet persisted until Joyce left the club in tears. Carey got her home safe, but he was not there to witness Fante's drunken homecoming, or Joyce's fury at being trifled with in public. More and more of late Joyce had felt the brunt of John's neglect, of his lingering preference for being one of the boys rather than a real husband, of his occasionally active hostility. Now she stayed up waiting for her tormentor, and when he entered, as she recalls, "I beat him up with my shoes. I poured water over his head, did everything I could. He slapped me. He never touched me any other time. But [after that] he was covered with bruises." In fact, they were both covered with bruises—both ended up with blackened eyes—but the worst injuries were the invisible and lasting wounds to their relationship.

The bruises on John's face had healed a month or so later when he took Carey downtown to Main Street's Liberty Bar, a skid-row magnet for out-of-work drifters, blackout drunks and the assorted down-and-out. Eschewing last names, John introduced Carey to Audrey, the wild and perhaps mentally disturbed waitress who with Marie Baray had served as the composite model for Camilla Lopez in *Ask the Dust*. While Fante caught up on old times with Audrey in the semiprivate shadows of the Liberty, McWilliams dutifully looked away, edifying himself by observing a "pathetic old drunk, completely whacko, talking nonsense." And when on the way home later Fante asked McWilliams to pull over, the unflappable Carey never missed a beat. "As usual," McWilliams noted dryly in his diary that night, "he picked up a stray cat along the way."

Meanwhile, the world reeled onward, disaster-bound. James Joyce had died blind in January of the year, and in April 1941 came news of Virginia Woolf's suicide. "I feel certain I am going mad again," Woolf wrote toward the end. "I feel we can't go through another of those terrible times." Late in May President Roosevelt declared a national state of emergency, and as the conflict in Europe spread with Germany's June attack on the Soviet Union, the whole California coast seemed to bristle with military convoys of soldiers and ordnance preparing for America's entry into the war.

Fante's response to the situation was not to bear down on his novel as he knew he should but to team up with a new writing partner in an effort to make a killing in the movies. Norman Foster had started out as a stage actor in the 1920s, married and divorced his leading lady Claudette Colbert before marrying Sally Blane, sister of Loretta Young, and overcome an undistinguished film-acting career to become a prolific director of B movies, including many of the Mister Moto and Charley Chan whodunits. Now he and Fante were collaborating on no fewer than three screen stories, including an adaptation of *Ask the Dust* and another of Fante's unsold story "Woman Is Fickle." Overextended once again, Fante was also at work with Ross Wills on an original screen story set in the Wilmington fish canneries. As if all of these projects weren't more than enough, Fante somehow also found the time to write a comical but sympathetic profile of William Saroyan for *Common Ground*, as well as a review of *Home Is Here*, a San Francisco–based novel about Italian-Americans by Jewish American writer Sidney Meller.

No matter how optimistic he might have been about his prospects at this time, Fante could have had no hope that any of these ventures would compete on the same rarefied level as the movie that had astonished critics when it premiered in May, the one touted by the lighted blimp in the sky over Hollywood's El Capitan theater: IT'S TERRIFIC—ORSON WELLES—CITIZEN KANE. But Fante and Foster had retained an energetic agent, and by July, H. N. "Swanie" Swanson had succeeded in getting his clients interviews all over town: with King Vidor, at MGM and at Orson Welles's home studio, RKO, among others. Not every lead clicked but they needed only one, and in the end the timing was perfect, for when Fante and Foster signed a two-week contract in July with Culver City's MGM at $200 a week, Joyce had just learned that she was pregnant.

"Man of Tomorrow," the ninety-one-page treatment which Fante and Foster rushed through in those two weeks, was a transparent attempt at prewar Hollywood drumbeating. It told the rambling story of an all-American farm boy who goes from tinkering with a Model T to designing the B-21 bomber in the nation's drive for air superiority in the coming fight against Hitler. Alien to Fante's true interests, the treatment still evidenced his hand. An impoverished but beautiful love interest named Camille bore an unmistakable resemblance to *Ask the Dust*'s Camilla, for example, while a pair of scenes involving an automobile accident and a surgery were clearly modeled on Fante's own recent personal experience. But the story went nowhere, and when the two weeks were over the writing partners were out of work.

But not for long. Thanks to the boost H. N. Swanson was giving them as a pair of talents with story knack, by the beginning of August they were again employed for a weekly salary of $300 apiece, this time at RKO. Located at 780 Gower Street, RKO was the studio where only a few months earlier Orson Welles had completed *Citizen Kane*. Following the sensation created by his masterpiece, Welles was at the apex of his career. All things seemed possible, and the twenty-six-year-old wunderkind still had five pictures to go on a six-picture contract, two of which he had already begun, *The Magnificent Ambersons* and *Journey into Fear*. He was now about to launch into an ambitious multipart documentary of sorts, to be called *It's All True*, and it was for that project that Fante and Foster had been enlisted. RKO paid the partners $1,000 for rights to an original treatment on which they had been working and they plunged into writing the script of "Love Story."

A reworking of material Fante had often used, "Love Story" told the bittersweet tale of the meeting, courtship and marriage of a rough-edged Italian bricklayer and an innocent Italian-American girl. Central to the tale, set in the San Francisco of 1909, is the lie Rocco tells Della in order to win her love, namely, that he has built her a beautiful dream house. When Della discovers that there is no such house, it is too late to escape a life of poverty, for she and Rocco have already married. But rather than destroy what she has gained, Della determines to live by her love for the flawed but well-meaning Rocco.

That such a quintessentially Fante-esque fantasy fit into Welles's grand plan tells us something about the nature of *It's All True*, long known as "one of the great mysteries of film scholarship" and "perhaps one of the greatest feature documentaries never made." Originally entitled *Pan-American*, *It's All True* was a joint venture between the Brazilian government's Motion Picture Division, the United States Inter-American Affairs Committee, headed by Nelson A. Rockefeller, and RKO. As such, the film was meant to depict key aspects of life in both North and South America as a way of helping to ensure good relations in the face of impending world war. If only indirectly, and in spite of his long-standing disengagement, Fante was being drawn toward the intersection of politics and art.

Welles's central conceit for *It's All True* was to tell several dramatized stories which in all essentials would be factual rather than fiction. Among these was a segment called "The Story of Jazz" featuring episodes from Louis Armstrong's life, with music by Duke Ellington. Two other segments were to have been adapted from stories Welles had optioned from legendary documentary filmmaker Robert J. Flaherty: "The Captain's Chair," about the life-and-death struggles of a Hudson Bay trader; and "Bonito the Bull," based on an incident in Mexican bullfighting history when thanks to the crowd's acclaim a bull had been pardoned from death owing to its extraordinary bravery. Also planned was a segment about the phenomenon of the samba, to be filmed in Rio de Janeiro during Carnival, and a segment re-creating the journey of four Brazilian fishermen who had rafted nearly two thousand miles through shark-infested waters to bring their people's plight to the world's attention. Of these six segments, all linked by Welles's claim that each was true, it fell to Fante and Foster to write "Love Story" and an adaptation of Flaherty's "Bonito the Bull" which they titled "My Friend Bonito."

Not everything that was to go into *It's All True* was as true as it was said to be, however, starting with "Love Story." In fact, the task Fante and Foster had been hired to perform—to write a story about a love based on a bold-faced lie—was itself a job gotten on the basis of a strategic untruth. "All stories we do for Welles for this picture are supposed to be *true* stories," Fante wrote in explanation of the legal release RKO's legal department was requiring of Nick and Mary Fante as the purported models of Rocco and Della. "Well, my story of the Italian bricklayer isn't exactly true, but I had to tell them it was true in order to sell it. . . . Please do as I say and sign the papers which RKO sends you. I will take care of the rest."

If Welles knew about Fante's sham there is no indication that he objected. On the contrary, it stands to reason that the mastermind of the century's most notorious case of fiction masquerading as truth—the Mercury Theater's 1938 national radio broadcast of "The War of the Worlds"—would if anything have admired his writer's willingness to subordinate mere facts to the higher purpose of putting on a show.

When they finished "Love Story" Fante and Foster set to work on "My Friend Bonito." Making the most of Flaherty's spare story about a Mexican boy and his beloved bull, the partners crafted a gemlike tale of friendship and courage, nearly mythic in its affirmation of life. Nor did deadline pressures lessen their sense of humor, as the playful note at the end of their script indicates: "The authors hope that somewhere in Mexico there can be found a bull so intelligent, so literate, and so moviestruck that he will perform the miracles that are required of Bonito in this script." The completed script was dated September 17. Within the week Norman Foster was in Mexico, where for the next three months he would struggle to direct a film worthy of the script he had created with Fante.

The same day that the script was completed, Fante wrote Pascal Covici. Complaining that he did not like the work he had been doing for Welles, he asked for either $200 a month for the next seven months in order to complete his Filipino book or a release from his Viking contract. Covici's response was to urge Fante to keep working for Welles until he had saved up enough money to fund the writing of the novel, in which everyone at Viking still firmly believed. With Joyce's due date approaching, Fante complied, going to work for *The Lady Esther Show*, a CBS radio program narrated by Orson Welles.

A mélange of drama, comedy and music sponsored by the cosmetics line of Lady Esther beauty products, the show was performed by Mercury Theater regulars and guest artists such as Ruth Gordon, Betty Field and Welles's lover Dolores Del Rio, with music conducted by Bernard Hermann. In the next several weeks Fante ground out nine short radio dramas. All were adaptations, two from Fante's own stories ("The All-American Team" and "None So Blind") and one from *Ask the Dust*. From our remove today the conjunction of artistries might strike us as auspicious—Orson Welles doing Arturo Bandini! But this radio writing, little more than glorified assembly-line work, was even less to Fante's liking than the scriptwriting had been, and all the more so since his pieces were not even being aired.

Fante's short-lived contact with Orson Welles bore few lasting results. "Love Story" never made it to the casting stage, although Welles would later cannibalize the Crystal Maze scene in that script for his famous mirror scene with Rita Hayworth in *Lady from Shanghai*. And while in the words of one Welles biographer "My Friend Bonito" was "firmly on its way to being a masterpiece," it too would remain incomplete, canceled in December by RKO when a desperate Welles recalled Foster from Mexico to direct the foundering *Journey into Fear*. By then Fante had moved to Paramount, where from November 10 until December 4, 1941, he was in harness at a salary of $350 a week toiling on the script for yet a third remake of the durable melodrama *Mrs. Wiggs of the Cabbage Patch*.

Thrust by the course of world events and his own talent for self-inflation into the role of hemispheric goodwill ambassador, Orson Welles would go to Rio in February under the auspices of the Inter-American Affairs Committee to work on the two Brazilian segments of *It's All True*. He would succeed only in turning the grand effort into a disaster, thereby initiating the cycle of unfinished masterpieces, so called, that would dog him for the rest of his life. How Welles bungled this project is a complicated story peripheral to John Fante's life and thus not germane to our business here. But when Fante was an old man he summed up the debacle of *It's All True* in a vivid and telling way. Fante's version does not agree with any of the published accounts of Welles's tumultuous stay in Brazil, but it nonetheless rings true, if not perhaps strictly of Welles himself then of the feelings of the writer whose work on what was possibly one of the greatest movies never made ended up forgotten because of someone else's megalomania. Fante claimed that as Welles stood watching the spectacle of Carnival from a Rio balcony, the great man yielded to an excess of Carnival spirit "and peed on the people down below. . . . And that was the end of that particular project."

In five frustrating months Fante had again wearied of Hollywood, and when he had completed his Paramount chores and collected his check he left Los Angeles again for Roseville. As she had done the year before, Joyce had traveled northward ahead of her husband, for on November 13 her mother had suffered a heart attack and died. Now John agreed to move back to Roseville while Mrs. Smart's estate was being put in order. Fante arrived at the house on Lincoln Street in time to hear the news of December 7. The Japanese had attacked Pearl Harbor, inflicting incalculable damage to the American fleet and killing untold numbers of American servicemen. Three days later Germany and Italy declared war on the United States. The terrible time that Fante had long anticipated had finally come. He would respond to it in unexpected ways.

On January 31, 1942, Joyce gave birth to a healthy boy, Nicholas Joseph, at Sacramento's Sutter Maternity Hospital. Like his father before him, John Fante was bursting with pride, but he was also concerned about how the added expense would affect the other necessities of life, for example, gambling. "Confidentially," he wrote in a letter asking his Hollywood agent H. N. Swanson for a hundred-dollar loan,

I lost that amount in a poker game last week, and the money is now overdue. . . . I will have to deceive my wife a bit in returning the loan, but that's my affair, and it can be done easily. Please help me out in this, will you? Merely send a check, so that if she should see it, I can tell her it was for option money or something.

But no option money was coming. Swanson was trying to sell "Home Is the Hunter," a treatment Fante had cowritten with Carey McWilliams before leaving Los Angeles. But with the onset of war, who wanted a socially conscious drama about a populist Los Angeles mayor who awakens the city's Mexican population to its political potential? Swanson advised that it would be hard to land John a studio job without his being in town for interviews. But Fante had no desire to rejoin that game so soon after quitting it.

Nor did the once-pretty town of Los Angeles appeal to him now, with the ongoing evacuation of Japanese-Americans who were considered threats to national security. Almost overnight, in the days after Pearl Harbor, Terminal Island had been swept clean of its largely Japanese-American population, which would never return to the ghost town. This was not the L.A. Fante had loved, with its motley thrown-together peoples at least abiding each other. No, instead of going back to L.A. Fante would hunker down in the Roseville house he and Joyce were renting at 214 Shasta Street and get back to work on the Filipino novel. Doing so would help him sort through his feelings about the war.

For starters he took up the character of another migrant Filipino worker, this time in a story called "Mary Osaka, I Love You." Like Julio Sal in "Helen, Thy Beauty Is to Me—," Mingo Mateo starts out in a downtown Los Angeles setting, washing dishes in a restaurant in Little Tokyo during the time leading up to December 7. Like Julio Sal, moreover, Mingo also falls in love, but his is an even more impossible love than Julio's infatuation with the taxi dancer, for Mingo has fallen in love with a Japanese-American girl whose blustering old-country father will not hear of his daughter being with a mere Pinoy. The lovers elope to Las Vegas, where they spend one blissful night, only to wake to the nightmare news of Pearl Harbor. Returning to Los Angeles they find that in a single day the war has taken over every aspect of life, and that their dream of a life together is now impossible. Faced with a heartbreaking choice—between internment and separation—Mingo proves himself a true American to Mary's father by deciding to join the Marines. The story ends with Mary and her family being relocated to a desert camp as Mingo prepares to go fight the Japanese.

Fante had done it again. "Mary Osaka, I Love You" was a triumph not only because of its singing prose and ingenious plotting but also because of the complexities of the patriotism it portrayed. The story would run in the October *Good Housekeeping* with a special Editor's Note: "The War Relocation Authority in establishing its Relocation Centers has acted for the protection of loyal Japanese-Americans. These Centers are *not* internment camps." In the escalating war even a piece of short fiction could now be used as a propaganda tool.

Fante did not object. No longer merely a detached observer of human folly, by the time "Mary Osaka" appeared he had already enlisted in the war effort. Driven by "the cold fire of hatred . . . against the enemy," Fante had taken a job in San Francisco with the Office of War Information. On his Application for Federal Employment, Fante boosted his height to five feet four inches but for the first time since leaving home for Regis, he told the truth about his age, stating his birth date as April 8, 1909. Odd as it may seem in light of his earlier cynicism about "the end of this civilization," the war was bringing out the citizen long hidden behind the sneer. He was thirty-three years old.

Fante took his Oath of Office in Roseville on August 31, swearing to defend the Constitution against all enemies, foreign and domestic. Working as a radio news editor for the Overseas Branch of the OWI's Pacific Bureau John would not see line-of-fire service such as his brother Tom would serving as an Army lieutenant in Europe, but that was all right with Fante. He wanted to play his part but he did not look forward to being drafted. Until that time arrived, he would do his duty as a civilian. Only three weeks earlier he had moved his family into their new home in Roseville at 215 Coronado, paid for with Joyce's inheritance. Now he wasted no time in relocating wife and son to San Francisco. There he rented the upper floor of a charming Victorian at 414 Shrader Street, and at an annual salary of $3,800 joined the cause of Allied victory.

The Office of War Information had been created on June 13, 1942, by order of President Roosevelt to control the flow and slant of war-related information. Under the direction of three-time Pulitzer Prize winner and FDR speech writer Robert Sherwood, the Overseas Branch molded its broadcasts to maximize Allied successes and induce enemy defeatism. In weekly directives Sherwood coached his writers to emphasize the ruggedness of the American fighting man and the unity of purpose among Americans of all classes, faiths and parties. The newscasts Fante wrote for dissemination to the Southwest Pacific were thus a mixture of stratagem and artifice—not the wholesale manufacturing of truth but creative interpretations of selected facts. In Sherwood's phrase, Fante was part of the Nerve War.

Fante's compatriots on the fourteenth floor of 111 Sutter Street were a talented lot, including China expert Owen Lattimore, newsman Larry Fanning of the *San Francisco Chronicle*, and public relations expert Richard Diggs, a graduate of the Yale School of Drama who would go on to manage the career of Hollywood gossip columnist Louella Parsons. Fante's experience as a writer accustomed to reshaping facts into fiction served him well in the OWI, as did his years as a contract studio scenarist inured to writing to the specifications of others. But as he had discovered through his experience with his studio contract writing, Fante was temperamentally unsuited to the self-limiting nature of this kind of employment, in which personal contributions were subordinated to anonymous news production. Soon he was unhappy with the work.

In late October Fante applied for a change in position to feature writer, indicating his willingness to travel (and possibly a desire to escape) to South America. When that request failed he began lobbying for a transfer to the OWI's New York office, where he envisioned himself relearning Italian for the propaganda fight against the Fascists. But the wheels of the OWI bureaucracy turned slowly, and rarely in the desired direction. By late December Fante was fed up with the administrative infighting that plagued the OWI, and with the rampant "toadying to frauds" all about him. He had taken the job in the hope of serving his country, but now he could think only of protecting himself from the humiliation of working beneath incompetent and self-interested superiors.

The details of his ensuing troubles with the OWI remain obscure. Fante took seriously his security clearance, which prohibited discussion of work outside the office. But Joyce could tell something was wrong. Leaving her with the baby and a loaded pistol for protection, Fante would come home after his 5:30 p.m.–2:30 a.m. shift exhausted and out of sorts. If Joyce asked what the matter was Fante would clam up; but evidence exists to suggest there was cause for real concern.

One man who knew of Fante's situation and shared his mounting unhappiness with the OWI was Humphrey Cobb, author of the World War I novel *Paths of Glory*, which was later made into the classic Stanley Kubrick film with a script written by noir novelist Jim Thompson. Working out of the OWI's New York office, Cobb wrote to Carey McWilliams about "the John Fante matter." "Tell him he is not alone," Cobb said in one of his letters, "and get his report on paper." Cobb urged Fante to file a report with the chairman of the Writers' War Board, novelist Rex Stout, thus helping Cobb substantiate his own charge that "things are not all jake up at the mill." The problem with Cobb's request was that the Espionage Act required OWI employees to sign a statement promising never to write any account of the OWI. Evidently Fante took that draconian stricture to heart as well, for he never filed any such report.

What he wrote instead was a letter accusing one of his superiors of homosexuality. One day soon afterward there was a knock at the front door and two agents from the FBI demanded to speak with Fante about a possible breach of national security. Only after a tense time did he manage to persuade the agents that the whole thing was a terrible joke. But was it? Fante never disclosed to Joyce the truth behind this incident, which remains shrouded in official government secrecy. But after the G-men had departed Fante understood something important about the era his job at the OWI was helping to usher in: everything was evidence, and it was either for you or against you. It was going to be a long and drawn-out Nerve War, indeed.

On January 8, 1943, Fante temporarily solved the problem of his unhappiness with the OWI by requesting and being granted a sixty-day leave without pay "for personal reasons." Without the assistance of Swanie Swanson, whom he had fired for failing to find him movie work, Fante had managed to get back on the Warner Bros. payroll at $350 per week for six weeks. It was an exciting time to be at Warner Bros., for the story department included some of the best writers in the business: Frederick Schiller Faust and Frank Gruber, specialists in the western; W. R. Burnett, author of the crime classic *Little Caesar*; James Hilton, renowned for his best-selling novel *The Lost Horizon*; Albert Maltz and Dalton Trumbo, Screen Writers Guild activists and later two of the Hollywood Ten named during postwar congressional investigations into alleged Communist infiltration of the movies; Fante's old pals Jo

Pagano and A. I. Bezzerides; and no less a literary light than William Faulkner.

Within days Fante was back in Burbank collaborating with a writer named David Wear on "Marine Story," a morale-boosting ensemble piece about a battalion of leathernecks fighting their way back from Wake Island. The Auburn draft board had informed Fante that he would be called up by late summer, a prospect he did not relish. But for now at least he would write by day about the war from the perspective of fictional foot soldiers, while by night he would "go to a bar or a movie or gamble" to overcome the malaise of being back on the Hollywood treadmill.

What happened next may help us to understand the depth of that malaise, and how Fante's own actions contributed to it. As is often the case with movie stories in development, "Marine Story" was changing from day to day. Soon it was being called "The Fighting Marines" and Fante, working under producer Jerry Wald, was reteamed with Al Bezzerides. Together Fante and Bezzerides pounded out a ninety-eight-page treatment, and given its balanced portrayal of Americans pulling together—an Italian, a Mexican, a Jew, a WASP, an atheist, a priest, a veteran, a kid—it might have been sanctioned by the OWI's chief propagandist Robert Sherwood. Certainly there were thematic similarities to work Fante had done while at the OWI under Sherwood's editorship. But there were also other, more troubling similarities.

On February 24, eight days after their treatment was submitted, Fante made out a notarized statement affirming that he and Bezzerides had written "The Fighting Marines" pursuant to their employment agreement. Warner executives had reason to doubt Fante's word about who had authored the treatment and had thus requested a statement as a way of limiting the studio's liability. It seems the studio was in a precarious position, because a series of radio scripts by another writer had surfaced with unmistakable and extensive likenesses to "The Fighting Marines." Whole sections of description, story line, character development and dialogue were virtually identical. Though the word was never used in a flurry of interoffice memos among studio executives, plagiarism was suspected and Fante, not Bezzerides, was the suspect. Without so much as a word of reprimand—let sleeping dogs lie was the studio's legal attitude—Fante was quietly removed from the project and replaced by Alvah Bessie, veteran of the Spanish Civil War's Abraham Lincoln Brigade and another future member of the Hollywood Ten. Under Bessie's influence, the next draft of "The Fighting Marines" showed the war as less a series of personal vendettas for individual soldiers than an interlocking network of political struggles. Neither version was ever filmed.

Fante returned to San Francisco and his job with the Office of War Information as if nothing untoward had happened. But between his encounter with the FBI and this apparent brush with professional suicide, it would seem that Fante was picking his way through a potentially lethal minefield of no one's making but his own. Still, life went on. On March 14 one-year-old Nicky was baptized at San Francisco's Saint Agnes Church. Soon afterward John came up for performance review at the OWI. The Report of Efficiency Rating which went into his personnel file indicated that he was doing an "outstanding" job. On a scale of 1 to 9, where 1 equaled "Excellent," his overall rating was an almost perfect 2.

He continued working for the OWI through the spring of 1943, still hoping for reassignment to the New York office, where he would brush up on his Italian until he was fluent enough "to deal with the big Italian population in Casablanca, or Tripoli, or wherever they propose to send me." It would be exciting work, shuttling between North Africa and Italy to win back the hearts of the Italian people after the Allies' victory—and far better than packing a gun as a private in the infantry. Such romantic eventualities were not to be, however. When his draft status was changed to a temporary hardship deferment because of baby Nick, Fante put all such notions behind him. In early July, again citing "personal reasons," Fante resigned from the OWI. He engaged a sleeper car berth and he and Joyce and the baby were soon training south to Los Angeles.

Impressed with the work he had done for Orson Welles, RKO producer Val Lewton now hired Fante for $350 a week to work on a youth-oriented story that had been in and out of development since the early 1930s. Variously called "Cockeyed Youth," "Are These Our Children?" and "Youth Runs Wild," this oft-written but as-yet-unproduced project focused on the problem of "modern youth" living under the negative influences of city life. Fante's job was to resituate the story against a wartime backdrop. His script would focus on the underlying social and psychological causes of delinquency—the parents in Fante's story would put in so much overtime at an unnamed munitions plant that they would neglect the needs of their children—as well as on the effects such rebelliousness had on both families and communities.

Such social advocacy writing was a stretch for Fante. He knew that RKO was angling to cash in on the news value of juvenile delinquency, always good for a lurid headline in the Hearst chain of dailies, which had found that stories of marauding teenagers sold papers. He also knew that RKO had a deal with Hearst for a series of synchronized news and magazine features on the subject of delinquency, free advertising at its best. Still, flimflam aside, it was possible that under Val Lewton something more interesting than a mere exploitation picture might emerge. Lewton had been gaining a name with his string of cheap but effective psychological thrillers, including *Cat People*, *I Walked with a Zombie* and *The Seventh Victim*. So with Joyce again pregnant and the rent on their new house at 951 North Oxford Street $125 per month, Fante leaned into the task, writing and repeatedly rewriting first a treatment and then a screenplay about teens gone wrong, all under Lewton's eye.

"My job at the studio is very pleasant," Fante wrote to his parents on July 29. "I have an excellent story, with [a] good director and a satisfying producer."

Not for the first time, Fante was putting a positive spin on an unhappy situation for his parents. For although the story had possibilities, and the assigned director, Mark Robson, was proficient, Fante's producer was far from satisfying. In fact, Val Lewton proved extremely difficult. According to others who worked at RKO in Lewton's unit, the nephew of silent film icon Alla Nazimova could be as charming, supportive and loyal as he could be insecure, authoritarian and vindictive. Edward Dmytryk, then an up-and-coming director, would vividly recall the day when Fante submitted yet another set of revisions. "You're like a dog," Lewton spat, "going back to eat its own puke." The wonder is that in the wake of this remark Lewton did not have to spit out a few teeth of his own. But Fante needed to keep the job, and so he contained himself.

That is, he contained himself on the job. Off the lot he was drinking and gambling more heavily than ever. Two episodes from this time, both involving Al Bezzerides, reveal the direction Fante's life was taking. Still under contract to Warner Bros., Bezzerides had become friends with his fellow Warner Bros. contract writer William Faulkner. In fact, Faulkner, who was then forty-six years old, was living with the Bezzerides family at their West Los Angeles home at 621 North Saltair. On more than one occasion in the last year or so Fante had joined Faulkner in sipping Old Bushmill's at Musso Frank's on Hollywood Boulevard—"The way a Christian goes to church on Sunday," Fante later recalled, Faulkner "would go to Musso Frank's on Friday for the bouillabaisse"—but the two never really let loose together until the night Bezzerides picked Fante up for a night on the town with the future Nobel laureate.

According to Bezzerides, the party started out at Musso Frank's with "a lot of drinks," proceeded to several other places where the writers likewise had "a lot of drinks, and before you knew it we were the drunkest three people you ever saw. . . . But I never saw anyone as drunk as Fante was." Before the night was over, the three had their arms around each other—this despite Faulkner's inbred reserve—and were singing "the dirtiest song you ever heard in your life: 'The fucking in the cowshed, the fucking on the bricks, you couldn't hear the music for the swishing of the pricks.'" Bezzerides knew both Faulkner and Fante well, liked both of them very much, and appreciated their wit and their way with words, yet he had never enjoyed what he called a really "jolly" time with either of them. "But this was a really wonderful night, and I've never forgotten it."

The second episode is darker. After a birthday party for W. R. Burnett, Fante told Burnett and Bezzerides that he was going to take them to a place he knew where they could have some real fun. The place was on the second floor of a building on Sunset Boulevard, and the fun Fante had in mind was shooting dice. Bezzerides was not a gambler, but, as can happen, not long after he started he hit a hot streak. As he continued winning, the other players, professional gamblers who knew when to fold, all bowed out. At which point Fante stepped up to the table and announced, "I'll take him on."

Bezzerides's hot streak wouldn't cool. The more Fante lost, the grimmer he became, insisting that the game go on. Time passed. W. R. Burnett left, and others left too, until only a few onlookers remained. Fante kept losing, and his debt climbed crazily: $50,000, $60,000, $70,000, $80,000. Bezzerides grew afraid Fante would panic and quit and then it would all be over between the two of them, so he promised to keep playing until Fante had won it all back. Fante was stone-faced as he took up the dice. They kept playing, and finally Bezzerides's touch began to fade, and the momentum swung around to Fante. It was nearly four in the morning before they were even. Bezzerides was exhausted and relieved. But Fante wasn't ready to quit. Rather, he

> got this evil glint in his eye and he said, in a voice that I had never heard before, "Now we play." And I thought if he had won $80,000, my life would have been in jeopardy. I would have lost everything I owned because he'd demand to collect it. So I said to him, "John, if you win $80,000 from me, will you let me play until I win it all back?" And his eyes shifted in a lot of directions, boy, my lucky streak had ended and he was going to take advantage of that. And I said, "This is it, we quit." And I remember leaving the place.

It should be noted that Joyce Fante disputes this story. Conceding that John was a problem gambler and an alcoholic, she maintains he was not so irrational as to run up such an impossible debt. Be that as it may, this was the last time Bezzerides and Fante saw each other on a friendly basis for years to come, an indication that Fante's behavior was again turning self-destructive. Owing to the strain of such behavior, Joyce admits, their marriage "began to fall apart." Fante was rarely at home in the evenings anymore, though he kept showing up for work at RKO, enduring Val Lewton's martinet oversight and handing in pages in exchange for a paycheck. Although he had not worked on the Filipino novel for a long time, when October came Fante submitted his third application for a Guggenheim, enclosing as samples of his work the stories "Helen, Thy Beauty Is to Me—" and "Mary Osaka, I Love You," the beginning and end of the novel as he now saw it. His contract at RKO would end at Christmastime, and he wanted to get back to work on his fiction. But the third attempt to secure foundation largess would not be the charm. His application was again unsuccessful.

Nor would the holidays offer any real respite from the downward spiral of his marriage. Joyce's second pregnancy was proving more difficult than the first, and John was even less help than before. Early on they had dared hope for a daughter, but the way this one was kicking, at times making Joyce cry out in pain, no one knew what to expect. They spent Christmas with Carey and Iris McWilliams, a welcome enough diversion from all the tensions. The war was still raging but it was pleasant to get drunk with old friends. When the time came to exchange gifts, however, certain underlying hostilities were barely veiled. Joyce gave John an expensive set of poker chips, and John gave Joyce a beautiful fur coat made of sharp-eyed, razor-fanged lynx. The dog tore up little Nicky's stuffed bear.

On February 19, 1944, at Saint Vincent's Hospital in Los Angeles, Joyce gave birth to a second son, Daniel. Despite his growing family, Fante's draft status was now 1-A, and within a month he received the notice for his preinduction physical, which he passed on March 19. Expecting to be in the army by summer, Fante decided to pour himself into the Filipino novel during what little time remained. Toward that end he again uprooted his family for the move back to the house in Roseville. Louise Smart's estate had been settled on December 27, the upshot being that Joyce could expect a permanent monthly sum in excess of $200, as well as rental income from several Roseville properties. For the first time in memory Fante could afford not to work for a while.

Once in Roseville Fante set his mind on avoiding the draft. In the aftermath of the stabbing incident involving his father, Fante had cultivated the acquaintance of Placer County District Attorney Lowell L. Sparks, persuading the D.A. to write in support of his latest Guggenheim application. That acquaintance helped pave the way for Fante's approach to the chief clerk of the Auburn Draft Board, L. F. Morgan. Flattered to be meeting a published writer friend of the district attorney, Morgan led Fante to understand that a letter from his publisher indicating the vital morale-boosting service his novel would provide the nation might help keep him in civilian clothes. Fante wrote to Pascal Covici with this information, and Covici, hoping Fante was at last ready to write his great Filipino novel, dutifully composed and sent such a letter requesting the Draft Board's consideration. On May 31 Fante was granted a permanent deferment. Now nothing stood in the way of his writing the book.

The year before, "Helen, Thy Beauty Is to Me—" had been reprinted in *New Stories for Men*, an anthology that included stories by Sinclair Lewis, Paul Gallico, James Thurber, John O'Hara, John Steinbeck, Nunnally Johnson, John Huston and others. "This piece represents the first chapter of a novel I am writing entitled *Little Brown Brothers*," Fante explained in his author's introduction.

It will be a good book, and I hope the people who enjoy this story will follow the adventures of Julio Sal in a wider field. The reaction to this story (when it appeared in *The Post*) was pleasingly incredible. It ranged from threatening letters to lugubrious predictions that "the curses of the Filipinos" would follow me to the grave, to banquets given by Filipinos in my honor. One aspect of the criticism which disturbs me, however, is the notion among a few Filipinos that I am "condescending." If that is really so, then God forgive me, for I have always gone to my typewriter with a sense—not of dignity, for that would be pompous and churlish— but of sympathy and decent good humor. The Filipino is a very sad little guy. His role on the American scene is a bitter tragedy. Yet in his tragic adventures there are so many amusing facets that a writer finds them irresistible. In the novel I am doing my level best to see the thing as a whole. My conscience is clear. The writing so far seems to me to be intact. And that, I assume, is all that a novelist can expect.

But was his conscience truly clear? Given his alternating tone of defensiveness and, yes, condescension, no matter how inadvertent it may have been, one must certainly wonder.

With his house on Coronado Street freshly insulated against the summer heat, Fante settled into his first extended effort to write the novel that he believed would seal his reputation as a major American writer. Such was his ambition for *The Little Brown Brothers*, unpromising title and all. With two young sons making their presence felt—a local reporter who came to interview Fante during this time found "Danny . . . shrieking mightily, [while] Nicky had to be admonished by the charming Mrs. Joyce Fante to get off the grand piano"—Fante took to puttering around the yard by day, and working late into the night.

The schedule suited him and soon the pages were piling up. At the core of the story, which took Julio Sal by bus from the Los Angeles dance hall of "To Helen" north through Bakersfield and on into Sacramento, Fante would set a bitter truth, namely, that despite all of America's worthy attractions American racism lived on. During that crowded bus ride, for example, Julio Sal's offer of the empty seat beside him is rejected by a white American girl, who would rather stand than sit beside a Filipino. But such genteel, unintentional cruelty is only the most obvious level of racism under examination in *The Little Brown Brothers*; for once Julio Sal arrives in Sacramento the story becomes a far more convoluted exploration of the consequences, both comic and tragic, of America's racist legacy.

For starters, Julio is reunited with his old friend from the asparagus fields, the unforgettably named Purificacion Goldberg. Son of a Russian hat peddler and a mother from Cebu Province, Purificacion is the only Filipino Jew in California, and though by working hard and succeeding in business he has made a place for himself in America—or at least in the Filipino-Negro-Chinese-Mexican-Japanese quarter of America he is allowed to inhabit—he knows from experience what it means to be near the bottom of the racist equation. As he tells Julio Sal, "Many time, I wish to die. Many time I say to myself, 'Purificacion, you are Filipino, and you are Jew. Is too much. Is better you kill yourself.' Even Filipino spit on me, because I am Jew."

But that is only the beginning. For unlike Julio Sal and the vast majority of his countrymen in California, who live the joyless lives of single Pinoys, Purificacion Goldberg is married. (Because of immigration restrictions designed to maximize the exploitable labor pool of incoming foreigners during the 1930s and 1940s, over ninety percent of California's Filipino immigrant population was male.) Moreover, Purificacion is married not just to anyone, but to a member of one of America's oldest families, the Winthrops of Virginia—*black* Americans descended from slaves owned by George Washington. Intertwined with a subplot about Chinese gambling dens, the novel's main story line involves on the one hand Purificacion's self-interested attempt to pair Julio Sal off with his wife's sister Alice, the sex-starved hunchback widow of a notorious Filipino pimp who died at a poker table with a knife in his back; and on the other hand Julio Sal's purer romantic yearnings for Goldberg's beautiful young Japanese housemaid.

It should be clear from this précis that in writing *The Little Brown Brothers* Fante was out to render a vision of life in his times that would not fit comfortably with conventional views, least of all the views originating in the WASP bastion that was largely New York publishing. It should be equally clear that his fictional vision was a comic one, albeit steeped in real concerns. But while Fante was cooking up his comical race stew, someone else was addressing his same concerns from a serious historical perspective.

For much of 1944, while Fante was writing about Julio Sal's screwball reunion with Purificacion Goldberg, Fante's best friend Carey McWilliams was working on a study of anti-Semitism that would be published in book form in 1948 under the title *A Mask for Privilege: Anti-Semitism in America*. Prior to this McWilliams had researched and written *Prejudice—Japanese-Americans: Symbol of Racial Intolerance*, a copy of which, when it appeared in 1944, McWilliams had inscribed, "For Old Nick Fante—'Jap Lover'—Carey." (Aware of Fante's inescapable spiritual bond to his father, and sympathetic to its implications, Carey had long called John "Nick," with affection.) In 1943 Carey had published *Brothers Under the Skin*, an impassioned argument that racial discrimination was a national problem with international ramifications, and a call for civil rights legislation that would not be enacted for more than twenty years. And before the decade was over he would publish *North from Mexico: The Spanish-Speaking People of the United States* (1949). In all, McWilliams would write four important books growing out of the mounting interest in racial and ethnic minorities stimulated by World War II. And whenever he could, in the midst of it all, he would spend time drinking, gossiping and sharing ideas with his novelist friend John Fante.

The point is that Fante's fictional treatment of American racism in *The Little Brown Brothers* paralleled McWilliams's historical investigations to a significant degree, and certainly owed much to Carey's example as tireless defender of civil and human rights. This is not to say, however, that Fante succeeded in his attempt to address the issues as McWilliams did in his. In fact, despite Fante's best intentions, despite his self-avowed "clear conscience," *The Little Brown Brothers* failed to live up to its author's ambitions. Fante was simply not ready to write this novel without dipping to a certain level of condescension. In this respect the language of his own self-explanation in *New Stories for Men* had already given him away, or he never would have referred to the Filipino who was his central subject as that "sad little guy," or to the merely "amusing facets" of his tragic existence. In writing this novel Fante may have been trying to clear his conscience of the residual racism of his youth, which was a product of his painful experiences as a boy. He knew what it felt like to be called "wop" and "dago," but as Steinbeck had cautioned him, he did not know enough of the Filipino to translate what he knew into fiction without distorting it to cartoonish proportions. Most telling was the fact that of all the different ethnic groups included in *The Little Brown Brothers*, there was not a single Italian-American. Fante was not writing about what he knew best.

Nor was he allowed to continue after he submitted the first ninety-three pages to Viking in the fall of 1944. The two readers' responses Covici sent to Fante on November 10 were in substantial agreement: aside from the first chapter, which was almost verbatim the beautiful short story "To Helen, Thy Beauty Is to Me—," there was little there to warrant publication. Covici himself did not disagree, though as a sensitive editor he did his best to soften the blow. "My feeling," he wrote Fante after quoting the negative responses, "is that this is not your story. This doesn't mean that you haven't a great many short stories and novels in you. Not only am I convinced that you have, but I am convinced that you will write them and very successfully. Great authors have thrown away novels before."

Fante was numb. After reading Covici's letter he did not throw away *The Little Brown Brothers* but he immediately stopped working on it, abandoning a project he had cherished for years. A more crucial moment in his career would be difficult to pinpoint, for it marked the end of his concentration on prose fiction for a long, long time. The war was almost finished, and so was Fante.

When an offer from Hollywood reached him in Roseville soon afterward, he turned it down, refusing a second offer even when the pay scale was upped. Having lost his dream of writing a novel that would break him onto the national scene, he had nothing to lose in saying no. But when the third offer came with an even greater sum attached, Fante stopped resisting. By December 12 he was back in Hollywood at Paramount again, where he signed a ten-week contract at $500 per week to write a screenplay entitled "South American Story." The project was a gypsy trifle meant for Hollywood's "Sarong Girl," Dorothy Lamour, herself the emblem par excellence of Hollywood's inability to deal with matters of race. Separated temporarily from Joyce and the boys and no doubt longing for some kind of family contact, Fante wrote a holiday letter to his Denver cousin Jo Campiglia, with whom he had been out of contact for quite some time. In this letter he claimed falsely that his weekly salary at Paramount was $600, adding, "I like the assignment." More honest was the self-flaying inscription he wrote not long afterward in a friend's copy of *Dago Red*:

> For Esther, from that Hollywood whore, that stinking sell-out artist, that sublime literary pervert, that aborted lyricist—that stinking scenarist—that Paramount cunt-lapper who gets paid for the sweet-scented vomit whispered by Dorothy Lamour— Dedicated with the hope that some day soon he can write some less bitter inscription on the fly leaf of a really great work. Love . . . John Fante.

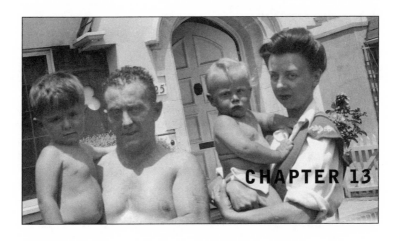

In the spring of 1945, after half a decade of total war, a kind of peace seemed finally at hand. But after the brutality and the fascism of this world war—after Pearl Harbor and Dresden and Dachau and Hiroshima—whatever peace might come would be a jittery and fragile one. And once it came, John Fante would be no more immune than the rest of the nation from the lingering strangeness of the postwar period.

During the last year of the war Fante went to his job every day at Paramount Studios like any other factory worker, inured to the brain-numbing nature of the assembly line. Instead of shell casings or ship armor, Fante was helping to rivet together that other mass product so vital to national defense, escapist film entertainment. Such was the stuff he was concocting for Dorothy Lamour and her slated costar Arturo de Cordova. A typically mercurial studio enthusiasm that would never be produced, this project metamorphosed while Fante was attached to it from his frothy but fully imagined seventy-page treatment, entitled "Flamenco," to an unabashed song-and-dance routine boiled down to fifteen turgid pages and called alternately "Gypsy Honeymoon" and "For the Love of Picaro."

It was a far cry from the work he had done at RKO the year before, which as it turned out had earned some very high praise indeed. Writing in *The Nation*, James Agee had called 1944's *Youth Runs Wild* one of the two "best fiction films of the year." (Agee's other pick, *The Curse of the Cat People*, had also been produced by Val Lewton.) But that had been last year. As far as this year went, Fante made no pretense about the work he was doing, but he was a professional and thus faithful to the machine he was paid to serve, apologizing for his actions with only a roguish self-contempt. "I know you're mad at me for being a Hollywood whore," a shameless Fante declared to his new agent Elizabeth Otis when she wrote from New York inquiring about his serious writing. "But it's fun while it lasts."

At least he was being paid relatively well for his services. Far from the princely sums showered on the industry's top-level screenwriters, Fante's was nonetheless a quite livable income, rising from $500 to $550 per week in April and remaining at that level until his release from Paramount in October. Having known poverty in his boyhood and hunger in his early days as a writer, Fante harbored no romantic notions on either subject, least of all with a wife and two children to support. On the contrary, Fante liked money, liked what it could do for a person, and he made no bones about his commitment to earning it.

One thing money could do was provide stability. In February, after fifteen years of constant shuttling between rented quarters in Los Angeles, San Francisco and Roseville, Fante made a $2,700 down payment toward the $15,000 sale price for a home where he now intended to stay. Located at 625 South Van Ness Avenue just north of Wilshire Boulevard at the southeastern edge of Los Angeles's exclusive Hancock Park, the house was a two-story twin-gabled English Tudor with five bedrooms, a fireplace and a large yard. Despite the rocky nature of their marriage, John and Joyce had their minds set on making a go at family life. What better place to do so than in such a made-to-order all-American dream house?

Trouble was, as Fante would soon discover when his father came down from Roseville to make a personal inspection, the dream house was rotten at the foundation: termites, Papa Nick said, and hungry ones. Fante was furious, threatening to sue the inspector who had proclaimed the house pest free. Rather than going off half-cocked, however, for once Fante took a deep breath and arranged for another inspection. But the second inspector went Nick one better. Not only were termites devouring the house's supporting wood construction; there was also significant fungus damage to the joists, girders and underflooring. Major restorations were indicated.

None of this bad news prevented Fante from moving in with Joyce and their two young sons. They needed a roof over their heads and room to stretch out in, so they settled in even though John was working too hard at Paramount to come home and put in a second shift battling pests. After a long day at the studio he was so tired, as he put it, "I have to drink to stay awake." Joyce set about furnishing the house with antiques purchased from high-end auction galleries, and the termites went unmolested.

Further evidence that Fante was settling down came with the March publication in Woman's Home Companion of "Scoundrel." A deft exercise in Catholic nostalgia, the story told of young Jimmy Toscana's enlightenment in the wake of his arrest for smashing street lamps. Arriving at the jail to take Jimmy in hand, Sister Mary Agnes admonishes him to pray, and pray Jimmy does—that she won't tell on him to his father. Holding that exact threat over him, Sister Agnes brings Jimmy to the parish pastor, who agrees to treat the boy severely. This the priest does by giving Jimmy a big piece of cake and nearly putting him to sleep with a sermon about "the light of faith" before sending him to the convent. There Jimmy is plied with warm pie and ice cream by sister cook before Sister Agnes reappears, stamping her foot and calling Jimmy a scoundrel. The miscreant finds himself trying to cry, an imperfect act of contrition but enough to soften Sister Agnes, who chucks him under the chin and promises not to call his father after all. As Jimmy hurries home elated by his luck he pulls up short, awed by the miracle of prayer, for he realizes how he has been saved from a beating. The feeling is too much, and standing alone on the street he cries "a real cry that shook me all over. . . . Then I started for home again."

The story was vintage Fante, a sign that he still had the old magic. It was also a sign of his inexorable drift back to the faith of his youth. Unlike "Hail Mary," that cynical meditation on the efficacy of prayer from his years as a disciple of Nietzsche, "Scoundrel" ends not with a smirk but with an authentic welling up of gratitude in the face of God's generosity. Although Fante's relationship to the Church would remain for the most part removed and often prickly, the return of his unironized Catholic sensibility was like nothing more than a prodigal's return home. And it was in his serious writing that this sensibility best expressed itself.

The hours that Fante devoted to such writing, however, were ever fewer and farther between. Rather, he logged his time at the studio cranking out piffle and drank himself stupid at every chance. "Spent the afternoon with Nick Fante," Carey McWilliams wrote in a typical diary entry for Saturday, May 12, 1945, "and wound up at the hour of 6:30 'kaput' and with a stunning and colossal hangover." It was also during this period that Fante took up golf again, now with a passion verging on vengeance. He golfed on weekdays after work, squeezing in as many holes as he could before nightfall, and he golfed all day Saturdays and Sundays; and when he was released from Paramount at the end of October, he golfed every day of the week, at Rancho, at River Park, at Sunset Fields and Fox Hills, wherever and whenever he could work himself into a foursome.

No matter how therapeutic the hours spent walking the fairways, addressing the ball and watching its flight, the sheer amount of time he poured into the game over the next several years took its toll in other areas of his life. Specifically, Joyce felt neglected, indeed, at times all but abandoned, as John's golfing grew obsessive. True, she might see him occasionally when she accompanied him as Carey's guest to a cocktail party at the Russian American Club honoring the new Russian consul, for example, or to the Royal Palms Hotel for dinner with Carey, Iris and Orson Welles. But these were mere occasions, social exercises at best, and not the day-to-day contact that a husband and wife should rightly share. In the absence of such contact they survived on the staple of sex, although it was rarely much more than that, raw passion and anything but tender. For all practical purposes Joyce was on her own, the married but solitary mother of two small and demanding children.

John was of no help whatever. While he was out golfing and drinking and gambling away his wages, Joyce remained behind to take care of "the demolition crew," as she fondly but wearily called Nicky and Danny. Left also to her attention were the cleaning and marketing and cooking and bill paying and balancing of unbalanceable accounts. (Fante still refused to divulge to Joyce the particulars of his expenditures, on the principle, inherited from his father, that a man did not stoop so low.) And when the termites chewed their way clear through the woodwork, exposing themselves in swarms to her horrified eyes, it fell to Joyce to treat the big dream house with murderous clouds of DDT.

In all it was a difficult time for Joyce, those lonely and harried years on Van Ness. She still worked on her poetry when she could steal precious moments, but she was cut off from contact with anyone who might share an interest in her struggles, whether poetic or personal. Sometimes she succeeded in capturing a glimpse of earlier, happier times, but more typical was her poem "Waking," with its chilling, fitful observations about a husband who wasn't there.

> He stirs and mutters, the heavy scent of dreams
> Grows thin, the dusky fragrance of her flesh
> And coiled hair drug him again to sleep
> Outside the birds awake, the mist falls fresh.
>
> Something almost remembered, almost found
> Disturbs him. Seaward into self, alone,
> He plunges, down through foam to quiet depths,
> Almost he sets his naked foot on stone.
>
> Tossed up again, he gasps and shakes his head,
> Opens his eyes: the clock—his trousers—the dust—
> Look back, establish their relationship.
> The curtains brighten, spring to flower. Disgust
>
> Returns, coiled in his stomach like a snake;
> The flesh slips firmly on, snaps shut, once more
> A vast machine whirs softly into gear,
> And worlds revolve, beyond the bedroom door.

Left behind in the big house Joyce was haunted by a mental image of a primitive hut in the midst of a barren desolation, with great dark birds circling in the clouds overhead. The feeling of portent accompanying this image was too often hers in these days, but she would not allow herself to speak of it. What she could not confide to anyone else she poured into her diary, which remains her witness to the hardships of this time — as well as to the few fleeting pleasures, for example, a rare evening out with John and the boys.

We went to dinner tonight with the children. We drove down Wilshire just at dusk. The sky was a luminous pinkish grey, and all the signs had been lighted. . . . The restaurant was quiet and pleasant. Whenever I am with John in different surroundings I begin to notice him again as a person. He has always baffled and rather frightened me. He seems scarcely aware of my existence. We look at each other and talk, scarcely seeing. And then I notice his face and the things about him that have always fascinated me. The rather thin but sensuously curved mouth, the heavy-lidded eyes, the fine texture of his hair, the delicately tilted nose. . . . We talk in a desultory fashion, stopping to urge the children to eat, or to tuck a napkin under a small chin. I discuss D. H. Lawrence with enthusiasm, comparing his style to John's. But John's mind is plainly elsewhere, although he agrees to read "Sons and Lovers" again. I am always a little uncertain in even a casual conversation with John, always watching him, taking my cue from him, my mind always searching out any lack of interest on his part, idly wondering what is going on in his mind that he does not express. He scarcely ever concentrates on me or watches my mood. I seem to be typed, to be a fixed and certain entity. I am always looking for the unknown in him. I wonder if he ever looks for the unknown in me.

More usual than such bittersweet evenings were all those evenings when Fante was simply not around. After getting the boys in bed for the night Joyce would fill the vacuum of these evenings by reading: Lawrence, Fitzgerald, Byron, and e. e. cummings, among others, as well as the philosophical writings of Alfred Korzybski. The latter's *Science and*

Sanity: An Introduction to Non-Aristotelian Systems and General Semantics appealed to Joyce with its argument that humanity's problems were the result of fundamental epistemological misunderstandings, and that in order to overcome these misunderstandings nothing short of a new and revolutionary way of thinking was required. Joyce was excited to discover a set of views that so thoroughly reinforced her own intuition; but she was also just as quickly frustrated. "I read a great deal," she wrote to her only confidant, her diary, "but feel it does me little good because ideas must have some relation to action in order to be effective." It was not possible to make an interpersonal revolution alone.

One arena where ideas and action did come together was the Hollywood strike of 1945. Starting in the spring and dragging on through summer, when Fante was still working at Paramount, the strike pitted factions of the American Federation of Labor against each other over various guild issues, including studio hiring and firing practices. With studio bosses playing the opposition against itself, the dispute continued escalating into the fall. In flashpoints of violence cars were overturned outside studio gates, water cannon deployed, and protestors hauled off by riot police.

As usual, Fante remained relatively disengaged, while Carey McWilliams poured himself into organizing. On October 7 Fante attended a mass meeting at Hollywood Legion Stadium to hear Carey speak, and the two friends went out afterward to drink with Ross Wills and Carlos Bulosan. Fante sympathized with the strikers, and as a card-carrying guild member he attended other meetings as well, and not only for the chance to get plastered afterward. At one such meeting of the Screen Writers Guild Fante voted to strike. The vote carried, but owing to machinations by the Trotskyite wing of the guild the vote was repudiated. As he was leaving that meeting Fante was disappointed, but he was even more surprised to learn how he was viewed by certain members of the far left when Lester Cole, one of the founding members of the guild, hissed at him, "You fucking fascist!"

Years later Fante would wonder if he had been denounced not only for failing to reverse his vote per the party's directive but also for the more rarefied crime of having been influenced by the wrong literary predecessor. By urging the Norwegians not to resist German occupation and by lending his name, wittingly or not, to the Nazi cause, Knut Hamsun had scandalized the world of letters which for so long had lionized him. Now, Fante felt, he, John Fante, was being singled out because of the projected connection between his writing and another writer's treason. Small matter that Hamsun's influence on Fante had taken root years before the war started: in the minds of some ideologues, even guilt by association could be retroactive. A bitter time of internecine political turmoil was hard upon the land. It would grow more bitter still.

The incident with the Writers Guild diminished Fante's already scant appetite for politics. While Carey McWilliams was deepening his commitments on many fronts—appointed contributing editor of *The Nation* in January 1945, during this period Carey would be involved in the Sleepy Lagoon murder case and the so-called Zoot Suit riots that ensued, the Hollywood witch-hunt, and the struggle for the rights of the foreign born, not to mention hard-fought if ultimately unsuccessful drives to elect friend and state attorney general Robert Kenney to the governorship of California and Henry Wallace to the presidency of the United States— Fante withdrew to his familiar position on the sidelines. Once again he was registered with the state Employment Service, but he was doing little to acquire gainful work. Truth be told, he preferred to concentrate on his backswing, play poker with old cronies Fenton and Wills, and maintain an alcoholic line of demarcation between himself and the battle royal that was the political world.

Still, martinis before and after dinner notwithstanding, Fante was not a complete wastrel in these postwar years. He wrote a whimsical sequence of bedtime stories for Nicky and Danny, one- and two-page nonsense tales about talking cats and mice and bugs and boys with names like Bitsy and Binky and Toots and Zip which delighted his sons when he read them aloud. He also succeeded in an avuncular role with Carey McWilliams's first son by an earlier marriage. Then verging on adolescence, Bill Carey, Jr., found himself one day in the stands at Los Angeles's Wrigley Field, then at the corner of 41st and Avalon, sitting between his father and Fante. The L.A. Angels were playing the Portland Beavers, but what would remain clearest in the memory of Carey, Jr., today a professor of history at Rutgers University, more so than the game itself, would be the experience of being in the company of his father and his father's close friend.

I don't remember whether the Angels won or lost—it wasn't a particularly good year for them—but that's partly because my more vivid memories are of John. I was very much up on baseball data for the year, and my father encouraged me to show off, but John's command of baseball stats went a long ways beyond mine. It was part of his charm that he engaged me in a very high level, technical conversation about various teams and players—I remember, especially, talking about Vince DiMaggio's propensity to strike out—that left my father more or less a spectator. As you can imagine, it was a very delicious experience for a not-quite-twelve year old, and it was clear that John got his own mischievous pleasure out of it. But for me, it was at least a minor rite of passage.

Calling Fante "a wonderfully sardonic bridge to my father," Carey McWilliams, Jr., helps us to appreciate an aspect of John's character that eluded Joyce's view. What Joyce tended to see was colored by her experience of Fante's ways toward her, and of his generally sullen presence when about the home. Unfortunately, what she tended to see was also most often the truth. When the Fantes' next-door neighbors, the Strobels, seemed to stop talking to them, for example, Joyce noted the sudden silence. What manner of ill behavior could John be guilty of now? The fact was that the families had been quite friendly to each other, the boys playing with young Mary Strobel, whose nickname was Ribbets, and John golfing now and then with Mary's father, Richard, an Associated Press photo editor who among many career highlights had been at the New Jersey airfield on the night of the fiery Hindenberg zeppelin disaster in 1937.

In December of 1945 Fante had made a handshake agreement with Strobel to cowrite a light family-oriented story based on an idea by the veteran photojournalist. Dore Schary, vice president of RKO and later studio chief at MGM, had recently expressed an interest in seeing whatever Fante might be writing, and Fante was eager to seize the opportunity. Smelling a quick kill, he encouraged Strobel to understand that they should write fast, cut out the middlemen and deal directly with the producer. This in fact the two neighbors did, arriving on the doorstep of Schary's home one evening with manuscript in hand.

Schary invited the men in and had them sit down while he skimmed through the freshly typed pages. Soon Schary was laughing, but in a tone to freeze blood, for he seemed amused not by the story but by the writers themselves. Recently released from his long stint concocting low-brow Paramount product, Fante had misread Schary, a liberal intellectual with a taste for message films. In expressing interest in Fante's work Schary no doubt had been hoping for something along the lines of the socially aware *Youth Runs Wild*, but this script by Fante and his next-door neighbor was something else, mere tripe. Curtailing the conference the producer showed his visitors the door, the humiliating conclusion of a partnership that more than fifty years later would still pain Dick Strobel to recollect. But this was not the reason that his family stopped talking to the Fantes.

Rather, the reason was similar to the reason that Nick Fante's neighbors back in Boulder would have as little as possible to do with the gruff bricklayer. John's sometimes rough-edged behavior around the neighborhood kids, his penchant for barking at them to be quiet, to get off the lawn, to go play somewhere else when they were disturbing his thoughts, endeared him to neither the children nor their parents. Then one day Joyce's cat gave birth to a litter. The neighborhood children, young Ribbets Strobel among them, were wide-eyed at the squirming miracle. But they were not allowed to marvel for long. Without a word of explanation Fante banished the children to Joyce's backyard victory garden and closed the screen door to the service porch behind him. He filled the cast-iron sink with water and then as the children peered through the screen he drowned the mewing kittens one by one. After that incident the Strobel children were forbidden to come over, and soon their parents had stopped talking to John and Joyce.

Little Danny began running away. One time it took the police more than three hours to find him, and when they finally did he was hiding in a garage down the street, "terribly scared" and yet screaming in protest at the officers' efforts to bring him home. Nicky for his part stuck around, displaying evidence of a precocious intelligence—he had been reading from books, his father's among them, since he was three—even as he expended prodigious amounts of energy tearing up the house. Across the street Nicky had a friend named Petey Parkin whose father, an army officer during the war, had brought home a collection of German battlefield memorabilia, including Nazi flags, a Mauser or two and a cat-o'-nine-tails that he had requisitioned from one of the liberated death camps. Mr. Parker would show the kids the blood on the braided whip ends and then they would play war, or jungle, or cowboys and Indians not a hundred feet from Wilshire Boulevard's Miracle Mile.

In addition to his war trophies Mr. Parkin owned an early home-movie camera, and under the direction of Petey, who would go on to a career in theater, the Fante boys and neighborhood playmates would enact their favorite fantasies for Petey's movies. Although Fante despised actors and rarely made himself available to his children, there came the day when he volunteered to help the kids with their moviemaking. As Pete Parkin would recollect many years later, the scene called for someone to die. John told the kids to watch and he would show them how. He took a deep drag on his cigarette, immersing himself in the part, and then he fell to the ground, shaking and kicking for a time, before going rigid and still. Smoke oozed from his nostrils and his mouth, curling skyward. He lay there without moving.

We must die to live again, as Saint Paul reminds us. But in the late 1940s Fante was enduring a sort of day-to-day death in life. Unable to focus on his writing, he was instead losing himself in his golf game for the greater part of each day; most nights he was also drinking and gambling to excess. Whether he knew it or not he was thereby preparing the way, paradoxically but predictably, for his eventual return to Mother Church. It is an old story, of course, older even than the Church herself, the mythic return to one's deepest source. But given the nature of Fante's beginnings and their roots in antiquity, it was also just as inevitable.

In this development Joyce was a significant influence. Her own search for a meaningful way to live in this world, and to coexist in the face of John's strangeness, had led her to begin reading works of Catholic theology, the Fathers of the Church, and certain lives of the saints. Long convinced of the existence of invisible worlds of immaterial and timeless spirit, Joyce increasingly felt the inadequacy of her own commonsensical Lutheran upbringing to answer the whisperings within her. More concretely, she was drawn to the dark, handsome gothic church a few blocks north on Van Ness at 3rd Street, Saint Brendan's, thinking it would be a good place to send the boys to school. When she mentioned this thought to John he immediately agreed. Even more surprising, he responded with enthusiasm when she told him that she felt she might want to convert. Within days Fante had contacted one of the priests at Saint Brendan's, Father Walter Martin, who arranged for Joyce to begin her conversion studies. Fante basked in this unexpected turn of events. As difficult as their marriage had been for the last several years, suddenly it seemed to have been made in heaven, if only with respect to this meeting of the minds.

Nor did John keep the secret of their newfound compatibility to himself. At a party hosted by Carey and Iris McWilliams in February 1948, John announced to all present—a distinctly irreligious gathering including Louis and Stella Adamic, Los Angeles political figure Joe Aidlin and his wife Mary, California gubernatorial candidate Bob Kenney and the ever-skeptical Ross Wills—that he was returning to the Church, and that Joyce was following in his footsteps. Three months later Joyce was baptized and made her first confession, and on May 21, a Monday, she and John took communion and renewed their marriage vows at a nuptial mass, making their union at last official in the eyes of the Church. The following week Danny was baptized, albeit reluctantly. Old enough to be afraid of what might be done to him in that strange dark place, he agreed to set foot in Saint Brendan's only on the condition that he could enter armed with his cowboy gun. So he was received into the Church holding the priest in his gun sights and threatening "to shoot anybody who hurt him."

Fante must have felt something of the cyclical nature of men's lives when Nicky started school at Saint Brendan's under the Sisters of the Blessed Virgin Mary, the same order of nuns who had taught him in Boulder. To his parents John reported that he was attending Sunday mass again, a claim that Joyce says was not true for long. In fact, the afterglow of their second honeymoon was short-lived. In the wake of his spiritual reawakening Fante had wasted no time in slipping back to his old ways, staying away from home every day playing endless rounds of golf and spending most nights with his friends over drinks and cards. Enthusiastic new Catholic that she was, Joyce wrote to John's old friend Father Paul Reinert in St. Louis seeking professional advice on the mystery of divine beneficence, for how could God be all good if He created some people who were going to hell?

His dissolute behavior notwithstanding, as Fante approached forty his mind was full of good intentions. He announced and undertook one writing project after another—movie ideas, short stories, an experimental novel that would allow him "absolute and limitless freedom," another novel on the birth-control theme which he had been circling for years but which now related directly to Joyce's third and latest pregnancy— only to pull up short and go back to golfing, time and again. With his old friend and nemesis Ross Wills he did manage to complete a movie treatment with the off-putting title "A Panty-Girdle for Mrs. Illytch," of all things a spoof of the Marshall Plan set in a remote Soviet village. To no one's surprise except perhaps that of its coauthors, however, "Panty-Girdle" failed to inspire any bidders. But then again, in a world where it felt "as if all life today has disintegrated into atomic fragments," as Fante wrote in a letter to Pascal Covici, who knew anything anymore?

In all it was a time of fitful dreams and false starts and misjudgments of the market, which was undergoing accelerated and drastic transformations. "The whole picture has radically changed here in Hollywood," Fante wrote in explanation.

The movie people are not making movies the way they did before the war. There used to be 30,000 people working every day in the studios. Now there are less than half of that number. There are supposed to be about 2,000 writers in Hollywood. No more than 150 are working. The whole trouble lies in the uncertain future. The coming of television has greatly changed the situation. Everybody is afraid to spend money. There are even some who believe the movie industry is finished for good, just like the old silent pictures ended when talking pictures were introduced.

Such doomsday concerns were in significant part a product of the snowballing congressional investigations in Washington into alleged communist infiltration of Hollywood. Anxiety had always been an accepted side effect of working in the industry, but these days everyone was more nervous than usual. A new kind of self-censorship was asserting itself as people grew more and more fearful of being investigated, and of the consequent potential for damage to—or even the loss of—their careers. As studios scrambled to persuade the ticket-buying public that there were no Reds on their lots, Father Daniel A. Lord's venerable "Code to Govern the Making of Motion and Talking Pictures" was giving way to "The Screen Guide for Americans," written by that arch-apologist of the American way, novelist Ayn Rand. In place of the Code's idealistic suggestions that in American films the "just rights, history, and feelings of any nation are entitled to consideration and respectful treatment," or that the "treatment of bedrooms must be governed by good taste and delicacy," Rand's Guide offered an inflexible list of commandments. "Don't Deify the 'Common Man,'" "Don't Glorify Failure," "Don't tell people that man is a helpless, twisted, drooling, sniveling, neurotic weakling. Show the world an *American* kind of man, for a change." It was an insidious time, for as often as not the people enforcing these commandments were the liberal-minded likes of producer Dore Schary, who with other leaders of the film industry agreed in the infamous Waldorf-Astoria Declaration of November 25, 1947, to blacklist the ten writers who the day before had been charged with contempt of Congress for refusing to disclose to the House Un-American Activities Committee their political affiliations. In the words of Lillian Hellman, it was a scoundrel time.

Working in the chilling atmosphere of these postwar developments, by the end of the decade Fante had succeeded in writing no books, selling no movie ideas and placing only three short stories, all with *Woman's Home Companion*. "Papa's Christmas Tree," appearing in December 1946, was a sentimentalized reversal of the Christmas scene in *Wait Until Spring, Bandini*: instead of ruining the family's Christmas through his selfishness, the reconstructed papa figure saves the day with his pure-hearted selflessness. "The Dreamer" (June 1947) was likewise a watered-down revision of something written long before, in this case "Helen, Thy Beauty Is to Me—," with bits adapted from *Ask the Dust*. Only "The Wine of Youth" (December 1948), a beautifully developed variation on his old theme of mismatched Italian-American lovers and their families, rose at points to the level of artistry Fante could muster when he was writing well.

Generally, though, failure was topped by ever more bizarre failure. At the very time he was writing "The Wine of Youth," for example, Fante was also collaborating with a physician acquaintance on a melodramatic mishmash about a magician's doomed quest to learn the secret of raising the dead. Aptly named "The Long Nightmare," this spec movie treatment combined hoked-up elements salvaged from the Dorothy Lamour South American hulk Fante had helped sink at Paramount four years earlier with an exceedingly creaky murder-mystery plot. It was at about this time that Fante wrote another story even more suggestive of his desperation, "The Case of the Haunted Writer."

The writer who narrates this story buys a house where the previous resident has died, a man by the lugubrious name of Coffin. No sooner does the narrator move in and try to start writing in the Coffin house, however, than he discovers that he can no longer find the words. While his wife redecorates, the narrator slides into a deepening paranoia. He purchases a handgun for protection against the noises that keep him awake at night, but even then he cannot escape into sleep. "I lay in the bed of a dead man, felt the curvature of the mattress that had once pressed against his body, and stared at the very ceiling which had been his last view of this world." One of the strangest stories Fante ever wrote, "The Case of the Haunted Writer" reads like unwitting but disturbingly accurate self-psychoanalysis. The story was never published in his lifetime.

He was casting about, plunging into one spur-of-the-moment, hit-or-miss writing scheme after another, and when one missed, and then the next one, he retreated to the twin refuges of golf and drink. Ten years had passed since the publication of Ask the Dust, a novel that, more than anything else he had ever written, still resonated. True, the book had been long out of print, but Norman Foster had recently called to express his reawakened interest in making a movie adaptation. Moreover, in yet another of the important studies Carey McWilliams published in the 1940s, Southern California: An Island on the Land, Ask the Dust had been singled out as one of the few works of fiction "that suggest what Southern California is really like." Such praise would not change the decision of the Dell Publishing Company, which would rebuff Fante's suggestion that *Ask the Dust* be reissued in paperback, explaining that "[w]hat people seem to be looking for today is escape of one kind of another, and the Dell Book list is therefore confined principally to murder mysteries, westerns, and love stories." (Not until 1954 would Bantam finally release *Ask the Dust* in a twenty-five-cent paperback edition, complete with lurid dimestore cover art and the come-on "He was young, broke and driven by a raging thirst for life.") But at least Carey still believed in him, and Carey was someone whose views Fante respected, even if his temperament did not allow him to share Carey's enthusiasm for politics.

In early 1949 McWilliams was more deeply immersed in politics than ever before. Among countless other commitments, he was helping to build a defense for the Hollywood Ten, working on the amicus curiae brief for (John Howard) *Lawson and* (Dalton) *Trumbo* v. *the United States*. Still, he always had time for John Fante. The two had recently taken a trip to Catalina Island, where they had laughed themselves silly at the Wrigley Memorial and jeeped around admiring the quintessential California landscapes and solitudes.

Fante had recently grown a mustache, which a good-humored McWilliams called "ridiculous," but which John himself admired, aware that it made him look uncannily like his father. A few months later, when news arrived from Roseville via the family's old friend Doc McAnally about Nick's deteriorating eyesight and heart, Fante must have looked at himself in the mirror in a new way. His own young Nick was growing up, about to make his first communion, while his father was putting him in mind of the last rites. For someone who knew what it felt like to lie in a dead man's bed, the sudden need to face up to the inevitable fact of mortality put Fante in a somber and reflective mood when he wrote his father on the first of May.

Believe in your children, and your grandchildren. Be courageous and strong, so that they will be proud of you. I have already told Nicky and Danny what a brave fighter you are. I have told them how strong you are. I have said that their grandpa would live forever. You must keep fighting. Don't pity yourself. Remember how you used to say that nobody could get the best of Nick Fante. You must still believe that, because it's true. And none of this will get the best of you, either. Your eyes will be well again soon. You will see again soon. You must have faith. Don't drink too much. Be the strong, brave father I know you are. . . . It is very hard on Mama. She is not well. Be nice to her. Be a good friend to her, because she has always been so good to you.

Once again he might have been writing to himself. He could have used the advice.

"**L**os Angeles is the capital of all the termites in America, a place where the greedy, noisy little monsters are endlessly consuming the rotting timbers of jerry-built homes."

Writing in 1946, the devilish Carey McWilliams may have been thinking of his friend John Fante, owner of a classic American dream home turned nightmare. McWilliams could not have known that three years later the termites would still be feasting, or that one morning Joyce, heavy with child, would plunge through the rotten floorboards of her kitchen, narrowly escaping injury. The Fantes' home life was no longer a fit subject for jokes.

Fed up with the neglect of her family's most basic needs—a floor to walk on, for God's sake—Joyce let Fante have it. She turned on him righteously and made him look at the hole in the kitchen until he saw it for what it was. Then she challenged him to take some stock: how dare he piss away his life playing golf while the house crumbled? Yielding to her fury, Fante vowed to face up at last to his responsibilities.

Toward that end, late in the summer of 1949 Fante signed a contract with independent producer Joe Gottesman, who needed a low-budget script and in a hurry. It was the first job Fante had held in years, but it was also an embarrassing step down: the deal was for an original feature script, with revisions, for a paltry $2,500, with the always-elusive incentive of an additional $2,500 should cameras ever roll on the production. Fante needed the money, but his heart had never been less in a project. Soon he was back on the golf course instead of writing.

On October 9 at Saint Vincent's Hospital Joyce gave birth to a daughter, Victoria Mary Fante, named after Hamsun's *Victoria* and John's mother. With another mouth to feed, Fante knew what he needed to do; but knowing was one thing, doing another. Through much of Joyce's pregnancy and even in the wake of his daughter's birth Fante had hardly tried to conceal the fact that he was again seeing the flamboyant waitress Audrey, behavior that suggests a desire to be punished. Eleven days after Victoria's birth, producer Gottesman fired Fante for breach of contract, citing his "turtle pace" and the "inadequacy of what script we have."

Except for Joyce's modest income, Fante was again all but broke. Instead of tackling the situation head-on, however, he took to staring at his new television. Long a fan of baseball and boxing, Fante seized on the new medium's potential for escape, watching every sporting event broadcast on the bluish black-and-white screen, and whatever other shows came on in between. Like Carey McWilliams, with whom he enjoyed getting drunk in the pulsing glow of the picture tube, he was especially fascinated by televised wrestling matches. These overacted morality plays, featuring the likes of pretty boy Gorgeous George and villainous Freddy Blassy, somehow fit with President Truman's recent order to proceed with production of a hydrogen bomb. Between no-holds-barred bouts the television was reporting that in case of war with Russia the FBI had a plan to round up as many as four thousand known Communists. The decade was dawning in stark black and white, the good guys and the bad guys indeed.

Then in the middle of February 1950 Joyce became pregnant for the fourth time. The timing could not have been worse. Aghast at the prospect of another child, Fante flew into a rage which lasted for weeks, standing over Joyce and shouting obscenities, demanding that she undergo an abortion. When she refused, Fante decided the time had come to leave his family, as his own father had once left his. Fante now saw his wife and three children as roadblocks. How much worse would it be with four children? But where to go? And how to finance his getaway? After a time his resolve began to falter, and in the end he did not go anywhere; but a lingering bitterness set in. He withheld any show of tenderness for his expectant wife, staying out night after night for weeks on end and then returning home so drunk that Joyce sometimes had to help him up the stairs. More than forty years later Joyce would resort to the third person in relating her experiences of this time, as if she still had to distance herself from the hurt—a brutally true reflection of how Fante's behavior affected her.

It was an impossible situation, as self-destructive a brink as Fante had come to in years—but it was also the catalyst he needed. Daggers drawn and with nothing to lose, Fante started writing again. By early April he had astonished himself with forty pages of a new novel, and enough momentum that he was hoping "to finish it in sixty days." Even more surprising was the discovery that, despite his bloody-mindedness throughout the writing, the story was turning into an affirmation of love, a comic paean to the joys and the heartaches of marriage, procreation and family.

He was calling the book *The White Balloon,* and in it he was resurrecting Arturo Bandini, now a successful writer suffering the pangs of expectant fatherhood. When the buoyantly pregnant Emily, a Protestant, falls through the termite-infested floor of the couple's kitchen, Arturo brings his tippling stonemason father to Los Angeles to undertake home repairs. Papa has other ideas, however, and while Emily experiences a quirky conversion to Catholicism, the faith from which Arturo has long since drifted, Papa builds them a fireplace for the ages, leaving the kitchen to the termites and driving Arturo to wonder at the looniness all about him. But when Arturo's rediscovery of faith coincides with his son's birth, life is full and again all of a piece.

In three previous novels the figure of Arturo Bandini had provided Fante with the lightning rod for some of his strongest efforts, the mouthpiece for what he knew how to say best. Now, in the heat of the writing and against the debacle of his life, John was using Bandini to construct a comical reverse image of the way things were. Four years after the failure of *The Little Brown Brothers* and his ensuing crisis of confidence, Fante was steaming through a story rich with family lore—the legend of Uncle Mingo, Nick Fante's garlic bulb virility charms, Joyce's autodidactic search for meaning—and as warmhearted as only fiction could be, given the state of Fante's personal affairs.

So charming was this tale of a young couple's first pregnancy and the comedy of their spiritual rebirth that before Fante was finished writing Elizabeth Otis had sold the book to *Woman's Home Companion* for $5,500. It was still early summer when Otis notified Fante that she had placed his story "The All American Team" with *The Saturday Evening Post* for another $1,500. To celebrate, Fante took a night off from his pig-headed drinking and went with Carey to see two films which greatly moved him, Roberto Rossellini's *Paisan* and *Open City*. For her part, Joyce went to Frederick's of Hollywood and purchased some sexy underthings. Then, with an enthusiastic letter from Pascal Covici to bolster his belief in the novel, Fante packed up his long-suffering wife and children for the flight to Catalina Island and two weeks' vacation in Avalon.

Long days of swimming, hiking and fishing made for a welcome respite from all the recent tensions. When the Fantes returned to the mainland two weeks later, however, the world was as tense as ever. While Fante had been escaping these tensions in the ironic domestic comedy of *The White Balloon*, Carey McWilliams was attacking their causes in *Witch Hunt: The Revival of Heresy*, his study of the new age of fear. Finished days before the June outbreak of the Korean War, McWilliams's book dealt, among other issues, with the Hollywood Ten, assaults on academic freedom, the anticommunist obsessions of Senator Joseph McCarthy and the House Un-American Activities Committee (HUAC), and the panic triggered by the disappearance from a Chicago laboratory of thirty-two ounces of uranium. Ironic novels and island idylls aside, it was a savage and depressing time.

Fante responded to the era's escalating pressures by teaming up in the fall of 1950 with Jack Leonard, an alcoholic screenwriter who lived in an apartment above the carousel on Santa Monica Pier. Between drinks, Fante and Leonard knocked out a treatment about a migrant farmworker from Mexico who cherishes his new American citizenship like life itself.

An alternately hard-hitting and saccharine tale filled with touches from the wreckage of *The Little Brown Brothers*, "Letter from the President" was custom-made for nervous studio executives looking for HUAC-proof scripts. It was making the rounds of the studios when just after midnight on November 15 Joyce went into labor.

Again Fante turned monstrous: refusing to drive to the hospital, he gave Joyce the cab fare instead and thus was not present for the birth of his son Peter James, later called Jimmy. Nor did he display much affection when, later in the day, he first laid eyes on mother and child. Ever the dutiful son, however, he did telegram his parents in Roseville with the news, signing the cable "Love Johnnie."

Five days later Johnnie's father, the inimitable Nick Fante, suffered a massive heart attack and died. Leaving Joyce at home with the four children, Fante rushed north to Roseville, where record-setting rains had been falling for seven days. On the day of Nick's requiem mass at Saint Rose of Lima Church the sun reappeared, but Roseville Cemetery was still mired in mud as the coffin was lowered into the ground. Papa had not lived forever after all. After all the neglectful, abusive years John's mother was heartbroken, and so was John; but he did not stay long to comfort her. The next evening Fante was back in Los Angeles. He and Joyce went to dinner at the McWilliams's, where Fante kept everybody up late drinking bourbon and telling stories about his father, how far he had traveled, how hard he had worked, how much he had done, in spite of himself, for the whole grief-stricken family.

A bad winter was upon the city, poisonous with smog. On December 12 Fante and McWilliams went downtown to the Olympic Auditorium to take in the fights, several strong Mexican cards. Afterward they fell into the notorious nightclub at Pico and Western called Strip City to have a few drinks and witness what the thick-skinned McWilliams would call "the most unpalatable strip teases" he had ever seen. It was past midnight when the two old friends stepped out into the night. A pall of fog and smog enveloped them. The brew was thick and it dripped, Carey observed, like the atmosphere overhanging stockyards.

On April Fool's, 1951, John and Joyce attended a going-away party for Carey McWilliams, who was moving with Iris to New York. Ever since his appointment as contributing editor to *The Nation* six years earlier, Carey's involvement with the venerable left-wing journal had been deepening, and now he was going east to work there full-time. It was a hard-liquor party and Fante partook liberally if not with joy. Fewer than five months had passed since his father's death and now his best friend was leaving too.

To fill the vacuum of these departures Fante was soon writing to H. L. Mencken for the first time in more than a decade. Mencken, Fante knew, had been immobilized by a stroke in 1948, and now here was the great skeptic's once ardent disciple sending prayers for his recovery. "Myself, when I read of your rough going, came up with a few prayers which might have helped a bit for all I know. I have returned to the Church, which I find as cantankerous as ever, as unyielding and irritating as in the days of my adolescence. But I must face it: the Church is my home. I love it." He mentioned his children and the loss of his father, then said he intended to dedicate his first novel in a decade to Mencken, "in undiminished admiration."

In May Fante had left Viking to sign with Little, Brown and Company's Angus Cameron, who had offered a more lucrative contract for the completed manuscript of *The White Balloon* than the one Pascal Covici had offered. (Carey McWilliams, whose *Witch Hunt* was then in press at Little, Brown, joked that he was going to charge Cameron a finder's fee for persuading Fante to switch.) Fante received a $2,000 advance, and although a scheduling conflict caused *Woman's Home Companion* to reverse its acceptance of *The White Balloon* and thus withhold all but $1,000 of the $5,500 sale price, Fante could see that he had a valuable commercial product on his hands. In order to maximize the book's value Fante readily agreed when Cameron suggested a few simple name changes which would enable the novel to cross over into the lucrative nonfiction market; and so with a canny stroke of the editor's pencil *The White Balloon* became *Full of Life* and "Arturo Bandini" became "John Fante."

In lending an air of fact to his fiction by fictionalizing his own name, Fante was following through on the autobiographical impulse that had always animated his creative writing. He explained the move to Mencken as a "rather embarrassing compromise," but his sheepishness was at least in part a pose. To hide behind his own name, to take credit for his own evasions, and to make a pile of money besides: Fante was too self-aware a writer and too sharp a professional to be embarrassed by such junctures of wit. Closer to the truth of how he felt was the detached irony of his observation that "by virtue of this absurd change in names, the book is no longer fiction but fact." Absurd indeed: the confessional writer was disappearing into his own self-revelation.

With his eye peeled for profit, Fante got a copy of his manuscript to the King brothers, independent low-budget producers Maurice and Frank, who submitted it for inspection to the Breen Office. A conference was arranged between Fante and a Breen representative to discuss the delicacies involved in treating such Code-sensitive subjects as pregnancy and religion. Fante listened carefully as changes were suggested in his story, some more drastic than others. It did not take long for Fante to respond. In the words of the Breen representative, Fante "accepted [the suggestions] willingly and said he would go about the business of drafting a 15 or 20 page treatment that would meet the requirements of the Code." Two days later Fante delivered the promised treatment to the Breen Office, accompanied by a cover letter with salutations in church Latin. "Pax vobiscum! I hope this comes near what you want. Needless to say, we shall be in close touch throughout the writing of the script (if there ever is one)." He signed off, "Affectionately, John Fante."

A calculating Fante wanted to write the script in part at least because Academy Award nominee Edward Dmytryk was interested in directing the project. Odd man out among the Hollywood Ten, Dmytryk had served prison time in 1950 before signing a shrewdly worded affidavit asserting that he was not a member of the Communist Party, thereby alienating himself for life from the other members of the Ten but also making himself employable again. Prior to prison Dmytryk had been living in semi-exile in London, where he had directed a film based on Pietro di Donato's novel of an Italian-American bricklayer, *Christ in Concrete.* Now, as Fante saw it, Dmytryk was seeking further to untaint himself of Communist associations by directing as wholesome a family film as he could find—*Full of Life.*

Before Fante could reach a deal with Dmytryk and King Brothers, however, free-spending producer Stanley Kramer appeared on the scene, throwing more money at the still unpublished *Full of Life* than the others could ever dream of. Terms "in the neighborhood of $40,000 plus a percentage agreement" were reported in the *New York Times* of July 31. Carl Foreman, another left-wing American writer-director who like Dmytryk had fled to England in order to keep working, was said to be Kramer's director of choice. Again Fante suspected that cynical political motivations were behind the rush to embrace *Full of Life*, but again he was glad to oblige.

Press releases indicated that Fante would write the adaptation himself, but for some reason the screenplay assignment went to Earl Felton, a writer whose credits included the fine 1945 Fred MacMurray comedy-drama *Pardon My Past*. Unfortunately, Felton's fortunes had slid far enough by 1949 that he was making the newspaper as a failed suicide, rescued by police at a Santa Monica Boulevard motel after overdosing on pills. Whether or not personal troubles were undermining his writing efforts now, the script Felton submitted in November was execrable, an anchored pleasure boat in Balboa Harbor substituting for the termite-infested house of Fante's novel and not a word about either a conversion to Catholicism or an Italian bricklayer father. When Kramer's attention shifted to the production of *High Noon*, *Full of Life* slipped out of development.

Still, Fante had made a bundle with the sale of his novel to Kramer. Now "Letter from the President" sold to MGM for another $10,000 and Fante was suddenly flush enough to consider moving out of the decrepit House of Usher–like pile where two of his four children had been conceived. This time he would go in style. A real estate agent whom Fante knew mentioned an oddity far out on Malibu's Point Dume, a custom ranch house on an acre of land priced far below market value. The current owners felt too cut off from civilization there, but to Fante the remoteness was appealing. The house faced the ocean, and at night you could hear the waves hitting the shore. There was hardly another house for miles around.

Like a high-rolling gambler Fante plunked down $10,000 toward the $29,500 sale price for the house—the year before it had listed at $92,000—and on September 15 he moved Joyce and the children in to their new home at 28981 Cliffside Drive. Suddenly he was somewhere new, and yet somewhere very old as well. Misnamed in the 1790s by explorer George Vancouver after a Franciscan priest named Dumetz, Point Dume was a place apart. For one thing, it was pronounced "doom," the premonitory burden of which John counterbalanced by nicknaming his new hideaway Fante's Folly. By that he meant the sheer extravagance of his purchase, a curiously Y-shaped rancho of 5,000 square feet featuring four bedrooms, three baths, a rumpus room, a four-car garage, a sun-roof and two fireplaces, all protected by a stout cinder-block wall enclosing the entire acre. The surrounding landscape was breathtaking, a sweeping promontory giving onto secluded sand beaches well seaward of the Pacific Coast Highway. There were seals, dolphins, whales, hawks, foxes, raccoons, and possums, as well as a friendly family of skunks.

Writing to Carey McWilliams in New York a month after moving in, a playful Fante imagined his new situation as the last line of defense against a world gone mad.

Now look here, McWilliams, when you deal with a man like me, you ain't dealing with just plain shit. You're dealing, rather, with just plain shit and I'm here to tell you, right here in the Malibu, where I now live—yes, McWilliams, the Malibu—I'm here to tell you that this blessed little spot I now own fronts the Pacific Ocean like a fortress, and every night I'm out there with my binoculars (I own binoculars now, McWilliams) scanning the horizon for enemy ships, and when I say enemy I don't mean the Japanese, McWilliams, I mean a country in Asia, the capital of which starts with an M. And I stand on my property with my binoculars, and if they come, and come they will, McWilliams, I want you to know, and your wife, and your child, and your mother, that John T. Fante, a pretty fair cunt-tributor (that's spelled right, McWilliams) to American letters, is out there ready to fend off them Slavic hordes, ready to drop in his tracks in order to keep men like you and your kind in business, the business of writing the truth, emblazoning it like a beacon light to guide the whole world down the perilous path of human liberty. The house cost me 29 thousand, Bub.

Kidding aside, Fante knew that he had gotten out of L.A. while the getting was good. The Van Ness house sold for $15,000, but only after the listing agent had lost money getting it in salable shape. "Had we known the real condition of the house," the realtor wrote Fante on December 20, "we would not have entered into a deal to do what we did do. As you know, the north part of the house in the kitchen almost fell apart because of dry rot and termites. . . . The deal was hardly worth the effort and the time involved."

At the age of forty-two Fante had learned a thing or two about making deals, and now he had a cliff-side fastness from which to view the nightly setting of the sun on God's creation. Serenity could not be far away.

But it was and always would be. In February of 1952, for example, Fante went to dinner at Frascatti's on Sunset Strip with Joe Petracca, a fellow Italian-American novelist and story writer then working his way into television, and Knox Burger, fiction editor of *Collier's*. As the drinks kept coming, good cheer presided until Fante turned surly, then belligerent. He insisted on fixing up Burger with a woman, an offer Burger declined on the grounds that he had come from New York to talk with writers, not pimps. Fante spun into a rage, calling Burger a faggot and moving to take their differences outside. As they exited the restaurant Fante was reeling, but before any punches were thrown he fell to the ground, hitting the curb with his head. Yet the next day Fante called Burger at his Beverly Hills Hotel room, no worse for wear and again entirely amiable.

Nor was there anything serene about Fante's March appearance in Santa Monica Court as a witness for William Saroyan in his second divorce from Carol Marcus, the mother of their two children, Aram and Lucy. It was a nightmarish situation, with charges and countercharges of infidelity, insanity and violence. In the widely syndicated newspaper photograph from the court proceedings, a rigid Fante sat between a murderous-looking Saroyan and his estranged wife—there but for fortune, it seemed.

Despite such tumult in Fante's personal affairs, *Full of Life* was published in April to strong, even glowing reviews. "In a world and time that hurries deathward," Christopher Morley wrote of Fante's success, "this biology of love and goodness praises the generosity of life." Such warmth was typical of the book's many reviews, and soon the novel was climbing best-seller lists nationwide. Interest continued to rocket in May when the book appeared as a Book-of-the-Month Club selection and, in condensed form, in *Reader's Digest*, which paid $7,000 for the rights. The triumph that had so long eluded Fante was finally his to enjoy.

Rather than pausing to savor his success, however, he plunged ahead. By June he was back at MGM, where "Letter from the President" had been filmed under the direction of William Wellman, from a screenplay by top screenwriter Marguerite Roberts. When Roberts and her novelist husband John Sanford were blacklisted for refusing to cooperate with the HUAC proceedings, screen credit for the film was changed to "Written by John Fante and Jack Leonard." (In August the film was released to polite reviews as *My Man and I*, with Norman Foster's brother-in-law Ricardo Montalban as the patriotic Chu Chu Ramirez and Shelley Winters as the fallen woman he saves.)

After several seasons out in the cold of studio disfavor—largely owing to his long self-induced golf stupor—Fante was now back in the good graces of MGM studio brass, including producer Stephen Ames and chief of production Dore Schary. In June Fante submitted "Silver Lode," an outline about Mexican mineworkers and the heartless conglomerate that occupies their land. And then in July Fante submitted "Orca," an unabashed Hollywood turn in four pages on the epic American novel of them all, Herman Melville's *Moby Dick*. With a one-armed protagonist named Lefty, engaged in an obsessive hunt for the whale that maimed him, and a shamelessly romantic subplot, this outline netted Fante the first long-term contract for a writer since Hollywood had come down with the political jitters. In addition to granting Fante $6,000 for his outline, the contract—signed by Dore Schary, who was no longer laughing at Fante—called for a starting salary of $1,000 per week for a minimum of forty weeks, with provisions for contract extensions over seven full years, annual raises included. The yarn was Hollywood claptrap and Fante knew it, but the money was awfully good.

When he got depressed he could turn for relief to the autumn 1952 issue of *The Thinker's Digest*, the Catholic journal that had reprinted "A Nun No More," or to the August *Collier's*, where despite the February altercation on the Sunset Strip, Knox Burger had seen fit to publish "The Big Hunger," a winsome story about an imaginative seven-year-old named Danny, his big brother Nick and their baby sister Vicky. Fante was playing again with the lines between fact and fiction in order to redraw himself. "Gee, Dad, you're great," Danny bubbles when his father sits down beside him and puts his arm around the boy's shoulder to listen to his problems. Gone was the rough-edged, even abusive ur-Svevo, replaced by this dreamy opposite number who, given the chance, might have played himself in a fifties television show where father always knew best and did nothing but the same. Danny's father in "The Big Hunger" would never be mistaken for John Fante, the real John Fante, who was often as distant from his children as his own father had been from him, but it was a good story nevertheless, in its contrary way as revelatory of its author's wishes, or perhaps regrets, as any he had ever written. In more practical terms, with the $1,500 he got from *Collier's* on top of his weekly MGM salary, Fante was laughing all the way to the bank.

He wasn't laughing when he heard that the old baseless charge of his being a Communist had come back to haunt him. Unwilling to allow the nation's mounting anticommunist mood to derail his career now that it was going somewhere, Fante moved to quash the charge in an open letter.

My attention has been directed to a claim made by one Rena Vale that in 1939 she identified me as being a Communist Party member and described me at that time as being employed by RKO in the Orson Welles unit.

I was employed by RKO in 1939 in the Orson Welles unit. I had heard the name of Rena Vale at that time. I did not meet Rena Vale at that time nor at any time since. I was not a member at any time in my life in any Communist organization nor in any Communist front organization.

I am a Roman Catholic in addition to being an American citizen and it is philosophically and emotionally impossible for me to associate myself with any group that is even remotely identified with Communism or Communist front organizations.

I wish to repeat again—I never have been, I am not now and under no circumstances would or could be a member of any Communist or Communist front organization.

I am strongly and unalterably opposed to any ideology foreign to our American form of Government.

Hounded publicly by the Hearst press for alleged Marxist commitments, Orson Welles had made a similar declaration nearly ten years before. In fact, Fante and Welles had been linked in secret FBI files as early as 1944. In a memo to FBI director J. Edgar Hoover reporting on "the extent of Communist infiltration into RKO Radio Pictures," Fante was wrongly described as "an Italian by birth [who] is believed to be a naturalized citizen. He is . . . very close to Orson Welles, and collaborates with him in scenario writing." Now in 1952 the old besmirchments were resurfacing.

Unlike many others during the height of the Red Scare, Fante never suffered consequences to his livelihood beyond the nerve-rattling annoyance of having to counter false charges in pro forma terms of disavowal ("I never have been, I am not now . . ."). Much less was he driven to such extremes of despair as was his friend Louis Adamic, whose death by a reportedly self-inflicted gunshot Ross Wills termed "assassination by suicide." On the contrary, Fante was entering the most profitable phase of his career, the flip side of his starvation years. As if to underline the fact of his new prosperity, on December 6 Fante signed and returned a Responsible Relative form to the Placer County Welfare Department, agreeing to take upon himself the entire support of his mother. In some ways he was growing up.

For much of the rest of the 1950s John Fante lived the life of a prolific if infrequently produced Hollywood screenwriter. He bought a Jaguar MK VII, the first of a long line of racy sports cars, and he took to playing poker with a Malibu crowd of mostly television writers, producers and directors, among them Jackson Stanley (*The Art Linkletter Show*), Leo Townsend (*The Donna Reed Show*), Buckley Angell (*Rawhide, Maverick*), Quinn Martin (*Desilu Playhouse*) and William Asher (*I Love Lucy*), and including the actor Jack Warden and the chess grand master Herman Steiner. The children were enrolled in parochial school, first at Corpus Christi in Pacific Palisades and later, when it was built, at Our Lady of Malibu, where Fante became a loyal contributor to the parish if not a regular at Sunday mass. On the rare occasions when John did accompany Joyce and the children to church, if he heard something that rankled him during the priest's homily he would stand up and leave to spend the rest of the hour outside, pacing and smoking his pipe. Afterward they would attend Sunday-afternoon barbecues and family softball games at Buckley and Grace Angell's canyon home, sometimes attended by *Los Angeles Times* sportswriter Jim Murray, who lived nearby, as well as the family of *Times* restaurant critic Lois Dwan and her husband Robert Dwan, a writer for Groucho Marx's *You Bet Your Life*. In all, it was a far cry from the way Fante had grown up in Boulder. And yet it was also far from perfect.

Again Joyce's diaries attest to the challenges of married life with a husband who could still sometimes act like one of the children. "I worried most of the day," she wrote in a representative entry. "My mind is like an open wound." And the reason for such anguish? "John lost his temper because Vickie kept talking throughout a t.v. program." Rather than despair over John's ingrained selfishness, however, Joyce set to learning the optimistic habits of mind outlined in Norman Vincent Peale's *The Power of Positive Thinking*. She also began cultivating an interest in psychic phenomena and the occult, an interest that would deepen in the years to come.

As much as they loved the children in their own ways, John and Joyce felt that their lives were being engulfed in the chaos of parenthood. Against the commotion John struggled to keep his concentration intact, and when he failed he could be insufferable. Still, during this time Fante confided to a friend that "the bright moments" were those he spent with his children, while "the sad, confusing, painful, frightening, even horrible hours" were those he spent writing. For her part, Joyce still bore the burden of day-to-day chores ranging from toilet training and feeding to bathing and arbitrating among four very active offspring. But John still had his escapes. Surprisingly, at least one of these involved neither cards nor hard liquor.

The Serra Retreat, a hilltop Malibu sanctuary conducted by Franciscan Friars, provided a respite from the world as well as scholarly support when in late 1953 Fante was researching Christmas customs from Spanish California for a television series he was trying to develop. *Saints Alive* was to be a weekly showcase based on *Butler's Lives of the Saints*, a four-volume source of dramatic material from two thousand years of Christendom. Fante's enthusiasm for this project led one of the friars to translate a traditional Spanish Christmas pageant for the guest from Point Dume,

John Fante, c. early 1950s

The corner of 3rd and Hill, downtown Los Angeles. The Fay Building, where Fante worked in the early 1930s, is at center. Angel's Flight rises in the foreground

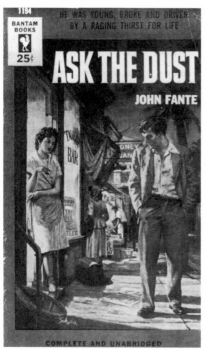

A 1954 Bantam paperback

(*above and below*) Fante in the home office, Malibu

625 South Van Ness Avenue, Los Angeles, a young couple's all-American dream home, paid for by Hollywood and, as the elder Nick first discovered, infested with termites

John Fante at the ranch, Joyce and children in car, mid-1950s

Nick, Dan, Joyce, John, Jimmy, and Vickie, early 1950s

Rancho Fante. 29981 Cliffside Drive, Malibu

Santa Monica Courthouse, March 1952. Fante served as a witness for his friend William Saroyan during divorce proceedings between Saroyan and his wife, Carol Marcus, who had already divorced and remarried once

Fante, second from left, with unidentified
Italian colleagues, Italy, c. 1959

Fante, c. 1960s

John Fante and his mother, Mary
Fante, c. 1960

John Fante and the donkey he kept at the Malibu
ranch for inspiration, c. mid-1960s

Jim, Dan, Vickie, Joyce, and John Fante, late 1960s

Fante, early 1970s

John and Joyce Fante at Vickie's wedding, 1972

John and Joyce Fante, mid-1970s

John Fante, golfer, sports car enthusiast, c. early 1970s

Blind and legless, with Vickie, in a rare moment of joy, c. 1980

John Fante's last signatures

and long after the proposed series had failed to find a home network Fante would keep the basic idea in mind.

To appreciate the depth of Fante's attachment to the lives of the saints we need only glance through the long list of screenplays, teleplays and treatments he wrote in the next several years. Among these are "The Second Thief," a teleplay cowritten with Buckley Angell and based on the legend of the so-called Good Thief, Dismas, who was crucified next to Jesus; *Mother Cabrini*, a feature script cowritten with Joseph Petracca and based on the life of the first American saint, the Italian nun who was Mary Fante's childhood inspiration; "Thorn in the Flesh," a treatment cowritten with Joseph Petracca and based on the life of Margaret of Cortona, patron of fallen women, who "would first have to descend into the hell of herself before she could emerge to glimpse the gates of paradise"; *Father of the Son*, a screenplay written by Fante from a Frank Capra story about Joseph, Mary's husband; "The Divided Horsecloth," a monologue written for television's *The Hour of Saint Francis* exemplifying the virtues of the Fourth Commandment, Honor Thy Father and Thy Mother; "A Hero Returns," a teleplay about an Italian priest who in the last days of World War II persuades a revenge-minded partisan to forgive his enemies; "Gold in the Streets," a treatment based on the autobiography of the Italian priest Mario Borrelli, who dedicated his life to the homeless orphans of postwar Naples; and *The Saint of the Satellites*, another screenplay collaboration with Joseph Petracca based on the life of the levitating thirteenth-century Italian monk St. Joseph of Cupertino.

Only the last of these would be filmed, in 1962, and released as *The Reluctant Saint*. If *Saints Alive* had succeeded, Fante would have gone on writing about holy men and women *in saecula saeculorum*. Among the litany of those listed in his notes were St. John Bosco, St. Joan of Arc, St. Thomas More, St. Perpetua, St. Anthony of Egypt, St. Augustine of Hippo, St. Brendan, St. Columbkille, St. Bede, St. Boniface of Mainz, St. Dominic of the Rosary, St. Francis of Assisi, St. Anthony of Padua, St. Catherine of Genoa, St. John of God, St. Vincent de Paul, and many others. Even as he strayed during these years along the ways of self-centered excess, Fante was possessed with a veneration for the canonized saints of the Church and their triumphs over the world, the flesh and the devil. From his mother he inherited a special devotion to St. Teresa, the Little Flower, whose holy card he kept near his bedside. For years, moreover, he was haunted by a novel about the aging Arturo Bandini, now a resident of Malibu who, in his comical struggle to write a novel about the donkey that carried the expectant Virgin Mary into Bethlehem, buys just such a beast to help inspire himself. Fante would have been familiar with the adage "Hands to work, hearts to God," equating fidelity to one's vocation with correct living. Perhaps he regarded his work, the often all-consuming work of writing, as tantamount to prayer.

Throughout their marriage Joyce would occasionally discover John sitting in an attitude of pure abstraction, staring into the distance, as if he was not even there. These fuguelike intervals could last for minutes or hours, his face as if lighted from within and reflecting an eerie beauty. Afterward he would remember nothing; if asked he would say straightforwardly that he had not been thinking, but rather that he had been in the presence of God. "Here was a man," Joyce later recalled, "who would as soon insult you as reassure you, whose ordinary speech was laced with obscenities, who was from time to time a liar and a petty thief, somehow rising above the limitations of the flesh [to look] at eternity." And every once in a while he would turn a sheet of his fiction over in the platen and continue typing in this other register:

> Dear Blessed Lord,
> Please help me. I am far away from you now, but I am trying to bridge the distance, for you are within me too, Oh Lord, inside my heart, my blood. Come to me with the wonderful clarity of my boyhood. Help me, Lord. For I need it desperately. I am alone now, more than ever. Each day and hour and year brings me deeper into the forest of loneliness, farther away from the days of light. I cannot go blindly through the darkness. I must have help, and there is none to give it but you. I ask you to consider me very seriously. I ask you, I beg you, to know that I cannot live without you. Please come to me, Oh precious God, with your love and kindness, for then will I know true peace and then will I be able to carry on the work thou hast set for me to do.

Such transports were seldom in evidence in Fante's interactions with family, friends and neighbors: certainly not at the twenty-four-hour poker and drinking marathons at Bill Asher's beachside hideaway, nor at the meetings of the Malibu Democratic Club occasionally hosted by Joyce and attended by locals Bill Saroyan, screenwriter Philip Dunne, and Will Rogers, Jr., among others. More likely to be seen in such private and semipublic arenas would be Fante's fun-loving cockiness and his penchant for braggadocio, or, conversely, his prickly aggressive-defensive side, as when he let his contempt be known for poker players and Democrats the likes of Jack Stanley and Philip Dunne because they were mere picture writers and not novelists.

And yet despite his efforts to write prose during this time—he had tried a novel about a boy who wants to run away from home and become a big league ballplayer, and he was beginning to toy with an idea about his father that he would not succeed in turning into a novel for more than twenty years—Fante was nothing during this time if not a picture writer. When the option on his MGM contract was not renewed, Fante signed with Frank Capra Productions in late 1954 to write something called "Hemo the Magnificent." This was an attempt to adapt for film a two-volume opus called *Man in Structure and Function* by the German physician Fritz Kahn. What emerged was an extended dialogue about the heart's role in the circulation of the blood, with a motto from the seventeenth-century English anatomist William Harvey: "When I first tried experimentation for the purpose of discovering the motions of the heart, I found it so truly difficult that I almost believed that it was understood by God alone." Far from conventional screenwriting, Fante's efforts on this project seemed like some strange meditation on mysteries beyond the physical. After all, heart failure had caused his father's death, leaving within his own breast "a deep heart wound that will never disappear." But after six weeks of the experiment—nothing came of this job for Capra— Fante was again on his own.

But not for long. In February 1955 he was hired by Universal Pictures at $1,000 a week to write an oddly hybrid action-romance with distinctly religious overtones—the hero was a former hellrake turned ordained man of God—set against the backdrop of the tuna fishing industry. Two decades earlier, the godless Arturo Bandini of *The Road to Los Angeles* had boasted emptily that he was writing a book, complete with footnotes, on the California fisheries. Now Fante was writing the movie, significantly titled "Miracle of the Fishes," complete with the canneries, labor tensions and dockside gambling dens, which he remembered, and high sea adventures, which he invented. But God was far from absent in Fante's fictional Clipper City: at the end of his fifty-eight-page treatment the cannery owner and workers join union bosses and rugged individualist fishermen in a lusty chorus of "that universal hymn, respected by Catholics and Protestants alike, 'Holy God, We Praise Thy Name.' " Fish story, indeed. The gulf between the grittiness of his serious fiction and the sentimentality of his movie hackwork could be bridged only by someone for whom contradiction was second nature.

The same month that Fante went to work writing "Miracle of the Fishes," radioactive fallout from an atomic bomb test in the Nevada desert drifted as far as Chicago and Upstate New York. An outline for a play that Fante cowrote with Harry Essex about this time dealt with a Jewish Italian-American, his wife and bricklaying father, and the upside-down family romance of building a bomb shelter in the backyard; titled "A Roof over My Head," the piece might as well have been called "Full of Death." Soon the papers would be carrying ominous articles about a place called Vietnam.

All of these horrors must have seemed remote when in April Fante went to the doctor for a routine checkup. But the doctor's findings were far from routine: Fante had diabetes. The good news was that he had been hit by a disease that could be managed by heeding certain dietary restrictions, starting with giving up alcohol, and by taking daily self-injections of insulin. Fante gritted his teeth and went back to work at Universal.

The news was met with less steely resolve in northern California, where Ross Wills had retired after leaving the film business. Carey McWilliams had learned of Fante's condition in a phone conversation with Joyce during a recent swing through Los Angeles. When Carey met Ross at a San Francisco saloon he was visibly dejected over their old companion's fate. "He still couldn't quite believe it," Wills wrote to John about his evening with Carey,

and still less could I. But Joyce had spoken of insulin and diet, etc. The waiter came and went twice without orders, while we considered this absurdity, hoped it would prove a false alarm, or turn into a simple pneumonia or the like, at worst, which you might shuck off in a week or so. Then we got to remembering the occasions when the martinis and cocktails piled up by the dozen, or the empty scotch and bourbon bottles burdened the sink, and we started ordering again and sort of taking on your share. . . . At 9 p.m. I drove [Carey] thru the rain to the airport and poured him on the plane for N.Y. So, if you felt a sort of vicarious amiability about that time . . .

What Fante may have been feeling is anyone's conjecture. Suffice to say that if it was alarm it would not have felt false; nor would it be shucked off in a hurry.

CHAPTER 15

On January 29, 1956, H. L. Mencken died. Saddened though he was by his first champion's passing, Fante could not dwell on the loss, for like some overdue bundle of moneymaking joy, *Full of Life* was stirring again. Columbia Pictures had acquired rights to the novel, and in February Fante began driving in every day from Point Dume to his new office on the studio's North Gower Street lot, where he went to work on the screenplay at the rate of $1,000 per week. Mencken would have approved.

In adapting his novel Fante worked closely with the film's director, former child actor Richard Quine. Back in 1935 Quine had performed in Fante's first credited picture, *Dinky*. Twenty years later mutual friend Bill Asher, on his way to directing over one hundred episodes of *I Love Lucy*, had introduced Fante to Quine. The two hit it off, and Quine had insisted on having Fante as his writer. The association proved congenial.

Fante would spend a day or two writing, then he and Quine would go over the pages together. The only problem was that Fante tended to go off on tangents. He "was re-writing himself too much," Quine would recall. "And I'd say, 'No, John, let's do *Full of Life*,' and he'd say, 'Oh, okay,' " glad to have such a sure guiding hand.

But in writing the screenplay for *Full of Life* Fante did manage to rewrite himself. In the first place, he renamed his writer hero yet again. Originally named Arturo Bandini in *The White Balloon* before being transmogrified into the John Fante of *Full of Life*, the protagonist of Fante's film script of the same story was now Nick Rocco, Nick after Fante's father and Rocco after his favorite pit bull. More to the point, Fante departed from the book by adding a scene in which Nick reads aloud a passage of his novel in progress for his expectant wife, Emily. Notably, the passage Nick reads is in the process of being rewritten; even more so, it is a passage from Fante's own *Ask the Dust*, Arturo's account of his desert foray in search of the lost Camilla: "Across the desolation lay a supreme indifference, the casualness of night and another day, and yet the secret intimacy of those hills, their silent consoling wonder, made living a thing of no importance." Emily interrupts Nick's reading with a suggestion: "Wouldn't it be better if you said 'made *death* a thing of no importance' instead of '*living*'?" To which a thoughtful Nick responds, "Maybe. . . . Yeah, I think you're right. Thanks, honey."

It is an intriguing conjunction of American literary and cinematic histories, this revisionary moment of self-quotation. For one thing, it marks *Full of Life* the film for what it truly is, namely, a quintessential Hollywood product of the 1950s deep inside which beats the heart of a depression-era literary sensibility, layered over with the trappings of middle-class respectability but still beating after all the years. Further, the nesting of fictional voices one inside the other reveals Fante's self-awareness of how far he had come as an autobiographical writer by staying so close to home. His own life had always been his best raw material. Now, since his life was so bound up with the transformative art of his writing, it was natural that his writing should again become raw material, the palimpsest upon which he would continue rewriting his most deeply written, writing self. From such a self-regenerating perspective, death could be a thing of no importance.

On April 18 Fante turned in his final draft of *Full of Life*. Two weeks later MGM president Harry Cohn wrote to thank him for the good work, expressing confidence that they would soon have a fine motion picture. In fact the filming went well from the start. The first-rate cast was headed by Judy Holliday, a star of considerable magnitude since winning an Academy Award in 1950 for her performance as the original dumb blonde in George Cukor's classic *Born Yesterday*. Playing Nick opposite Holliday's blond but now intelligent Emily was Richard Conte, stretching himself comically against the grain of his tough-guy persona. And weighing in as a rotund Papa was Metropolitan Opera luminary Salvatore Baccaloni, making his Hollywood debut and bringing with him a touch of high international culture.

After toiling for so long in Hollywood's minor leagues, this was the big time for Fante. He visited the set only rarely, playing paisano with Conte, but he was a regular at nightly rushes with Quine, who would recall Fante as his best audience, laughing out loud at his own scripted humor. It seems just as likely that Fante also may have been laughing at the strangeness of watching his fantasies take such elaborately sunny shape, especially since the reality behind them—his rage six years earlier in the face of Joyce's pregnancy—had been so morbidly dark.

A shrewdly orchestrated publicity campaign prepared the nation for *Full of Life*. Housewives turned the pages of their morning newspapers from reports of H-bomb tests in the Pacific to six-column spreads featuring the picture of a giant safety pin and the reassurance that "In a CHANGING world, this motion picture is joyously dedicated to the heartwarming fact that BABIES still come in the same old, wonderfully old-fashioned way!" Other ads announced, "All 6 Macy's stores are ready for your baby," accompanied by photo layouts of Judy Holliday's cuffed maternity smock ("Wonderful washable gray Dynel," $17.94) and a selection of other expectant-parent essentials, including an imported English Pedigree Continental coach perambulator ("Proud grandparents' privilege," $69.95), a box of fifty Saybrooke Perfectos ("Papa's passing out the cigars," $7.29), and a fifty-nine-cent jar of Lily White kosher gherkins ("Is she yearning for pickles?"). "You'll like *Full of Life*," Macy's assured its film-going customers, "and we're sure you'll agree with us that it rates an extra round of cheers for treating pregnancy as naturally as . . . a walk in the country."

Released in time for the Christmas rush, *Full of Life* was an immediate smash. *Time* observed that though the film was "sentimental," "John Fante's script, based on his novel, is full of happy touches, and Richard Quine's direction makes the most of them." Knowing a hit when they saw one, the trade papers waxed enthusiastic. *Variety* called the picture "wholly satisfying," while *The Hollywood Reporter* headlined it a "Winner." Equally approving, *Parents' Magazine* conferred upon the movie a coveted Outstanding Family Picture of the Month Award. For Columbia Pictures, Inc., and its assorted business partners, it was a merrily profitable Christmas.

On the day after Christmas southern California's delayed fire season erupted, and Malibu was ablaze. Walls of flame raced across the countryside. Up in the tinder-dry hills the fire lines were visible from Fante's Folly, not to mention the towering clouds of ember-reddened smoke. From where Fante stood in the dwindling daylight upon his verdant and circumscribed acre, it could have been a view from paradise upon some hellish dreamscape envisioned by Hieronymus Bosch. Depending on the devil winds, anything could happen: a stray spark—the right kindling—immolation. What you needed in this world was your ration of God's grace, and gizzard enough to start shoveling when the time came.

Full of Life continued its banner business well into the new year, thanks in part to Fante's own self-promotion. Late in January, for example, he wrote Francis Cardinal Spellman, Archbishop of New York, modestly recommending the picture. "I shall make arrangements to see your picture," His Eminence wrote back to promise, "through . . . the Legion of Decency office."

More heartening still was the February letter from Writers Guild of America president Edmund North informing Fante that his fellow guild members had nominated *Full of Life* as the Best Written American Comedy of 1956. Cowriter (with Andrew Solt) of *In a Lonely Place*, the classic 1950 Nicholas Ray thriller starring Humphrey Bogart as an embittered screenwriter caught up in the coils of poison luck, North knew as well as Fante did the jagged peaks and valleys of the business; but now he joined in congratulating the nominee on receiving this sign of respect from his professional peers.

The Writers Guild of America's Ninth Annual Awards Dinner was held on March 7 at the Moulin Rouge. Wittily distinguishing the writers' evening from the more crowd-pleasing Academy Awards held later in the month, the evening's menu featured as much culinary variety as verbal horseplay, ranging from Pâté de Chayefsky and New England Clam Chandler to Hashed Braus Paganos and Strawbezzerides and Cream. As one of the nominees Fante found himself in distinguished company including Tennessee Williams (for *Baby Doll*, lately denounced from the pulpit of Saint Patrick's Cathedral by none other than Cardinal Spellman); Ernest Lehman (a double nominee for *Somebody Up There Likes Me* and *The King and I*); the blacklisted Michael Wilson (for *Friendly Persuasion*); John Patrick (another double, for *High Society* and *Teahouse of the August Moon*); Abe Burrows (for *The Solid Gold Cadillac*, also directed by Richard Quine); and the team of James Poe, John Farrow and S. J. Perelman (for *Around the World in 80 Days*, which won the award for Best Written Comedy).

Though he had not been nominated for an Oscar, on March 27 Fante climbed back into a tuxedo to escort Joyce to Hollywood's RKO Pantages Theater for the annual Academy Awards ceremonies. Entering to the flash of cameras, Fante guided Joyce to their seats near *80 Days* producer Mike Todd and his new wife Elizabeth Taylor, the latter resplendent in a blinding diamond tiara valued at $25,000. Fante was less interested in Liz's finery, however, than in the year's various writing nominations, which he found notable for reasons ranging from the ridiculous to the wrenching.

In the first place, Jean Paul Sartre was up for *The Proud and the Beautiful*, a French film based on his novel *L'Amour Redempteur*. In a priceless gaffe, the grave existentialist had been pitted in head-to-head competition with the team of Elwood Ullman and Edward Bernds, cowriters of a Bowery Boys laugher mistakenly nominated for Best Motion Picture Story. (At the last moment Ullman and Bernds withdrew themselves from consideration to help spare everyone the embarrassment.) A second reason for Fante's interest in the writing awards was the absence of Michael Wilson's name from the nomination for *Friendly Persuasion*, the Quaker Civil War epic of conscience adapted from Jessamyn West's novel. Though Wilson had won the Writers Guild Award for Best Written American Drama three weeks earlier, the Academy had a policy of refusing to honor anyone tarnished by the blacklist, so Wilson's name had been replaced by the chilling words "Writer ineligible for nomina-

tion under Academy bylaws." Last, and combining the ridiculous and serious elements of these two cases, a person unknown in the small world of
Hollywood screenwriters had been nominated for Best Original Story, the
mysterious Robert Rich.

This nomination interested Fante the most. The film in question was
The Brave One, a King Brothers production about a Mexican boy and his
beloved bull, which fights so courageously in the ring that he is spared
death at the point of the matador's sword by the thunderous acclaim of
the crowd. Fante was unperturbed when Jean Paul Sartre did not win in
his category, nor was he surprised when Michael Wilson's name remained unspoken. But when Deborah Kerr called out Robert Rich's
name for Best Original Story, Fante waited to see who would go up to accept the award. An expectant hush fell over the audience, but no Robert
Rich materialized, and the statuette went unclaimed. Driving home afterward Fante could not help wondering if he should have jumped on-
stage and grabbed the award himself, for he suspected that Robert Rich
was a front—a front for John Fante himself.

Hollywood was still buzzing about the identity of the mystery writer
when two weeks later the story went national in a *Life* magazine article
entitled "Hollywood Whodunit." Claiming to know the answer to the rid-
dle, Orson Welles pronounced in this article that the story was "Robert
Flaherty's invention. I bought it from him and in 1941 I shot thousands of
feet of film on it." Acting on Fante's request four days after the *Life* piece
appeared, Norman Foster sent a copy of "My Friend Bonito" to Margaret
Herrick, Executive Secretary of the Academy of Motion Picture Arts and
Sciences. Foster explained that he and Fante had written the script about
a Mexican boy and his bull for Welles's ill-starred *It's All True*, and he expressed the hope that the Academy would "go into it further" in order to
determine who really deserved the Oscar.

A circuslike atmosphere soon enveloped the controversy, as a mixed
bag of cranks, pranksters and other pretenders rushed to lodge claims of
having written *The Brave One*. (Robert Rich, it turned out, was a nephew
of the King brothers, an impecunious young man who was no Hollywood script master but an unassuming assistant bookkeeper.) For their
part, the Kings remained mum, settling one $750,000 suit out of court
rather than disclose the identity of their writer. For the next several

months, other claimants continued to come forward, some more credible than others; but it was the Fante-Foster claim that was taken most seriously by the Writers Guild, which finally proposed an arbitration to determine the truth of the matter.

It took two years, but by the time the arbitration was proposed the Academy had lifted its ban against honoring victims of the blacklist. Soon afterward Hollywood Ten member Dalton Trumbo, author of the antiwar novel *Johnny Got His Gun* and of many fine films, declared in a KNXT television interview with reporter Bill Stout that he was the real Robert Rich. There then appeared in the office of the WGA's legal counsel a formidable sheaf of affidavits supporting Trumbo's declaration. Corroborating evidence included synopses of eight separate but strikingly similar fictional versions, dating as far back as 1928, of incidents reported in Mexican newspapers where fighting bulls had been spared for their bravery in the ring. The argument was that even if Trumbo's script did parallel "My Friend Bonito," the resemblances were owing not to plagiarism but to the writers' reliance on similar sources that had collectively passed into Mexican folk culture.

Following the presentation of this evidence it appears that Fante and Foster's case never reached arbitration. Trumbo would not receive his Oscar for *The Brave One* until 1975, when, seriously ill, he accepted it at a special ceremony. In all, the case was emblematic of a time—the Time of the Toad, as Trumbo would brand it. In pushing for a decision on the truth of the matter, John Fante and Norman Foster played a role, peripheral but not unimportant, in exposing the absurdity of a terrible era, and in exposing it they helped in some small way to undo its decades-long grip on the nation.

His Columbia salary now a solid $1,250 per week, Fante earned another screen credit in 1957, this one for his work on *Jeanne Eagels*. An earnest bio-pic designed as a vehicle for the voluptuous Kim Novak to wear lacy corsets while playing the actress who in her day, the American 1920s, was as famous for the incandescence of her stage presence in Somerset Maugham's *Rain* as she was notorious for her alcohol and drug addictions, the job was not one that Fante relished. Still, he got to share credit for the screenplay with the well-regarded Sonya Levien, winner of the WGA's prestigious Achievement Award for 1953, and novelist Daniel Fuchs, whose Williamsburg Trilogy (*Summer in Williamsburg*, 1934; *Homage to Blenholt*, 1936; and *Low Company*, 1937) did for Jewish slum life in New York something of what *Ask the Dust* had done for the lower depths of Los Angeles. Fante and Fuchs worked well enough together, though they never became close friends. Perhaps each man recognized a bit too much of himself in the other, both being novelists of the 1930s who were writing novels no longer. But it was a different world than it had been back then, and you wrote what you had to write, even if, like Fante, you often hated it.

Often but not always: for once in a great while the rare studio project came along that engaged Fante's passion to almost the same degree as did his fiction writing. One such project was *The Roses*, a screenplay adaptation of Félicien Marceau's story, to which Fante was assigned after *Jeanne Eagels*. *The Roses* was a love story involving an American sailor and a poor Italian girl amidst the squalor—and the splendor—of postwar Naples. As success breeds success, Fante was again paired with *Full of Life*'s Richard Quine, who was to direct Jack Lemmon in the starring role. Fante's ebullient first draft, dated June 27, showed so much promise that Quine was dispatched to Italy by Columbia chief Harry Cohn to scout locations and test Italian actresses for Lemmon's costar. Within the month Quine was sending for Fante to join him in Naples to continue work on the script.

Although *Full of Life*, the novel, had found its way around the world through translations into Portuguese, German, Swedish, French, Hebrew, Japanese and Italian, Fante had never set foot outside the United States. Reading *The Roses*, however, you would never suspect that its author wasn't intimately familiar with Naples and the Neapolitans. A testament to Fante's ability as a writer to inhabit his material when it engaged him, the intensity of the writing in this script was the truest mark of his enthusiasm for the story: a full-blooded young American in a vibrant city discovers love for a poor girl who has complicating attachments. Though it would be misleading to overemphasize particular connections, the thematic echo that one hears in reading *The Roses* comes from *Ask the Dust*. But unlike the Los Angeles of that novel's setting, which Fante knew from within, the Italian atmosphere of *The Roses* was known to him only indirectly, through his reading and his blood's absorption of his father's sensibilities. But now here he was at age forty-eight, embarked on a flight bound for Copenhagen and from there on to Rome and Naples, about to discover how close he had come in his imagination to the real thing.

In fact he had come very close, and he would come closer still. Though everything in Italy was new to him—"he walked around just looking at everything, devouring it," Quine would recall—there was also the delicious sense of having been here before. Fante moved in next to Quine at the luxurious Hotel Vesuvio, his third-floor room giving onto an ironwork balcony overlooking the Via Carracciolo, the bustling seawall promenade skirting the bay. As soon as he was settled in Fante took to working nights with Quine on the script. Days he spent wandering the streets alone, soaking up every sight and sound and ancient odor of the city. "By September I shall probably be insanely homesick," he wrote Joyce soon after arriving; but for the time being he was captivated by his new surroundings.

No part of Naples captivated him more than the poor section of Monte Calvario, to which he returned again and again. As part of a well-heeled contingent of American filmmakers—in Copenhagen Fante had gone sightseeing with director Stanley Donen, while at the Rome airport he had been royally received by representatives of both MCA and Columbia—Fante put in appearances at a number of tony luncheons and soirees, including one at a yacht club where he got drunk and insulted an Italian duke over a literary disagreement. But it was to the slums of Monte Calvario that Fante found himself drawn back, enthralled by the people's poverty. There he moved through lightless alleys and basement stalls, past swarming tenements and pitiful shacks as if to witness the kind of life that might have been his had his father not boarded the steamship *Friedlander* half a century before.

Now that he was in his father's homeland, however, Fante drank it up not only for the mesmerizing power of its poverty but also for its breathtaking beauty. With Quine he made location-scouting excursions to the islands of Capri and Ischia, and in the company Fiat he drove down the coast past Castellamare, Sorrento, Amalfi, and into Positano, through the lava-rich farm country beneath Mount Vesuvius. He attended mass in a little church on the Via Santa Lucia, finding the central rituals familiar and the incidental differences fascinating, and he ate as he had never eaten before. It was all enough to make him muse about buying an apartment and reestablishing his family in this beautiful and tragic country.

Most fascinating were the people he encountered. From hotel and restaurant workers, to members of the ruined aristocracy employed in various preproduction capacities, to the poorest orphans on the street—one sickly nine-year-old by the name of Vincenza became his favorite—Fante found the Italians "civilized, sophisticated, generous, kind, polite, gallant, and terribly brave people." Only the rich did he detest. And as for the women of Naples, "each with the face of the mother of God," Fante claimed to have only admiration. Asked if Fante remained "the family man" while helping to interview countless young Italian actresses, Richard Quine answered, "Oh yes, very much so." After Fante himself was interviewed for an article in a Naples newspaper, a distant family connection appeared in the person of "a fine old gentleman" who came calling to introduce himself as the grandson of Nick Fante's Uncle Mingo. In this relation's account the notorious Uncle Mingo had not died on the gallows but rather had escaped to America—an intriguing twist in the family legend.

Aside from such diversions, the seven weeks Fante spent in Naples were devoted mostly to work. By August 11 he had written fifty new pages; six days later he had written seventy-four, with sixty or so more to go. The strain of being confined to the hotel working long, intense hours, and—surprisingly—the sadness of being separated from his wife and children were beginning to tell on him, as was the incessant begging whenever he stepped outside. At first he had showered the urchins of Monte Calvario with lire simply for the asking, but now he was being chased through the streets by one shoeshine "boy" in particular, a wrinkled old man with rotten teeth and a goiter who would not desist until Fante had bought him a new pair of shoes. And so Fante took to staying in his hotel room, working even harder on the script, which in spite of it all was turning out extremely well. No matter that his stomach was going bad and his throat always hurt, for he was finishing a script he could be proud of when the film was finally released.

Only it was not to be. One day Quine received a telegram: "COME HOME IMMEDIATELY HARRY COHN." Indignant, Quine fired back the even terser "WHY?" To which came Cohn's reply ending all such small talk: "BECAUSE I SAID SO." And that was the end of *The Roses*.

Fante would later doubt the explanation that Quine gave him, namely, that Cohn had run out of money and could not afford to put another picture in production that fiscal year. Rather, Fante suspected that Cohn had cut off support when Quine began leaving the producer out of crucial preproduction developments. Whatever the case, Quine and Fante were soon on a plane flying home. "Fante was shattered," Quine recalled. "He was broken-hearted. And it was a *good* script. It really was."

Interviewed the following summer by a local Malibu reporter about his Naples experience, Fante would sound a philosophic note. "[F]ailure is good," he said. "Not the kind that crushes you, but the kind that inspires you, the kind that drives you on. Failure is a challenge. It is healthy. In a field where all you need is a paper and pencil, what have you got to lose? I like to fail. I learn by failure."

In the case of *The Roses* Fante had not failed, but perhaps that was why he needed to assert such heroic levels of resilience. Thirteen-year-old Danny Fante's scrapbook for 1958 confirms this view in two separate entries, both accompanied by clippings from local newspaper sports sections. In the March 8 running of the Santa Anita Derby a colt by the name of Silky Sullivan staged a rousing come-from-behind victory, about which Danny observed: "This derby is one of the most fabulous derbies my dad says he has ever seen because of the heart attack horse coming from 10 lengths behind to win." Then on December 10 veteran fighter Archie Moore defeated Yvon Durelle in a thrilling light-heavyweight championship bout at the Montreal Forum. "My father said that this is a good fight for this reason. Archie was down three times in one round. And for a guy to finish a fight like that would have been a feat. But to win by a KO no less is a terrific feat for a man of his age."

It was no coincidence that between these two emblematic sporting events Fante teamed up with Harry Essex, screenwriter of such quintessential fifties what-iffers as *Creature from the Black Lagoon* and *It Came from Outer Space*, to cowrite a teleplay called *The Comeback*. From his own career in the boxing ring Fante knew what it was to be knocked down and to get back up again. A man of his age, he was still in there bobbing and weaving.

The Comeback was not Fante's only collaboration with Harry Essex, nor was it unusual for Fante to seek out other writers to work with when it came to the grind of speculative screenwriting. Denied the pleasures of prose by the restrictions of the medium—"I have never met a person in the film business who enjoys reading a screenplay," says no less an authority than Francis Ford Coppola—Fante turned regularly to the expedient of teamwork in order to keep himself going. Joyce Fante's files are filled with dozens of such ventures—outlines, treatments, teleplays, features—the vast majority of them never produced and relatively few ever purchased. A partial listing of titles unmentioned so far suggests the staggering amount of time Fante used up in harness with other writers who were content to divide their credits: *Satin Dolls*, *The Rialto Kid*, *How to Kill a President*, *The Walls of Heaven*, *The Strange Adventures of Dr. Jackal and Mr. Hide*, *The Betrayed*, *The Golden Gown* and *The Chicanos*, all with Harry Essex; *The Great Diamond Hoax*, with James L. Henderson; *The Dark Laughter*, *The Two Lives of Sam Salem*, and *Dancer on the Run*, with Frank Fenton, and *The Dark Mountain*, with Frank Fenton and Jack Leonard; *Saint Anthony's Forty Blondes*, with Carey McWilliams, rewritten as *The Hispano Blondes*, with Buckley Angell; *Chinese Gordon* and *Thunder in the South*, with Buckley Angell, and *The Ballad of Whistler's Mother*, with Angell, based on a story by Frank Fenton; *Two for the Money*, with Hernani Monte; *Gloria in Excelsior*, with Jo Pagano; *The New World of Carmen Columbo*, with Leo Townsend; *The Lawbringers* and *The Fabulous Feud* with Edmund Morris.

As depressing as this list is—so *Thunder in the South* sold for $3,250 to John Wayne's Batjac Productions, which never developed it: so what?— can anyone charge that Fante denied the world masterpieces because he poured so much of his life into the sinkhole of Hollywood spec writing? The question is an open one, and vexing. In considering it we will do well to remind ourselves that any masterpiece is a gift, as well as its own justification. That said, it is reasonable to wonder, as Fante himself sometimes did, what might have emerged from his typewriter had he never gone to work for Hollywood, the stories and the novels and the sheer prose of it all, and yes, maybe another masterpiece or two. It is a tantalizing thought but in the end that's all it is, a thought, perhaps a wish, but far removed from the life that John Fante lived.

Between studio assignments in June of 1958, Fante leased an office at 309 Santa Monica Boulevard by the old Santa Monica Mall. There he set to work on "Papa," a pilot script for television that he hoped to sell as a weekly half-hour series. In essence, "Papa" was an ode to the memory of Fante's father, fictionalized here as Vico Ramponi, who came to America "from the hills of Vesuvius with a passion for a new life in a land wild with opportunity[, who] worked like a horse, dreamed like a poet, and spoke English like a Dago." With Bill Asher interested in producing, Fante's hopes were again high; but in the end this project too came to nothing.

By September Fante was back on a studio payroll. This time it was 20th Century-Fox, the head of which, Buddy Adler, had signed Fante to adapt Mary Renault's best-selling novel *The King Must Die*, again for $1,250 a week. Adler had taken over the studio in 1956 when 20th Century-Fox cofounder Darryl F. Zanuck had resigned as head of production in order to move to Paris and produce his own films. Long a believer in strong screenplays, the legendary Zanuck summoned Fante to New York the following February for a private viewing of his son Richard Zanuck's first produced film, *Compulsion*, starring Fante's former boss Orson Welles. After drinks and dinner at the Blue Ribbon with Carey McWilliams, Fante and his old friend appeared for the screening, and Fante promptly fell asleep, snoring loudly enough through most of the movie for everyone, including Zanuck, to hear. Fortunately Zanuck was preoccupied, "all eyes and ears" for Juliette Greco, the free-spirited French beauty who during this time owned the monopoly on Zanuck's attention.

Bad manners aside, Fante made a good impression on Zanuck, who was not the only big producer courting the writer's talents. In a bit of movie mogul rivalry, Italian producer Dino DeLaurentiis was lobbying for Fante to come to Italy to write not one screenplay but two, novel adaptations of Ulrich Mohr's *Atlantis* and Bernhardt Rogge's *Under Ten Flags*. But by the end of May 1959 Fante was flying not to Rome but to Paris, where he checked into the Hotel Prince de Galles at 33 Avenue George V. There he would spend the next six weeks writing a script for Zanuck called alternately *High Tide* or *The Fish Don't Bite*, and, as he had done in Naples the year before, seizing every opportunity to roam the city.

Initially Fante found Paris less to his liking than Naples. On the night of his arrival he got so drunk wandering alone from bar to bar that he "lost track of all time and locale," waking the next morning to discover that he had been rolled for $400 in traveler's checks. Miraculously, his blood sugar level remained within bounds, as he was relieved to find when he checked. Still, it was not the most promising way to start out his stay in the City of Light. Thereafter he made an honest effort to stay off the booze, though in a culture where people drank wine and liquor instead of water he had to try especially hard.

Joyce came to stay with him for two weeks, which helped. Since Fante was immersed in writing, Joyce spent much time on her own, shopping and sightseeing before joining him for dinners with Zanuck, Juliette Greco, William Saroyan, and a revolving cast of others. Saroyan had recently moved to Paris under contract to Zanuck to write a play for Juliette Greco, and he was staying in the hotel next door to Fante's. The situation proved a little too close for comfort, however, with Zanuck sharing his doubts with Fante about Saroyan's play, and Saroyan confiding that Greco was finished with Zanuck, and both Zanuck and Saroyan going on about how important Fante's script was going to be. For Fante it all added up to an uncomfortable feeling that maybe something was not quite right.

The script should have been the last of his worries. Once again it was a love story and once again Fante was producing a fine piece of work. It was another romantic comedy set outside the United States, this time in Spain, about an earnest youth returning home to his coastal village after two years at the university, only to discover that in his absence his ageless fisherman father, long a widower, has married a fiery young gypsy girl the same age as the son. Fante kept the complications charmingly off-kilter, crafting a conclusion that soared into the realm of the poetic.

Having finished the script but still on Zanuck's payroll, Fante found himself at loose ends. To occupy the time he wrote a short story, something he had not done in nearly a decade. "The First Time I Saw Paris" turned out to be a small gem. In this story Fante's alter-ego narrator encounters not the romance so often associated with the city but rather unspeakable tragedy. Walking along the Avenue George V one evening, he comes upon an old woman, "the oldest and lousiest and ugliest human being I ever saw," weeping inconsolably against the wall of the French Red Cross. He tries to evade the unexpected roil of emotions by walking away, tossing back a couple of highballs, and hauling out the conventional suspicions—"it's a racket, she's a beggar you dope." But when these defenses fail he returns to find the woman still standing there weeping, invisible to the hurrying throngs. He overcomes his revulsion and tries awkwardly to help, but there is nothing that he can do, for as he learns from a passing Frenchman whom he begs to intercede, "She wishes nothing, except to be alone with her pain."

Fante sent "The First Time I Saw Paris" to Art Buchwald, who was then writing a Paris column for the *International Herald Tribune*, but the story would remain unpublished until after Fante's death. Meanwhile, other writing possibilities proliferated. Anthony Quinn's agent approached to ask if Fante was available; Dino DeLaurentiis was still courting Fante to come to Italy; and an American producer, Charles Feldman, proposed that Fante write a screenplay adaptation of Nelson Algren's novel *A Walk on the Wild Side*. About the only person who did not inquire about Fante's writing services in Paris that summer was Elvis Presley, who was also staying at the Hotel Prince de Galles. Every evening the street outside would fill with teenagers waiting for a glimpse of their idol, whom Fante found "quite a nice kid" when the two were introduced.

In the end Paris, like Naples before it, proved a fiasco for Fante. In a doomed effort to regain the romantic interests of Juliette Greco, Zanuck opted to produce the play that he had hired Saroyan to write for her, and *The Fish Don't Bite* was canceled and forgotten. Fante missed California—he had consoled himself in Paris by writing frequently to his youngest son Jimmy about the pitching exploits of Sandy Koufax, Don Drysdale and Johnny Podres of the Dodgers, who had moved from Brooklyn to Los Angeles the previous year and were now on their way to winning the 1959 World Series—and so it was without regrets that he left Paris on the ninth of July. He laid over in the muggy heat of New York for a day and a half, staying at the Gotham and joining Carey McWilliams for dinner and a long walk up the embankment of the Hudson River all the way to the yacht harbor. And when he returned home to Malibu he spent $445 on a deluxe Exercycle, determined to work off the lingering effects of his Paris sojourn.

In September Fante went to work on *A Walk on the Wild Side* for Charles Feldman's Famous Artists Productions. Ten years earlier Feldman had produced A *Streetcar Named Desire*, and this was his chance to repeat that film's success with another hard-hitting tale of love gone wrong set in steamiest New Orleans. Thirty-five pages into the script, however, Fante found himself at an impasse, baffled as to how he should proceed. Then one day in a Santa Monica bank he ran into Edmund Morris, a former playwright turned screenwriter whom he had met at Columbia while working on *Full of Life*. Fante knew that Morris had had a hit on the London stage with his play *The Wooden Dish*, which Fante appreciated for its honest portrayal of an aging father and his son. Fante was also aware that Morris happened to know Nelson Algren from their days together with Studs Terkel in the WPA's Illinois Writers' Project. Standing in line at the bank Fante told Morris about the problem he was having adapting Algren's novel into a script. Sympathetic to Fante's plight, Morris agreed to help break the news gently so that instead of firing Fante, Charley Feldman would hire Morris to collaborate. The plan worked, and soon the two writers had rented an office in Santa Monica's Wilshire Professional Building and were setting to work on a fresh adaptation.

Like every other writer who has described working with Fante, Edmund Morris recalls their collaboration fondly. "I never heard a harsh word from him. And you know, you collaborate, you sometimes disagree, but our disagreements were gentle. . . . We didn't walk out on each other, we didn't call each other names, we didn't throw paper or typewriters. We worked and we had a common goal. And it was a pleasure working with him."

The goal that they shared was a challenging one, not least of all because of the Code-breaking nature of Algren's novel, set in a depression-era whorehouse. Complicating matters was Feldman's insistence that there be a major role for the French actress Capucine, an insistence matched in degree of difficulty by that of Joan Cohn, Harry Cohn's widow, that the starring role of Texas drifter Dove Linkhorn go to her husband-to-be, the Lithuanian-born English Jew Laurence Harvey. (Fante and Morris had no way of knowing that a third major role, that of the sluttish Kitty Twist, would go to newcomer Jane Fonda in her first major screen appearance.) Nevertheless, the writers attacked the adaptation with relish. Chief among their innovations—and daring for its time—was the lesbian angle, which Barbara Stanwyck would play to the hilt as the brothel's hard-boiled madame, helping to make the resulting film something of a camp classic among later gay and lesbian audiences.

Studs Terkel later told Edmund Morris that when Nelson Algren saw the film, directed with a heavy hand by Edward Dmytryk and released in 1962, the novelist said, "I've been raped." Reviewers agreed. Despite a largely negative reception—Saul Bass's stunning credits sequence earned the only consistent praise—the film helped clear the way for the increasing frankness with which Hollywood movies would treat sex in the later 1960s. Vexed by all the sexual and moral ambiguities, the Legion of Decency assigned the film to a "Separate Classification," commenting that "[a]lthough the theme of redemption of a prostitute is moral, numerous elements of treatment require caution for a mass audience." Newspaper ads for the film foreshadowed today's ratings system with a discreet warning in the lower left-hand corner: "This is an adult picture! Parents should exercise discretion in permitting the immature to see it."

When they finished A Walk on the Wild Side, Fante and Morris continued working for Charles Feldman, adapting S. N. Behrman's play The Cold Wind and the Warm for $15,000. The collaboration was again a happy one, and when it was finished Fante and Morris cowrote a spec television pilot for a series based on Mark Twain's Roughing It. Nothing came of either of these latter endeavors, however, and two more writing projects with Fante's name on them were consigned to the death of oblivion.

But life went on, and as had long been the case with Fante, life and writing were inextricable. His son Nick was now a senior at Santa Monica High School, and though Nick had his wild side—an adolescent overlay, Joyce was convinced, to disguise a deeply warm and caring sensibility—he was showing signs of interest in both writing and art. As for Fante, he wanted only to do right by a son who must have reminded him of himself at a younger age. So that when an admirer of Fante's early works wrote to ask how the author's attitudes toward writing and education had developed since 1942, when the autobiographical blurb in Twentieth Century Authors had stated flatly, "Hated school, all the time," Fante fell into a thoughtful mood.

I don't know whether or not I can satisfactorily answer your letter of March 11. Times change—glands change—there is death in the world, and life—children to be born, books unwritten—love and hate and aspiration and despair. My statement in Twentieth Century Authors now seems embarrassingly crude, headstrong and rather gamey. Perhaps it has to do with the boldness of phrasing, the arrogant youthfulness, the cockiness of myself at that time. But I hasten to add that fundamentally my thinking remains unchanged about a college education in relation to creative writing.

I will say this: a high school education *is* necessary. A college education is *not*. But so much depends on the teacher. Better that future writers have no formal schooling at all than be chopped down by inferior teachers. And what is an inferior teacher? One who is afraid of the new, the daring, the challenging. Conversely, a good teacher welcomes the new, the daring, and anything that tries to break fresh ground.

But philosophies are no good unless one is ready to live by his own. For myself, the father of four children, two sons in high school, I am holding fast to what I believed in the Thirties. My oldest son is a senior at Santa Monica High School. He has some talent for writing. And he has my permission to quit school when he terminates at Samohi. I make only one condition—that he goes out in the world and earns his bread by the sweat of his arms, and that he makes no attempt to publish until he is thirty. No man under thirty has any sense, and damned few have any wisdom past that. But there is such a thing as publishing too young. Most of the dreadful stuff in print today comes from young people who are merely talented. That is not enough. Humanity, humility, reverence for one's fellow man, respect for women and the first real grasp of God does not come until thirty, or even later. By then a writer is ready to write. And all the days of his life he should be reading, as faithfully as his partaking of food; reading, watching, listening. It seems to me that college is a poor substitute for this kind of preparation. If Hemingway, Faulkner, Saroyan, Steinbeck had all walked away with B.A.'s it would have been a great loss to literature. It is a matter of over-compensation, and I would rather have written A Farewell to Arms than attained the highest scholastic eminence a university has to offer.

What I have said here has no bearing, of course, on the student whose inclinations are not in the sphere of writing, which is peculiarly personal and not subject to the discipline and training needed in other professions. Medicine, science, law, and most all the other professions require heavy doses of textbooks and classroom training. The giant enterprise known as colleges are built specially to grind out these professionals. But they are calculated to destroy a first rate artist.

Your continuing interest in my earlier writings is something that gives me great personal satisfaction. Thank you for telling me about it, and good luck with your kids.

He might not be writing the same kind of stuff that in the hungry years of the 1930s had helped shape his philosophy, but at the dawn of the 1960s he could remember how he felt, and still feel it. As for young Nick, like his father before him he would have to find his own way. Fante was not going to push him. By this time in his life Fante knew that there were plenty of forces in the world calculated to destroy artists. He would do his best not to do that to his own son. It was true that he had hated school and failed at it repeatedly, but even a college drop-out could try to become a good teacher.

On August 2, 1960, Fante finally succumbed to the blandishments of Dino DeLaurentiis. Signing a contract for ten weeks—$15,000 plus the lire equivalent of $250 weekly for expenses—Fante flew first-class to Rome to work on a screenplay called *Black City*. For the third time in a row, Fante found himself in Europe working on a story that brought out his best as a screenwriter. The story featured Don Pepino Navarra, the so-called King of Naples, an Americanized Italian who, after working as a bricklayer in Chicago, returns to Italy to become the biggest black-market boss in Europe during World War II. With the war almost over, this crooked but benevolent godfather is chosen by the Bishop of Naples to go to Rome to recover the jewels of the city's patron, San Genarro, which for the last several years have been locked in a Vatican vault to protect them from the depredations of war. The story follows Navarra's picaresque quest to recover the jewels, including an encounter with a bandit closely resembling Fante's great-great-uncle Mingo, and culminating in the good thief's experience of grace during the miracle of the liquefaction of the martyr San Gennaro's blood, the annual recurrence of which Fante traveled to Naples to witness on September 19.

Rod Steiger was DeLaurentiis's first choice to play Navarra. Soon after Fante's arrival in Rome, the flamboyant producer—pound for pound and inch for inch Fante's match—dispatched Fante and the film's assigned director, Duilio Coletti, by plane to confer with the actor, then staying in Berlin. After talking with Steiger, whom Fante found vain, Fante and Coletti hired a cab to take them through the Brandenburg Gate so that they could see East Berlin. "To hell with Marxian dogma," Fante remarked after this side trip. "What the eye looks upon in E. Berlin answers all questions. You get very uneasy driving those deadly quiet streets. . . . In all the world there is no Sunday afternoon like it."

Such was not the case in Rome. Now that he was living there, Fante found the Eternal City "almost too perfect," even more beautiful than Paris. See Rome and die: so said the proverb. But in addition to its beauties Rome was swarming with life, for 1960 was the year of the Rome Summer Olympics. Oddly enough for such a diehard sports fan, Fante remained unmoved by the Olympic spirit, preferring instead to follow the Dodgers from afar in the *International Herald Tribune*. He settled into an apartment at Via Rusticucci 14, where Raphael was said once to have lived, and with a view of Bernini's colonnades and Saint Peter's Square he plunged into the work of writing.

Joyce did not come to visit John this time but their eldest son Nick did, in part to distance himself from the bad influence of his crowd of friends. As thoughtful as he was intelligent, Nick had always been a high-spirited boy. Now, however, since failing to complete high school despite his father's wishes, Nick had been drinking too much, driving too fast— following a serious accident his license had been revoked—and in general courting trouble with his increasingly irresponsible behavior. He arrived in Rome on August 13 and moved into his own room in the big apartment; but because Fante was working hard on *Black City*, father and son saw little of each other apart from the suppers they shared. They took in an outdoor opera together, dined with an Italian set designer known as The Cricket, who moonlighted as a robber of Etruscan graves, and visited the Catacombs, where the bones of countless Christians lay. For the most part, however, Nick was on his own, reading *Lolita*, hanging out in the

Piazza Barberini ("where all the hookers hang out") and gravitating toward the Roman equivalents of his rowdy Malibu companions. When the date Fante arranged for Nick with the beautiful nineteen-year-old sister-in-law of another Italian film worker turned out to be chaperoned by a stern-faced old woman in black, Nick hightailed it out of Rome for Madrid.

Fante was writing steadily but this script was a difficult one, and De-Laurentiis and Coletti kept questioning the pages he submitted. Twice burned in his previous European writing stints, Fante now dared "not grow optimistic" about the script's chances, aware how it was "with the hopes of writers in this treacherous medium." Still, he kept "grinding away," and had completed 127 pages by September 5. The temperature in Rome was over 100 degrees during the days and Fante missed his swimming pool. He also missed the younger children, but most of all he missed Joyce, who tantalized him with the news that she had been shopping again at Frederick's of Hollywood. "Goodnight my love," he closed one letter. "I can see you now in that mirror, and if you're not careful I'll pop right through it!"

To help fill this absence, when he was not writing Fante walked all around the city. Every corner he turned offered "a dash of the marvelous, an elegance, a dignity" which he longed to share with Joyce, and he bought and sent home for her many fine gifts of gloves and sweaters and jewelry. After several weeks' resistance he also finally succumbed to the grandeur of the Vatican. On first arriving in Rome he had been repulsed by the spectacle of the Sunday-mass multitudes scurrying around the sacred site like so many observant mice. But after devoting some solitary time to the majesty of it all, he grew so enthused that he composed a "stirring letter" about his experience and sent it to a friend, Father Mark Falvey of Our Lady of Malibu. Soon he heard back that the priest was going to read the letter aloud to his whole congregation—at Sunday mass!

Though he had been making good money Fante was increasingly concerned about his future livelihood as a writer. As he explained to Joyce, "The complexities of film writing today, with the decline of production in Hollywood and the resulting bulge in Europe, are almost too much to think about." Once again he was considering the possibility of relocating the family to Europe, if only he could get a decent contract instead of these piecemeal salaried jobs. But the contract system was becoming a thing of the past, replaced by the traveling-hired-gun way of doing business which Fante was helping to define. More often than not he felt less like a regular wage earner than a far lower kind of worker, a faceless member of the eternal laboring masses: "So we bend our necks to the yoke," he wrote to Joyce near the end of his stay in Rome, "grinding out cigarettes and cars and phonograph records for a breed that asks for nothing except our very lives." He ended this letter by signing himself "John S. (Slave) Fante."

Before Fante left Rome in the middle of October, word reached him that the script he had cowritten about Saint Joseph of Cupertino might be filmed, though nothing, as ever, was certain. He lunched with director Michael Curtiz, of *Casablanca* fame, in Rome to prepare for a film about a far more popular saint, Francis of Assisi. Things in Hollywood were lousy, Curtiz reported, all the more reason for Fante to say yes when Curtiz asked him to fix a scene in the Francis of Assisi script, an hour's work for $350. After all, you never knew when your next job would be your last.

In his meandering walks around the city in the last three months Fante had given himself over to "the color of Rome," a rose-and-gold tint suffusing the ruins of the Eternal City that lent it "an almost suffocatingly beautiful aspect." During these walks he had also experienced a troublesome recurrent pain in his left foot. His diet in Rome had been a dangerous one for a diabetic, "too heavy, too much oil, too much pasta." Now he was returning home to an uncertain future, past the age of fifty and getting no younger in a business that cherished only youth. On October 10 he walked into a sporting goods store on Via Principe Eugenio and purchased a .22 caliber automatic Beretta handgun and one cartridge clip. He had seen Rome.

Whatever plans Fante may have had for his .22 Beretta were thwarted when the gun was seized at Customs in New York as a violation of the International Traffic-in-Arms Act. Airliner hijacking having yet to become the terrorist's statement of choice, Fante was simply questioned by airport security and sent on his way. He spent one night at the Airport Hotel Continental battling jet lag, then flew home to Malibu.

To say that Fante was now a failed gun smuggler would be to put too fine a point on the incident, but the question of failure would soon be dominating his thoughts once again. In the middle of November his oldest son Nick disappeared, leaving a note imbued with a gnawing sense of failure—Nick had been running the mechanical horse-race attraction on the pier at Pacific Ocean Park, a manifest case of underachievement—and asking his parents not to try to discover his plan of action or whereabouts. Hoping to communicate a father's concern without setting off any alarms, Fante wrote to a friend of the family who he hoped might know something about Nick's flight. "We . . . want to tell him that whether he fails or not in this world is not important to us. Success is too vague a challenge. Maybe even failure is better; certainly it is more beautiful." Before the year was over Nick had found his way into that perennial refuge for the lost and confused, the United States Navy, and father and son were exchanging affectionate letters, John among other things reminding Nick of his Sunday mass obligation, and Nick wrestling honestly with the advice. But Nick's troubles were not over yet.

With his holdover reputation from *Full of Life* as wholesome family-oriented writer, Fante signed a contract on December 19 with Paramount Pictures for $1,500 per week to work on a Debbie Reynolds confection, *My Six Loves*. He remained on payroll twenty weeks laboring through six drafts and suffering for his sins, for this was the most despicable assignment he had ever completed, a cloying farce about an actress who adopts six abandoned waifs. One day he visited the set, only to come home in a rage at having helped perpetrate such trash. (The resulting film would be described as drowning "in its own treacle" and would be singled out for its "cliche-ridden script.") Fante hated everything about it except the paycheck.

A strange time was taking shape. The Russians had launched a dog into orbit and now President John F. Kennedy was exhorting the nation to believe that within the decade an American would walk on the moon. If only indirectly, these Cold War thrusts and parries helped propel *The Saint of the Satellites* into production. In an age filled with images of supersophisticated rocket shots and missile launchings, what better time could there be to tell the story of a medieval monk so childlike in his faith that he levitated during prayer, thus gaining the name several centuries later of the Patron Saint of Flyers? With his cowriter Joe Petracca, Fante split the $25,000 that their script fetched from the independent team of producer Sam Weiler and director (once again) Edward Dmytryk.

Cameras were soon rolling on location in Italy. In an intriguing overlay of screen personae, the starring role of Joseph of Cupertino, the village-idiot-turned-saint, went to Maximilian Schell, fresh from his Academy Award–winning performance as the defense attorney for Nazi war criminals in Stanley Kramer's *Judgment at Nuremberg*. When the film appeared (as *The Reluctant Saint*) in theaters the following December, opinions were mixed, ranging from "embarrassingly inept" to "ultimately touching." There was nothing mixed about the response of the National Catholic Theater Conference, however, which honored the film with its Religious Drama Award, sending Fante a plaque and his producer a statuette of Saint Genesius the Comedian.

Early in 1962 Fante contracted to write yet another religiously oriented story, this one for the Gene Kelly television series (based on the Bing Crosby movie) *Going My Way*. In "A Man for Mary," parish priests Kelly and Leo J. Carroll persuade a beautiful and sexy actress to forsake her career and marry a widower with a houseful of children. The comedy earned Fante $6,000, a small part of which went to purchase a copy of *Justine, or Good Conduct Well Chastised*. From *A Walk on the Wild Side* to *The Reluctant Saint*, from Father O'Malley to the Marquis de Sade: Fante was swinging from one pole of the emotional and aesthetic compass to the other, hesitating no longer before contradicting himself than he did before trading in one barely used car after another. Between 1960 and 1962 Fante bought and sold a Citroën, a Porsche, a Chrysler, a Dodge, a Studebaker, a Volkswagen, a Pontiac, a Chevrolet, a Metropolitan, a Cadillac and a Packard. The last of the Pacific Electric Red Cars had been removed from service in 1961, the final vestige of a saner Los Angeles which for all its suburban spread had been a more connected place to live than the increasingly alienated metropolis of isolated commuters, John Fante of Point Dume among them. It was at this time that Fante turned briefly to an abortive foray into pornography, sketching out and then abandoning a highly derivative tale of two naughty sisters named Juliette and Justine. Just as scattered were Fante's professional writing prospects at this time. In the guise of a friendly "pending projects" list, a memo from his agent at International Management Associates suggests the dangerous degree of fragmentation looming over any effort Fante might make to gather his concentration:

1. *Thorn in the Flesh*—property under consideration as vehicle for either Gina Lollobrigida or Shirley MacLaine.
2. *Papa*—Idea for a television series submitted to Don Fedderson.

3. A *Man Is Greater Than a Town*—Potential screenplay at Universal with Gordon Kay.

4. *Seven Arts*—Assignment pending subject to Ray Stark's approval.

5. Hecht-Hill-Lancaster—Possible project with respect to one of several reactivated stories.

6. Ross Hunter—Both *Next Time We Live* and *Chalk Garden* definite possibilities for assignment.

7. Irving Briskin—Considering assignment for *Scandal's Child*.

8. Frank Ross—Considering assignment for rewrite of Norman Vincent Peale script.

9. 20th Century-Fox—Discussions for two projects coming up the first part of January, *Illicit* and *Fate Is the Hunter*.

10. The Hitchcock Presents TV producers are awaiting submittal of your original story or idea for your possible assignment in adapting it.

11. Bud Kay of Four Star Theater is awaiting a submittal of original story or idea so that he may discuss with you your assignment to adapt it.

12. Goodson-Todman—You are being considered to write in connection with the Richard Boone Anthology series.

13. Carl Stuckie of Warner Bros. TV is awaiting activation of the series entitled *Ready for the People* which should occur sometime in January, 1963, at which time he will consider your assignment to it.

14. *Sand Pebbles*—Robert Wise, producer for the Mirisch Company, is considering your assignment to write the screenplay.

15. *Spinner*—You are being considered by Walt Disney Productions to write the screenplay.

It was an impossible juggling act of unrealities, a subjunctive whir of high-wire agent-speak. Fante had recently spent a month at the Park-Sheraton Hotel in New York struggling to adapt Rodolfo Sonego's *An Italian in America* for Dino DeLaurentiis. While in New York Fante capitalized on the opportunity of seeing Carey McWilliams as often as possible, frequently joining him for dinner (where both old friends typically drank too much), strolling around Greenwich Village, and helping to celebrate the publication of Iris McWilliams's novel *Jeeney Ray*. But the experience of working for DeLaurentiis again proved difficult. Before the script was finished Fante's inability to satisfy the producer's demands resulted in his firing, leaving him dependent on the anxiety-inducing insubstantialities catalogued in the memo from his agent. In short, Fante's fears about the changing nature of the movie business were turning out to be all too true, and there seemed to be little that he could do to calm them.

Then on March 12, 1963, John's mother died. For the past several years Mary Fante had been living with John's family at their home in Malibu, where she had become an increasingly feeble old lady. As time passed her presence in the house had become a burden especially on Joyce, who lived up to her role as dutiful daughter-in-law as best she could. But when Mary deteriorated to the point that round-the-clock care became necessary, she was admitted to the Santa Monica Lodge Convalarium, where she succumbed to a coronary occlusion. John made the arrangements for his mother's body to be shipped north to Roseville, and then he grimly followed for the funeral and interment at Roseville Cemetery next to Nick, the bane and the great love of both their lives.

Faulkner had died the year before, and the year before that Hemingway had blown his brains out, and in years before that Sinclair Lewis, Sherwood Anderson, Mencken and Knut Hamsun had all passed on, not to mention the bookseller Stanley Rose and the sportswriter Art Cohn, who had loaned Fante his typewriter all those years before in the basement of the *Long Beach Press-Telegram*, killed in the same 1958 New Mexico plane crash that took the life of epic movie producer Mike Todd. Then in June came word of the death of Pope John XXIII, architect of the Second Vatican Council, which was redefining the Church, and a man about whom even the irreligious Carey McWilliams would write in admiration: "a very good man; amazing the almost universal enthusiasm and affection for him."

All of which helps explain Fante's snap decision in the summer of 1963 to board a train bound for Denver with his youngest son, Jimmy, then twelve, on a pilgrimage back to his beginnings. Ironically, of all his children it was the one he had demanded Joyce abort with whom Fante had grown the closest, playing catch, golfing and taking in Dodger games together. Now, three decades after having last seen his home state, it was a reflective Fante who spoke with a reporter for the *Denver Post.* Describing himself as "stuck" at 35,000 words on a novel he was calling *The Left-Handed Virgin* (published posthumously as *1933 Was a Bad Year*), Fante openly wondered "what would have happened if I hadn't gone to work writing for pictures. . . . I know for sure that I would probably have a dozen novels published, instead of four." Fante took Jimmy around to call on old friends like Jack Keeley in Boulder and to show him the various stone and brick buildings that Grandpa Nick had helped build. Among these buildings one was missing, the steepled church of the Sacred Heart of Jesus. The great sandstone edifice had been torn down the year before to make way for the modern cruciform structure that in the summer of 1963 was being erected in its place. Even the past, it seemed, was changing before Fante's eyes. All in all, this visit home was bittersweet. Asked by the *Post* reporter why he had come back to Colorado, Fante replied, "It was just impulse."

Back in California Fante passed the rest of the summer trying to get *The Left-Handed Virgin* back on track, without much success. He had been stung by the rejection of the manuscript by his old Viking editor Pascal Covici, who found the story to be "without the poetic spontaneity of your earlier books." As if to challenge that assessment, in October Fante took a job writing a one-hour teleplay for *The Richard Boone Show*, reworking materials and themes on which he had worked many times before. "Captain Al Sanchez" told the story of a dreamy cannery worker who pretends to be a rich tuna boat captain in order to impress a poor Mexican girl. Effective enough for what it was, namely, commercial-driven network television, the script could boast little of the poetic spontaneity that Covici had lamented. Nor would Fante's next writing project give him the likeliest opportunity to recapture that quality, though he would not be kept from trying to do so in spite of the considerable odds.

This project was again with King Brothers, a feature script that Fante contracted to write in November 1963. Returning to the successful pairing of courageous boy and animal, à la "My Friend Bonito," *Maya* went the formula one better by focusing on two boys—one a blond American youth, the other his dark-skinned Hindu counterpart—and two elephants, one of them a sacred albino—on an adventuresome quest through the jungles of India seeking to fulfill their respective destinies, and in each boy's case coming to terms with the father who started it all.

Maya was obviously a departure for Fante. Still, he managed to infuse his story with characteristic concerns, in particular the compounded father-son tensions throughout, while extending himself in the construction of a story form and structure that for him were entirely new. (New if not exactly original: Fante had been brought onto the project to rewrite a screenplay by Gilbert Wright, itself an adaptation of Jalal Din's story "The Wild Elephant.") Fante worked long and hard on this project, writing seven different drafts in the course of the next calendar year. He also worked cheap, at the low-budget salary to which one acceded in working for the cost-conscious Kings. (His original contract stipulated a flat fee of $15,000 for the screenplay plus revisions.)

When Maya the Magnificent was released in 1966, the critics found much to admire. "A timeless odyssey of boys with a mission to fulfill and a father to be redeemed," enthused the Los Angeles Times, while Variety observed approvingly that "John Fante's script takes on the aspect of a saga." The success of both the script and the on-location production values notwithstanding, John Berry's film would not stand up well over the years. For contemporary viewers of a certain age, the casting of two minor icons of early 1960s television—the ever-stolid Clint Walker (Daniel Boone) as the fallen great white hunter father and the adolescent Jay North (Dennis the Menace) as his son—lends a retrospectively distracting cast to the movie, undermining the strength of the story. But for better or worse that was the story to which Fante devoted the greater part of a year of his life.

While Fante worked on this fablelike story of failing fathers and brave sons, his second son Dan had fled California hitchhiking for New York after the birth of his own first son, Jeffrey Mistofsky. Eldest son Nick, by this time out of the Navy, still had a year to go on a sentence of two years' probation for being convicted of marijuana possession. President Kennedy had been assassinated; Vietnam was heating up; yet who could say with any assurance why all of a sudden the whole world felt so different?

Snubbed by Who's Who in America for 1962 and 1963 after having been included for several years—when he wrote to inquire about the oversight he was told there was simply not enough "new material . . . to be added" to his entry—Fante countered by making sure he was listed in *The American Catholic Who's Who* for 1964. That he belonged in the latter directory was confirmed when Frank Capra hired him back in June of that year to write the story of Saint Joseph for a television Christmas special; and reconfirmed when Father Ellwood E. Kieser, C.S.P., invited him to consider contributing a teleplay to *Insight*, the popular Paulist Productions weekly showcase for quality religious drama.

With the failure of *The Left-Handed Virgin*, Fante seemed to lean more and more away from his fiction and in the direction of purely mainstream film and television entertainment writing. When a new Malibu neighbor came to introduce himself one day in the early 1960s, however, Fante was surprised and pleased to meet a genuine fan of his books. Rudolph Borchert had studied Fante's novels in an English class at Ohio State University, along with novels by John Dos Passos and Malcolm Lowry. Now Borchert was managing a security systems company while trying his best to write. When Fante offered to read Borchert's work he was impressed by what he saw. Soon Fante was confiding that he had just bought the last twenty-four copies of *Full of Life* for thirty-two cents apiece from Little, Brown and Company, which after ten years was deleting the book from its active list. This development depressed Fante but his acquaintance with the younger Borchert, who would often stop by for morning coffee and stay to talk books and tell stories, soon led to another collaboration.

While living in Mexico Borchert had heard a story, reputedly true, about a young boy and his courageous burro. Whether or not the story was based in fact, it was clearly related to the same basic folk material that had informed "My Friend Bonito" and for that matter *The Brave One* as well. Together Fante and Borchert crafted a detailed film treatment around a boy and his burro involving a fighting bull, a daring mountain rescue, and the redemption of a father's lost dignity. No sooner had they registered *Black Mountain* with the Writers Guild on February 2, 1965, however, than Fante suggested reworking the story into a children's book. The task of this rewriting fell largely to Fante, who soon had a new novel, albeit cowritten, to bring to market. It would take five years but *Bravo, Burro!* would finally appear in print, today the least known of all Fante's published fictions.

With dogs Mingo, Sam and Mitzi roaming the enclosed acre, Furry the cat overseeing the dogs, and Vickie's jumping horse Stardust corralled in the back—Fante's braying model for the failed novel about the Blessed Virgin's donkey would soon join the menagerie—Fante's Folly had truly become Rancho Fante. It was appropriate then that Fante should sign yet again with the King brothers, for $20,000, to write another script about the relationship of a child and an animal, this time an adaptation of the Marguerite Henry novel *King of the Wind*, about a mute Moroccan stableboy and his fearless black stallion. But no movie would result.

The smell of horse sweat that permeated Fante's script notwithstanding, writing this screenplay wasn't the same as being at the Turf Club at Santa Anita, where during this time Fante often escaped with Bill Asher to yell his picks down the stretch and drink; but it was a job and it helped cover his losses. Watts burned, Joe Petracca had died, and Joyce was delving seriously into the occult—no coincidence that at this time Bill Asher was producing a hit television comedy, *Bewitched*, starring his wife Elizabeth Montgomery as a suburban witch—while on the other side of the country Carey McWilliams was introducing a jangling new voice in the pages of *The Nation*, a writer by the name of Hunter S. Thompson who was reporting on the hair-raising rituals of a California motorcycle club that styled itself the Hell's Angels. From the kaleidoscopic bugginess of all these developments Fante remained withdrawn, as he did from his own vocation for serious prose fiction, provoking a jab from son Dan in faraway New York which must have touched a nerve.

I notice one thing immediately about your letters; they are flawless. My old man don't make any mistakes in punctuation, spelling, grammar, nothing. Your letters read like they were from the inside four pages of chapter six of the novel you didn't publish. You write good stuff. It flows almost flawlessly from your stubby hands. . . . But my old man isn't a boy anymore. And it isn't 1938. He doesn't write any books. He writes that shit I see that comes out of the skin mill. How come, Dad? . . . What gives?

Rather than striking back, Fante withdrew even further, privately expressing both his pique and his bewilderment at the way the world was going in a letter to Carey McWilliams.

We are all as well as can be expected for a family living in a tree house on the mouth of an active volcano. Danny found himself a Jewish bride in New York and I think is properly shackled in the prison of some Bronx apartment. He is driving a cab. I can't imagine a more loathesome job, but it must be that somewhere in my genes there was a strain that drove donkeys on Abruzzian trails, and now that the donkey is being retired one moves on to taxi cabs.

As for Nick—oh my God. I can only say that he is not in jail. We have a terrible time with that kid. He makes Rimbaud look like an Eagle Scout. He has a fatal fascination for black women, and what they have done to him would throw Governor Wallace into a fit of ecstasy. I tell you Carey, when Joyce and I sit down to dinner with Nick we have the feeling that our terrible white skin disgusts him. . . . He is the very quintessence of today's revolution. I am thinking of calling my house Watts by the Sea.

Fante's Folly, Rancho Fante, Watts by the Sea: the river was flowing, treacherous and swift, and it was all Fante could do to keep his head above the churning surface. One moment the suddenly nubile Vickie was surfing tandem with a boyfriend at Zuma Beach, and the next moment that same boy was off fighting in Vietnam. In 1966 Fante earned $3,000 from Universal Pictures for an untitled treatment about four United States Marines—one a California surfer—plucked from the blood and the muck of the Vietnam War for five days of flesh-searing, soul-searching R and R. Fante was now driving a '59 Corvette, which could often be found parked outside the Cottage, a neighborhood saloon owned by a former striptease artist and devout Catholic who had donated the church organ to Our Lady of Malibu. Fante continued to brawl: one fight at the Cottage ended with the man who had attacked him with a pool cue lying facedown in the crushed-shell pathway outside, his face looking like so much ground beef. Meanwhile, Free Speech was in the air, and there on national TV was motormouth pundit Mort Sahl broadcasting the hearsay that Carey McWilliams of *The Nation* had come into possession of key facts surrounding President Kennedy's assassination so "perilous and calamitous" that he was suppressing their publication.

No wonder that Fante's aborted novel from this time—the one about the writer trying to write a novel about the Virgin Mary's donkey—was called *The Confusion of the Times*. No better emblem could have been found for the entire country; and yet out of all the confusion of family and work and country and world something was percolating upward in Fante's imagination, a new novel he would soon be tackling.

First, however, he would team up with his old writing partner Frank Fenton for one last collaboration. Once tall and urbane, Fenton had been reduced to an alcoholic wreck, sitting down drunk at his typewriter and grinding out assembly-line westerns in the wake of a vicious divorce. Thirty-two years had passed since the two writers had worked together on *Dinky* and now here they were, two aging minor figures who found themselves in the *Times* Sunday supplement magazine listed in an elegiac survey of Los Angeles writers who had gone Hollywood.

In fact, a note of elegy was apt in light of the script that Fante and Fenton now cowrote, an anti-western about a giant of a dreamer who quotes from Emerson's "Self-Reliance" while trying to raise a derailed steam engine from the depths of the American River. To do so he builds a dam in a quixotic effort to hold the river back—the script's central conceit tantamount to what Fante and Fenton would have done had they been able to hold back the flow of time while they did some much-needed salvage work on their careers, their lives, their souls. Appearing opposite Susan Clark and Warren Oates, Dan Blocker (Hoss Cartwright on television's *Bonanza*) played Big John Killibrew in the Universal Pictures television movie *Something for a Lonely Man*, the last film that would bear Fante's name in his lifetime.

"It is only as a man puts off from himself all external support, and stands alone, that I see him to be strong." Emerson's words might have seemed a curious motto for as collaborative an exercise in anonymity as a movie of the week, but they were exactly to the point when Fante sat down by himself to undertake a new novel about an aging and life-befuddled screenwriter. Originally titled *Sad Dog* and featuring Harry and Sarah Banducci and their four grown but out-of-control children, this project had recaptured Fante's old writing spirit, and soon he was working on the story with a concentration that was once again intact and ferociously focused.

Nearly twenty years had passed since he had written his last novel, *Full of Life*, that benignly sanitized reverse-image of the way things were with his life as a husband and father, albeit true enough to itself as fiction. Now he had embarked on the effective sequel to that novel, but this time his story would play no such games, aiming rather for an emotional honesty that, despite fictional liberties, would be true to the life that had overtaken him as husband, father and writer twenty years later.

Henry and Harriet Molise (as Harry and Sarah Banducci were soon renamed) live in a rambling Y-shaped ranch house on Malibu's Point Dume, beset by the encroaching challenges of matrimonial commitment, the waning days of parenthood, and late middle age. A sold-out novelist-turned-screenwriter facing the fact that his professional prime is behind him, Henry Molise resists the noisome new world of his four ingrate children, each more feckless than the next. When a libidinous misfit dog strays into his life, Molise takes what comfort he can in identifying with the beast while suffering the loss, one by one, of his children as they leave the nest.

The saddest of comedies, by the time it was finished *My Dog Stupid* had amounted to a personal triumph for Fante. He had managed to finish writing a novel again, proof positive that he had not squandered his talent irrevocably on the movies. The cliché of the sold-out writer's ruination to the contrary, Fante had again demonstrated with this novel that his life remained his best raw material—and here was the most beautiful part— even when that life seemed to prove the legitimacy of the cliché. In writing *My Dog Stupid*, Fante saturated the story with an awareness of these tensions, making it among other things a meditation on the responsibilities a writer shirks or shoulders in choosing what and how he will write.

> Screenwriting was easier and brought more bread, a one-dimensional kind of scribbling asking no more of the writer than that he keep his people in motion. The formula was always the same: fightin' and fuckin'. When finished you gave it to other people who tore it to pieces trying to put it on film.
>
> But when you undertook a novel, the affair was awesome. Not only were you the writer but the star and all the characters, as well

as the director, producer and cameraman. If your screenplay didn't come off you could blame a lot of people, from the director down. But if your novel bombed, you suffered alone.

The virtue being discerned here—the courage to stand alone and if necessary suffer for one's actions—is perfectly Emersonian. As such, it lends itself to the kind of self-critical inwardness that the easier, more lucrative life of screen scribbling tends to deny. "I've done a little soul-searching," Henry Molise confesses at one point to his wife, "and what I've found isn't pleasant. I'm a rotten husband, a lousy father, a bad provider, a total failure." As recognitions go, this is a painful one, all the more so for being so many-headed; but only by meeting the gaze of the faces that stare back at him in reflection can Henry reach an even deeper and ultimately liberating recognition: "To write one must love, and to love one must understand." And that is what finally most permeates *My Dog Stupid*, a love for family earned through the compassionate understanding of all the laughable foibles that make any family its own greatest source of heartache.

Paradoxically, almost as soon as he was finished writing this paean to real writing, Fante set about trying to sell it to television. With Bill Asher's encouragement he sent the manuscript to weekly-comedy-show magnate Sheldon Leonard (*The Andy Griffith Show, Gomer Pyle U.S.M.C., The Dick Van Dyke Show, The Real McCoys,* and so forth). But *My Dog Stupid* would fare no better with Hollywood television producers than it would with New York publishers, no matter how enthusiastic his New York agent might be. "[I]t almost makes me weep to think of the many years you haven't been writing," Elizabeth R. Otis confided to Fante upon reading the manuscript. "Please, John, don't ever stop writing again for publication. It is terribly important for you not to keep hiding your light under a bushel." Despite Otis's best efforts, however, *My Dog Stupid* would remain unpublished during Fante's lifetime. The personal triumph of completing a first-rate novel that could not find an audience thus became just another misfire, to be filed away with all the other misfires of a long and jinxed season, the unyielding years of John Fante's unfulfillment.

In 1968 the Vietnam War was at its ghastliest. For many, such a word no longer sufficed to describe the phantasmagoria of the American scene. When Fante signed a contract for $20,000 with Roger Corman's American International Pictures to rewrite a typically derivative AIP exploitation picture entitled *Lola*—about a writer of pornographic novels who falls into an affair with a sixteen-year-old nymphet—he assuaged the pain of the self-inflicted affront by treating himself to a 1965 Mustang. Joyce was now fully immersed in the serious study of the Tarot, astral projection and Wicca, or white witchcraft, attending meetings of a coven and going so far as to request and receive a letter from Carey McWilliams credentialing her as being on assignment to *The Nation* to write an article on the southern California occult scene. For his part, Fante kept his own counsel, briefly collaborating with Harry Essex on a new screenplay of *Ask the Dust*, which both writers were forced to admit only gutted the story of all life. With his focus again shot, Fante retreated once more to the al fresco escape of golf. Limited now in his ability to walk long distances by a recurrent pain in his foot, Fante took to playing at Santa Monica Shores, a three-par course where he could work on his short game without going too gimpy. He was spending more and more money on vitamins and dietary supplements in an effort to control his health, which, while stable, was as precarious as only a diabetic's health can be.

Then on Christmas evening, 1969, Fante foolishly tried to intervene in a dogfight between his 105-pound Akita and two Doberman pinschers belonging to a neighbor. In the snarling confusion Fante was severely bitten on the lower right leg by one of the dogs. The suppurating wounds were months in healing, and he found himself unable to work. Like *My Dog Stupid's* Henry J. Molise, Fante kept harking back to the glory days of Rocco, his beloved white pit bull who would have torn those Dobermans limb from limb, if only he were alive. The memories were still sweet of Rocco's ferocity, of Rocco the cat killer, the terror of Cliffside Drive. John had hung a tire from a tree branch, and Rocco would attack the tire and swing there from his massive locked jaws in a paralysis of rage. But like so many other loved ones, Rocco was long dead. Fante had buried him with his own hands behind the corral at the back of the property, where he would go now at times to think, and think back, beneath the whispering pines.

A plague of blackbirds soon took to infesting those pine trees, the ceaseless chatter driving John to distraction; so that when Vickie's surfer boyfriend, Bill Berkholtz, returned from Vietnam a seasoned veteran and a dead shot, Joyce put him to work on the sunroof of the garage picking off the noisy pests with a rifle. Though all he could do was rest, it was not a restful period for Fante, who was growing jumpy and strangely suspicious. Fante put little stock in his wife's trafficking in magic, white or otherwise, but when one night, unbeknownst to him, Joyce recited the ceremonial incantation summoning Apep, the fierce Egyptian dog-demon, Fante reported feeling a looming canine presence in his room, as if the ghost of Rocco had come back to visit him. Even spookier was the night when Bill Berkholtz brought a friend to dinner, a crop-haired Green Beret known as Captain Z whose specialty in Vietnam had been nocturnal assassinations. Joyce enjoyed the opportunity to entertain a professional killer, whose stories grew more and more harrowing, but Fante was not amused. After listening uneasily to the drift of the conversation, Fante folded his napkin and excused himself. He retired early for the night.

CHAPTER 17

At six o'clock in the morning of February 9, 1971, a magnitude 6.4 earth-quake centered in the San Fernando Valley struck greater Los Angeles. Buildings toppled, freeways collapsed and scores of people perished. Rid-dled with faults though southern California was, the region had not been hit so hard since the great Long Beach quake of 1933, which had left the young John Fante trembling with terror and in repentant mind of the Last Things. But far removed from the epicenter of this latest cataclysm, Rancho Fante was spared major damage. No one on Point Dume died.

Three days later Vickie was married to Robert Gardner at Saint Augustine-by-the-Sea Episcopal Church in Santa Monica. Fante showed up in a vested suit and striped pants to give the bride away. "I never thought it would happen to John Fante," he had written to Carey McWilliams, but now it had happened, and soon Jimmy, the youngest of his four children, would also be married and gone. "Then we shall be alone, Joyce and I, and I am sure we shall discover some interesting things about one another."

Such contemplative moments came over him rather frequently these days with the passing of other major life events. "My little black and white granddaughter is now three," he wrote of Angela Fante, born in 1968 to Nick's first wife Edith Baker, and "a very beautiful child" she was in her grandfather's eye. Dan's second son, Peter Fante, would soon be born in New York, and in 1973 Vickie would give birth to Bobby Gardner, brother Scott following in 1974. Despite California's four seasons of natural catastrophe—earthquake, fire, flood and mudslide—life went on.

But there was also death. Ross Wills died in April 1971, followed by Frank Fenton in August. Reports of these losses took time for Fante to assimilate. No man liked to think death would come for him, but such reminders of others' ends, and of the shared life thus concluded—those trips to the desert with Ross in the early thirties, all the golf and poker and drinking with Fenton—made the fact impossible to deny.

On a brighter note, prospects appeared to be opening up for a couple of long-delayed screen projects, *My Dog Stupid* and *Ask the Dust*. Four years after failing to interest American television producers, *My Dog Stupid* had captured the fancy of film comedy genius Peter Sellers. Writing to Fante from his estate in County Kildare, Ireland, Sellers said that he was setting "to work trying to get my end of the project together," failing which he would "return to my old love of Amateur Coal Mining." Five months later Fante signed a contract for $15,000 with Bill Asher's Ashmont Productions to write a screenplay adaptation of the novel, and casting suggestions were drawn up including such A-list actors as Carroll O'Connor, Edward Asner, Jack Lemmon, Walter Matthau, Jackie Gleason, Ernest Borgnine, George C. Scott, Jason Robards, Alan Arkin, Frank Sinatra and Peter Falk.

In the meantime, an up-and-coming young screenwriter by the name of Robert Towne had stepped forward to take up the cause of *Ask the Dust*. Researching 1930s Los Angeles for an original screenplay he was then developing—Roman Polanski's *Chinatown*, as it would turn out, the classic neo-noir detective film starring Jack Nicholson and Faye Dunaway—Towne had come across *Southern California Country: An Island on the Land,* and in it Carey McWilliams's favorable mention of Fante's long-out-of-print novel. When Towne read a copy of *Ask the Dust* from the Los Angeles Public Library he was so moved that in the best Hollywood tradition he contacted his agent, who connected him with Fante. Towne and his then-wife Julie met John and Joyce for dinner and soon Towne's Tortoise Productions had paid Fante $1,000 for the initial six-month option, which took effect in late 1971.

All of these developments gave Fante reason for hope. So too did the rebirth of interest in long-neglected works by friends Carey McWilliams and Carlos Bulosan, whose books were reappearing in new editions for new generations of readers. Hope as Fante might, however, his books remained all but unread for the simple reason that they remained out of print or, what was worse, unpublished. Longing for a second life for *Ask the Dust,* Fante struck a desperate note when he wrote McWilliams in early 1974: "The [University of Washington Press] reprint of Carlos' book is a beautiful job, and I would give both testicles if the editors could be persuaded to do my Ask the Dust for their list." Despite Carey's efforts, however—he arranged for the book to be seen at the University of Washington Press and Salt Lake City's Peregrine Smith, both of which returned it—*Ask the Dust* was to remain unavailable to all but the most adventurous readers for several more years to come.

What little attention was being paid to Fante outside the rarefied and frustrating arena of Hollywood deal making came from an earnest young graduate student. Marilyn Murphy-Plittman had approached Carey McWilliams for information about Fante's background, indicating that she was "particularly interested in the immigrant experience." After getting Fante's ironic permission to cooperate—Fante insisted that nothing be disclosed about any of his friends but that otherwise Carey should "by all means let her have the truth with both barrels blasting"—McWilliams downplayed Murphy-Plittman's emphasis on "the new ethnicity" as merely a "current intellectual fad." In place of the ethnic oversimplification, McWilliams stressed "that *many* factors—personal, social, political, etc."—bore on the question of Fante's life and writing. To underscore his call for a balanced and rounded approach, McWilliams asserted that in his view, "for what it may be worth, John is as American as Huckleberry Finn," and he went on to apply to Fante John Jay Chapman's marvelous comment on another quintessential American, Walt Whitman, namely, that at his best Fante "ate cold pie and tramped the earth in triumph."

For his part, Fante remained skeptical about Murphy-Plittman's biographical endeavor. "A curious fact about biographers of writers is their stubborn resistance to reality," Fante told McWilliams, citing the well-intentioned degree candidate as "a good example of a biographer wearing blinkers as she gallops toward her goal." Fante was no more in a mood to begin pigeonholing his life than he had been to reinforce the romantic view of the old Stanley Rose Bookshop when Jay Martin came to interview Fante in his Santa Monica office for Martin's biography of Nathanael West. "Indeed," Fante wrote to Martin after the interview,

> the whole romantic business about the fabled Stanley Rose Bookshop is hogwash. It was just a store where, once in a blue moon some lonely writer out here to do a picture ventured in to buy a book. If you have the notion that the store was a little cultural oasis in the desert of filmdom, do not be misled. There were, and are, thousands of such stores all over the country. The writers who visit them are less important than the product they sell.

Central to this debunking is the properly defensive, that is, self-protective, view that what matters most in the long run is the integral work, not the writer's artificially extrapolated personality. In a writer who tended so often and so thoroughly to conflate his personal life with his fiction as Fante did, the point may seem a tortured one; but to miss it or, worse, to dismiss it as merely self-serving is to fail to apprehend Fante's deeply felt sense that the man and his work were ultimately inseparable, were, indeed, ultimately one and the same.

To help keep these verities in perspective, Fante took to raising garlic in his backyard, not far from the marijuana patch that a friend of Jimmy's, then residing there in a tent, maintained with equal devotion. With garden soil under the nails of his blunt fingers, Fante could maintain some relation to the earth, even as the worlds of literature and film found him increasingly irrelevant. Even when Fante made a conscious effort to be relevant, in fact—or, what was worse, contemporary—he encountered much the same response. When, for example, with Leo Townsend he cowrote a film treatment set in the rough-and-tumble world of San Pedro commercial fishermen but focusing on the gay son of a rich Italian-American cannery owner, the strain was all too obvious. Self-conscious phrases such as "a cat like Carmen," "Wow! Weird!" and "a young, hip priest who dug the scene" gave the aging writers away. "You said it one day," Harry Essex had written Fante about the failure of their many collaborations, "not to add the name of Edna Mae Oliver to one of our treatments because it would date us. . . . While we're not really very old the muscles of our creativity creak a little." And so Fante bent to his garlic bulbs, as if in practicing such an old man's avocation he might rediscover the youthful virility associated with the herb since time immemorial.

Garlic cloves in the pocket had been Papa's prescription for male offspring as far back as *Full of Life*, a superstition traceable through Fante's father Nick back to the old country of the Abruzzi. Now Fante found himself writing about yet another old bricklaying philanderer who owed as much to Nick Fante as did all of the author's other fictional father figures. This time, however, the novel Fante was plotting would center on not the birth of a son but the death of the father.

Preliminary titles for this novel included *The Last Supper* and *Our Father Who*, but before the first draft was finished Fante had settled on the less overtly religious *The Brotherhood of the Grape*. Still, tucked in the typed and penciled-over pages of the manuscript Fante kept a holy card, printed in Italy, of Saint Teresa of the Child Jesus, known as the Little Flower, with the Roman Missal's Prayer to Saint Teresa on the reverse: "Oh Lord, who hast said: 'Unless you become as little children, you shall not enter into the kingdom of heaven'; grant us, we beseech Thee, so to walk in the footsteps of thy blessed Virgin Teresa with a humble and single heart, that we may attain to everlasting rewards."

At first Fante reported being bored by this novel, which he claimed to be writing only for the money. As he worked deeper into the bruising comedy of the Molise family, he grew more and more attached, calling it "a tale revolving around my father." Later still he would call it his favorite novel, confessing that as he wrote it he would often be overcome by tears.

Certainly *The Brotherhood of the Grape* is an emotional novel, but

what John Fante novel isn't? (When the novel was published in 1977
Larry McMurtry called it "a study of the resources and the limitations of
an absolutely rampant emotionalism.") Here, however, more than in any
of Fante's earlier works, the emotion is intensified by a presiding awareness of death. It is the autumn of the year when fifty-year-old writer Henry
Molise journeys north from Point Dume to the fictional town of San
Elmo (Roseville in Fante's early drafts) in order to arbitrate his aging parents' lifelong lovers' quarrel. Once there he allows himself to be cajoled
into helping his father build a brick smokehouse up in the Abruzzi-like
mountains, where he witnesses his father's death; or rather, as he soon realizes, where he beholds a vision of the death that lies nested inside every
pulsing moment of life:

> Then a peculiar thing happened. My father died. We were work-
> ing away, swirling in mortar and stone, and all of a sudden I
> sensed that he had left the world. I sought his face and it was writ-
> ten there. His eyes were open, his hands moved, he splashed
> mortar, but he was dead, and in death he had nothing to say.
> Sometimes he drifted off like a specter into the trees to take a piss.
> How could he be dead, I wondered, and still walk off and pee? A
> ghost he was, a goner, a stiff. I wanted to ask him if he was well, if
> by chance he was still alive, but I was too tired and too busy dying
> myself, and too tired of making phrases. I could see the question
> on paper, typewritten, with quotation marks, but it was too heavy
> to verbalize. Besides, what difference did it make? We all had to
> die someday.

In a novel brimming over with drinking, fighting, weeping and sex,
not to mention more delectably described cooking and eating than in all
Fante's other novels combined, this is a remarkable passage. It is also a
passage that must be seen as emblematic of Fante's concern throughout
the novel to capture in his hand the throbbing heart of life's tragicomic
reversibility. "The whole world had turned into a graveyard," Henry re-
members feeling when he was a boy and his father, gruff with wine,
would make him be late for his baseball games in order to show off his favorite tombstone carvings: angels and crosses and one "fashioned like an

open book, [the] vital statistics chiseled on a stony page." Vital, indeed, but far from stony are the pages of *The Brotherhood of the Grape*, Fante's maturest, indeed, wisest work.

Later in the novel Nick Molise does die, granting Henry the opportunity to begin discovering the answer to that most filial of questions, "How could a man live without his father?" In taking up the death of his father in the fictional death of Nick Molise, who is characterized significantly as a diabetic, Fante was also facing up to the fact of his own declining years and the end they portended. Yet when compared to the ultimate sadness of *My Dog Stupid*'s comedy, the sadness of *The Brotherhood of the Grape* is tempered with what can only be called the happiest of unhappy endings. In short, it is a little divine comedy, something for our age, a death and a burial but with life bursting through—beneath the black cassocks of the altar boys Henry glimpses the green-and-white stripes of their baseball socks, "and you knew that somewhere in the town their teammates were waiting for them"—followed by a home-centered paschal feast of lamb, new potatoes and the life-enabling absurdity of hope.

Fante had done it again, bounced back from the mat to write a beautiful novel, and this time he found his audience. On January 5, 1975, he received a soft-cover advance of $35,000 from Bantam Books, and on March 15 Robert Towne optioned the film rights for $1,500. Towne was enthralled with his discovery of both Fante and Carey McWilliams and eager to demonstrate his indebtedness. About *Southern California: An Island on the Land* Towne had written McWilliams to affirm that "your book really changed my life. It taught me to look at the place where I was born, and convinced me it was worth writing about." Towne soon brought Fante to the attention of renaissance man Francis Ford Coppola, who agreed that *The Brotherhood of the Grape* would make a fine film. First, however, Coppola would launch the novel by serializing it in his weekly San Francisco–based magazine, *City*. Prefaced by Towne, who compared Nick Molise to no less formidable a figure than Jehovah—"two very powerful, very grumpy old men who won't take shit from anybody"—the novel ran in five consecutive installments between July and August.

Once again Fante was in the public eye, with prospects for something big to happen. About the likelihood of a movie emerging from the Towne-Coppola enthusiasm he indulged a cautious optimism. After all, these two young Turks were the best possible auspices for an obscure old-ster like himself, both white-hot Academy Award winners for films Fante admired, Towne for *Chinatown* and Coppola for *The Godfather*. More-over, as famous as Fante was within his own family for walking out on movies that bored him—and, like Sunday sermons, most movies bored him stiff—he had been so impressed when he went with his son Dan the year before to see Coppola's *The Conversation* that he had stayed for the entire film. Still, who could tell? "Moneywise," he wrote to Carey McWilliams, "something very dramatic may happen to me." But experi-ence had taught him the dangers of optimism, so he covered himself with a hard-boiled shell. "Needless to say, I am horribly cynical and expect the deal to blow up at the very last moment. But Towne insists it's all true."

In the meantime, with Buckley Angell, Fante was knocking out *The Hispano Blondes*, a spec screenplay based on the same recycled material he and Carey had scripted more than twenty-five years before, from the true incident described in Carey's *North from Mexico* about an idealistic priest and his efforts to place forty blond orphans in adoptive Mexican-American homes. Fante was also heeding the advice of his Bantam editor who, citing the successful use of flashbacks in *The Godfather*, had sug-gested he write more such scenes for *The Brotherhood of the Grape*. In a notable instance of the reverse influence that cinema can exert on litera-ture, Fante embraced the idea, adding to the manuscript Henry's memo-ries of Wilmington and the Toyo Fish Company, extended scenes that would ultimately constitute chapters 9 and 10 of the novel. But with these relatively minor writing chores out of the way, Fante felt out of sorts, a novelist without a novel to write.

A nasty diabetic ulcer between the toes of his left foot, which would not seem to heal, was making him testy with his doctors and fearful of the probabilities. When despite physical ailments of his own Carey McWilliams jetted west for one of his last whirlwind swings through the Southland—cocktails in San Diego with young mayor Pete Wilson, in-troductions courtesy of the *Los Angeles Times'* Art Seidenbaum at a speech in the San Fernando Valley—Fante was unable to join Carey and Robert Towne for dinner at Dominick's on Beverly Boulevard because of the diabetes. Restless, he prowled the house on Point Dume trying to come up with an idea for a new book. Nothing seemed to come, however, and when he wearied of failing he limped out to the backyard and swung a rope over a tree branch. Testing the branch against his suspended weight, he satisfied himself that it would hold. Then he tied on an old tire and swung for a while, a little surprise for the grandkids.

The last story Fante would publish in his lifetime appeared in the fall of 1975. Written as early as 1966 and then unread for nearly a decade, "My Father's God" was one of the finest stories of his career, a profoundly simple but elegantly plotted tale of obligation and honesty centering on the issue of fatherhood and the miracle of writing.

In this story, in order to persuade the narrator's papa to make his first confession in thirty years, new parish priest Father Bruno Ramponi cuts an unorthodox deal: rather than having to force himself inside the coffin-like box of the confessional, Papa is given the dispensation of chronicling his sins in writing. For days he toils over the massive work, blackening page after page, and when he is finally finished he charges his son, the story's narrator, with the task of delivering the fearsome package to the rectory. Trudging through the snowy streets of Boulder, the boy resents the imposition—"They weren't *my* sins, they were his"—but more than resentment he feels the inherited weight of this strangely spiritual occasion.

All of this wickedness, every human being he had injured, every sin against God's commandments were congealed in a block of ice burning against my stomach as I crossed town, under dripping maple trees, around grey mounds of mud-splattered snow, my toes picking their way with the delicacy of bird's feet, across the town, the awful responsibility of my burden hurting my flesh, too sacred, too heavy for my life.

Crafty enough to have gotten this far with his apostate parishioner, Father Ramponi is shocked to discover that he has been outfoxed by the even craftier bricklayer: Papa's outpouring of transgressions great and small has been written not in English but in Italian, which the American-born cleric cannot read. Although he is angry at this upstaging, like the knowing priest in "The Wrath of God" Father Ramponi is also a good enough sport not to push the issue. He orders Papa to burn his confession, and then to kneel for absolution. Since biblical times burnt offerings have signified expiation for sins and praise for the divine Father on high. Less conventional but just as efficacious here is the conjoining of Papa's written confession and his son's dutiful delivery of same, all of it leading up to the ritual immolation. In "My Father's God" Fante was bearing witness to the soul-cleansing powers of confession, if not confession by the rules then the kind of confessional writing he spent so much of his life practicing, truthful in spite of all the evasions and written in a language all his own. "Suddenly my father laughed. 'I feel good,' he said. 'Real good, Father.' " And then, pouring a glass of wine, "He raised it heavenward and drank." Close your eyes for a second and then look again: even the sacraments could surprise you.

With his own health deteriorating from the onset of cancer, Carey McWilliams stepped down from his position as editor of *The Nation* on January 2, 1976, ending a quarter of a century of indefatigable commitment to one of the country's most irreverent and influential journals. Never a man to slow down, he kept up as demanding a schedule of travel and lectures as his condition would allow. He also set to work on his autobiography, *The Education of Carey McWilliams*, loosely modeling it on that classic critique of American convention *The Education of Henry Adams*. But in the quiet after yet one more keynote address or the latest honorary degree, the Colorado cattle baron's son turned radical social reformer was forced to realize that his long and eventful life was drawing to a close.

Instead of hard-liquor toasts, old friends John and Carey now exchanged ironic airmail updates on their respective medical developments, bucking each other up with irascible descriptions of inattentive doctors and incompetent Social Security drones. It was a far cry from their youthful days of helling around California together but it was how they now helped themselves deal with the inevitable.

In a different kind of effort to stave off the inevitable, one day Fante took his youngest son Jimmy out golfing. Over the decades few activities

had afforded Fante more pleasure than golf, the chance to be outside under the sky knocking the ball around. After only a couple of holes, however, Fante was in such pain from walking that he told Jimmy he was
heading back to the clubhouse. Jimmy protested that he would go too,
but when he saw his father's eyes flash Jimmy knew he would have to
tough it out and complete the round without him. He watched his father
get smaller and smaller as he slowly hobbled away down the fairway,
knowing that they would never go golfing again.

Troublesome lesions now on both feet kept Fante careful about how
he walked and made him a frequent visitor at his doctors' offices. His eyesight was also failing, and in July 1976, with his left eye all but useless,
he underwent laser surgery on his right eye for diabetic retinopathy at
UCLA's Jules Stein Eye Institute. The operation was a success, enabling
Fante to see clearly enough when in August he signed the hardcover contract for *The Brotherhood of the Grape* with Boston's Houghton Mifflin
Company. Like Bantam's Ted Solotaroff, Fante's editor at Houghton Mifflin, Robert Cowley, was enthusiastic about the novel, inspiring Fante to
wish less for medical miracles than for a good solid idea for a novel. Every
day now he was learning new truths about pain, not least among them
that "[t]he compulsion to write without the substance of an idea can get
very painful." And yet the ideas continued to elude him.

In January 1977, Francis Ford Coppola invited John and Joyce to San
Francisco for a dinner in John's honor. Fante had been ill for some time
now but he knew that Coppola was home only briefly from the Philippines, where he was struggling against the elements to make *Apocalypse
Now*, his epic film adaptation of Joseph Conrad's *Heart of Darkness* set
against the backdrop of the Vietnam War. Despite his continuing poor
health Fante accepted the invitation in the hope of learning Coppola's
plans for *The Brotherhood of the Grape*, and he and Joyce flew to San
Francisco. They were taken to a drafty downtown theater where while
waiting for Coppola they listened to his father, the composer Carmine
Coppola, rehearsing Puccini's *La Boheme*. Later that night at Coppola's
twenty-two-room Victorian mansion in Pacific Heights, John and Joyce
sat down to a sumptuous meal and much lively talk alongside San Francisco mayor Joseph P. Alioto, among others, and afterward a surprise
screening of *Full of Life*. Yet when they left the city to return home the

next day, Fante was still uncertain what Coppola's plans might be for his novel.

In an effort to enlighten himself Fante made a phone call to his Malibu neighbor Martin Sheen, then also home from the Philippines to wait out the monsoons during the filming of *Apocalypse Now*. Sheen, who as Fante knew had starred in the powerful 1973 television film adaptation of Brian Moore's novella *Catholics*, came to Fante's house and the two talked affably for some time. Sheen had read and loved *The Brotherhood of the Grape*, especially its treatment of the father-son theme, and he encouraged Fante to think of Alan Arkin for the part of Henry J. Molise. Fante indicated that he thought Coppola had Robert DeNiro in mind for that part and Sheen agreed that the choice was an interesting one. When Sheen returned to the Philippines he spoke to Coppola about his visit with Fante, expressing Fante's concern about whether *Brotherhood* would be filmed or not. But the director was so consumed with the maelstrom that *Apocalypse* was becoming that Fante would hear nothing from him anytime soon.

On January 12 Fante was admitted to Santa Monica Hospital for five days of extensive tests. His daily insulin injections were now up from 15 to 55 ccs, and the ulcerations on his feet had continued to worsen, ominous signs he knew too well how to read. He was all the more relieved then to be home two weeks later when the advance copy of *The Brotherhood of the Grape* arrived, the first new book of his own that he had held in his hands in twenty-five years.

Critical reception of the novel was exceptionally warm. Asserting that Fante had managed "to span every emotion, to transcend every regional, ethnic limitation," Carolyn See in the *Los Angeles Times* called the novel "[h]eart-rending and hysterically funny." Similarly, *The New York Times* found Fante's latest offering "alternately full of cleansing laughter and as comical as a toothache." And in *The Washington Post* Larry McMurtry made comparisons to *The Brothers Karamozov* and *King Lear* in support of his point that *"The Brotherhood of the Grape* belies the myth that screenwriting is destructive. John Fante has been doing it for a great many years, and his talent for the novel is, if anything, more vigorous than it was when he was young."

The book went into its second printing in late March but by then Fante's health had taken a turn for the worse. The diabetes was slowly choking off circulation to his lower extremities, and the pain was all but unbearable. One night John and Joyce stayed up late together, talking about what was now clear to both of them, crying and holding each other. Then on May 23 Fante checked himself into Santa Monica Hospital, where three days later he underwent the first of his amputations, losing one toe on either foot. A month later he was back in the hospital, feverish but alert and manfully cooperative, though one whole foot had gone black to gangrene. As awful as he knew his condition to be, he still struck the attending physician as "a delightful gentleman with a rather desperate problem." On June 25 his left leg was amputated below the knee, and when that measure failed to halt the spreading necrosis, on August 3 the surgeons took what remained of the leg, in all a grisly series of choppings which left Fante badly shaken and Joyce praying for the strength to endure.

When he was able to hold a pen for any length of time—typing was out of the question—Fante scrawled a letter to Carey McWilliams. "The first great loss after a leg," he confessed, "is the ability to write. It is like struggling with a heavy rubber tire hanging from your neck. Don't ask me why. All I know is the hopeless great weight crushing your arms." Trying to master the use of an ungainly metal walker upon his return home from the hospital, Fante had fallen backward, crashing down hard on his stump. Ever since then the pain had been constant, as had Fante's sense of indignity at his diminishment. Youngest son Jimmy was marrying his Japanese-American fiancée Jennifer Kato in September, but Fante could not bring himself to face all the staring wedding guests should he agree to be wheeled into the reception. He was fearful, moreover, that he would break down crying in front of everyone, "for," as he went on to explain to Carey, "I cry a lot these days, and for no particular reason." He later apologized to Carey for this "insufferably maudlin and disgusting letter," blaming it on too many glasses of grenache rosé, and going on gamely to describe the "glorious ease" in which, instead of attending his son's wedding, he had stayed home alone peering at televised football with his one remaining serviceable eye.

Even the blurry escape of watching television was threatened when in early November Fante's eyes began to water and grow painful in the light. Upon visiting his ophthalmologist he was immediately admitted to St. John's Hospital in Santa Monica, where he underwent the "absolute hor-

ror" of an operation upon his right eye to reverse the rapid onset of glau-
coma. Two weeks later it appeared that his sight was returning, but by
June of the following year he had gone irreparably blind. Then on June 6
he lapsed into insulin shock. Emergency admission to Santa Monica
Hospital helped pull him through the crisis, but after he was released, a
long and frightful period of disorientation ensued.

At 4:30 on the morning of July 10, Fante woke screaming for the police, in the grip of severe hallucinogenic paranoia. When he reentered
the hospital the following day he was still shouting incoherently and had
to be restrained, succumbing finally to a tranquilizer shot. He was very
thin, incontinent and seemed near death, but when on July 15 a visitor
stepped into his hospital room Fante was able to recognize his old friend
Carey McWilliams. In Los Angeles to contribute several days' worth of
videotaped interviews to UCLA's Oral History Project, Carey had come
to the hospital with his wife Iris and Joe and Mary Aidlin. Fante's recog-
nizing Carey was the first positive sign in a long time, and Joyce was
vastly relieved. But when Fante was transferred by ambulance to the Motion Picture and Television Country House Hospital in Woodland Hills
on July 20, the grave-faced admitting physician advised Joyce that, realis-
tically speaking, her husband had only a week to six months to live.

Yet by August 7 Fante was well enough to go home again. His mind
had cleared and he had put on some weight, as if to make liars of all un-
smiling realists. Fante certainly must have smiled when on September 14
he received a letter informing him that he had been selected for induc-
tion into the Long Beach City College Hall of Fame. As evidence of the
life he still had inside him, Fante's response is worth quoting in full.

Dear Sirs:

In the Spring of 1932 I sat in the English class of Miss Florence Carpenter at Long Beach City College. Miss Carpenter was
a buxom, kindly mother-type who loved her students even more
than she loved the English language, and every outstanding theme
submitted by her brood brought enthusiastic gurgles from this
wonderful, kindly, dedicated woman. She paid small attention to
me until I turned in an innocuous assignment on campus love.
The thing left her ecstatic. A dedicated romantic, she could be

breathless over the turn of a phrase, a colorful adjective, or [any] ringing positive statement about life.

From the time of that theme onward I was her favorite, her pet, her genius. Wherever we met on the campus, in the hallways, in the classroom, her face brightened with an endearing smile. She loved me—no, not an emotional love or anything like that; rather a deep affection and a respect for a talent I did not even know I had. But it worked like magic. I suddenly discovered the English language and the pleasures of manipulating it. I joined a campus literary society and spent all my waking hours writing short stories, essays and critiques. One night I arrived at the society's monthly meeting with a brand new short story. Miss Carpenter was enthralled. She stood before our little group and read my yarn aloud. To my surprise it sounded much better than I had expected. Everybody was impressed. Fellow members congratulated me, patted me on the back, urged me to submit the story to a publication.

My first thought was the Saturday Evening Post, but lurking in the back of my mind was my hero and literary god, H. L. Mencken, editor of the American Mercury, and my loyalty to him prevailed. I sent the story to Mencken, not by way of the editorial offices, but directly to his home in Baltimore. The manuscript was not typed, it was in longhand, which will give some idea of how unprofessional I was at the time. A week later I received a bulky envelope in the mail and opened it to find my story inside. I assumed it meant a rejection, but there was a small note from Mencken attached to the front page. It read:

"Dear Mr. Fante:
    What do you have against a typewriter? If you will transcribe this manuscript in type I'll be glad to buy it.
                                                Sincerely yours,
                                                H. L. Mencken"

That was all—two or three lines, but it made me dizzy with joy. My first thought was Miss Carpenter. I ran all the way from a downtown poolhall to the campus. Miss Carpenter was at her desk correcting papers. I shoved my triumphant scrawled manuscript and Mencken's note under her nose. It was a high moment in my life. I wanted to weep, to kiss her, to kiss one of her dear hands, to kneel and thank her, but I did none of those things. I simply walked away crying quietly. And all of this if you will is my everlasting memory of Florence Carpenter and Long Beach City College.

Due to his illness Fante was unable to attend the Hall of Fame reception luncheon but that hardly mattered, for in good time he received a neatly handwritten letter that must have melted his heart:

Dear John,

I'd be either sub- or super-human if I didn't tread on air for a while after reading the copy of your letter sent to me by the Associated Student Body Office of the City College. I have delayed in telling you so for lack of your address. But the other day in our Glendale Library I discovered a huge volume, I–K, of *Who's Who in America*, recounting the Fante facts and titles and awards beside which our poor little LBCC Hall of Fame grows pale. Your Malibu address was there.

Of course I know of your genius in fiction. I know that only kind, nostalgic eyes could see in me the person you have built up like a character in one of your novels. But it feels good to be glamorized. I give you a grateful, humble A+ as of old for your composition.

It is hard for me to picture you in this new role of father of a family. You were always family-oriented. But it was as son and brother. Now you have sons of your own. How many times, to how many fascinated classes I have read the table dialogue of "Home Sweet Home"! It is still fresh in my memory. Listen:

"Any work in Sacramento?"

"No, no work in Sacramento."

and

"Let's be nice today. Let's not have any fights."

and

"Cutton, cutton, who's got the cutton?"

and

"Look it up, Squirrel Eyes."

I could even repeat the four-letter word in the last paragraph which in those prehistoric days I altered delicately. What would I have done with the four-letter words in *The Brotherhood of the Grape?*

Will you let me add one little bit? You remember Kipling's lines about meeting triumph and disaster and treating "those two impostors just the same"? Well, I am proud of the way you have met your triumphs. But I honor you still more for the unflinching courage and good will with which you have met the second impostor.

And now my greetings to Mrs. John Fante, the comrade-wife whom I have never met but whom I accept on faith. To you, affection and gratitude from

Your very old friend,

Florence Carpenter

This was not the only heartfelt recognition Fante received during the otherwise terrible year of 1978. Appearing in the November issue of *Westways*, Carey McWilliams's "Writers of the Western Shore" featured Fante prominently and affectionately. Earlier in the year, moreover, Robert Towne had shown his true feelings for *The Brotherhood of the Grape* by exercising his option and purchasing the film rights for $44,500. By far the most consequential show of appreciation for Fante during this time almost went unnoticed, however, a throwaway line of dialogue in a novel entitled *Women* by renegade Los Angeles street writer Charles Bukowski.

Second to no one, not even Robert Towne, in his admiration for Fante's works, Bukowski probably read the same borrowed library copy of *Ask the Dust* as had Towne. Bukowski had read it a quarter of a century earlier, however, in a rented room in downtown Los Angeles where he was trying to become a writer, drinking to excess, starving and in general driving himself if not strictly mad then ever further from accommodation with convention, literary or otherwise. Before winding up in the charity ward of County General Hospital in the mid-1950s hemorrhaging from a bleeding ulcer, Bukowski had published only one short story. "Aftermath

of a Lengthy Rejection Slip" had appeared in the March–April 1944 issue of *Story* when Bukowski was twenty-four years old, a conscious
homage to the two writers who had most influenced him, Knut Hamsun
and even more so John Fante. Since beginning to publish again in 1960,
Bukowski had treasured Fante's works, especially *Ask the Dust*, for literally saving his life. Before the old neighborhood of Bunker Hill was razed
to make way for all the steel-and-glass skyscrapers of today's downtown, he
had often walked past the rooming house where he imagined Fante had
lived in the days of his early struggle to write, fantasizing that he, Charles
Bukowski, was Arturo Bandini, the self-proclaimed greatest writer who
ever lived. Now, with more than twenty published volumes to his name
and a growing international following, Bukowski had fictional alter-ego
Henry Chinaski speak his author's mind in responding to another character's curiosity in *Women*:

> "Who was your favorite author?"
> "Fante."
> "Who?"
> "John F-a-n-t-e. *Ask the Dust, Wait Until Spring, Bandini*." . . .
> "Why did you like him?"
> "Total emotion. A very brave man."

Fante had never heard of Bukowski until another Los Angeles poet,
Ben Pleasants, appeared at his front door, tape recorder in hand and hoping for an interview. Fante invited him in, and between December 1978
and February 1981 Pleasants would visit Fante at home several more
times and conduct five wide-ranging interviews. A knowledgeable man of
letters, Pleasants had discussed with Bukowski the possibility of getting
Ask the Dust back into print, and Bukowski had indicated his willingness
to write a preface to the novel if and when the happy moment came to
pass. Now Pleasants asked Fante's permission to bring the book to the attention of poet Lawrence Ferlinghetti, owner of San Francisco's fabled
City Lights Bookstore and publisher, via his City Lights Books, of Jack
Kerouac, Allen Ginsberg, William Burroughs and many others, including the early Bukowski. Fante readily agreed.

Before the Ferlinghetti initiative could move forward, however, Bukowski's own publisher, John Martin of Santa Barbara's Black Sparrow

Press, happened to ask Bukowski about the passing reference in *Women* to this Fante character. In a phone conversation that would prove to have long-lasting and widespread consequences, Bukowski assured Martin that Fante was not only real but also one of the great unrecognized writers of the century. Arrangements were made for a photocopy to be made of the now increasingly well-thumbed copy of *Ask the Dust* belonging to the Los Angeles Public Library. This copy was sent to Martin, who read it and got back in touch with Bukowski agreeing that the book was a classic and indicating that Black Sparrow would be honored to publish it. Fante needed no prodding, and soon it was agreed that *Ask the Dust* would be on the earliest possible list upcoming from Black Sparrow. After disappearing from print forty years earlier, Arturo Bandini would have a second life after all.

Out of respect for his idol, Bukowski had never dared approach Fante. Now that they were both engaged with John Martin on the same project, however, Fante received tribute from Bukowski in the form of several books and an LP recording of Bukowski's readings from a German poetry tour, each gift inscribed with heartfelt expressions of Bukowski's gratitude. On the title page of *Love Is a Dog from Hell: Poems 1974–1977*, for example, Bukowski wrote, "For John Fante—who taught me how. Hank." At this time Bukowski was writing the screenplay for *Barfly*, which would star Mickey Rourke and Faye Dunaway, for French film director Barbet Schroeder. Feeling cramped by the unfamiliar format and Schroeder's need to oversee the script's page-by-page development, Bukowski wrote to Fante asking for an old pro's advice. Fante obliged, with gusto.

> Your French director who stands over your shoulder measuring the screenplay at one minute per page sounds like a kook to me. It seems to me that subject matter determines style and time. Maybe you might want to break some rules. . . . You need limitless horizons and distances. You cannot be bound by the Frenchman's rules. You are the writer, so write a unique, an unorthodox screenplay.

When Fante received Bukowski's draft preface to *Ask the Dust* in early May, he was back in the Motion Picture Hospital suffering from an infected ulcer on his right foot. His spirits could only have been lifted, however, when Joyce read to him the four typewritten pages with Bukowski's penciled-in corrections. First Bukowski recounted the despair of his youthful search through the L.A. Public Library for something braver than the "comfortable contrivance" of so much modernist writing, most of which he considered mere "word tricks." He had been looking for a book that captured the passion and "the gamble" of the life he knew, but no matter how much he read he had found little of either, whether in philosophy, religion, mathematics or geology. And then he described the eureka moment in the library's big Fiction room when he had pulled *Ask the Dust* off the shelf

and there it was. I stood for a moment, reading. Then like a man who had found gold in the city dump, I carried the book to a table. The lines rolled easily across the page, there was a flow. Each line had its own energy and was followed by another like it. The very substance of each line gave the page a form, a feeling of something *carved* into it. And here, at last, was a man who was not afraid of emotion. The humour and the pain were intermixed with a superb simplicity. The beginning of that book was a wild and enormous miracle to me.

Fante met his new champion for the first time when Bukowski and his future wife Linda Beighle came to visit him at the Motion Picture Hospital. Both Hank and Linda would later claim to recall an aged Johnny Weissmuller, the most famous of all screen Tarzans, "running up and down the halls" of the somnolent facility giving his King of the Jungle call. Mostly, however, Bukowski would remember Fante's bulldog tenacity in the face of his plight as they talked of writing and baseball but never death. Tied as it was to the reappearance of *Ask the Dust*, the visit did Fante a world of good.

Despite such uplifting moments, however, Fante's health remained a crushing cross to bear. His right foot now showed the same signs of deterioration that had led to the loss of his left leg in pieces, macerated running sores that refused to heal. Moreover, his spirits were subject to the blackest of visitations, periodic fits when he was reduced to terrified animal raving. Joyce's meticulous daily record of her ministrations to John and of the fluctuating state of his illness bear grim testimony to the hell his life had become. Upon returning home from the doctor one day in September—Fante had confounded the medical experts once again by improving enough to be released from the Motion Picture Hospital the month before—he developed an extreme paranoia. He was convinced that Joyce had taken him not home to Malibu but rather to a shadowy warehouse filled with sinister sacks and packing crates, and that she was holding him there against his will. Less severe but just as taxing in its way was the recurrent lower-level paranoia that led Fante to wheel himself to the open front door of their home where he would sit sentry, beneath his lap blanket gripping a loaded handgun. And then the terrors would return, the disorientation so complete and the rage so extreme that Joyce could only note in her medical log, "baring teeth and snarling like a dog."

Savage brush fires throughout the Southland in the fall of 1979 had blackened the skies and filled the air with ghostly wisps of floating ash. The medieval horridness of his afflictions notwithstanding, however, it was not all unadulterated misery for Fante. Francis Ford Coppola had reestablished contact, sending Dennis O'Flaherty's screenplay adaptation of *The Brotherhood of the Grape* and inviting Fante's response. Bukowski too, no longer a down-and-out poet haunting the back streets of East Hollywood but a financial success owing in large part to his popularity in Europe, kept up his moral support with encouraging notes from his new home in San Pedro, telling Fante that he was finally "in the big time . . . up there with Goethe, and rightfully so." And Carey McWilliams, too, long a stranger since he had moved to New York, was back in Los Angeles for an extended stay in order to teach a class at UCLA.

All of these factors cooperated to improve Fante's outlook even in the midst of his physical agonies. Early in October John told Joyce to get a pad of paper and a pen and to wheel him out to the back patio. There, where he could smell the breeze in the tall pines and feel the warm autumn air, he began to dictate a story that took him back to his beginnings as a writer and to his favorite alter-ego protagonist, Arturo Bandini. Inside Fante's mind the year was no longer 1979 but 1934 and the place was not Point Dume but downtown Los Angeles. As had the young John Fante once, Bandini had just had his photograph splashed across the front page of a Los Angeles newspaper. The photograph was accompanied by a feature story about the hardworking kid from Colorado and his first literary success with the sale of a short story to *The American Phoenix*, "edited by the most renowned personage in American literature, none other than Heinrich Muller."

After the terrible barren stretch of the last three years it was as if Fante was reborn with the excitement of an idea. No one was more keenly aware of the change in him than Joyce. "I now have a unique opportunity to observe the making of a novel," she wrote to a relative in Roseville. "[John] has been dictating his latest work to me. . . . John's work *is* his life — it literally keeps him alive. Beyond that is incredible persistence and a passion for excellence. He is not satisfied until a passage is right. He is part master craftsman and part instinctive artist."

Over the next two months Fante's craft and instinct would combine to create the fourth and final installment in what has come to be called the Saga of Arturo Bandini. Originally entitled *How to Write a Screenplay*, the novel taking shape in his mind's eye told the story of how Bandini comes to exchange his old Bunker Hill stomping grounds for the gaudier purlieus of Tinseltown. The migration is a comical one, as Bandini moves up the job ladder from busboy in a downtown deli to editorial assistant in a crooked literary agency to highly paid but underutilized scenarist at Columbia Pictures. There amidst the real-life likes of Ben Hecht, Tess Slesinger, Dalton Trumbo, Nathanael West and Horace McCoy, he is ushered into the do-little life of contract screenwriting by Frank Edgington, a lightly fictionalized character based largely on Frank Fenton, with elements of Joel Sayre worked in.

Again blending fact into the fiction — Fante assured one interviewer, for example, that Bandini's screaming encounter with Sinclair Lewis was written exactly as it had happened to Fante — the novel traces the evolution of regret and the ingrowth of longing that Fante himself knew so well. When Bandini recognizes the sham behind the masquerade of so much Hollywood glamor, he wishes for "the reality of Bunker Hill" once again, for his beloved hotel room and his beloved desk clerk, Mrs. Brownell. Indeed, it is to Mrs. Brownell — affectionate, understanding and five years older than his mother — that Bandini makes haste to return. But in this novel one return leads to another, each as numinous as it is impossible to sustain. Thus when Mrs. Brownell can no longer bear the sadness of an affair with a man thirty years her junior, Arturo vacates his room and returns to the Los Angeles Harbor of his youth. There he settles on Terminal Island, a paradise of white sand beaches and seaside cottages. But paradise is soon invaded in the person of the Duke of Sardinia, a professional wrestler and veriest caricature of the Italian ethnic, all accent and onions and olive oil. As if sprung fully formed from Arturo's deepest emotional insecurities, as well as from Fante's bodily incapacitation, the superbly physical Duke soon drives the young scribbler off the island, and "Like a homing bird I flew to Bunker Hill, to my old hotel, to the kindest woman I had ever known."

But he is not yet truly home, for in his absence his room has been rented out to someone else, and Mrs. Brownell remains firm in her resolution to end their affair. Cut off from his anchorage in Los Angeles, Arturo is left seemingly with but one place to return to, and he boards a Greyhound bus for Boulder, Colorado. He arrives in a snowstorm, no patly blinding affair but rather a revelation, for out of the swirling white cold steps the figure of his father. No longer dead as in *The Road to Los Angeles* or simply absent as in *Ask the Dust*, Arturo's father has rematerialized for the first time since *Wait Until Spring, Bandini* to offer his son the coat off his back. "The overcoat felt warm from the heat of his body," Arturo tells us; and suddenly "[i]t was all of a piece, a part of my life, like an old chair, or a worn fork, or my mother's shawl, the things of my life, the precious worthless treasured things."

There follows a joyous reunion with his mother, sister and two younger brothers, then lasagna for dinner, and a soothing procession of days lazing about his childhood home. But Bandini would not be Bandini if he could leave well enough alone. Like all his earlier returns, this one must fail too, for he makes the mistake of bragging about his Hollywood life to old hometown acquaintances, and suddenly home is again the place he must flee.

Bandini is thus left with the need to make one last return, and it is inevitable that he make it, the return to Los Angeles, his Eternal City, where all roads in his saga lead. On his third return to his old hotel, however—that place of longed-for permanence, "that lobby that would last forever"—he learns that Mrs. Brownell has died of a stroke while he was away. So he walks down to Temple Street, as solemn as any priest, and takes a room in a Filipino hotel. "It was my kind of room," Arturo tells us, as if his kind of room is always available to the kind of person who perennially needs it. "I deserved it—the smallest, most uninviting room in Los Angeles." And there he sits down at his typewriter, says a prayer to Knut Hamsun, and sets to writing again, "for a man had to start someplace."

No parable could be clearer. The one thing that survives in a world forever changing is the good dream—the real dream—of human connection, be that connection through romantic love, or family, or art. The dream *is* the reality, the novel seems to say, a surprisingly Platonic notion for a writer so rooted in the palpable guts of existence. Lest we forget, however, Fante was in the throes of leaving that existence as he imagined and dictated this novel, deprived of his sight and one of his legs and with the other slowly rotting away. Before he could leave his body, his body was taking leave of him. Only his imagination remained intact, and for a final few weeks it enabled him to soar free of the wreckage of his once-vital corpse-to-be in dream-visions that he captured in words.

Remarkably, less than three months after Fante had started dictating, the novel was completed by the beginning of December and Joyce had typed the manuscript by December 7. Even more remarkably, there was not the slightest hint anywhere in the novel of bitterness or resentment or self-pity. Over and over near the end of his life Fante told people that bitterness was the writer's worst enemy. Representative are his words to Ben Pleasants: "I believe the one thing a writer must avoid is . . . bitterness. It is the fault that can destroy him. It can shrivel him up. . . . Bitterness is the one thing a writer must fight. I've fought it all my life."

Having fought and overcome nearly incomprehensible obstacles in writing *Dreams from Bunker Hill*, Fante called the book a "black comedy, scandalous, grotesque, bizarre." There can be no doubt that it was all of those things, but it was also something more, a testament we might say to Fante's sustaining faith in his writing as the one way he knew how to make miracles. Charles Bukowski certainly felt the miraculous effects of Fante's writing when over the phone he listened to Joyce reading the book's last chapter. Bukowski had been in what he called an "impotent period" but hearing Fante's words gave him to believe that "because of Celine and Dos [Passos] and Hamsun but mainly because of you" he would come out of it again. "You have meant, do mean more to me than any man living or dead," Bukowski confessed to Fante. "I had to tell you this. Now I am beginning to smile a little."

It rained hard all day on Christmas Eve that year. The downpour did not deter Dan Fante from picking up Carey and Iris McWilliams in Los Angeles, however, and driving them north on the shining Pacific Coast Highway to spend the evening in Malibu with the Fantes. While in Los Angeles during the last several months Carey had maintained his usual headlong pace, teaching, giving speeches and granting interviews to television reporters Tritia Toyota and Kelly Lange and a longer, more strenuous session to *Los Angeles Times* editorial writer Kay Mills. (Compounding Carey's status as a media favorite during his stay in Los Angeles, the television movie *Act of Violence*, starring Elizabeth Montgomery and based in part on Carey's experience of being mugged in New York, aired on CBS in November.) Through it all he had been enduring radiation treatment for his advancing cancer every day before going to UCLA's Bunche Hall to meet his class of forty students, who on the last day of the term had given him a standing ovation. Now, however, it was time to slow down as the two old friends, Carey and John, met for the first time in years. Given the dire state of their respective conditions, they were both painfully aware that it would also be the last time they met.

All four Fante children were present that night, as were assorted spouses and most of the grandchildren, and there was Joyce in a shimmering yellow gown overseeing the assemblage like the benevolent witch-mother that she was. (Earlier Carey had made a gift of *The Education of Carey McWilliams*, inscribing it "For John Fante, 'dear friend and evil companion,' and Joyce, the Witch of Malibu.") The Christmas tree was bright with ornaments and thick underneath with presents, and the dinner Joyce served was delicious. Someone turned on a tape recorder, and though it is difficult at times to make out the talk through all the sounds of a family celebration, the warmth comes through in the voices of John and Carey, both of whom were in excellent spirits. After dinner eldest son Nick, who since before he was ten years old had been reading his father's books, read aloud three chapters from the dictated novel, with Fante listening closely throughout. It all came off beautifully, the dinner, the reading, the long-delayed reunion. And when it was over John and Carey clasped hands and told each other goodbye.

The Black Sparrow edition of *Ask the Dust* appeared in January of 1980. In its wake came a flurry of high praise. Newspaper articles began to appear with titles such as "The Great Los Angeles Novel" and "The Consummate L.A. Novel," and by early March the *Los Angeles Times* was asserting that "a cult has formed" around Fante's long-neglected masterpiece. As for himself, Fante was no longer neglected, at least for now, by grateful readers both old and new. Letters began arriving from people Fante had not seen since the 1930s, among others J. V. Cunningham, Fante's poetic classmate from Regis College, now University Professor of English Literature at Brandeis University; Herman Cherry, a former clerk at the Stanley Rose Bookshop who had gone on to a painting career in New York; Marjorie Brown Shneidman, a fellow member of Skalds at Long Beach City College who had typed the first story Fante had had accepted by Mencken; and Muriel D. Bradley, whom Fante had helped get hired in the Stenographers Department at Warner Bros. and who went on to become a published writer of suspense and historical novels. One and all, they were thrilled to know that Fante was alive and that the book they remembered so vividly and with such fondness was receiving a second life.

Strangely enough, the only person who seemed to be neglecting Fante now that he had returned to the public's attention was one of those most responsible for the resurgence of popular interest, Robert Towne. For some time Fante had been trying to contact Towne about *Ask the Dust*, the film rights to which had reverted to Fante, but Towne was not returning his calls, leaving Fante disturbed and mystified. In February of 1980 Fante wrote Coppola's right-hand man Tom Sternberg in San Francisco to report that Towne "obviously . . . is ducking me," and to indicate that he would thus like for Coppola to take *Ask the Dust* under consideration, independent of Towne. Wishing to keep the air clear between Coppola and Towne, Sternberg immediately wrote to Michael Ovitz, Towne's agent at Creative Artists Agency, apprising him of Fante's feelings and asking that he likewise so apprise Towne. But Towne would remain mysteriously incommunicado for some time to come.

Fante's thoughts were now running toward the darkness. To a young writer, Tom Christie, who had taken it upon himself to begin visiting the ailing author at home, Fante intimated that he was considering a new novel about going blind, but that he hated the thought of writing a depressing novel. Since the luminous interlude he had been granted while writing *Dreams from Bunker Hill*, Fante's health had fallen to a new low, marked by sporadic mental disorientation and constant wracking physical pain. He was back in the Motion Picture Hospital for two weeks in late April and early May because of the acute deterioration of his right foot. Then, inexplicably, he was released to go home, there to suffer the macabre experience of observing himself decay.

It was during this time that Charles Bukowski and Linda Beighle drove out to Malibu to have lunch with John and Joyce. It happened to be trash day, and as the great city truck rumbled past the house on Cliff-side Drive Fante tried telling a joke. On trash days, he said, Joyce had to hold on to him to keep the trash man from tossing him in with the rest of the neighborhood's garbage. When nobody laughed he excused himself and rolled away to his room. A few moments passed, and then an unearthly moaning started up.

On July 22, with gangrene again having set in, Fante's right big toe was removed. The doctors were only trying to help, certainly, but they could have caused no more physical pain or mental anguish had they gone out of their way to be intentionally cruel; for nine days later Fante was again back in surgery, this time to have what remained of his right leg amputated above the knee.

On June 27 in New York City Carey McWilliams had died. Within the next year, on May 18 in Fresno, William Saroyan would also be dead, another victim of cancer. By then Joyce Fante would have survived her own brush with the disease, while John would have outlasted another long-term bout in the Motion Picture Hospital, from late September 1980 to early February 1981. In April both John and Joyce came down with the flu, an otherwise inconsiderable coincidence of upset stomachs and long naps. Given John's nearly total dependence on Joyce, however, it is unnerving to imagine the feverish details with which husband and wife now had to grapple, the spiking fire-and-ice temperatures, the nausea, the vomiting. As John had predicted ten years before, they were discovering interesting things about each other, not least of all the expanding bounds of their mutual endurance, and enabling that, their faithfulness and, yes, their love.

In 1981 Bukowski dedicated his latest poetry collection, *Dangling in the Tournefortia*, "To John Fante." Because of Bukowski's reputation around the world as the reigning American literary outlaw, the gesture was guaranteed to boost Fante's sales and spark additional book-buying interest. Already the Italians were inquiring after translation rights to Ask the Dust, and the Germans were interested too, and when the French got involved, as they would before long, Fante would be another Black Sparrow phenomenon. Sure enough, with Ask the Dust selling briskly, in April John Martin sent a publishing contract for Dreams from Bunker Hill, along with a stack of blank pages for Fante to autograph. As Martin explained, signed editions were an important part of the independent publisher's business, so it was important that John keep signing. When he got tired Joyce made sure to give him a break, but she also made sure that, having written his books, he did as much as he could to enhance their value yet further in the worldwide literary marketplace. As she had plainly announced to a friend two years earlier, "I think that Ask the Dust is a major American novel, and I intend to see that it is recognized as such."

Aside from autographing blank sheets, Fante was trying to get another novel under way, but he was encountering "considerable difficulty." Writing to a distant East Coast relation, Fante explained that the "worst result of blindness is its effect upon memory. I forget things. I dictate a sentence and in five minutes I can't remember what it was . . . but I blunder on." He was trying to write about two brothers in Boulder, one a baseball fanatic, the other a chain-smoking scholar. When that story went nowhere he tried something different, one in which the widow of an ex-convict cares for the mute parrot brought back by her husband from Folsom Prison. And when that story failed he started on another, rarer still, this one about an Alaskan husky, the favorite pup of his mother's nursing litter, sired by a great black brooding beast named Diablo.

Needless to say, none of these projects was ever finished. To fill the time when he was not writing John took to listening to the radio more and more. Country and western music seemed to appeal to him for some reason, and Dodger baseball games, announced by Jerry Doggett and the great Hall of Famer Vin Scully, provided his one true joy in the constant darkness that was now his.

In late September 1981 Fante received a letter postmarked Paradise, California, from someone he had not seen in decades. The letter was from his aged aunt Dorothy, Uncle Ralph Capolungo's ex-wife, with whom John had briefly shared an apartment when he first moved to Los Angeles half a century earlier. They had both been penniless then, Aunt Dorothy recalled, but now those days seemed golden, what with her health just as broken as John's. Did he recall all the fun they used to have playing Chinese checkers every night? And Uncle Paul's violin? There were so many questions to ask and so much to remember, but she did not want to tire him and so she signed off, hoping to hear from him sometime soon.

"Dear Aunt Dorothy," Fante wrote in response, "How did you arrive in Paradise? Did you spend much time in purgatory? I wonder if you ran into my father. I am certain that he spent at least 25 years in purgatory, and may be in Heaven at this time." Even in extremis Fante remained capable of mustering a whimsical sense of humor, as he went on to describe the plight of a man confined to a wheelchair amidst all the dogs and the fleas but blessed with four children and, most of all,

the woman who brought all of this on—all of my problems, my travail, my bitterness, my true love, my dear and beautiful wife, who is without shame, a born hussy, who mistreats me, reviles me, and loves me in return. We are truly an odd couple, bumping into one another from time to time, cursing one another, and quarreling day and night—but love we never lack, and the moment our quarreling ceases we are in one another's arms again. It's a hard life, but I can't think of any other that suits me so well.

After more than fifty years of writing letters Fante would never write another. In the predawn darkness of December 28 he awakened Joyce, screaming insanely for her to get up out of bed and make coffee. The next night the moaning and the screaming and the obscene imprecations began just after midnight and did not cease until he had exhausted himself. After years of such unpredictable flights of abuse, as well as the all-too-predictable daily horrors of John's illness, Joyce was exhausted. She suffered from diverticulitis, high blood pressure and constant worry, and at last she could take it no longer. Setting her mind on the steps that had to be taken she made the necessary phone calls, then with son Jim's help she got John in the car for the curving ride north through beautiful Malibu

Canyon, back to the Motion Picture and Television Country House in Woodland Hills, where he was admitted to the hospital for the last time.

The last seventeen months of John Fante's life were spent almost exclusively in a private hospital room equipped with a television, which was useless, and a radio. Because the Country House was filled with retired show business people, a variety of entertainment-oriented activities took place regularly for the residents, an array of games and socials and film screenings. Fante took part in none of these, preferring instead to stay in his room and listen to his radio, and emerging only for his biweekly haircut. It was, he told one visitor, as if someone had stuck him in a barrel and then clamped the lid on. He had even stopped trying to write.

In January 1982 Black Sparrow's *Dreams from Bunker Hill* appeared to consistently warm notices. Word of Fante's rediscovery was now steadily spreading, and letters from far-flung readers smitten with the irrepressible quality of his writing were piling up, testaments to Fante's unwavering gift for affecting people. At Joyce's suggestion John Martin expressed interest in publishing a volume of John's stories, but first Martin wanted to make sure that Fante was still able to sign blank pages in his present state of health. When Joyce assured him that this would not be a problem, Martin set about preparing a collection that would add to the stories in *Dago Red* several previously uncollected pieces. Rallying at the news that his work was still alive, Fante proposed that the new book be called *The Wine of Youth*; and when he heard that Black Sparrow was going to do a new edition of *Wait Until Spring, Bandini* as well, he knew that he was in the right hands. He tired quickly now but that didn't matter: he set to signing pages again.

Joyce visited Fante several times a week, and not always simply to sit by his bedside. One day as she appeared in the doorway, before she had even said hello, Fante inclined his head in her direction and said, "I've been thinking of fucking you." He had other visitors as well. His four children came when they could, bringing along assorted grandchildren, including the newest Fante, Morgan, Nick's daughter by his second wife, Sharyn; the child was a redhead like her grandfather, who held her in his arms. Vickie brought her second husband, Michael Cohen. Fante also had visits from friends good enough to overcome the ambient fear of death which makes any hospital a hard place to visit. Harry Essex and Richard Quine and Edmund Morris and Tom Christie came to see him, and so finally did Robert Towne, emerging from his seclusion bearing a gift of expensive cigars and inspiring Fante to pretend that Towne was there simply as his personal tobacconist. (Another time, when Fante lay in his room as if dead to the world, he was brought back to life by a thoughtful phone call from Towne, better medicine than any doctor could prescribe.) No matter how good the talk was, however—Fante could still rise to the occasion with vigor and wit for brief but precious moments—these visits had about them the unspoken sadness of goodbye. Comparisons are odious, but as wrenching as any of these was the visit by Fante's old friend and collaborator Al Bezzerides.

When Bezzerides entered the hospital he found Fante sitting in a wheelchair near the nurses' station with his two stumps sticking out, gazing blindly as if into space. Bezzerides said, "John," and Fante turned his head. "Al?" he said.

So I went over there and we hugged each other and talked our heads off and I said, "Jesus, I'm sorry this is happening to you." And he says, "Aw." And I said, "Well, what do you do sitting here in this goddamn wheelchair all the time?" And he said, "I'm writing a book." I said, "You are? That's wonderful. What's it about?" And he says, "You know, my writing. You want to know what the title is?" I said, "Yeah." Now comes the pinch, boy: "*Fante's Inferno!*" Man, I sat there and looked at this guy that had been wrenched out of his life and was in a hospital and was doomed to die there. And he told me more about his suffering and his torture with a joke.

It was late February 1983 when the new Black Sparrow edition of *Wait Until Spring, Bandini* arrived in the mail at Rancho Fante. Writing John Martin to thank him for all he had done and all he still planned to do, Joyce confessed, "I am afraid my copy is splashed with tears. I remember the day the first edition came out, and John and I opened its covers. What a day that was!" It was a different kind of day when John held the second edition in his hands in his Country House hospital room, but a day worth surviving for. "I am sure I shall never read this book again," he had written for the Preface to the new edition. "But of this I am sure: all of the people of my writing life, all of my characters are to be found in this early work. Nothing of myself is there any more, only the memory of old bedrooms, and the sound of my mother's slippers walking to the kitchen."

Aunt Dorothy had died in Paradise on Saint Valentine's Day. After a long fall and winter, however, spring was almost in the air, and with it the promise of Vin Scully and the Dodgers on the radio. It was the same promise of spring training and endless baseball that had given hope to Arturo Bandini when he was a boy and he had made up just the right story to persuade his prodigal father to come home again and make his long-suffering family whole again . . .

And then somebody stole Fante's radio. One day it was there and the next it was gone, and with it something of Fante's spirit. No one knew who could have done such a thing, stolen a blind man's one pleasure. But after the theft John was never quite the same.

To try to cheer him up some well-meaning staffer sent a volunteer in to see him, a big-voiced male candy striper named Hal. Hal barged in talking with his tape recorder going—why a tape recorder it is impossible to say; but the evidence exists of how Fante's long nightmare had come to this: a laughing stranger invading his room to try to tickle his spirits, uncalled for but there all the same.

—*Good morning, John Fante. This is Hal. . . . I'm one of the Blue Angels here, or Blue Devils as you call them. And I just wondered, I read an article in the Book Review where it said you were about to complete another book. Is that true, John?*

To which Fante answers simply,

—*No.*

—*You're not going to complete another book?*

To which Fante answers,

—*Not in the immediate present . . .*

At which the Blue Devil prattles on in his stagy upbeat voice, trying to draw Fante out. But Fante refuses to play along, or perhaps he simply cannot, for his voice sounds so tired and absent. He cannot remember the title of one of his novels, *something about the vineyard*, nor does he think he ever knew a young man whom Hal insists he helped learn to write.

—*Did you know a fellow by the name of Bukowski?*

—*Bukowski* . . .

—*Yeah. Did you help Bukowski write?*

—*No, I didn't.*

—*Oh, he was a pretty good writer too, wasn't he?*

—*Yes, he was. He is. He's a current writer.*

—*He's a current writer.*

—*Yeah.*

—*Have you any idea what your book is going to be about, your last book that you're going to write?*

At which Fante takes a breath, as if struggling to make some kind of sense out of this ghastly intrusion.

—*My last book,* he says, *is probably going to be about myself engaged in this particular hospital* . . .

At which the Blue Devil cannot suppress a giggle.

—*You got a little room for me in your book, John?*

—*I guess so, sure.*

—*What would you write about me?*

—*Well, I'm not sure.*

—*You're not telling your books.*

—*Well, I don't know. I like to write one thing today and not write it to-morrow.*

—*But you're in great hopes of finishing another book?*

At which Fante, sounding wearier than ever, sighs,

—*Oh, yes.*

—*Oh, very good!*

And now it's time for the Devil to go.

—*The book that John was referring to, "In the Vineyard," was called Brotherhood of the Grape. That is about all, I think, for this interview. Thank you, John.*

At which the tape recorder is turned off.

The last fragment of dictation that Joyce took from Fante at the Motion Picture Home evinces a mind sinking back into its deepest fears. Fante had spent much of his creative life transforming these fears into lasting literature, but as they resurfaced now they were stripped of anything artful, demons rampant against a backdrop of remembered hate.

In the winter of 1890 a startling development was the cause of much bloodshed on the Italian-American front. Several thousand Italians in America broke into internecine war and brought about the death of hundreds of Italians and Americans. A war so far apart consuming the lives of so many thousands of native Italians was an unprecedented occasion, and many Italians, both men and women, suffered. The main cause seems to have been the savage attack of Americans against Italians. . . .

At that he stopped short. Joyce sat with pen poised, ready to continue writing. Had he fallen asleep? Or was he just resting his eyes? But why should he rest his eyes?

> *There was an old man of th'Abruzzi*
> *So blind that he couldn't his foot see.*

Only a nonsense rhyme like the one by Edward Lear could seem to hold any meaning at this late date in the horror. Fante's hand had become too unsteady to sign his name clearly, *John Fante, John Fante,* and so he had finally stopped his blind signing of blank pages. He was seventy-four years old, what little the surgeons had left of him, and now his condition took a turn for the worse. It was pneumonia in the lungs, and so the vigil began, one day, two days, three days, four. The family was there, in and out of the room, Joyce, Nick, Dan, Vickie, Jim and a number of others, moving about in a dreamy fog. At one point John squeezed Joyce's hand and told her that he loved her. A priest was called to administer the last rites and deliver viaticum, but according to eldest son Nick, instead of receiving the Host Fante spit it out for the simple reason that he was not ready to leave this life. And then, shortly afterward, he left it.

It was May 8, 1983, at three o'clock in the afternoon. Elsewhere children were gathering papers and pencils and bursting out of classrooms. It was spring. You could feel it in the air all around you.

EPILOGUE

"**I** can say honestly: there was only one John Fante, and Heaven will be a different place because of his arrival."

So wrote Paul Reinert, the big Clover Club first-baseman become Jesuit priest, upon hearing of his old friend's long and agonized dying. In the time following Fante's death, others wrote to say much the same thing in their own words. A couple of examples will suffice.

"He was a gritty warrior, a fine writer, and a man in every sense of the word," was how John Martin put it. "A writer creates books so that his vision of the world will not be lost. John's vision of the world is permanently and beautifully preserved in his books."

And Edmund Morris: "I had the privilege and honor of working with John; every day of our collaboration was rewarding. Let his children know they were fathered by an authentic man whose authentic voice produced some of the finest lyrical prose in American literature. God bless the Fantes."

On May 11 at Our Lady of Malibu Church a requiem mass was conducted in the traditional Latin. None of the big Hollywood names who had been associated with Fante managed to show up, but a few lesser known writer friends came to pay their respects, including Edmund Morris, Harry Essex, Rudy Borchert and Ben Pleasants. Ill at ease in the incense-heavy atmosphere, Bill Asher was anxious to get away in time to make the first post at Hollywood Park. In a rear pew, by contrast, Martin Sheen attended closely to the liturgy, rising and kneeling and responding in Latin to all the antiphonal prayers. Charles Bukowski sat apart from family members and friends, grieving privately in a rumpled brown sport jacket.

Afterward, the funeral procession traveled south down Pacific Coast Highway, ending in Fox Hills at Holy Cross Cemetery. The plot was at the foot of a grassy slope with a view of Culver City's industrial backside. After the interment a considerable time passed before the grave received a marker, but when one was laid the image upon it was perfect, a traditional depiction of the Virgin Mary standing atop planet Earth, arms extended in welcome, one bare foot crushing the head of a serpent. It was a simple illustration, its lines almost childlike, but something about it was strange: unlike the thousands of other such images throughout the vast cemetery, the Virgin on Fante's headstone was smiling.

Less than two weeks later, the first attempt at a comprehensive consideration of the writer's life and career appeared, Kathi Norklun's "John Fante (1909–1983) and the Great L.A. Novel." This article was the first of many other such overview-appreciations published in the popular press over the next decade and a half, evidence that readers continued to find their way to Fante's works without benefit of academic or corporate publishing support.

By the end of the year in which Fante died, Paris publisher Christian Bourgois had begun making arrangements with Joyce Fante and John Martin to bring out translations of Ask the Dust, Wait Until Spring, Bandini, and Dreams from Bunker Hill. Fante was thus launched onto French best-seller lists, which helped prepare the way for the larger European audience that soon came to embrace him. That embrace continues to this day. As I write these words in the summer of 1999, handsome new editions of Fante's works are being released in Italy, where the son of Nick Fante of Torricella Peligna is regarded by readers as one of their own American kin; while to the north in France, Germany, the Low Countries and Scandinavia, the names of John Fante and Arturo Bandini live on, as indeed they do elsewhere, in country after country around the world.

Until his death of leukemia in 1994, Charles Bukowski continued to commemorate Fante's courage and his legacy in such typically rough-hewn poems as "The Passing of a Great One," "Suggestion for an Arrangement," "Result," "The Wine of Forever," and "Fante." Bukowski's esteem for Fante remained unflagging, as would the expressions of his indebtedness to *Ask the Dust*, the novel he always thought was unsurpassed.

Critical recognition of Fante, while slow in catching up with his posthumous popularity, has recently begun to coalesce. In May 1995 it was my privilege to help organize a three-day conference devoted solely to Fante which drew scores of writers, filmmakers, artists and scholars, as well as all of Fante's immediate surviving family, to California State University, Long Beach. Academic respect does not always translate into undergraduate enthusiasm, but in Fante's case there seems to be little contradiction between the two as professors and students alike discover the delights and the challenges of Fante's works.

As for Fante and film, the relationship goes on, subject to the same industrial vagaries as ever. Robert Towne has written a script based on *Ask the Dust* and continues his efforts on behalf of both that project and *The Brotherhood of the Grape*. Peter Falk has purchased the film rights to *My Dog Stupid* and is working to mount a film adaptation with actor-director John Turturro. Other Fante titles in various stages of development—always a slippery word, that—include *1933 Was a Bad Year*, "A Wife for Dino Rossi" and, so it is rumored, *Full of Life*, the remake.

If today you go to Pershing Square in the heart of downtown Los Angeles, you can see Carey McWilliams's words engraved on a commemorative stone wall. The words, excerpted from *Southern California Country: An Island on the Land*, describe the epiphany Carey experienced one morning after an "extremely active evening in Hollywood." Emerging from the Biltmore Hotel to make "the rocky pilgrimage through Pershing Square to my office in a state of miserable decrepitude

. . . it suddenly occurred to me that, in all the world, there neither was nor would there ever be another place like this City of the Angels."

For Carey McWilliams, that city would not have been itself without the vibrant presence of his friend John Fante. For some of us who have come later it is just as true that the city would not be the Los Angeles we know without John Fante's legacy. In 1984 Mayor Tom Bradley was presented with a proposal from the chairman of the County Board of Supervisors that a Los Angeles street be named in John Fante's memory. As matters turned out, no street was then available to be accorded the honor, and the proposal was eventually forgotten. Perhaps someday it will be raised again, or perhaps someone will propose that the inscription from Carey McWilliams's book be joined by the lover's demand in *Ask the Dust*: "Los Angeles, give me some of you! Los Angeles come to me the way I came to you, my feet over your streets, you pretty town I loved you so much, you sad flower in the sand, you pretty town." Whether or not any such civic-minded gesture comes to pass, however, it is clear that the resurgence will continue for the writer now recognized as the "father" of the Los Angeles novel, and as "the patron saint of . . . L.A. writing." As Fante himself observed, after all, "saints can be the strangest of people in the damndest of places."

No such rebirth would be taking place without the faith and vision of one person more than any other. Since their secret marriage in 1937, Joyce Fante has never wavered in her belief that John Fante was a great writer. For forty-six years she stayed by his side, even during his long periods of inactivity and illness, when he often treated her brutally. Since his death in 1983 Joyce has been tireless in her efforts to secure for her late husband the legacy that he earned through his writing. She continues to see him in her dreams.

In the summer of 1974 I was living in a rented room in Los Angeles. I was twenty-four years old, unemployed and unattached, and I was trying to teach myself how to write. I had a radio and for entertainment I listened to Dodger games, nothing else. There was a woman I knew who worked at the State Hospital in Camarillo. Once or twice I drove up there to see her, or so I told myself, though the real reason was to walk the grounds of the asylum where, as I understood it, my blood father had been institutionalized before getting out and shooting himself to death. Those memories were hazy—I had been a very young boy at the time of his death—but if only for that rented room and my typewriter and those trips to Camarillo, the summer of 1974 would have remained clear in my mind. But there was also something else.

One August day I came across an article in the *Los Angeles Times* about a new movie I had admired. The movie was *Chinatown* and in this article the screenwriter Robert Towne mentioned a novelist whose name was new to me, John Fante, and a novel of his called *Ask the Dust*, which Towne said simply was the best novel ever written about Los Angeles. I could not rest until I had tracked down a used copy of that book to see if Towne's assertion was true; and when I had finished the book I could not sleep, so amazed was I at its beauty.

Without really knowing what I was doing I wrote what I took to be a review of a novel that had been out of print for over thirty years, and then I sent what I had written to the *Los Angeles Times Book Review*. I then went to the library and like Florence Carpenter I found John Fante's address in Malibu. I wrote him a letter saying how much I had been moved by the story of Arturo Bandini and how I wished everyone could read the novel. And when I went back to trying to teach myself how to write I could feel I was changing in some way that was important.

Time passed. The review I had submitted came back from the *Times* with a note thanking me for my effort but declining it. I wasn't too disappointed because deep inside I had expected it would be rejected. And besides, by then another letter had arrived.

Dear Steve:

Thanks very much for your generous thoughts about Ask the Dust. I wish I could spare a copy for you but they are rare indeed. . . .

Writing is a great joy but the profession of writing is horrible. I wish you all the good luck in the world.

Sincerely yours,
John Fante

I have felt his wish with me all these years.

NOTES

AD	*Ask the Dust*. Santa Rosa: Black Sparrow Press, 1980.
BG	*The Brotherhood of the Grape*. Santa Rosa: Black Sparrow Press, 1988.
DBH	*Dreams from Bunker Hill*. Santa Rosa: Black Sparrow Press, 1982.
Fante/Mencken	*John Fante & H. L. Mencken: A Personal Correspondence 1930–1952*. Ed. Michael Moreau and consulting ed. Joyce Fante. Santa Rosa: Black Sparrow Press, 1989.
FL	*Full of Life*. Santa Rosa: Black Sparrow Press, 1988.
RLA	*The Road to Los Angeles*. Santa Rosa: Black Sparrow Press, 1985.
SL	*John Fante: Selected Letters 1932–1981*. Ed. Seamus Cooney. Santa Rosa: Black Sparrow Press, 1991.
WR	*West of Rome*. Santa Rosa: Black Sparrow Press, 1986.
WSB	*Wait Until Spring, Bandini*. Santa Rosa: Black Sparrow Press, 1983.
WY	*The Wine of Youth: Selected Stories*. Santa Rosa: Black Sparrow Press, 1983.

CHAPTER 1

4. In order to write the scene: *SL*, p. 280.
4. "a nightmare of stones": Anne MacDonnell, *In the Abruzzi* (London: Chatto & Windus, 1908), p. 212. This book informs much of the chapter's discussion of deep historical background.
5. "with valor and honor": Cosmo di Cicco, abbot of the parish of San Giacomo Apostolo in Torricella Peligna, November 7, 1924. In this letter to Domenico Fante of Philadelphia, Father di Cicco traces the Fante family genealogy through his investigations in the parish archives and at the Bureau of Heraldry in Rome.
6. war of national unification: Information on the Bourbons and the Risorgimento comes from Benedetto Croce, *History of the Kingdom of Naples*, ed. and trans. H. Stuart Hughes (Chicago: University of Chicago Press, 1970); and Gay Talese, *Unto the Sons* (New York: Alfred A. Knopf, 1992).
7. His first bid to succeed: Interview with Joyce Fante, July 21, 1994.
7. the once thriving economy: William A. Douglass, *Emigration in a South Italian Town: An Anthropological History* (New Brunswick: Rutgers University Press, 1984), 96.
9. "our major meditative novelist": Jay Martin, keynote address at "John Fante: The First Conference," California State University, May 5, 1995. See also Martin's essay "John Fante: The Burden of Modernism and the Life of His Mind" in *John Fante: A Critical Gathering*, ed. Stephen Cooper and David Fine (Madison, N.J.: Fairleigh Dickinson University Press, 1999), p. 25.
9. "the finest novel written in all time": Charles Bukowski in an unpublished letter to Joyce Fante, December 18, 1985. See also Stephen Cooper, "John Fante's Eternal City" in *Los Angeles in Fiction*, ed. David Fine (Albuquerque: University of New Mexico Press, 1995), p. 97.
9. "[i]f there's a better piece of fiction": Robert Towne, quoted in Wayne Warga, "Writer Towne: Under the Smog, a Feel for the City," *Los Angeles Times Calendar*, August 18, 1974, p. 22.
9. Nick Fante sailed: *Index to Passenger Lists of Vessels Arriving at New York, New York, June 6, 1897–June 30, 1902*. National Archives and Records Administration, Pacific Region, Laguna Niguel, California.
9. a document . . . notarized: Giovanni Fante's *Consenso d'espatrio* was notarized on October 20, 1900.
10. a pamphlet like the one: John Foster Carr, *Guide for the Immigrant Italian in the United States* (Garden City, N.Y.: Doubleday, Page & Co., 1911), p. 77.
10. With a turn-of-the-century population: Thomas J. Noel, *The City and the Saloon: Denver, 1858–1916* (Lincoln: University of Nebraska Press, 1982), p. 116.
10. "You gotta buck?": John Fante told the story of the Denver reunion of his father and grandfather in an undated audio recording made in the late 1970s, in conversation with his wife Joyce and son Dan.
11. "Death to the Dago!": Noel, *The City and the Saloon*, p. 61.
11. The 1890s had been: Carl Abbot, Stephen J. Leonard and David McComb, *Colorado: A History of the Centennial State* (Boulder: Colorado Associated University Press, 1982), pp. 205, 267–72.
12. plans for the auditorium's construction: Frederick S. Allen, Ernest Andrade, Jr.,

Mark S. Foster, Philip I. Mitterling and H. Lee Scamehorn, *The University of Colorado: 1876–1976* (New York: Harcourt Brace Jovanovich, 1976), pp. 55–56.

13. Mary's devotion to Saint Teresea: After her death in 1897, devotion to the French Carmelite nun Thérèse or Teresa of Lisieux grew rapidly, leading to her early canonization in 1925 as Saint Teresa of the Child of Jesus. Devotees like Mary Capolungo would have considered her a saint even before she was officially named one.

13. In two published stories: "A Kidnapping in the Family" and "A Nun No More." The unpublished manuscript was called "The Man from Rome," an early version of materials that would eventually become *Wait Until Spring, Bandini*. With Norman Foster in 1943 Fante cowrote "Love Story" for Orson Welles, a screenplay based loosely on his mother and father's courtship.

13. the Latin culture of an overwhelming masculine mystique: See Andrew Rolle, *The Italian Americans: Troubled Roots* (New York: The Free Press, 1980), p. 111.

14. her uncle Rocco Capolungo's saloon: The address of this saloon, 3659 Navajo Street, was later the address of the Pirate Art Oasis, a venue for contemporary music, arts and open readings by local poets and writers. On May 18, 1983, ten days after John Fante died, a memorial reading dedicated to his memory took place there, proceeds going to the American Diabetes Society.

CHAPTER 2

16. "He was a handsome man": Interview with Edward Campiglia, September 16, 1996.

18. Giovanni Fante died: Information on Fante's grandparents comes from his unpublished manuscript "Grandma Versus America." Although family names have been changed to Fante's favorite alternates—his grandfather Giovanni is called Arturo—Fante pointedly refers to this piece as an "essay."

19. "But Mamma": WY, 123.

20. "gentle and generous": WY, 129.

20. "I am crying, Mike": WY, 131.

20. "sucking it down greedily": WY, 132.

20. a profile of Fante: Richard Donovan, "John Fante of Roseville," *San Francisco Chronicle*, March 9, 1941, "This World" section, p. 14.

21. "to quicken the spirit": Raymond C. Dobson, ed. *History of the Order of the Elks* (Chicago: Benevolent and Protective Order of the Elks, 1978), p. 430.

22. Rinn's famous and frequent toasts: "M. M. Rinn Dies in Los Angeles Where He and Wife Were Vacationing," obituary in *Boulder Daily Camera*, February 24, 1958.

22. True, he was away: Interview with Tom Fante, September 17, 1996.

22. a resourceful and energetic lawyer: In an interview with the author on September 18, 1996, Nick Fante's niece Della Minici Friedman recalled that Nick "had a pal here. His name was Mike Rinn. He was a prominent attorney. They belonged to the Elks Club. . . . Anyway, they gambled a lot and they drank a lot together and he kind of got into a kind of mess, my uncle did. But whatever he did Mike would get him out of it. It was one of those kind of things."

24. "the hooded figures of the knights": Robert Alan Goldberg, *Hooded Empire: The Ku Klux Klan in Colorado* (Urbana: University of Illinois Press, 1981), p. 14. Information on the Klan in this chapter comes from Goldberg's valuable study and from *The In-*

visible Empire in the West: Toward a New Appraisal of the Ku Klux Klan of the 1920s, ed. Shawn Lay (Urbana: University of Illinois Press, 1992).

24. "a whore like all Catlickers": WY, p. 171.
25. "there would be a string of beads": Goldberg, *Hooded Empire*, p. 9.
26. Nick "was drinking": Interview with the Reverend Paul C. Reinert, S.J., November 3, 1995.
27. "highly sensitive": WSB, p. 74.
27. "fun": WY, p. 138.
28. a former member of the Creekside Gang, Jack Keeley: Information in this paragraph comes from a letter to the author from Jack Keeley dated November 18, 1996.
29. "friendly, generous": Interview with Jack Keeley, October 24, 1996.
29. "He was a good bricklayer": Interview with Jack Keeley, October 24, 1996.
29. "He was a mean old man": Interview with Della Minici Friedman, September 18, 1996.
30. "He was very abusive": John Fante in interview with Ben Pleasants, December 18, 1978.
30. "There were scenes": John Fante in interview with Ben Pleasants, July 20, 1979.
30. "that skunk": WSB, p. 99.
30. "I'll get you": WSB, p. 99.
30. "*Dio cane*": WSB, p. 13.
31. an apparition of the Virgin Mary: "John swore this happened, and repeated the story many times. [His brother] Pete confirmed it." Joyce Fante in a letter to the author dated March 9, 1999.
31. "Oh, she was keen!": WY, p. 58.
31. "After his twelfth year": WSB, p. 114.
32. so much brickwork in lieu of so much tuition: "Even though there was no money for tuition . . . Nick did make a deal with the Jesuit priests to let John enroll in school providing [Nick] did some building or stonemasonry for the school in return. Nick never lived up to his pledge, but the priests did allow John to stay in school." Letter from John Fante's cousin Edward Campiglia to Scott Edward Anderson, December 14, 1991.

CHAPTER 3

34. declaring the year of his birth: It has been assumed mistakenly that Fante took to shaving a year off his age in the early 1930s, in an effort to impress H. L. Mencken. In fact, the inaccurate date on Fante's Regis enrollment card preceded his first contact with Mencken by six years.
34. a handful of Neapolitan Jesuits: Information in this chapter about the history of Regis College comes from Harold L. Stansell, S.J., *Regis: On the Crest of the West* (Denver: Regis Educational Corporation, 1977).
35. "a scrappy little fellow": Interview with the Honorable James J. Delaney, September 17, 1996.
35. Ominously, this brazen act: Interview with Paul C. Reinert, S.J., November 3, 1995. See also Goldberg, *Hooded Empire*, p. 31.
35. the Ignatian ideal: See George E. Ganss, S.J., ed., *Ignatius of Loyola: The Spiritual*

Exercises and Selected Works (New York: Paulist Press, 1991); and John C. Olin, ed., *The Autobiography of St. Ignatius Loyola* (New York: Harper and Row, 1974).

36. "hard-nosed": Interview with the Honorable James J. Delaney, September 17, 1996.

36. "presented many thrills": *The Red Jug*, n.d.

37. "John went after this guy": Interview with the Reverend Paul C. Reinert, S.J., November 3, 1995.

37. Fante would write often and well about sports: Fante's passion for baseball is examined in an essay by Richard Collins, "Stealing Home: John Fante and the Moral Dimension of Baseball," *Aethlon: The Journal of Sport* 12, no. 1 (Summer 1995): 81–91.

38. More than simply an inspiring speaker: See Daniel A. Lord, S.J., *Played by Ear: The Autobiography of Daniel A. Lord, S.J.* (Chicago: Loyola University Press, 1955). Lord reviewed films for *Catholic World*, a publication that attracted discriminating readers as unlikely as that scourge of organized religion H. L. Mencken. See Mencken's *The Philosophy of Friedrich Nietzsche* [1908] (Port Washington, N.Y.: Kennikat Press, 1967), p. 295.

39. the Klan-sponsored "ex-nun" Mary Angel: Goldberg, *Hooded Empire*, p. 47.

39. "to walk with mind and heart": Daniel A. Lord, S.J., Preface to *Strength through Prayer*, vol. 2 of *With Heart and Mind*, by Sister Helen Madelein, S.N.D. de Namur (New York: Benziger Brothers, 1938), xi.

39. "something simple about devotional practices": Jay Martin in Cooper and Fine, eds., *John Fante: A Critical Gathering*, pp. 24–25. Martin's analysis informs this chapter's discussion of Jesuit influences in Fante's life and writing.

40. "If Eliot and Stevens": Cooper and Fine, eds., *John Fante: A Critical Gathering*, p. 25.

40. Tellingly, when John: This fact is noted in Denise Jacobson's article "Writer John Fante Says He Never 'Felt Famous' Until He Went to Italy for 'The Roses,' " *Malibu Times*, n.d., c. summer 1958.

41. "genuine American boy": Francis J. Finn, S.J., *Tom Playfair, or Making a Start* (New York: Benziger Brothers, 1891), p. 13.

41. Finn, another Jesuit: See Daniel A. Lord, ed., *Father Finn, S.J.: The Story of His Life Told by Himself for His Friends Young and Old* (New York: Benziger Brothers, 1929).

41. This resentment would resurface: It is reasonable to read early Fante stories such as "Altar Boy," "First Communion," and "The Road to Hell" as ironic reworkings of — and effective revenges on — various Father Finn stories involving similar Catholic materials.

41. "The Poet": This early unpublished John Fante story survives in a six-page typescript; page 3 is missing.

42. his classmate James Vincent Cunningham: Discussing first-rate poets who write "outside the mainstream" and thus remain obscure, Dana Gioia refers to J. V. Cunningham as "the crown prince of unpopularity, but nonetheless a contrarian master." See Dana Gioia, *Can Poetry Matter? Essays on Poetry and American Culture* (St. Paul, Minn.: Graywolf Press, 1992), p. 65.

42. "trouble": *WY*, p. 143.

43. "I look squarely at him": *WY*, p. 144.

43. Although Nick had managed to buy the house: On January 6, 1923, a loan of $1,000 was taken out for the purchase of the house in the name of Mary Fante, to be repaid

in monthly installments of $13. Given Nick's habit of letting his wife take care of household finances as best she could in the face of his perennial profligacy, one wonders if he had Mary sign for the loan to shield himself in the case of default. See Deed of Trust No. 183092, Boulder Building and Loan Association, Boulder County Assessor's Office.

43. Unmellowed with age: Interview with Edward Campiglia, September 16, 1996.

44. Again he committed the fiction: College of Arts and Sciences Registration No. 29971, University of Colorado at Boulder, University Libraries, Archives.

44. his father's presence loomed: It is not clear that Nick was the "building superintendent for the University of Colorado," as his obituary claims he had been. See "Catholic Rites for N. Fante," *Roseville Press-Tribune*, November 24, 1950. However, he may have had more influence in the development of the campus's distinctive architectural style than a mere laborer would have had. Most of the buildings erected after 1917 were designed by Charles Zeller Klauder, a Philadelphia architect. Visiting the site prior to beginning his designs, Klauder was so impressed with the character of the sandstone taken from a local quarry that "he evolved a distinctive style based upon that of Italian rural architecture." This style, "unsymmetrical in line, with red tile roofs sloping at various heights and angles," would have been familiar to at least one of the stonecutters on hand. With his gift for making good first impressions upon men of the world, it is possible that Nick was in some way responsible for inspiring Klauder's vision, which remains visible to this day. See *Colorado: A Guide to the Highest State*, compiled by Workers of the Writers' Program of the Work Projects Administration (New York: Hastings House Publishers, 1941), p. 108.

45. "had complete confidence": Herman Hansten in a letter to Joyce Fante, July 14, 1984.

45. "got very drunk": WY, p. 148.

46. "for each other's guilty throat": WY, pp. 148–49.

46. the Greek-style public library at 1125 Pine Street: When a new public library was erected on Canyon Boulevard in 1962, the Pine Street Library became the Carnegie Branch Library for Local History. Ironically, the former Fante residence at 959 Arapahoe was torn down in 1992 in order to make room for an addition to the new library, where John Fante's books can now be found.

46. "less men than intellectual machines": H. L. Mencken, *Prejudices: Sixth Series* (New York: Alfred A. Knopf, 1927), p. 114. This remark is from "The Emperor of Wowsers," Mencken's hilariously scathing assessment of American reformer Anthony Comstock (1844–1915).

47. his *Mercury* contributors: A partial list of contributors to *The American Mercury* between September 1927 and December 1929 includes Louis Adamic, Sherwood Anderson, Joseph Warren Beach, James M. Cain, J. Frank Dobie, George Jean Nathan, Jim Tully, Bernard DeVoto, Joseph Hergesheimer, James Branch Cabell, Sinclair Lewis, Vachel Lindsay, James Weldon Johnson, Carl Sandberg, Granville Hicks, Lewis Mumford, Josephine Herbst, John Huston, Margaret Mead, Carey McWilliams, Louis Untermeyer, Owen Francis, Michael Gold and George Milburn. Fante would eventually come into contact with several of these writers—Adamic, Cain, Tully, Lewis, Gold—and he would become the lasting friend of Carey McWilliams.

47. "I was delighted": Herman Hansten to Joyce Fante, July 14, 1984.

47. "skepticism and too much Voltaire": *Fante/Mencken*, p. 26. In an earlier undated let-

ter to Mencken, Fante claimed that he "was turned from Catholicism and the novitiate a week after I decided to become a priest by reading your *Treatise on the Gods.*" *Fante/Mencken*, p. 20. Since *Treatise on the Gods* did not appear until 1930, some three years after John's vocation evaporated, we must understand that this claim is based less on chronological facts than on the young writer's wish to please his new correspondent.

48. the virgin Mother of Sorrows: The Sorrowful Mother attracts such devotion within the church that the feast of the Seven Dolors of the Blessed Virgin Mary is celebrated not once but twice in the liturgical year, first on the Friday in Passion Week preceding Holy Week, and again on September 15.

48. "Of course Nick beat [Mary] up": Interview with Edward Campiglia, September 16, 1996.

48. Indeed, that blur may be the surest indicator: Interview with Tom Fante, August 22, 1994. The radically disorienting nature of Nick's injury to his family is vividly suggested by novelist Don DeLillo, one of whose fictional characters says of his own father, "He did the unthinkable Italian crime. He walked out on his family. They don't even have a name for this." See Don DeLillo, *Underworld* (New York: Scribner, 1997), p. 204.

49. "I'm for you, old boy": *WSB*, p. 166.

51. the Chrysler chimes: A bronze tablet at the church bore this inscription: "The Tower of Chimes—Dedicated to the Honor and Glory of God—A Gift of Walter P. Chrysler, A.D. 1928—May Religious Liberty Always Triumph." See "Fr. Agatho of Sacred Heart Church Dies," obituary in the *Boulder Daily Camera*, February 1, 1938. See also Warren Heidgen, O.S.B., *Centennial History of Sacred Heart of Jesus Church* (Boulder: Sacred Heart of Jesus Parish, 1976), p. 19. Thanks to Miss Hortense Brant for sharing her recollections of parish life at Sacred Heart of Jesus during this time, including Father Agatho Strittmatter's friendship with John Galen Locke and various captains of American industry. Interview with Hortense Brant, September 17, 1996. According to Father Paul Reinert, as a pastor Father Strittmatter was both beloved and "a little bit scandalous in lots of ways. The people didn't appreciate the fact that he seemed to be spending an awful lot of his time buying and selling and things like that." Interview with the Reverend Paul C. Reinert, S.J., November 3, 1995. See also the long obituary, "Father Agatho Was Man of Many Interests," *Boulder Daily Camera*, February 12, 1938.

CHAPTER 4

53. "Poverty drove me": Larry Tajiri, "Novelist Fante Comes Home," *Denver Post*, n.d., summer 1963.

54. The novel *1933 Was a Bad Year* would remain unpublished: *1933 Was a Bad Year* (Santa Rosa: Black Sparrow Press, 1985).

55. "Wilmington was paranoid": *BG*, p. 65.

57. Working for the Wrigley Corporation: John's uncle Paul lived at 1243 Lakme Avenue, while Uncle Mike lived at 1237 Cary Avenue. My thanks to John Fante's cousin Paul Capolungo for this and other information about Fante's Wilmington period.

57. In a city built to serve: For his California sojourns Wrigley maintained the palatial Wrigley Mansion on the hill overlooking Catalina Island's Avalon Harbor, directly across the bay from Zane Grey's rustic but well-appointed lodge, known as the Pueblo.

58. An enthusiastic supporter: Despite widespread sympathy in southern California for the Confederate cause, Banning was an ardent Unionist and Abolitionist. At his urging the federal government selected southern California as the center for Union Army supplies in the Southwest. Together with a business partner, Banning donated sixty acres of land as the site for Fort Drum. See Kilbee Brittain, *The General Phineas Banning Residence Museum*, a pamphlet published by Friends of Banning Park, P.O. Box 397, Wilmington, CA 90748. Surprisingly, Wilmington's Fort Drum was not the westernmost outpost of the Civil War in Southern California, for there was another Drum Barracks on Santa Catalina Island.

58. the fabulous Banning Residence: Occupied by members of the Banning family until 1925, the Banning Residence and its surrounding grounds were acquired in 1927 by the Los Angeles City Recreation and Parks Department. Today it is maintained as a museum.

61. Fante did not last long: For a reference to Fante's work at an ice company, see *SL*, p. 24. Tom Fante told me that John worked for the California Packing Company. Interview, February 14, 1998. As for Fante's working as a peanut butcher aboard the S.S. *Catalina*, I am indebted both to John's brother Tom and their cousin Louise Capolungo McLean, the daughter of Fante's uncle Mike Capolungo. Interview with Louise Capolungo McLean, May 16, 1997.

61. Later in life: The 1963 *Denver Post* profile has Fante working "as a hotel clerk, a longshoreman and as an oiler on a ship." See also the *Malibu Times*, c. summer 1958: "Fante has had a good taste of different types of work, such as labor in a fish cannery, digging ditches, working as a bus boy, being a night clerk in a hotel, and working as an oiler on a ship." Thanks to Larry Castagnola of Wilmington Transportation Company for his help in searching through company files for evidence of Fante's employment on board the *Catalina*. Interview with Larry Castagnola, January 21, 1998.

61. Perhaps he managed: My thanks to Bill Schwab of the Wilmington Historical Society for sharing his memories of working aboard the S.S. *Catalina*. Interview with Bill Schwab, January 13, 1998.

61. Issued by the Steamboat Inspection Service: United States Department of Commerce, Steamboat Inspection Service, "Certificate of Efficiency to Lifeboat Man," Serial Number 220828, File No. B2512, issued to John T. Fante, May 5, 1931.

62. If you impressed the man: Widespread dissatisfaction among the dockworkers led to a bloody strike in 1934, which led to a stronger union organization. My thanks to Bill Oleson of the Los Angeles Maritime Museum, ninety-four years old on the day he spoke with me, for sharing his memories of the old days in Los Angeles Harbor. Interview with Bill Oleson, January 17, 1998.

63. With the house on Arapahoe in foreclosure: Interview with Tom Fante, August 22, 1994.

63. When his family arrived: At exactly this time on the other side of the country Nathanael West was managing the Sutton Club Hotel on New York's 56th Street. See Jay Martin, *Nathanael West: The Art of His Life* (New York: Farrar, Straus and Giroux, 1970), p. 158.

63. Sitting on the beach: One of Fante's fellow cannery workers at the California Packing Company was named Bob Aiken. See *Fante/Mencken*, p. 34.
64. Ever ready to take offense: James Gibbons Huneker (1860–1921) was an important American critic in his day. The drama critic Jean George Nathan (1882–1958) collaborated with H. L. Mencken in various publishing ventures.
65. a clove in her mouth to sweeten her breath: Interview with Louise Crowe, Boulder, September 17, 1996.
65. Like all nuns of the order: Interview with Hortense Brant, Boulder, September 17, 1996.
65. "And so is Father Benson": These were all actual people in Fante's life. We have already encountered Benson and Reinert. Dan Campbell played baseball with John and Paul Reinert on the Regis Clover Club.
66. Seldom read today: In his 1930 Nobel Prize address, Sinclair Lewis named Cabell and the others listed here as writers who deserved the attention of the Swedish Academy. See Sinclair Lewis, *The Man from Main Street*, ed. H. E. Maule and M. H. Cane (New York: Random House, 1953), pp. 8, 16–17.
66. His romance *Jurgen: A Comedy of Justice*: See Joe Lee Davis, *James Branch Cabell* (New York: Twayne Publishers, 1962), p. 88. Davis calls *Jurgen* "a prose saga of nostalgic libertinism such as no one had attempted since Byron wrote *Don Juan*" (p. 37). *Jurgen* became a literary cause célèbre soon after it was published when it was banned for obscenity, only to be exonerated in court in 1922.
66. Indeed, Fante took the title: See James Branch Cabell, *The Works of James Branch Cabell*, Storisende Edition, 18 vols. (New York: Robert M. McBride & Company, 1927–30), vol. 6, p. 135. *Jurgen* evolved from Cabell's short tale "Some Ladies and Jurgen," published originally in Mencken's *Smart Set* in 1918 and reprinted in *The Smart Set Anthology*, ed. Burton Rascoe and Geoff Conklin (New York: Reynal & Hitchcock, 1934), pp. 182–95.
67. "Suddenly, I thought of Nietzsche": The narrator's command for Nietzsche to "get away" echoes Christ's command in Matt. 4:10, "Begone, Satan!"
68. "They called God that which": Friedrich Nietzsche, *Thus Spake Zarathustra*, Part 2, "The Priests," trans. Thomas Common in *The Philosophy of Nietzsche* (New York: The Modern Library, n.d.), p. 98.

CHAPTER 5

71. At their most charitable: Interview with Tom Fante, August 22, 1994.
71. "angry, very angry": Interview with Louise Capolungo McLean, daughter of Fante's uncle Mike Capolungo, May 16, 1997.
72. a "very pathetic character": Interview with Louise Capolungo McLean, May 16, 1997.
72. Before he had left Colorado: Herman Hansten to Joyce Fante, July 14, 1984.
73. With its crude writerly implications: See *Fante/Mencken*, p. 35. It is intriguing to wonder if the essentials of this incident were simply reversed during the writing of "Fish Cannery," with Fante the victimizer becoming the story's victimized narrator. If so, it was a more sophisticated if equally mean-spirited way for Fante to ink his revenge.
73. "Though I'm young": *Fante/Mencken*, pp. 30–31.

74. "Futilely," he blurted: *Fante/Mencken*, p. 21.
74. "I've got to have a god": *Fante/Mencken*, p. 42.
74. "the man who replaced God": *Fante/Mencken*, p. 21.
74. "I can imagine no reason": *Fante/Mencken*, p. 17.
74. "I would have done anything": *Fante/Mencken*, p. 141.
75. "I'll give you a kick in the pants": John Fante, untitled, unpublished manuscript fragment.
78. Unremarkable in his appearance: See Don Arturo Bandini, *Navidad: A Christmas Day with the Early Californians* (San Francisco: California Historical Society, 1958), p. 7. This is a reprint of Bandini's "Navidad," which appeared in the December 1892 *Californian Illustrated Magazine*. Don Arturo was old enough when he wrote "Navidad" to recall the gracious "adobe days" of old Los Angeles.
78. the kind of writing that Northrup Frye: See Northrup Frye, *The Anatomy of Criticism: Four Essays* (Princeton, N.J.: Princeton University Press, 1957).
79. "was sure a flop with her": *Fante/Mencken*, p. 30.
79. "was a character": Interview with Louise Capolungo McLean, May 16, 1997.
79. As for the other English class: The course description is from the Long Beach Junior College Catalogue for 1931–32, p. 10. The courses Fante attempted and his grades are from Fante's Permanent Record Sheet.
80. "From the time of that theme": Letter from John Fante to Jack Ging, Chairman of the Long Beach City College Hall of Fame, and John R. Fylpaa, Associated Student Body Advisor, September 29, 1978.
81. He also joined Skalds: From the campus literary society (Skalds, ancient Scandinavian poets) to the school's various sports teams (the Vikings), student organizations at Long Beach Junior College took their names from the Old Norse.
81. In two years he had gone: The student literary journal was named after the *Edda*, a thirteenth-century Norse collection of mythological, heroic and aphoristic poems in alliterative verse. I am indebted to Frank Gaspar of Long Beach City College for sharing his discovery in *Edda* of Fante's earliest published story, "Eleven-Thirty," which also won an Honorable Mention in a contest sponsored by *Writers' Digest*. While at Long Beach City College Fante also published a selection of doggerel co-written with fellow Skald Thelwall Proctor in the 1932 edition of *Saga*, the school yearbook. An example:

Cabellism

The theologians might do well
To read the sage Jim Cabell
He has no moral to sell,
But proves the sweetness of hell.

The poems were accompanied by caricatures of both authors, John looking especially ethnic in a heavy-lidded, dissolute sort of way. See Donald A. Drury, *Long Beach City College: The First Fifty Years* (Long Beach, Calif.: Long Beach Community College District, 1978), pp. 14–15. My thanks to Elizabeth Hoffman for bringing this book to my attention. The 1932 issue of *Saga* featured parodies of *The New Yorker*, *Vanity Fair*, and *The American Mercury*. Thelwall Proctor would go on to a career as a professor of Russian at the state college in Humboldt, California. Several unpublished Fante stories date from this time, including "It Was Funny," a story of brutal misogyny narrated by an ironically clueless oaf reminiscent of the narrator in

Ring Lardner's "Haircut"; "Look Out Strutting Man!," an essaylike foray, unique for Fante, into proletarian overwriting ("We, the languishing unskilled, whose hands were once as twisted and harsh as thorn vine through wielding of rope and shovel and pick, are gnawed by the ratty teeth of misery, but the aches in our bellies surely cannot taunt as much as the fear and hatred and hypocrisy that fester in the brains of some of our brother men, they whose armpits ooze sweat as never before, whose frightened eyes slink woman-like to the gang boss, lest by a trick of ego that is uniquely his, he leap upon them, flourishing a time-card that conscribes their emission into the ranks of the melacholy."); and "Charles Bates," no longer extant but rejected by Mencken for an indelicate reference to syphilis and thus its potential to disgust readers.

81. In the words of one person: Letter to author from Tom Cullen, December 18, 1996. Much of the information in the preceding two paragraphs comes from this letter and two others from Cullen: one sent from Cullen's home in London to John Fante and dated September 25, 1980; the other sent to me and dated January 8, 1997. Cullen went on from Skalds and the staff of *Edda* to work on Upton Sinclair's failed 1934 EPIC (End Poverty in California) campaign for California governor, and from there to the Los Angeles Newspaper Guild, where he rose to the position of secretary. Among other *Edda* contributors who would later be active in the Guild were Richard Emery, who in his time with the *Long Beach Press-Telegram* would help to boost Fante's nascent writing career; and Dolph Winebrenner. Cullen would later join the Communist Party. After serving as an infantry soldier in World War II, Cullen, who was gay, moved permanently to London to avoid the rising threat of McCarthyism. There he worked as a journalist and an author, writing books on Jack the Ripper and several other notorious English murderers.

82. "He really let his feelings be known": Interview with Ellenore (Boggegian Abowitz) Hittelman, January 13, 1997.

83. "He was living with Miss Carpenter": Interview with Ellenore (Boggegian Abowitz) Hittelman, January 13, 1997.

83. Perhaps he was telling the truth: On December 26, 1933, Fante made the following impressionistic entry in his writer's notebook: "Miss Carpenter's Victorian niceness—that awkward, old fashioned furniture in her parlor—Miss Carpenter in the kitchen while I wait for a glass of grape juice—the noise she made—Her girlish modesty when she handed me the glass." Far from proof of the claim that he lived with his teacher, Fante's words nonetheless suggest an incipient intimacy.

83. "Dear Mr. Fante": This Mencken letter does not survive. The letter quoted here is as Fante reconstructed it in his September 29, 1978, letter to the Long Beach City College Hall of Fame Committee. In a letter dated March 5, 1980, former schoolmate Marjorie (Brown) Shneidman wrote to Fante, "Those early years are so vivid in my memory. Long Beach Junior College, Skalds Literary Society . . . In fact, I typed that first article that Mencken accepted."

83. In *Ask the Dust: AD*, pp. 56–57.

84. In a strangely unexplained: *SL*, p. 24.

84. He was "staying with friends": *SL*, p. 25.

84. In talking about this time: Interview with Tom Fante, August 22, 1994.

85. "a book in process or in mind": Letter from Alfred A. Knopf to John Fante, June 8, 1932.

85. "Pretty hot stuff": *Fante/Mencken*, p. 26.

86. "John Fante, who studied in Catholic schools": Anonymous, "Listening In," front-page column in the *Denver Catholic Register*, August 4, 1932.

86. Fante did not see: *SL*, p. 41.

86. "I never have and never shall": *SL*, p. 40.

86. Not too many years earlier: Describing his sisters Grace and Josephine as "very good friends" with John, Edward Campiglia told me that as a teenager John often came to talk with them because "he wanted to know how girls felt and what they did and . . . how they handled every situation." Interview with Edward Campiglia, September 16, 1996.

86. "present little success": *SL*, p. 40.

86. After bouncing around: The tango joint reference comes from an unpublished letter from Fante to his mother dated June 24, 1932. The *Selected Letters* (p. 34) omits from a December 12, 1932, letter to his mother Fante's reference to the Long Beach "hotel at which I stayed and starved this summer."

86. "I would rather write": *Fante/Mencken*, p. 31.

87. "crazy with poverty": *Fante/Mencken*, p. 21.

87. "all of Hemingway": *Fante/Mencken*, p. 25.

87. "the immense music": *Fante/Mencken*, p. 31;

87. "bedding talents": *Fante/Mencken*, p. 68.

87. "cocksmanship": *Fante/Mencken*, p. 67.

87. a puff piece: "Publisher Seeking Book from Student," *Long Beach Press-Telegram*, June 18, 1932. This brief article quotes Knopf's letter in its entirety.

88. "write all night": Malcolm Epley's "Beachcombing" column, *Long Beach Press-Telegram*, April 18, 1957, B-1. Epley's description of Fante's typing habits were based on the recollections of retired city editor Frank Goss.

88. "anything . . . for $5 a week": Art Cohn's "Cohn-ing Tower" column, *Oakland Tribune*, n.d., c. September 1940. Unfortunately the letter from Fante to Cohn does not survive. Writing to his mother on November 14, 1932, about his prospects at the *Press-Telegram*, Fante claimed that "the lowest salary is $5 per day," a significant difference from the $5 *per week* that Cohn mentions. Both writers were probably exaggerating for effect. See *SL*, p. 31.

88. "a bad season": John Fante, unpublished letter to his mother, June 24, 1932.

88. "a last fling": *Fante/Mencken*, p. 25.

88. "barring death or blindness": *Fante/Mencken*, p. 26.

88. "I am coming home": John Fante, unpublished letter to his mother, July 26, 1932.

89. Soon after Fante arrived: Fante would hold a special place in his memory for "Home, Sweet Home," considering it "the best short story I ever wrote." John Fante, interview with Ben Pleasants, December 18, 1978.

89. "absurd": *Fante/Mencken*, p. 27.

89. "I never did study for the priesthood": *Fante/Mencken*, p. 26.

89. "I have been among my people": John Fante, untitled twelve-page manuscript. The title page of this story has been lost. Given the way Fante typically laid out his title pages, we must assume that the missing text would amount to the story's first twelve to fifteen lines.

91. "Anima naturaliter Catholica": The soul is naturally Catholic: this idea is developed in St. Augustine's *Confessions*, the most famous sentence of which the narrator's Jesuit correspondent seems to be paraphrasing. Addressing God, Augustine sums up his

whole teaching when he says, "Our heart is restless until it rests in you." *The Confessions of St. Augustine*, trans. John K. Ryan (Garden City, N.Y.: Image Books, 1960), p. 371.

91. "I'm forced to freight out of here": *Fante/Mencken*, p. 35.

CHAPTER 6

93. In 1933 Frank Lloyd Wright: Frank Lloyd Wright, *The Living City* (New York: Horizon Press, 1958). See also Richard Weinstein, "Wright's Vision of 'Broadacre City' Emerges in Today's Los Angeles," *Los Angeles Times*, August 31, 1997, M1, 6.

93. "Los Angeles is an epic": Harry Carr, *Los Angeles: City of Dreams* (New York: Appleton-Century, 1935), p. 5. See also Mark Laurila, "The Los Angeles Booster Myth, the Anti-Myth, and John Fante's *Ask the Dust*" in *John Fante: A Critical Gathering*, ed. Stephen Cooper and David Fine (Madison, N.J.: Fairleigh Dickinson University Press, 1999), pp. 112–21. As Laurila makes clear, Carr was no mere rogue visionary of the Aryan apogee in Los Angeles. Rather, he followed in the footsteps of such important pioneers of Los Angeles civic culture as Joseph P. Widney and Charles Fletcher Lummis. One of the founders of the University of Southern California, Widney wrote the two-volume *Race Life of the Aryan People* (1907), which Carr considered "[o]ne of the great books of modern times [and] an epoch-making work of standard and permanent value." See Carr, *City of Dreams*, p. 354. Lummis—among other things Los Angeles's tenth City Librarian from 1905 to 1910 and, with his idiosyncratic getup of corduroy suit, colorful sash and Stetson, the sartorial model for the character of Noah Cross (John Huston) in Roman Polanski's *Chinatown*, written by Robert Towne—used his magazine *Land of Sunshine* to boost ideas of the Southland's Aryan destiny. See Kevin Starr, *Inventing the Dream: California through the Progressive Era* (New York: Oxford University Press, 1985), p. 89.

94. "the man most responsible": Robert Gottlieb and Irene Wolt, *Thinking Big: The Story of the Los Angeles Times* (New York: Putnam, 1977), p. 126.

94. "A wonderful city": John Fante in a letter to his mother dated October 4, 1932. This quotation is from a passage deleted in *SL*, p. 31.

95. "this is a better town": John Fante, unpublished letter to his mother, October 11, 1932.

95. "The subject seems to obsess you": *Fante/Mencken*, p. 37.

95. "now that I'm actually": *Fante/Mencken*, p. 38. The Filipino story hung fire for several years, until Fante finally succeeded in writing "Helen, Thy Beauty Is to Me—" in 1941. Although he would use his own starvation experience of these days in order to write humorously about going hungry in *Ask the Dust*—influenced by Knut Hamsun's *Hunger*—"How to Go Hungry" never materialized per se.

95. Nephew and aunt: Letter dated September 20, 1981, from Dorothy (Capolungo) Shearer to John Fante.

95. "a hell of a poor Catholic": *SL*, p. 30.

95. There he became: Tully's *Beggars of Life: A Hobo Autobiography* (Garden City, N.Y.: Garden City Publishing Co., 1924) was dedicated to "Charlie Chaplin, A Mighty Vagabond." Much of the information in this paragraph comes from James Chinello, "Tully's Punch," *Westways* (November 1979): 41–45, 80.

96. "too young and too serious": *Fante/Mencken*, p. 38.

96. "It will be hard to sell": Jim Tully to John Fante, September 28, 1932.
96. "Thanks very much": *Fante/Mencken*, p. 40.
97. "a bit of a job downtown": *SL*, p. 31. In an unpublished passage of a letter dated December 3, 1933, Fante reassured his mother that despite Green's "hellraising," he was "really not such a bad fellow and as a co-worker on manuscripts he's a great help to me."
97. Seven stories above: See William Pugsley, *Bunker Hill: Last of the Lofty Mansions* (Corona del Mar, Calif.: Trans-Anglo Books, 1977), p. 66.
97. "all the good things": *SL*, p. 33.
97. "I want to settle down": John Fante, unpublished letter to his mother dated December 4, 1932.
98. "I have no love": This quotation, along with the reference to "the big galleries on Wilshire" and Japanese art is from John Fante's letter of December 24, 1932, to his cousin Jo Campiglia. The passage was deleted from the letter as published in *SL*, p. 35. In his diary entry of October 26, 1931, Carey McWilliams had mentioned two watercolors, Lee Blair's *Bunker Hill* and Eric Webster's *Buttresses of Bunker Hill*. "What I have thought for so long," McWilliams wrote, "that is[,] that people would begin to write about and paint this place, is true, only it seems that the painters have come first. I don't know any writing about Los Angeles as graphic as the two scenes by Webster and Blair." Fante and McWilliams, each in his own writing, would help to change that. The Carey McWilliams Collection, UCLA.
98. "vagrant bohemians": *SL*, p. 35.
98. "the boy is myself": *SL*, p. 39.
98. "He seems to be a very fine man": *SL*, p. 36.
99. "One day I got a letter": Carey McWilliams, "Writers of the Western Shore," *Westways* (November 1978): pp. 74–75.
99. He spent the rest of the decade: See Carey McWilliams, *The Education of Carey McWilliams* (New York: Simon and Schuster, 1978).
100. An astute appreciation: Carey McWilliams, "Notes on H. L. Mencken," *The Wooden Horse* 3, no. 2 (February 1925): 23–27.
100. a magnanimous biography: Carey McWilliams, *Ambrose Bierce: A Biography* (New York: Albert and Charles Boni, 1929). Two years before this book appeared Mencken had published the claim "There is no adequate life of Bierce, and I doubt if any will ever be written." H. L. Mencken, *Prejudices: Sixth Series* (New York: Alfred A. Knopf, 1927), p. 263. McWilliams's biography, which relieved Mencken of his doubt, remains to this day the standard work.
100. Wills had helped his friend Carey: See the letter from Ross Wills to Carey McWilliams dated April 5, 1930, and three letters from Wilson Follett to Carey McWilliams, dated April 23, 1930, July 7, 1930, and August 18, 1930. The Carey McWilliams Collection, UCLA.
100. Talk with Ross Wills: For an account of Wills's deafness—and of John Philip Sousa's role in it—see Louis Adamic, *My America: 1928–1938* (New York: Harper & Brothers, 1938), p. 521.
100. In addition to Wills: *SL*, pp. 38, 40.
101. Pausing only to consult with McWilliams: "Before I send [the synopsis] to him, I am having a Los Angeles lawyer friend go over it with me, so that should Knopf like my synopsis, and offer me a contract, there won't be any mistakes made." John Fante in

an unpublished letter to his mother, January 18, 1933. Fante's synopsis of *Mater Dolorosa* does not survive. In June 1933, Fante submitted an Author Card to the California State Library indicating that he had "In preparation—'Mater Dolorosa'—Knopf." In filling the card out in his own hand, Fante also continued the fiction that he was born in 1911.

101. "I am greedy to begin": *SL*, p. 39.

101. "The idea is that she": *SL*, pp. 53, 54.

102. the sporting events on which they both thrived: John Fante to his mother, January 2, 1933, in a passage deleted from the version published in *SL*, p. 44.

102. "I didn't care anymore": John Fante, "Washed in the Rain," *Westways* (formerly *Touring Topics*) (October 1934): 16–18 ff.

103. At Regis Fante would have learned: Besides inordinate ambition, the Capital Sins include uncharitableness, pride, greed, impatience, dishonesty and envy. The Cardinal Virtues are prudence, justice, temperance and fortitude. See William L. Kelly, S.J., *Youth Before God: Prayers and Thoughts* (Westminster, Md.: The Newman Press, 1958), p. 294. Under Nietzsche's influence Fante would have found the concept of inordinate ambition repulsive—and thus the tensions informing the story.

103. "I don't mean autobiographical fact": *SL*, p. 57.

104. Fante promptly talked: See *SL*, pp. 67–68.

104. He would also have been aware: See Phil Townsend Hanna, *Libros Californianos: Or, Five Feet of California Books*, revised and enlarged by Lawrence Clark Powell (Los Angeles: Zeitlin & Ver Brugge, 1958).

104. "I know that I could write": *SL*, p. 48.

104. When a new story: Whit Burnett's acceptance letter was dated February 8, 1933. See also Martha Foley, *The Story of STORY Magazine* (New York: W. W. Norton & Company, 1980).

105. "bumming around": *SL*, pp. 45–46.

105. "Say Mother": *SL*, p. 48.

105. Also on that day: Fante's letter to the American Consulate does not survive, but it is referred to in the response he received from American Vice Consul Livingston Harley dated March 28, 1933. There is no record that Fante followed up on the rather sketchy information provided in Harley's response. In the margins and on the reverse of Harley's letter Fante signed two names, J. Fante and Svevo (or S.) Bandini several dozen times, in signatures ranging from the elegant to the indecipherable. This is the letter that is reproduced on the jacket of this biography.

105. There he attempted: John Fante to his brother Pete, unpublished letter dated February 23, 1933.

106. His name was mentioned favorably: William Soskin, "Reading and Writing," *New York Evening Post*, March 1, 1933.

106. "No one can boost an author": The clipping files of the old *Los Angeles Examiner* are maintained at the University of Southern California's Regional History Center, where I viewed the clipping quoted from here.

106. "employed part-time": Anonymous, "John Fante Signs Contract to Write His First Novel," *Long Beach Press-Telegram*, February 21, 1933, B4.

106. back-to-back stories: "First Communion" appeared in *The American Mercury* in February 1933, followed in March by "Big Leaguer."

107. "There was something breathless": *AD*, pp. 97–98.

108. "a sinful woman": *WY*, p. 160.
108. his faith "was still there, strong as ever": *WY*, p. 162.
108. Carey McWilliams claimed: Carey McWilliams, "Writers of the Western Shore," p. 74.
108. "and I believe": Tom Cullen, letter to John Fante, September 25, 1980.
108. "drama interrupted fiction": "Writer Meets Actual Drama," *Los Angeles Examiner,* n.d., March 1933. In 1934 Fante told a colleague at Warner Bros. that he had lost his typewriter in the earthquake. Muriel D. Bradley to John Fante, March 7, 1980.
108. "A four-story apartment house": "Author to Visit at Home of Parents," *Roseville Tribune and Register,* n.d., March 1933.
109. the humorous piece: Carey McWilliams, "The Folklore of Earthquakes," *The American Mercury* (June 1933), pp. 199–201.
109. Though the earthquake had terrified him: In an unpublished letter to his mother dated October 27, 1933, Fante wrote, "The quakes still scare the living hell out of me. I don't suppose there's any cure for the fear I have."
109. "The result horrifies me": *SL*, p. 58.
109. "a man's room": *SL*, p. 64.
110. a flattering article: *Los Angeles Examiner,* August 7, 1933.
110. he had been let go: *SL*, p. 62.
110. He had spent an August night in jail: See *SL*, p. 61. Responding to a question about criminal convictions on his application for employment with the Office of War Information in 1942, Fante wrote, "Arrested for disturbing the peace in Los Angeles in 1933—was 24 years old. Pleaded guilty in Judge Brand's court—fined $10.00. However, I was *not* guilty of the charge."
110. he had swum naked in the ocean: On numerous occasions Joyce Fante told me about Audrey, whose last name John never mentioned. Fante reported the naked swim to his mother; see *SL*, p. 64.
110. By December he was being hailed: John S. McNamara, "These Here Highbrows," *Writers' Digest,* December 1933.

CHAPTER 7

111. "She has plenty of influence": *SL*, p. 69.
112. "the ancient fact": *Fante/Mencken*, p. 66.
112. The accident's other victim: "Local Men Seriously Injured in Car Crash," front page, *Roseville Tribune and Register,* February 9, 1934.
112. "a nasty piece of hypocrisy": *Fante/Mencken*, p. 74. This scenario does not survive. Seamus Cooney (*SL*, p. 79) asserts that the Dillinger story was a collaboration between Fante and Frank Fenton. However, in a letter written three days after Fante mailed his novel to Knopf on April 8, Fante told his mother that he and Wills were "going to begin soon to work on a picture," emphasizing Wills's potential connection to producer David O. Selznick. Two months later, in his letter to Mencken describing the Death Valley–Dillinger "motion picture slop," Fante said that he was collaborating with "a man who has a potent entree to the Selznick office." *Fante/Mencken*, p. 74. By late July, Fante was indeed collaborating with Fenton, but on a different story altogether, the one that would become the film *Dinky*. In Fante's July 27 letter to Carey McWilliams, the third-person pronoun in the sentence "He and I were un-

tangling a plot for a Death Valley story at the time," as ambiguous as it appears, must thus refer to Ross Wills.

113. "the obscene wails": *Fante/Mencken*, p. 74.

113. Ironically, the man responsible: See Daniel A. Lord, S.J., *Played by Ear: The Autobiography of Daniel A. Lord, S.J.* (Chicago: Loyola University Press, 1955). The chapter entitled "To a Member of the IFCA Board of Review," pp. 269–313, offers a behind-the-scenes history of the origins of the Motion Picture Code. Lord's original drafting of the Code is treated specifically on pp. 299–303.

113. "The hell of it is": *Fante/Mencken*, 74. The phrase "writing for the studios" has been taken to mean that Fante was a salaried contract writer as early as June 1934. However, the most reliable evidence indicates he received no such contract until early August. I understand the phrase to mean that he was "writing for the studios" in the sense that he was writing for what he took to be their wants and needs, hoping thus to gain employment.

113. "to think of the motion picture machine": *SL*, p. 78.

114. "the Crucified One": See Robert C. Holub, *Friedrich Nietzsche* (New York: Twayne Publishers, 1995), p. 13.

114. "heavy doses": *Fante/Mencken*, p. 74.

114. "truly . . . bad": *Fante/Mencken*, p. 75.

114. Soon he was revisiting: John Fante to his mother, June 14, 1934. Fante's reference to visiting the scene of the longshoremen's strike occurs in a passage of this letter that was deleted from *SL*, p. 77.

114. In mid-June of 1934: See Louis Adamic, *Dynamite: The Story of Class Violence in America* (New York: Chelsea House Publishers, 1958), p. 449.

114. In the week that Fante came: See the *Los Angeles Times* of June 6, 8 and 9, 1934, and especially the front-page article "Terrorism Grips Port," June 10, 1934.

114. Fante's sympathies leaned: "my sympathies lean toward strikers in most of their demands." John Fante to his mother, July 22, 1934, in a passage deleted from the letter published in *SL*, p. 81.

115. author and editor Louis Adamic: Louis Adamic was yet another protégé of H. L. Mencken and a contributor to *The American Mercury*. A native of Yugoslavia, after coming to the United States Adamic wrote many books and articles on the immigrant experience, including *Laughing in the Jungle: The Autobiography of an Immigrant in America* (1932). From 1923 to 1929 he worked as clerk to the port pilot at Los Angeles Harbor, where Carey McWilliams came to know him. See McWilliams's generous portrait, *Louis Adamic and Shadow-America* (Los Angeles: Arthur Whipple, 1935). A passage in Fante's unpublished short story "To Be a Monstrous Clever Fellow" goes thus: "San Pedro. Louis Adamic, the writer, lived there. I remembered how I had gone through telephone books and directories searching for his name; how I imagined myself arguing with him."

115. "every bohemian": *Fante/Mencken*, p. 76; "smelly slovenly radicals": p. 79. In the summer of 1934 novelist Upton Sinclair was running for Governor of California on a socialist platform meant to "End Poverty in California" (EPIC).

115. "My business in life": *Fante/Mencken*, p. 76.

115. "movie hokum": *SL*, p. 83.

115. "shrewdly inserted a Jesuit priest"; "the sight of a Jebbie in the movies": *Fante/Mencken*, p. 82.

115. Joe Breen and Cardinal O'Connell: Joseph Breen succeeded Will Hays as chairman

of the Code and Rating Administration. Boston's William Cardinal O'Connell was the founder of the Catholic Legion of Decency.

116. "Dinky" was being purchased: On August 5, 1934, screenwriter Samuel Gilson Brown cabled Warner Bros. from London asserting that the original story idea for "Dinky" was his, but offering to omit his name if it would facilitate the process and suggesting that he and Fenton be credited with the original story and Fante with the treatment. The August 13 Assignment of Rights to Warner Bros., for $1,500, includes all three writers' names. Warner Bros. Archives, University of Southern California.

116. "movies are very uncertain": This letter was written not in July, as estimated in *SL*, p. 79, but sometime soon after Fante signed the Warner Bros. contract in early August.

116. "I'm not going to last": *SL*, p. 84; "I may be out of a job": pp. 85–86.

116. "get something from the movie magnates": *Fante/Mencken*, p. 77.

116. "Dear Mr. Mencken": *Fante/Mencken*, p. 86.

117. "all I do is write and laugh": *Fante/Mencken*, p. 87.

117. "And the harpies of the shore": *Fante/Mencken*, p. 87. Holmes wrote "Old Ironsides" in 1830 to protest the proposed scrapping of the legendary frigate U.S.S. *Constitution*. My thanks to Ernie Sjogren and Doug Domingo-Foraste for helping me to identify this poem. It is likely that Fante saw the restored frigate during her ten-day visit to Los Angeles Harbor beginning March 10, 1933, the day of the Long Beach earthquake. See the editorial " 'Old Ironsides' May Come Again," *Long Beach Press-Telegram*, March 16, 1933. See also George Gordon, Lord Byron, *Childe Harold's Pilgrimage*, Canto IV, Stanza 179.

117. The surprise is that: "Bandini," fifty-five-page treatment dated September 29, 1934. Warner Bros. Archives, University of Southern California. There are several carbon copies of the treatment. On the title page of each copy Frank Fenton's name has been typed in belatedly, suggesting that he came onto the project only after Fante had worked through much if not all of the story on his own.

118. "Most of the ideas": *SL*, p. 85.

118. Despite the recommendation: In an interoffice memo to Hal Wallis dated February 14, 1935, Abem Finkel suggested that Bette Davis play the blond widow opposite Robinson, playing Svevo Bandini: "I see it as a sort of 'Human Bondage' in Little Italy."

118. a memo forbidding: interoffice memo from Hal Wallis to John Fante, September 27, 1934. Warner Bros. Archives, USC.

118. "Dago Mike Cantello": This was a fifteen-page treatment dated October 1, 1934. Warner Bros. Archives, USC.

119. "on impulse": *SL*, p. 87.

119. "bitter memories of a devilish boyhood": *SL*, p. 87.

119. a 1941 caricature: Ross B. Wills, "John Fante," *Common Ground* 1 (Spring 1941): 84–90. Reprinted in *SL*, pp. 329–38.

119. "felt very lost and sad": *Fante/Mencken*, p. 90. Known too is the fact that while in Denver Fante used the Marion Street mailing address of an acquaintance named Chet Carroll, then employed by General Motors and later, in 1936, to collaborate with Fante on a pulp novelette.

119. Two days later he arrived: Contrary again to Ross Wills's *Common Ground* profile, Fante did not end up in Denver so broke that he had to hitchhike back to California.

He rode the train as a paying passenger first to Roseville and then back to Los Angeles.

119. a tubercular young Jewess: Fante mentioned this woman to Ben Pleasants on December 18, 1978. The encounter led to a short story, "A Night in Venice," no longer extant. Though Fante failed to place this story for publication, he used it as the basis for the Vera Rivken subplot of *Ask the Dust*.

120. "It is a fine room": *SL*, p. 88.

120. If indeed he did go to midnight mass: John Fante to his mother, December 27, 1934, in a passage deleted from *SL*, p. 89.

120. "I often ask": *SL*, p. 89.

CHAPTER 8

121. "[not] such a bad looking devil": *SL*, p. 93.

121. "That novel . . . means everything": *SL*, p. 92.

122. "a competent hack-writer": *SL*, p. 92.

122. a project entitled *Stiletto*: The forty-nine-page treatment by Joel Sayre and John Fante was dated February 25, 1935. Warner Bros. Archives, USC.

122. The End: In the *Stiletto* file of the Warner Bros. Archives there is an undated article entitled "One Against Five Thousand" about the true-to-life crime-fighting exploits of one Joseph Petrosino in New York's turn-of-the-century Little Italy. Used as background for the story of *Stiletto*, this article was taken from *Black Mask*, the crime pulp magazine founded in 1920 by H. L. Mencken and George Jean Nathan.

122. "on fire . . . to make good": John Fante, interview with Ben Pleasants, December 12, 1978.

122. "slow and fat and lazy": John Fante, unpublished letter to his brother Tommy dated March 4, 1935.

123. Fante applied for and was granted membership: Letter from Tristram Tupper, Secretary of the Screen Writers Guild, to John Fante, March 26, 1935.

123. "The story is no great shakes": *The Hollywood Reporter*, April 22, 1935, p. 4.

123. "I don't like the movies": *SL*, p. 96.

123. "personal novel": John Fante to his mother, unpublished letter, April 19, 1935.

123. Again the pair headed for the desert: John Fante to his mother, unpublished letter, May 15, 1935.

124. "rest and read and let the sun burn": *SL*, p. 97.

124. "autobiographical, of course": *SL*, p. 99.

124. When his Denver cousin: Interview with Edward Campiglia, September 16, 1996.

125. "honest to the point of ghastliness": *Fante/Mencken*, p. 93.

125. "a religious talk": *SL*, p. 105.

125. "like a dog": *SL*, p. 106.

125. "The only war I care to fight": *SL*, p. 106.

125. "I nearly collapsed": John Fante to his mother, November 3, 1935. This passage was deleted from the version of the letter published in *SL*, p. 107.

126. something perilously close to a breakdown: This information comes from an undated and unpublished letter to his mother in which Fante described the details and aftermath of his three-day attack. Referring to his medical problems in an unpublished

letter to his mother dated December 12, 1935, Fante wrote, "I am convinced that most of my sickness is simply in my mind."

126. "every afternoon for exercise and nude sun baths": John Fante to his mother in an unpublished letter, March 27, 1936.

126. most likely Seal Beach: The Seal Beach Historical and Cultural Society has refurbished Tower Car No. 1734 and parked it permanently on the greenbelt near Main Street, where the forty-mile Pacific Electric L.A.–Newport Line operated from 1904 to 1950. Thanks to Elouise Shanks for this information.

126. "a highly excitable girl": SL, p. 112.

127. "too cruel": Elizabeth Nowell to John Fante, January 11, 1936.

127. "a spoiled little baby": Maxim Lieber to John Fante, February 4, 1936.

127. (Relations between the two men): Fante/Mencken, p. 75. No letter from Lieber survives that would substantiate Fante's claim of such a refusal, much less three of them—"This is the third time it has happened to me"—so it is not possible to say with certainty what story was thus refused, if any. It is unlikely that the story was one called "A Bad Confession," as Michael Moreau suggests in Fante/Mencken, p. 149, because the letter from Lieber that Moreau cites in evidence is dated July 25, 1934, whereas Fante's letter to Mencken complaining about the Lieber refusal is dated June 16, 1934, and refers to the event as having taken place "[a] month ago." Given the inherently Catholic nature of virtually everything Fante ever wrote, it could have been any of several stories. Or then again Fante might just have been displacing his frustration at another rejection by blaming the bad news on the messenger. Nevertheless, Lieber's half of the correspondence (Fante's has been lost) indicates that their relationship had been tense for a considerable time.

128. "wasn't a novel": Elizabeth Nowell to John Fante, April 1, 1936.

128. "Hollywood ending": Elizabeth Nowell to John Fante, May 11, 1936.

128. Fante would come to prize: "Pan is probably my favorite novel." John Fante in interview with Ben Pleasants, December 18, 1978.

129. George Egerton's 1921 English translation: Egerton's translation of Hunger was published by Knopf the year after Hamsun won the Nobel Prize for Literature.

129. the emotional ingrowth and homebound narrowness: On August 31, 1932, Mencken wrote Fante, "I have a feeling that you had better stop writing about your family. The subject seems to obsess you." See Fante/Mencken, p. 37. Thanks to Mencken's advice and Nowell's assistance Fante would go on to expand his fictional purview, but we can be thankful that he never truly stopped writing about his family.

129. "Dear Fante": Elizabeth Nowell to John Fante, April 11, 1936.

129. (An extended comparison): Elizabeth Nowell to John Fante, April 11, 1936.

130. "Now you, John Fante, are a sort of split personality": Elizabeth Nowell to John Fante, April 11, 1936.

130. "The more I think of it": Elizabeth Nowell to John Fante, April 11, 1936.

130. "constant struggle between religion and reason": Elizabeth Nowell to John Fante, July 1, 1936.

131. " 'Arturo's hatred for the Church' ": Elizabeth Nowell (quoting Fante himself) to John Fante, April 11, 1936.

131. "have bearing on all the muddled Catholics": Elizabeth Nowell to John Fante, April 11, 1936.

131. "stop fighting you like a tiger": Elizabeth Nowell to John Fante, April 11, 1936.

131. In an ill-conceived effort: See Fante's letter to Carey McWilliams about "this Nowel-Fante-Adamic-McWilliams squabble" in *SL*, pp. 123–25.
131. "[I]f I find I can't trust you": Elizabeth Nowell to John Fante, May 11, 1936.
131. She continued pushing: Elizabeth Nowell to John Fante, May 27, and June 24, 1936.
132. "I guess it'll hurt your feelings": Elizabeth Nowell to John Fante, July 29, 1936.
132. "all those roses": Elizabeth Nowell to John Fante, August 13, 1936.
132. "a beautiful Mexican model": John Fante in a letter to Steven Meloan, August 25, 1980.
132. "dress well and increase my own prestige": *SL*, p. 129.
132. he treated her shabbily: Interview with Yetive Moss, October 11, 1996.
133. "I bequeath her to you": *SL*, p. 127.
133. "be too strong": *SL*, p. 129.
133. Bancroft's multivolume *California Pastoral*: *SL*, p. 127.
133. "the finest thing ever written": *SL*, p. 125
133. "unworthy of publication": Bernard Smith to John Fante, August 6, 1936.
133. "extremely provocative": James Henle to John Fante, August 25, 1936.
133. "boring . . . effect of repetitiousness": Martha Foley to John Fante, September 16, 1936.
134. *Hunger* certainly must come to mind: An interesting comparison could be made between *The Road to Los Angeles* and another highly autobiographical first novel, Henry Miller's *Moloch or, This Gentile World* (New York: Grove Press, 1992), both published posthumously. Among other similarities, both are the products of self-obsessed young authors who dared treat highly risky themes and material, including the racism of their respective protagonists.
134. "I had a lot of jobs": *RLA*, p. 9
134. "Dictator," "Superman," "What guts! God, I was mad": *RLA*, p. 33; "Fuhrer Bandini": p. 35.
135. grandiose titles: See *RLA*, p. 29.
135. "nigger" and "Spick" and "slimy Oriental": *RLA*, pp. 65, 66, 69.
135. "alone for sure": *RLA*, p. 70.
136. "the kids used to hurt me": *RLA*, p. 64.
136. "the decadence of a fraudulent Christianity": *RLA*, p. 23.
136. "wheezy twaddle": *Roseville Tribune and Register*, September 18, 1936; "a crime really unforgivable," "hard on the eye": *Roseville Tribune and Register*, September 25, 1936.
136. "storehouse of enchantment": *Roseville Tribune and Register*, October 2, 1936.
137. "What has become of that magnificent vitality": *Roseville Tribune and Register*, September 25, 1936.
137. "characters who are one hundred percent American": August Lenniger to John Fante, October 22, 1936.
137. just such a story: "The Wonderful Bird," a sappy yarn about a rich child's mother having another baby, was published as "That Wonderful Bird" in *Good Housekeeping*, but not until May 1941.
137. "almost cured of the prostitution": *SL*, p. 133.
138. "I can't fuck enough": *SL*, p. 134.
138. "[i]f America went Soviet": *SL*, p. 133.

138. "toward marriage and a return to Catholicism": *Fante/Mencken*, p. 103.
139. "frauds and soap-boxers": *SL*, p. 136.
139. "sucker": *Fante/Mencken*, p. 107.
139. "a bad place," "young and violently": *Fante/Mencken*, p. 103.
139. "make a lot of money": *SL*, p. 139.
139. "very low and broke": *Fante/Mencken*, p. 110.
139. The correspondents went back and forth: Chet Carroll's surviving letters to John Fante about this collaboration are dated December 3 and 11, 1936. Fante's side of the correspondence does not survive.
140. back-to-back acceptances: Marian Ives, Fiction Editor of *Scribner's Magazine*, accepted "Charge It" in a letter dated December 10, 1936. Paul Palmer of *The American Mercury* accepted "The Postman Rings and Rings" in a letter dated December 15, 1936.
140. He did not receive a third acceptance: For Fante's claim that he received three acceptances on Christmas Eve, 1936, see *Fante/Mencken*, p. 110.
140. "loop-eyed": *Fante/Mencken*, p. 110.

CHAPTER 9

143. "mother was alarmed": Joyce Fante, "Beginnings," unpublished memoir.
144. "Nathaniel Hawthorne could have invented": Joyce Fante, "Beginnings."
145. "Breathless, we flung": Rupert Brooke, "The Hill," in *The Collected Poems of Rupert Brooke* (New York: Dodd, Mead & Co., 1954), p. 62.
146. the poem lent itself to republication: Newspapers reprinting the poem included the *New York Herald-Tribune*, the *Providence Journal*, the *Sacramento Bee* and the *Fresno Bee*.
146. "I want . . . a marvelous, fascinating man": Joyce Fante, undated Blue Bond Composition Book.
147. "triumphant departure": Joyce Fante in unpublished letter to John Fante, February 21, 1938.
147. calculated attempts at writing: During this time Fante had stories rejected not only by *Esquire*, *The Atlantic Monthly*, *Scribner's* and *The American Mercury* but also by *Mademoiselle*, *Women's Home Companion*, *Collier's*, *Pictorial Review*, *Columbia* (the monthly magazine of the Knights of Columbus) and, oddest of all, *The Army and Navy Register*. On May 14, 1937, John Lamont of *Women's Home Companion* did accept one of Fante's "smooth-paper" yarns, "None So Blind," which appeared in the April 1938 issue. An openly cynical Fante called this story "wonderfully contemporary, a sort of glorification of the man of labor, who overcomes all obstacles and realizes Utopia in the union with a daughter of Capitalism. Hokum, of course, but very good hokum." John Fante, unpublished letter addressed to "Felix," May 12, 1937. Fante spoke at length about his unsuccessful attempts to write for radio in an unpublished letter to William Saroyan dated ambiguously "Winter (Fall?) 1938." The contents of the letter indicate that it was most likely written in January 1938.
147. "monotonous," "wearing": James W. Poling of Doubleday, Doran and Company to John Fante, November 19, 1936.
147. One of the few successes: "The Road to Hell" appeared in *The American Mercury*, October 1937.

148. "this vicious little satire": David Zablodowsky in an unpublished letter to John Fante, December 16, 1937.

148. "I am very grateful": *SL*, p. 150.

148. "The letter may give you": William Soskin to Edward J. Stackpole, Jr., February 28, 1938. I am indebted to Stackpole's grandson David Detweiler of Stackpole Books for providing me with copies of this memo and other materials relevant to Fante's relationship with Stackpole Sons. Unfortunately, the Fante letter to which Soskin here refers has not come to light.

149. Fante took the precaution of registering: U.S. Department of Labor Employment Service, Applicant's Identification Card No. 0482-34177, March 4, 1938.

149. "Best of luck to you": Edward J. Stackpole, Jr., to John Fante, March 16, 1938.

149. "He is short, darkly handsome": From the unpublished papers of Joyce Fante, c. 1937.

150. "I was recently married": *Fante/Mencken*, p. 116.

150. "that living with a literary gent": *Fante/Mencken*, p. 119.

151. "Every week or so": Joyce Fante, "Early Days," unpublished memoir.

151. Joyce's efforts proved successful: Joyce would later credit John's intercession with helping her to land the job. Mrs. Maynard Shipley, an aunt of Joyce's who headed the San Francisco WPA, may also have been of some assistance.

152. an extensive guide to the city: See *Los Angeles: A Guide to the City and Its Environs*, compiled by Workers of the Writers' Project of the Work Projects Administration in Southern California (New York: Hastings House, 1941); Robert Brownell: Brownell had helped manage Upton Sinclair's unsuccessful EPIC campaign in the 1934 California gubernatorial race.

152. "frightened [and] worried": Carey McWilliams, diary entry for March 17, 1938. Carey McWilliams Collection, UCLA.

152. "The new title has a lilt to it": Edward J. Stackpole, Jr., to John Fante, May 16, 1938.

152. "We are hoping": Edward J. Stackpole, Jr., to John Fante, June 16, 1938.

152. "I have done an immortal work of art": John Fante to William Saroyan, unpublished letter, September 15, 1938.

153. "a more fitting gesture": *Fante/Mencken*, p. 121.

153. as McWilliams put it: Carey McWilliams, diary entry for September 20, 1938. Carey McWilliams Collection, UCLA.

153. "good friends, evil companions": In 1940 Fante would dedicate *Dago Red* thus: "For Carey McWilliams and Ross Wills—good friends, evil companions."

154. *The Long Haul* had just been published: *The Long Haul* was made into the classic 1940 Humphrey Bogart, George Raft and Ida Lupino melodrama *They Drive by Night*, directed by Raoul Walsh. Bezzerides is best known today for his screenplay adaptation of Mickey Spillane's *Kiss Me Deadly*, the 1955 noir thriller directed by Robert Aldrich which had a major influence on French New Wave directors.

154. It was only by keeping polite but firm pressure: Interview with A. I. Bezzerides, February 2, 1995. See also David L. Ulin, "Bezzerides Again," *Buzz*, October 1997, p. 57.

154. The small gallery in the back: Interview with Yetive Moss, June 13, 1997.

155. "nearest thing to a Left Bank": Budd Schulberg, "Saroyan: Ease and Unease on the Flying Trapeze," *Esquire* (October 1960), p. 86. In his short but valuable study of West Coast writers, *The Boys in the Back Room: Notes on California Novelists* (San Francisco: The Colt Press, 1941), Edmund Wilson took up a number of Stanley

Rose regulars. Included among these, although not named, is Carey McWilliams, described as "a highly intelligent Los Angeles lawyer who had come to California from Colorado." Never mentioned, by name or otherwise, is John Fante.

155. "[I]t was a glorious beginning": Quoted in Lois Dwan, "Musso and Frank," *Los Angeles Times West Magazine*, November 9, 1969, p. 44.

156. "devious and treacherous ways": Joyce Fante, "Early Days."

156. one ambivalent assessment: W.S., "Fiction," *Saturday Review of Literature*, October 29, 1938.

156. Ignazio Silone's: E. L. Walton, *The Nation*, January 14, 1939.

156. "clear as a Grant Wood painting": Iris Barry, "Growing Up in Italian Colorado," *New York Herald-Tribune*, October 16, 1938.

156. The Communist *New Masses*: "Four Novels," *The New Masses*, October 25, 1938; while Farrell himself: James T. Farrell, "The Bookshelf," *The Atlantic Monthly*, January 1939.

156. "the same qualities of humor": Joseph Henry Jackson, "A Bookman's Notebook," *San Francisco Chronicle*, October 17, 1938.

157. "the big boys in the shelves": *AD*, p. 13. Fante appeared in the Los Angeles Public Library on November 19.

157. a mansion on Temple Street: The address of this mansion was 3313 Temple, now the site of a Los Angeles landmark of sorts, the decorative-rat-encircled headquarters of Western Exterminator.

CHAPTER 10

159. Frank Fenton published a bitterly knowing article: Frank Fenton, "The Hollywood Literary Life," *The American Mercury*, November 1938, pp. 280–86.

160. who on November 20 wrote to admonish Fante: William Saroyan to John Fante, November 20, 1938.

160. "In reply to a frantic telegram": Edward J. Stackpole to B. A. Brown, in-house memorandum, November 29, 1938.

160. "of a girl I once loved": *SL*, pp. 151–52.

161. an "absolutely necessary novel": John Fante, undated application for a 1939 Guggenheim Foundation award, submitted in October 1938. Archives of the J. S. Guggenheim Foundation.

162. good, frivolous copy for a day's column: Westbrook Pegler, "Fair Enough," *Los Angeles Evening News*, December 15, 1938.

162. "Put it this way": John Fante, "Pegler's a 'Peeping Tom,' says Fante, for Gibe at Strip Tease Writing," *Los Angeles Evening News*, December 19, 1938.

162. an article detailing the "legend": Richard W. Emery, "Midnight Oil: Once Struggling Long Beach Man Turns Out Sparkling Novel," *Long Beach Press-Telegram*, front page, October 21, 1938.

163. "when you were in need": Mrs. W. R. Feiring to John Fante, unpublished letter, December 28, 1938. In an unpublished and undated letter to his mother written during the time he lived on Terminal Island, that is, June 1935, Fante mentions having dinner in Long Beach "with a girl I like very much. Her name is Evelyn Feiring. . . . She is quiet, attractive, with very golden hair and fine teeth. . . . I am seeing her again Sunday night."

163. The November evening: Carey McWilliams, diary entry for November 9, 1938. The Carey McWilliams Collection, UCLA.

163. the November night when Fante appeared: Carey McWilliams, diary entry for November 20, 1938. The Carey McWilliams Collection, UCLA.

163. Called to order in Washington: See Walter Goodman, *The Committee: The Extraordinary Career of the House Committee on Un-American Activities* (New York: Farrar, Straus and Giroux, 1968).

164. Carey McWilliams was named: *Hearings of the House Committee on Un-American Activities*, vol. 3 (Washington D.C.: U.S. Government Printing Office, 1938), p. 1996.

164. Following *Kristallnacht*: McWilliams referred to the appearance of swastikas throughout southern California in his diary entry for December 23, 1938. The Carey McWilliams Collection, UCLA.

164. Fante remained blithe enough: Carey McWilliams, diary entry for January 13, 1939. The Carey McWilliams Collection, UCLA.

164. "and a whole slew of people": John Fante to William Saroyan, unpublished letter, January 1939.

165. a farewell lunch at the hotel: Carey McWilliams, diary entry for January 27, 1939. The Carey McWilliams Collection, UCLA.

166. And then he plunged: Joyce Fante describes John's mania for second-hand tables in her unpublished memoir "Early Days."

167. "It's good. It's myself": When this piece was published by Black Sparrow Press as *Prologue to Ask the Dust* in 1990, Fante's original ending (page 17 of the manuscript) was missing. The entire prologue can be found in John Fante, *The Big Hunger: Stories 1932–1959*, ed. Stephen Cooper (Santa Rosa: Black Sparrow Press, 2000).

167. *Out of the Past*: For a revealing look at Frank Fenton's important but uncredited contributions to *Out of the Past*, see Jeff Schwager, "The Past Rewritten," *Film Comment* 27, no. 1 (January–February 1991): 12–17.

167. "He said, 'You can't mean it' ": John Fante, interview with Ben Pleasants, December 10, 1978.

168. "One night I was sitting": *AD*, p. 11.

168. "It was an easy book to write": John Fante, interview with Ben Pleasants, December 10, 1978.

168. a club-hopping tour of Negro nightspots: Carey McWilliams, diary entry for June 7, 1939. Carey McWilliams Collection, UCLA.

169. the rights to "Mama Ravioli": Assignment of All Rights, notarized and signed June 23, 1939. Warner Bros. Archives, USC. Fante and Wills received story credit when the film was released in the fall of 1940 as *East of the River*, starring John Garfield as a gangster who does the right thing in the end for the sake of his mother. The *New York Times* of October 28, 1940, branded the film "contrived and hackneyed." Late in his life Fante admitted that the film was "a hideous embarrassment to me." Asked to elaborate, Fante replied, "No, I'll vomit if I talk about it." Interview with Ben Pleasants, May 22, 1979.

169. a wan comedy: "The Golden Fleecing," thirty-eight-page treatment by Lynn Root, Frank Fenton and John Fante, dated October 13, 1939. Academy of Motion Picture Arts and Sciences, Special Collections. *The Golden Fleecing* was released in August 1940, story credit going to Root, Fenton and Fante, and screenplay credit to S. J. and Laura Perelman. Featuring Lew Ayres as a hapless insurance broker who gets mixed

up with the mob, the film drew criticism for Leslie Fenton's inept direction of a story with good comic possibilities. See the *New York Times*, November 7, 1940, and *Variety*, August 16, 1940.

169. Rena Vale . . . had filed an affidavit: Carey McWilliams, diary entry for April 18, 1939. Carey McWilliams Collection, UCLA. My attempt to locate this affidavit in the Culbert L. Olson Papers at Berkeley's Bancroft Library proved unsuccessful. However, McWilliams's diary entry is not the only reference to the affidavit. In his papers at UCLA is an extensive commentary on the Vale charge, which McWilliams indicates was notarized on March 10, 1939, in an attempt to block his appointment to the Division of Housing and Immigration. In 1952, as we shall see, John Fante was forced to respond in writing to Vale's accusation. For further information on Vale, see August Raymond Ogden, *The Dies Committee: A Study of the Special House Committee for the Investigation of Un-American Activities, 1938–1944* (Washington, D.C.: The Catholic University of America Press, 1945), p. 212. See also Eric Bentley, ed., *Thirty Years of Treason: Excerpts from Hearings before the House Committee on Un-American Activities* (New York: The Viking Press, 1971), p. 160.

169. to hear Carey speak: Carey McWilliams, diary entry for August 23, 1939. Carey McWilliams Collection, UCLA.

170. He prevailed upon Joyce: Chattel Mortgage, notarized October 16, 1939.

170. "none too fit": Carey McWilliams, diary entry for November 11, 1939. Carey McWilliams Collection, UCLA.

170. "an amazing evening": Carey McWilliams, diary entry for November 15, 1939. Carey McWilliams Collection, UCLA.

171. While reviewers were consistent: See Iris Barry, "Behind the Orange Blossoms," *New York Herald Tribune Books*, November 12, 1939, p. 9; *The New Yorker*, November 11, 1939; Joseph Henry Jackson, "A Bookman's Notes," *San Francisco Chronicle*, n.d.

171. "a character cut wholly": N.L.R., *Saturday Review of Literature*, November 25, 1939.

171. "[N]ow that he has written his Werther": E. B. Garside, *The Atlantic Monthly*, December 1939.

171. "particular vision of a modern inferno": Iris Barry, "Behind the Orange Blossoms," *New York Herald Tribune Books*, November 12, 1939, p. 9.

171. "quite an extraordinary piece of work": H. L. Binsse, *Commonweal*, December 1, 1939.

172. "I'm an American": *AD*, p. 49.

172. "the folks back home": *AD*, p. 46.

172. "I have seen them stagger": *AD*, pp. 46–47.

173. "hodgepodge": *Fante/Mencken*, p. 118.

173. "Fuhrer Bandini": *RLA*, p. 35.

173. "*Mea culpa*": *AD*, p. 96.

174. "about a few other Italians": *AD*, p. 90.

174. Cellini and his lover-model Caterina: See Benvenuto Cellini, *The Life of Benvenuto Cellini, Written by Himself* (New York: Phaidon Publishers, Inc., 1949), pp. 292–305.

174. two seminal southern California novels: Helen Hunt Jackson, *Ramona* [1884] (New York: Little, Brown, 1939); and Don Ryan, *Angel's Flight* (New York: Boni & Liveright, 1927).

174. From his explorations in California history: Jackson's story continues to fascinate

southern Californians, who since 1923 have flocked by the thousands each spring to the high desert town of Hemet in order to witness the story's reenactment in the Ramona Pageant.

174. "The first book came": *SL*, p. 157.
175. "Six weeks, a few sweet hours every day": *AD*, p. 113.
175. "Los Angeles, give me some of you!" *AD*, p. 13.
176. annus mirabilis: See David Fine, "John Fante and the Los Angeles Novel in the 1930s," in *John Fante: A Critical Gathering*, ed. Stephen Cooper and David Fine (Madison, N.J.: Fairleigh Dickinson University Press, 1999), p. 122. See also Chapter 1, "Welcome (1939)," of Otto Friedrich's *City of Nets: A Portrait of Hollywood in the 1940s* (New York: Harper & Row, 1986).
176. He optioned the film rights: *SL*, p. 154; hired a Hollywood agent: Fante signed a contract with A. George Volck Agency on December 18, 1939.
177. "For God's sake, honey": See William Saroyan, *Sons Come and Go, Mothers Hang in Forever* (New York: McGraw-Hill, 1976), p. 109.
177. Distracted by an expensive lawsuit: See John Tebbel, *A History of Book Publishing in the United States* (New York: R. R. Bowker Company, 1978), vol. 3, p. 453; and vol. 4 (1981), p. 2. Stackpole's *Mein Kampf*, which appeared on the same 1939 list with *Ask the Dust*, was the first unexpurgated edition in English of Hitler's hate-filled manifesto. As such, it was meant to afford American readers the chance of seeing for themselves what the earlier authorized abridgment from Houghton Mifflin had obscured.
177. In order to survive the financial blow: The lawsuit created a serious financial drain on Stackpole Sons, but it did not drive the publisher out of business, as has been stated, for example, in *SL*, p. 150. Compared to the twenty-seven titles published in 1938, the 1940 list contained only three. After the war the firm rebounded and survives to this day as Stackpole Books.
177. John's most recent meeting with Pascal Covici: On November 23, 1939, Fante wrote two letters in which he mentioned Covici's offer, one to his mother and the other to his cousin Jo Campiglia. To his mother he said that the offer was for $200 a month for one year, with an open account of $3,500, while in the letter to Jo Campiglia the figures had climbed to $300 a month for eighteen months, with an open account of $4,000. With bookkeeping like this typical of Fante, it's no wonder that Joyce assumed responsibility for the couple's finances, and disturbing to think what a responsibility it was to be partnered with someone whose understanding of financial realities was as tenuous and even illusory as his.
177. "No worry": *SL*, p. 315.
177. "smacko among writers": *SL*, p. 158.
178. "solacing conceit of immortality": *SL*, p. 315.
178. Fante's spirits were briefly lifted: Maximilian Becker of AFG Literary Agency informed Fante of the *Esquire* sale in a letter dated January 4, 1940.
178. "It was either murder and death, or life and love": "The Taming of Valenti," *Esquire*, April 1941, p. 170.
179. "magnificent idea": *SL*, p. 316.
179. "sick as hell": *SL*, p. 318.
179. "I am against death": *SL*, p. 318; "A sort of highly refined Christianity": *SL*, p. 319.
179. When the fight was over: *SL*, pp. 316–17. Showing me the chip in her tooth left by

Thornton's punching her, Ellenore (Boggegian Abowitz) Hittelman confirmed Fante's account of this harrowing night. I interviewed her on January 13, 1997.

179. "recurrent spells": *SL*, p. 318.

179. "sexual maladjustment": *SL*, p. 316; "inspired love affair": p. 319.

180. "bitter hangover depression": *SL*, p. 322.

180. "a terrific attack of melancholia": *SL*, p. 323.

181. "She could develop": *SL*, p. 324.

182. "lost control": John Fante to his parents in a letter dated only "Saturday," that is, February 3, 1940.

182. He underwent surgery: Fante's account of his accident to Pascal Covici in *SL*, p. 162, is corroborated in a letter from Joyce to John's parents dated February 3, 1940.

182. "Some people simply refuse to die": John Fante to his parents in an unpublished, undated letter written sometime in the first part of the summer of 1940.

CHAPTER 11

183. "I love war": John Fante in a letter to Pascal Covici, May 26, 1940. See *SL*, p. 165.

183. His German shepherd: John Fante in undated letter to his mother from early 1940.

183. And unlike Bill Saroyan: See Larry Lawrence and Barry Gifford, *Saroyan: A Biography* (New York: Harper & Row, 1984), p. 17. *The Time of Your Life* featured a character named Willie, described in Saroyan's play notes as "a marble game maniac," who was modeled after Fante and his pinball wizardry. See William Saroyan, *The Time of Your Life* in *Three Plays* (New York: Harcourt, Brace and Co., 1940), p. 17. See also Ross Wills's 1940 profile, "John Fante," in *SL*, p. 337.

183. a quickie film idea: The produce truckers story on which Fante collaborated with Bezzerides was called "Wholesale Terminal." Fante signed a contract with agent A. George Volck to represent this project on April 4, 1940.

184. "chafing to write": *SL*, p. 165.

184. "They can tear this over-rated civilization apart": *SL*, p. 166.

184. the Viking editor had sent Fante a check: Pascal Covici to John Fante, February 20, 1940; requesting release from his contract: John Fante to E. J. Stackpole, March 3, 1940.

184. Stackpole had agreed: E. J. Stackpole to John Fante, March 8, 1940.

184. as an advance on the collection: Pascal Covici to John Fante, May 29, 1940.

184. "Fante is an owlish": Carey McWilliams, diary entry for July 7, 1940. Carey McWilliams Collection, UCLA.

185. Toward that end he spent the entire day: Carey McWilliams, diary entry for August 20, 1940. Carey McWilliams Collection, UCLA.

185. "the most vicious system of race and class taboo": *SL*, p. 175.

185. "over each page bright as sunlight": Marianne Hauser, "The Portrait of an Italian Family," *New York Times*, September 29, 1940.

185. "This is a warm good book": Quoted in Joseph Henry Jackson, "Between the Lines," *San Francisco Chronicle*, October 6, 1940.

186. "perhaps 1940's best book": *Time*, October 7, 1940.

186. the Italian opus: *SL*, p. 175.

187. "I think you and I both agree: *SL*, p. 180.
187. Covici took Joyce's hint: Pascal Covici to John Fante, October 1, 1940.
187. "to go to the Philippine Islands": From Fante's application for a 1941 Guggenheim grant. In reapplying for a Guggenheim Fante described his plans to write "a novel of perhaps 75,000 words on the question of Filipinos in California, and the problem of Philippine Independence as it affects the Filipino both in California, and in the Islands." Archives of the J. S. Guggenheim Foundation.
188. Still, he wished him good luck: John Steinbeck to John Fante, undated letter. For another ironic view of the 1941 Guggenheim Awards competition, see the final section, "Addenda," of Henry Miller's *The Air-Conditioned Nightmare* (New York: New Directions, 1945).
188. "so that, should it succeed": John Fante to Pascal Covici, November 30, 1940. This part of the letter has been omitted from the version published in *SL*, pp. 185–86.
188. When Tom tried to intervene: Interview with Tom Fante, February 14, 1998.
188. "very broke": *SL*, p. 186.
188. His doctors were suing him: *SL*, p. 175.
188. Even his veterinarian: C. C. Sundstrom of the South Bay Dog-Cat Hospital to John Fante, December 1, 1940.
188. "in all critical truth, pretty bad": George Jean Nathan to John Fante, December 1, 1940.
188. on the outskirts of the Imperial County town of El Centro: Jay Martin, *Nathanael West: The Art of His Life*, pp. 7, 11.
188. "a wilder-than-usual mood": Carey McWilliams, diary entry for December 27, 1940. Carey McWilliams Collection, UCLA.
189. After Solari's: Carey McWilliams, diary entry for December 27, 1940. The Carey McWilliams Collection, UCLA. Herb Caen recalled the night as "bibulous" in a letter to me dated August 1, 1995.
189. A few weeks earlier: William Saroyan to John Fante, December 2, 1940.
189. screenwriter Budd Schulberg: Interview with Budd Schulberg, August 15, 1995.
189. RKO story editor Collier Young: Collier Young to John Fante, September 9, 1940.
189. "horrible dump": Carey McWilliams diary entry for September 15, 1940. Carey McWilliams Collection, UCLA.
189. "On desperate seas": Edgar Allan Poe, "To Helen."
189. "the hand that held the dagger": Russell D. Buhite and David W. Levy, eds., *FDR's Fireside Chats* (New York: Penguin Books, 1992), p. 152.
190. "a pro-Mussolini man": *SL*, p. 168.
190. called Nick a "fifth columnist": This was the name applied to rebel sympathizers in Madrid in 1936 when four rebel columns were advancing on the city. The term came to be used to designate any group of secret sympathizers or supporters of an enemy that engages in espionage or sabotage within defense lines or national borders.
190. For the next several days: "Local Man Held in Knifing Friday Night," *Roseville Press*, February 3, 1941, front page. This article identifies Nick as "a native of Italy and father of novelist John Fante."
190. As a result no charges were filed: "District Attorney Orders Release of Nick Fante," *Roseville Press*, February 5, 1941, front page.
191. Still, Fante stood accused: See the Ted LeBerthon column "Night and Day," *Los Angeles Daily News*, March 8, 1941.

191. "We had an unexpected dinner": Carlos Bulosan, *Sound of Falling Light: Letters in Exile* (Quezon City, 1960), p. 13.
191. "Once Carlos threw a party": Carey McWilliams, Introduction to Carlos Bulosan's *America Is in the Heart: A Personal History* [1943] (Seattle: University of Washington Press, 1973), pp. xix–xx.
192. "I beat him up with my shoes": Interview with Joyce Fante, July 21, 1994.
192. the composite model for Camilla Lopez: Although she was never certain, Joyce Fante suspected that her husband continued seeing both Audrey and Marie after he was a married man. Rejecting his claim that Camilla was based on a lesbian, Joyce contends that Fante said as much in an effort to obscure the facts of his infidelity. Fante made this claim in an interview with Ben Pleasants, December 10, 1978. Fante also told Charles Bukowski that Camilla's original was a lesbian. See Charles Bukowski, "Remembering John Fante," the *New Haven Advocate*, February 27, 1989.
192. "pathetic old drunk": Carey McWilliams, diary entry for June 13, 1941. Carey McWilliams Collection, UCLA.
193. James Joyce had died: Carey McWilliams noted the deaths of both Joyce and Woolf in his 1941 diary, on January 13 and April 19, respectively. The version of Woolf's words he quoted in his diary differs from the version in Quentin Bell's *Virginia Woolf: A Biography* (New York: Harcourt Brace, Jovanovich, 1972), p. 464. The reason for the discrepancy is unclear.
193. Norman Foster had started out: Don Miller, "Remember . . . Norman Foster," *Applause*, October 6, 1971, p. 9.
193. an adaptation of *Ask the Dust*: John Fante, unpublished letter to his mother, April 8, 1941.
193. "Woman Is Fickle": contract with literary agent H. N. Swanson, June 23, 1941.
193. Overextended once again: John Fante, unpublished letter to his mother, June 19, 1941.
193. profile of William Saroyan: "Bill Saroyan," in *Common Ground* 1 (Winter 1941): 64–66.
193. a review of *Home Is Here*: "Italian Home in San Francisco," *New York Herald Tribune Books*, July 6, 1941, p. 4.
194. Fante and Foster had retained an energetic agent: For evidence of Swanson's energies, see the H. N. Swanson Collection, Margaret Herrick Library, Special Collections, Academy of Motion Picture Arts and Sciences.
194. Alien to Fante's true interests: John Fante and Norman Foster, "Man of Tomorrow," ninety-one-page treatment, dated July 19, 1941. Margaret Herrick Library, Special Collections, Academy of Motion Picture Arts and Sciences.
195. "one of the great mysteries": Kenneth Turan, "The Lost Piece to the Welles Puzzle," *Los Angeles Times Calendar*, October 24, 1993, p. 4.
195. As such, the film was meant: See Charles Higham, *Orson Welles: The Rise and Fall of an American Genius* (New York: St. Martin's Press, 1985).
196. "All stories we do for Welles": *SL*, p. 195. In an unpublished letter to his parents dated August 7, 1941, Fante reiterated his disclaimer: "Norman Foster and myself made up the whole story. . . . It has nothing to do with your lives in any manner, shape or form." Nick and Mary Fante signed the waiver, which was dated August 2.
196. "The authors hope": Norman Foster and John Fante, "My Friend Bonito." Orson Welles Collection, Lilly Library, Indiana University.

196. Complaining that he did not like the work: See *SL*, p. 196.

196. Covici's response: Pascal Covici to John Fante, September 30, 1941.

196. A mélange of drama, comedy and music: See Frank Brady, *Citizen Welles* (New York: Charles Scribner's Sons, 1989), p. 333.

197. nine short radio dramas: The nine eight-minute scripts Fante penned for *The Lady Esther Show* in the fall of 1941, with the dates they were submitted, were "Ask the Dust" (September 19); "Black Marigolds," from the poem of the same name by the eleventh-century Sanscrit poet Bilhana (October 6); "The Lost Stars," from a story by French poet and novelist Catulle Mendes (October 8); "The All-American Team," from his own story, later published as "One-Play Oscar" in the November 1950 *Saturday Evening Post* (October 22); "Mr. Sampson," from a story by Charles Lee (October 28); "Eye Hath Not Seen," from his own story "None So Blind," published in the April 1938 *Women's Home Companion* (October 31); "Kangaroo Loves Me," from a story by the prolific novelist Geoffrey Household (November 11); "The Light in the Valley," from a story by Michael Manning (no date); and "Water of Iturrigorri," from a story by Geoffrey Household (December 3).

197. But this radio writing: I am indebted to Becky Cape of Indiana University's Lilly Library for information regarding Fante's radio scripts.

197. Welles would later cannibalize: My thanks to Welles scholar Catherine Benamou for calling my attention to this fact. Interview with Catherine Benamou, March 24, 1997.

197. "firmly on its way to being a masterpiece": Higham, *Orson Welles*, p. 190.

197. By then Fante had moved to Paramount: Paramount work contract, November 10–December 4, 1941. Academy of Motion Picture Arts and Sciences, Special Collections.

198. "and peed on the people down below": John Fante, interview with Ben Pleasants, December 10, 1978. In 1993 a documentary film entitled *It's All True* was released, a fascinating study of the Welles project of the same name. Employing footage undiscovered until 1985, this film incorporates stunning reconstructed scenes from the two Brazilian segments of Welles's unfinished omnibus, as well as from "My Friend Bonito." Codirected by Richard Wilson, Myron Meisel and Bill Krohn, *It's All True* is in nearly all respects a model of film history and preservation. Unfortunately, nowhere in the documentary is John Fante credited for cowriting with Norman Foster the script of "My Friend Bonito."

CHAPTER 12

199. "Confidentially . . . I lost that amount": Undated letter from John Fante to H. N. Swanson. H. N. Swanson Collection, Special Collections, the Margaret Herrick Library, Academy of Motion Pictures Arts and Sciences.

200. "Home Is the Hunter": This fifty-four-page treatment can be found in the Arts Special Collections of UCLA's Charles E. Young Research Library.

200. Swanson advised: H. N. Swanson to John Fante, March 9, 1942. H. N. Swanson Collection, Special Collections, the Margaret Herrick Library, Academy of Motion Picture Arts and Sciences.

201. "the cold fire of hatred": *SL*, p. 198.

202. the Nerve War: See David H. Culbert, ed. *Information Control and Propaganda:*

Records of the Office of War Information, Part II: Office of Policy Coordination, Series A: Propaganda and Policy Directives for Overseas Programs, 1942–1945 (Frederick, Md.: University Publications of America, 1986).

202. Fante's compatriots: I am indebted to novelist Oakley Hall for putting me in contact with Harle Montgomery, who during the war did contract work for the Pacific Bureau of the OWI. She shared with me her recollections of the people who worked there at the time. Interview with Harle Montgomery, September 24, 1998.

202. "toadying to frauds": *SL*, p. 199.

203. "the John Fante matter": Humphrey Cobb in a letter to Carey McWilliams, January 2, 1943. The Carey McWilliams Collection, UCLA.

203. "for personal reasons": Advice of Personnel Action, January 8, 1943. Fante's claim to Pascal Covici that the leave was "good for three months" seems to have been one of his characteristic exaggerations. See *SL*, p. 200.

203. Fante had managed to get back on the Warner Bros. payroll: Unpublished letter from Joyce Fante to Mary Fante, January 9, 1943.

204. "Marine Story": seven-page story by John Fante and David Wear dated January 21, 1943. Warner Bros. Archives, University of Southern California.

204. The Auburn draft board: John Fante to his parents, unpublished letter dated January 30, 1943.

204. "go to a bar": John Fante to his mother in an unpublished letter dated February 5, 1943.

204. the studio was in a precarious position: Interoffice memo from Carl Stucke to Steve Trilling, February 25, 1943. Warner Bros. Archives, USC.

205. On a scale of 1 to 9: Report of Efficiency Rating, March 31, 1943.

205. "to deal with the big Italian population": *SL*, p. 201.

205. When his draft status was changed: Auburn Draft Board Number 30, order no. 2284, indicates that as of May 15, 1943, Fante's classification was changed from 3-A to 3-B.

205. "personal reasons": According to the Advice of Personnel Action form detailing his resignation, Fante officially separated from the OWI on July 14, 1943.

205. Val Lewton now hired Fante: Fante's salary rate at RKO is recorded in a memo appended to his Paramount contract of December 12, 1944. Special Collections, the Margaret Herrick Library, Academy of Motion Picture Arts and Sciences.

205. Variously called "Cockeyed Youth": These scripts can be found in the RKO Archives of the Arts Special Collection, Charles E. Young Research Library, UCLA.

206. His script would focus: Assisting Fante at the story stage, that is, before Fante wrote the script proper, was documentary writer Herbert Kline, whose credits included *The Forgotten Village* (with John Steinbeck) and *Spanish Earth*.

206. RKO was angling to cash in: Joel E. Siegel, *Val Lewton: The Reality of Terror* (New York: The Viking Press, 1973), p. 60.

206. RKO had a deal with Hearst: RKO's promotional campaign for this socially conscious film was extensive and unabashedly cynical. Plans included coordinated articles in *Life* and *Look* as well as a steady barrage of front-page articles on the nation's supposedly rampant juvenile delinquency problem in newspapers around the country. All of this was gleefully considered "the equivalent of many thousands of dollars worth of free advertising." RKO's ultimate aim was to "force the approval and endorsement of child-welfare groups, parent-teacher associations, church and civic organizations, and the like. Such support if properly guided can mean a flood of dough

at the box-office." *RKO Radio Flash* xiv, no. 31 (January 1, 1944). Mayer Library, American Film Institute.

206. "My job at the studio": John Fante in an unpublished letter to his parents, July 29, 1943.

206. Val Lewton proved extremely difficult: For Joyce Fante's recollection of the Fante-Lewton relationship, see *SL*, pp. 202–3.

206. According to others: See Siegel, *Val Lewton.*

206. "You're like a dog": Interview with Edward Dmytryk, April 19, 1997.

207. "The way a Christian goes to church": Quoted in Joseph Blotner, *Faulkner: A Biography* (New York: Random House, 1974), p. 1134.

207. "a lot of drinks": I am indebted to Philippe Garnier for allowing me to use the transcript of his film interview with A. I. Bezzerides, from which this quotation comes. Garnier played a key role in introducing Fante's works to the French, through his translation of *Ask the Dust*, his many newspaper articles, and a documentary film co-produced with Claude Ventura that aired on French television's *Cinema Cinemas* in 1988. In an interview with Ben Pleasants on December 18, 1978, Fante called Faulkner "a good friend of mine. . . . I used to meet him at Musso Frank's and we used to go out and get drunk together, he and I and a guy by the name of Al Bezzerides."

208. "got this evil glint in his eye": A. I. Bezzerides in the 1988 interview with Philippe Garnier. I had not yet met Philippe Garnier, nor thus read the transcripts of this interview, when on February 2, 1995, I interviewed Bezzerides myself. He told me the same story then that he had told Garnier several years earlier. See also David L. Ulin, "Bezzerides Again," *Buzz*, October 1997.

208. "began to fall apart": *SL*, p. 203.

208. Fante submitted his third application: Archives of the J. S. Guggenheim Memorial Foundation.

209. the way this one was kicking: John Fante to his mother, December 15, 1943. The information about Joyce's pregnancy has been omitted from the letter as it appears in *SL*, p. 204.

209. when the time came to exchange gifts: John Fante to his parents, unpublished letter dated December 28, 1943.

209. Morgan led Fante to understand: *SL*, p. 205.

210. dutifully composed and sent such a letter: Unpublished letter from Pascal Covici to L. F. Morgan, May 19, 1944.

210. Fante was granted a permanent deferment: Auburn Local Board No. 30 Classification Advice, Order No. 2284, May 31, 1944. Fante was reclassified 2-A-L.

210. "This piece represents the first chapter of a novel": Charles Grayson, ed. *New Stories for Men* (Garden City, N.Y.: Garden City Publishing Co., 1943), n.p.

211. "Danny . . . shrieking mightily": Sparky Heilbron, "Roseville Author of 'Dago Red' Would Rather Have Lemonade." *Sacramento Union*, September 10, 1944, p. 18.

211. (Because of immigration restrictions): I am indebted to Dr. Linda N. España-Maram of California State University, Long Beach, for sharing her paper, "Brown 'Hordes' in McIntosh Suits: Filipinos, Taxi Dance Halls, and Performing the Immigrant Body in Los Angeles, 1930s–1940s," from which I take this information.

212. McWilliams would write four important books: See Carey McWilliams, *The Education of Carey McWilliams* (New York: Simon and Schuster, 1979), especially Chapters 5 and 6.

213. "My feeling . . . is that this is not your story": Pascal Covici to John Fante, November 10, 1944. Parts of this letter appear in *SL*, pp. 206–7.
214. he signed a ten-week contract: Paramount Collection, the Margaret Herrick Library, Special Collections, Academy of Motion Picture Arts and Sciences.
214. "I like the assignment": *SL*, p. 208.
214. "For Esther, from that Hollywood whore": Author's collection. Esther Blaisdell had been a lover of Carey McWilliams. The inscription is dated March 4, 1945.

CHAPTER 13

215. A typically mercurial studio enthusiasm: John Fante, "Flamenco," seventy-page treatment, Paramount Pictures SF 88666, February 7, 1945; John Fante and Sidney Field, "For the Love of Picaro," fifteen-page treatment, May 26, 1945. The alternate title "Gypsy Honeymoon" is written in pencil on the cover page of this latter treatment. In an unpublished interview in the late 1970s with Argentinian filmmaker Einer Moos, Fante said that this film project was canceled when Dorothy Lamour became pregnant.
216. "best fiction films of the year": James Agee, "Films," *The Nation*, January 20, 1945, p. 30. In the September 25, 1944, issue of *Time* Agee had also praised *Youth Runs Wild* warmly, indicating his enthusiasm for the film's "awkward grace" and its approach to showing "normal people in normal situations." Other critics were not so kind. Typical was the view expressed in *Variety*, June 28, 1944, which found the film little better than "a feeble sermon that fails to provide much entertainment." Most viewers today would side with *Variety*; it is difficult even for a sympathetic critic to recapture Agee's enthusiasm for *Youth Runs Wild*.
216. "I know you're mad at me": John Fante to Elizabeth Otis of the literary agency McIntosh and Otis, unpublished letter dated July 18, 1945.
216. a $2,700 down payment: Receipt from J. Warren Tatum, real estate broker, dated February 13, 1945.
217. Fante was furious: John Fante to his mother in an unpublished letter dated March 16, 1945.
217. Major restorations: Inspection report, Jewett, Inc., May 7, 1945. Photographs accompanying this report show that had Fante only glanced into the crawlspace beneath the house he would have been able to see for himself the extent to which his dream home was damaged goods.
217. "I have to drink": *SL*, p. 210.
217. Joyce set about furnishing the house: Receipts from Bimini Auction Galleries, April 29, July 22, 1945.
217. "the light of faith": *WY*, p. 206.
217. "a real cry that shook me": *WY*, p. 209.
218. "Spent the afternoon with Nick Fante": Sunday night, May 13, 1945. McWilliams followed up this entry with the brief notation that he had spent "all day recuperating." Carey McWilliams Collection, UCLA.
218. True, she might see him occasionally: Carey McWilliams, diary entries for May 6 and May 31, 1945. Carey McWilliams Collection, UCLA.
219. "He stirs and mutters": "Waking," from the unpublished poems of Joyce Fante.
220. The feeling of portent: Joyce Fante, diary entry, May 30, 1946.

220. "We went to dinner tonight": Joyce Fante, diary entry, August 19, 1946.
220. The latter's *Science and Sanity*: Alfred Korzybski, *Science and Sanity: An Introduction to Non-Aristotelian Systems and General Semantics* (Lancaster, Penn.: The International Non-Aristotelian Library Publishing Company, 1933). See also J. Samuel Bois, *Epistemics: The Science-Art of Innovating* (San Francisco: International Society for General Semantics, 1972). Korzybski's philosophy has influenced thinkers as divergent in their views as S. I. Hayakawa and Michel Foucault. I am indebted to the late Robert K. Straus for showing me his unpublished essay "My Map Was Not the Territory," about his long interest in Korzybski and general semantics. Interview with Robert K. Straus, February 8, 1997; letter from Robert K. Straus to author, February 11, 1997.
221. "I read a great deal": Joyce Fante, diary entry, April 17, 1946.
221. On October 7 Fante attended: Carey McWilliams, diary entry for October 7, 1945. Carey McWilliams Collection, UCLA.
221. Years later Fante would wonder: John Fante, interview with Ben Pleasants, December 18, 1978.
222. He wrote a whimsical sequence of bedtime stories: Six of these children's stories survive: "Toots," "Zip," "Little Car," "Binky," and two that are untitled.
223. "I don't remember whether": Wilson Carey McWilliams, Jr., in a letter to the author, September 1, 1997.
223. When the Fantes' next-door neighbors: Joyce Fante, diary entry, April 20, 1946.
224. Curtailing the conference: The story that Fante cowrote with Richard Strobel was entitled "The Day after Tomorrow." It was registered with the Writers Guild on January 15, 1946. No copy survives.
224. After that incident: Interview with Richard and Mary Strobel, February 13, 1997.
224. "terribly scared": Joyce Fante, undated diary entry, summer 1946.
225. He lay there without moving: Interview with Harry Pete Parkin, February 18, 1997.
226. At a party hosted by Carey and Iris: Diary entry for February 27, 1948. Carey McWilliams Collection, UCLA.
226. "to shoot anybody who hurt him": John Fante in an unpublished letter to his parents, c. June 1948.
227. Enthusiastic new Catholic: John Fante in a letter to his parents, September 15, 1948. The version of this letter published on pages 218–19 of *SL* omits the information about Joyce's writing Father Reinert.
227. "absolute and limitless freedom": *SL*, p. 217.
227. "as if all life today has disintegrated": *SL*, p. 217.
227. "The whole picture has radically changed": John Fante in an undated letter to his parents.
228. It was an insidious time: The information in this paragraph, including the quotations from Lord and Rand, is based on Lillian Ross's 1948 *New Yorker* article, "Introducing the Blacklist," republished in *The New Yorker*, March 21, 1994, pp. 176–84.
229. Aptly named "The Long Nightmare": John Fante and Ben Sacks, "The Long Nightmare," thirty-one-page treatment registered with the Writers Guild of America, August 23, 1949.
229. The story was never published: Candidly calling it "scattered," Fante's agent Elizabeth Otis nevertheless thought enough of this story to try to sell it. Elizabeth Otis to John Fante, February 1, 1949.
229. Norman Foster had recently called: *SL*, p. 220.

229. "that suggest what Southern California": Carey McWilliams, *Southern California Country: An Island on the Land* [1946] (Salt Lake City: Peregrine Smith, Inc. 1979), p. 364. The other three novels singled out by McWilliams in his classic study were Nathanael West's *The Day of the Locust*, Frank Fenton's *A Place in the Sun* and Mark Lee Luther's *The Boosters*. With its penetrating analyses of the region's many interwoven histories—cultural, social, ethnic, economic—*Southern California Country* sheds invaluable light on all of these novels, and especially on *Ask the Dust*. For an enhanced understanding of the vexed relationship between Arturo Bandini and Camilla Lopez, see especially Chapter 3, "Californios and Mexicanos."

230. "[w]hat people seem to be looking for today": Lloyd E. Smith to John Fante, in a letter dated March 22, 1949.

230. the amicus curiae brief: McWilliams's working papers for this brief as well as the brief itself can be found in the Carey McWilliams Collection, UCLA.

230. The two had recently taken a trip: Diary entries for January 27–28, 1949. Carey McWilliams Collection, UCLA. Cf. McWilliams's remark in the introduction to *Southern California Country*: "With Fante and Wills I have explored Southern California from the Mexican border to the Tehachapi Range, not once but many times. We were co-explorers of the region" (xx–xxi).

230. "ridiculous": Diary entry for January 23, 1949. Carey McWilliams Collection, UCLA.

230. "Believe in your children": *SL*, p. 221.

CHAPTER 14

233. "Los Angeles is the capital": Carey McWilliams, *Southern California Country: An Island on the Land*, p. 230.

234. "turtle pace": Joe Gottesman in a letter to John Fante dated October 20, 1949.

234. Like Carey McWilliams: Diary entries for January 6, February 8, and February 11, 1950. Carey McWilliams Collection, UCLA.

235. More than forty years later: For Joyce's third-person account of this period, see *SL*, p. 225.

235. "to finish it in sixty days": John Fante to his parents, unpublished letter dated April 9, 1950.

236. Elizabeth Otis had sold the book: Elizabeth Otis to John Fante, June 12, 1950.

236. *Paisan* and *Open City*: Diary entry for July 4, 1950. Carey McWilliams Collection, UCLA.

236. an enthusiastic letter from Pascal Covici: On July 20 Covici wrote Fante to say that he was "perfectly happy" with the half-finished manuscript sent him by Elizabeth Otis.

236. Long days of swimming: From August 11 to 25 the family stayed in a rented bungalow at 326 Eucalyptus Street. Unpublished letter from John Fante to his parents, no date.

236. Finished days before the June outbreak: Carey McWilliams, *Witch Hunt: The Revival of Heresy* (New York: Little, Brown and Company, 1950). See also *The Education of Carey McWilliams*, p. 140.

236. Fante responded to the era's escalating pressures: Less than five years later, at the age of forty-two, Leonard would die of cirrhosis of the liver. Obituary in *Variety*, January 12, 1955.

237. Nick's requiem mass: *Roseville Press-Tribune*, November 24, 1950.
237. The next evening Fante was back: Diary entry for November 23, 1950. Carey McWilliams Collection, UCLA.
237. "the most unpalatable strip teases": Diary entry for December 12, 1950. Carey McWilliams Collection, UCLA.
238. "Myself, when I read": *Fante/Mencken*, p. 135.
238. Fante had left Viking: Fante signed the contract for *Full of Life* with Little, Brown, and Company on May 11, 1951.
238. joked that he was going to charge Cameron: Carey McWilliams, unpublished letter to John Fante, June 17, 1951. In no small part for having published *Witch Hunt*, Angus Cameron would soon be forced out of Little, Brown, "perhaps the sole editor to be blacklisted in the publishing industry." See Griffin Fariello, *Red Scare: Memories of the American Inquisition* (New York: W. W. Norton & Company, 1995), p. 319.
238. "rather embarrassing compromise": *Fante/Mencken*, p. 137.
239. "accepted [the suggestions] willingly": Motion Picture Association of America memo, June 25, 1951. *Full of Life* file, Margaret Herrick Library, Academy of Motion Picture Arts and Sciences.
239. "Pax vobiscum!": Undated note from John Fante to the Motion Picture Association of America. *Full of Life* file, Margaret Herrick Library, Academy of Motion Picture Arts and Sciences.
239. A calculating Fante: Dmytryk had been nominated for Best Achievement in Directing for his engrossing 1947 drama *Crossfire*, which received four other Oscar nominations as well.
239. *Christ in Concrete*: Di Donato and Fante had already been linked as Italian-American novelists of the same generation whose best-known books had both been published in 1939. Dmytryk's film adaptation of *Christ in Concrete* was released variously as *Give Us This Day* or *Salt to the Devil*.
239. Now, as Fante saw it: For Dmytryk's version of events at this time, see his *Odd Man Out: A Memoir of the Hollywood Ten* (Carbondale: Southern Illinois Press, 1996). See also his interview in Fariello's *Red Scare: Memories of the American Inquisition*, pp. 294–305.
240. Again Fante suspected: For Fante's astute analysis of the political background to these developments, see his long letter of October 17, 1951, to Carey McWilliams in *SL*, especially pp. 229–30.
240. Unfortunately, Felton's fortunes: *Los Angeles Times*, August 26, 1949.
240. the script Felton submitted: A copy of the Earl Felton *Full of Life* can be found at the Margaret Herrick Library, Academy of Motion Picture Arts and Sciences.
240. When Kramer's attention shifted: On January 22, 1952, Stanley Kramer wrote to Fante not to "kill yourself" on the script. He said he was looking forward to seeing the material but that there was no deadline and no pressure intended.
240. Misnamed in the 1790s: See Ruth Ryson, "Tucked along the Coast," *Los Angeles Times*, August 31, 1997, K6. Monsignor Francis J. Weber, Archivist of the Archdiocese of Los Angeles, is cited as the authority for this historical background.
241. "Now look here, McWilliams": *SL*, p. 227.
242. "Had we known the real condition": Harry Miller to John Fante, December 20, 1951.
242. Yet the next day: Knox Burger in a letter to the author, January 23, 1995. In a letter to Fante dated February 18, 1952, Fante's agent Elizabeth Otis mentioned pointedly

that she had "heard a very racy account of your dinner with Knox! You two really did get off on the wrong feet with each other."

242. Nor was there anything serene: See Aram Saroyan, *William Saroyan* (San Diego: Harcourt Brace Jovanovich, 1983). See also Lawrence Lee and Barry Gifford, *William Saroyan: A Biography* (New York: Harper & Row, 1984), pp. 254–56.

242. "In a world and time that hurries deathward": Christopher Morley, *Book-of-the-Month Club News*, May 1952, p. 11.

243. When Roberts and her novelist husband: Despite the bitter experience of being blacklisted, Marguerite Roberts would remember her work on "Letter from the President" with fondness. "I did the script on *Letter* with great joy—Chu Chu was one of the two best characters I'd met in forty years of screenwriting; Rooster Cogburn of *True Grit* was the other." Marguerite Sanford in a letter to John Fante dated February 25, 1982. This letter is reproduced in John Sanford's *Maggie: A Love Story* (Fort Lee, N.J.: Barricade Books, 1993), pp. 380–81. My thanks to John Sanford for bringing this letter and his book to my attention when I interviewed him at his home in Montecito, California, on October 18, 1996. For further information on the blacklisting of Roberts and Sanford, see the interview with Sanford in Fariello's *Red Scare*, pp. 289–94.

243. In June Fante submitted "Silver Lode": Dated June 27, 1952, Fante's five-page outline for "Silver Lode" appears to have had nothing to do with RKO's *Silver Lode* of 1954, the anti-HUAC allegory directed by Allan Dwan.

243. And then in July Fante submitted "Orca": The Metro-Goldwyn-Mayer Pictures Reader's Report on "Orca" was dated July 22, 1952. The connections, if any, between Fante's "Orca" and the 1977 Dino DeLaurentiis film of the same title are uncertain. In the late 1950s DeLaurentiis would hire Fante to write screenplays for several different projects. Arthur Herzog's novelized *Orca* (New York: Pocket Books, 1977) was tied to the release of the film, which according to the credits was based on an original story and screenplay by Luciano Vincenzoni. Starring Richard Harris, Charlotte Rampling and Bo Derek, the film has been described as a "[m]indlessly imitative" twin rip-off of *Moby Dick* and *Jaws*. See David Bordwell and Noel Carroll, eds., *Post-Theory: Reconstructing Film Studies* (Madison: University of Wisconsin Press, 1996), p. 204.

243. this outline netted Fante: Fante's contract was newsworthy enough to be reported not only in the trades (for example, *The Hollywood Reporter*, August 19, 1952) but also in the *New York Post* of August 22.

243. In addition to granting Fante $6,000: This contract is dated July 30, 1952.

244. "My attention has been directed": John Fante, letter to the Stanley Kramer Company, dated July 25, 1952.

245. Hounded publicly by the Hearst press: See Frank Brady, *Citizen Welles* (New York: Charles Scribner's Sons, 1989), p. 293.

245. "the extent of Communist infiltration": Federal Bureau of Investigation memo, dated November 23, 1944, p. 15. Fante's FBI file, secured under the Freedom of Information Act, goes back to 1942, when his name appears on a list of possible guest lecturers purportedly lined up for the School for Writers, a series of creative writing classes sponsored by the Hollywood chapter of the League of American Writers. Fante never took part.

245. Now in 1952: On August 14, 1952, J. Edgar Hoover wrote to an anonymous infor-

mant thanking him for "letters written by Dore Schary, Richard Hale, John Houseman, [. . .] John Fante, [. . .] Laslo Benedek, [. . .] and Frederick March."

245. Unlike many others: Fante is said to have told Filipino activist Chris Mensalves "that he (Fante) was barred from working at MGM simply because of his association with Carlos [Bulosan]." See Susan Evangelista, *Carlos Bulosan and His Poetry* (Seattle: University of Washington Press, 1985), p. 22. Fante may indeed have been so graylisted after the war. He may also have used his suspicion in this regard, whether or not it was valid, as an alibi for his long unemployed period of golf and drinking.

245. "assassination by suicide": *SL*, p. 228. Adamic had long been shadowed by the FBI because of his suspected ties to the communist Marshal Tito of Yugoslavia. Although Adamic's death was officially termed a suicide, the circumstances surrounding it were suspicious: his body was discovered in his Connecticut farmhouse, which had been set ablaze as if to conceal evidence of the involvement of others. See Carey McWilliams's impassioned appreciation, "Louis Adamic, American," in *The Nation*, September 22, 1951, pp. 230–32. Besides Adamic, McWilliams lost at least one other friend to suicide during the witch-hunt years, F. O. Matthiessen, the beleaguered Harvard literary critic who jumped from a hotel window in 1950. See Fariello, *Red Scare*, p. 422.

246. *Los Angeles Times* sportswriter Jim Murray: "I lived near John Fante in Malibu and . . . we played in the parents' game against Little Leaguers a time or two." Jim Murray to author, April 4, 1997; *Times* restaurant critic: Interview with Lois and Robert Dwan, October 10, 1996.

246. "I worried most of the day": Joyce Fante, diary entry for January 27, 1954.

246. "the bright moments": John Fante in a letter to Jack Stanley, January 17, 1954. The Jackson Stanley Collection, Special Collections, UCLA. When I showed them a copy of this letter, Joyce and all four of the Fante children expressed the suspicion that Fante was being ironic in this letter by seeming to place the pleasures of fatherhood over his writing. Pointing out that the letter was written at 2:00 a.m., youngest son Jim Fante suggested that his father was probably drunk when he wrote it.

246. Fante's enthusiasm for this project: "Father Hugh was very happy about his visit with you and I find that his enthusiasm has affected me." Father Armand Quiros, O.F.M., in a letter to John Fante, September 24, 1953. Fante's interest in Christmas pageants would have originated in high school at Regis, where he may have seen or even performed in *The Pageant of Peace*, a popular Christmas play at Catholic schools of the time written by his old retreat-master, Father Lord. See Daniel A. Lord, S.J., *Pageant of Peace: A Christmas Masque* (St. Louis: Queen's Work Press, 1924). CBS Television returned Fante's proposal, including a pilot script entitled "The Second Thief" and cowritten by Fante and Buckley Angell, citing the project's "limited" sales potential to advertisers. Hal Hudson, General Manager of CBS Programing, in a letter to Joel Cohen, an agent at the Dick Irving Hyland Agency, August 13, 1954.

247. the long list of screenplays, teleplays and treatments: Originally written in 1953, *Mother Cabrini* continued to circulate for several years. In 1955 Bert Leonard, creator of *Rin Tin Tin* and *Circus Boy*, was briefly interested. As late as 1961 the script was at Warner Bros., and Susan Hayward was expressing interest in playing the title part. Letter from Warner Bros. Elstree Studios director G. L. Blattner to Warner Bros. West Coast executive William T. Orr, September 12, 1961. "The Second Thief" was written in 1954 and sold to the Hal Roach Studios in 1956 for $1,500.

"Thorn in the Flesh" is undated. *Father of the Son* is dated August 18, 1964. This script is referred to as *The Carpenter of God* in Joseph McBride's *Frank Capra: The Catastrophe of Success* (New York: Simon & Schuster, 1992), p. 639. "The Divided Horsecloth" is undated. "A Hero Returns," based on a story by Indro Montanelli, was written between October and December 1955 for $1,500 under contract to Revue Productions for the *Wyman-Fireside Theater*. *Saint of the Satellites* was written in 1955.

248. a novel about the aging Arturo Bandini: Fante was struggling to write this novel in the mid-1960s, when he actually bought and kept a donkey in his backyard. Alternately titled "The Confusion of the Times" or "A Change of Life," only a dozen pages of this aborted project survive.

248. "Here was a man": Joyce Fante, unpublished memoir.

248. "Dear Blessed Lord": Fante typed this prayer on a rough draft manuscript sheet of *Full of Life*.

249. as when he let his contempt be known: For evidence of Fante's contempt for mere screenwriters, see the interview with Phillip Dunne in *Backstory: Interviews with Screenwriters of Hollywood's Golden Age*, ed. Pat McGilligan (Berkeley: University of California Press, 1986), 165.

249. beginning to toy with an idea about his father: See the long letter Fante wrote outlining the basic idea of what would ultimately become *The Brotherhood of the Grape* in *SL*, pp. 231–40. This letter, dated February 9, 1954, is addressed to Stanley Salmen and Howard Cady, editors at Little, Brown.

249. When the option on his MGM contract: Fante signed the contract with Frank Capra Productions on November 17, 1954. His weekly salary was $250.

249. This was an attempt: Fritz Kahn, M.D., *Man in Structure and Function*, 2 vols. trans. George Rosen, M.D. (New York: Alfred A. Knopf, 1953).

249. "a deep heart wound": *SL*, p. 231.

249. Two decades earlier, the godless Arturo Bandini: *RLA*, pp. 56–57.

250. at the end of his fifty-eight-page treatment: "Miracle of the Fishes," Universal-International Pictures, February 10, 1955.

250. "He still couldn't quite believe it": Ross Wills to John Fante in a letter dated April 23, 1955.

CHAPTER 15

254. He "was re-writing himself": I am indebted to Philippe Garnier for pointing out the young Richard Quine in *Dinky*, as well as for sharing with me the transcript of the interview he recorded with Quine for his 1988 French television documentary on Fante.

254. a passage from Fante's own *Ask the Dust*: On April 20, 1956, E. J. Stackpole responded favorably to Fante's request for permission to quote from pages 233–34 of *Ask the Dust*, generously waiving any fee.

255. Two weeks later MGM president: Harry Cohn in a letter to John Fante, May 2, 1956.

255. "You'll like *Full of Life*": *New York Times*, February 11, 1957.

256. "sentimental": *Time*, February 18, 1957.

256. "wholly satisfying": *Variety*, December 19, 1956.

256. "Winner": *Hollywood Reporter*, December 19, 1956.
256. "I shall make arrangements": Francis Cardinal Spellman in a letter to John Fante, January 28, 1957. With its sympathetic portrayal of the parish priest Father Gandolfo and Joyce's conversion to Catholicism, *Full of Life* was a great hit among the clergy. On Christmas Day evening, 1957, the Jesuit community at Saint Louis University was treated to the film. As Fante's old friend Paul Reinert, S.J., wrote of that screening and his fellow Jesuits, "I don't think I have ever been present at a show which they enjoyed so thoroughly." Paul Reinert to John Fante, January 3, 1958.
256. More heartening still: Edmund North to John Fante, February 8, 1957.
257. Tennessee Williams: *Baby Doll*, which received the dreaded "Condemned" rating from Cardinal Spellman's Legion of Decency, concerned the attempted deflowering of a child bride by her husband's smarmy business rival. Spellman compared Elia Kazan's film of the Tennessee Williams play to Russia's 1956 invasion of Hungary. See Gail MacCall, ed., *Inside Oscar: The Unofficial History of the Academy Awards* (New York: Ballantine Books, 1987), p. 272.
258. the mysterious Robert Rich: *Inside Oscar*, p. 273.
258. Hollywood was still buzzing: "Hollywood Whodunit: An Oscar, Whowonit?" *Life*, April 15, 1957.
258. "go into it further": Norman Foster in a letter to Margaret Herrick, April 19, 1957.
258. For their part, the Kings: "Kings Settle $750,000 Suit over 'Brave One,' " *Los Angeles Times*, April 9, 1957.
258. For the next several months: Thomas M. Pryor, " '57 'Oscar' Writer Sought by Guild," *New York Times*, February 4, 1959.
259. Soon afterward Hollywood Ten member: "Now It's Official: Trumbo Owns Up He Was Robt. Rich of '56 Oscar Fame," *Variety*, January 21, 1959. On the same day that Norman Foster sent "My Friend Bonito" to the Academy (April 19, 1957), thus initiating this two-year tug-of-war, Trumbo wrote a long letter to Frank King expressing gratitude for the King brothers having kept Trumbo secretly working during the long and ugly height of the blacklist. See Dalton Trumbo, *Additional Dialogue: The Letters of Dalton Trumbo* (New York: Lippincott, 1970), pp. 394–95.
259. Following the presentation of this evidence: The affidavits were sent to attorney Melville B. Nimmer by Ross R. Hastings of the firm of Hastings and Lasker on March 13, 1959. Special Collections, Margaret Herrick Library, Academy of Motion Picture Arts and Sciences. Since the WGA maintains strict confidentiality in arbitration matters, it is not possible to ascertain whether the Fante-Foster case was actually heard; but it would appear that in fact it wasn't.
259. a special ceremony: "Trumbo Finally Gets 'Brave One' Oscar—Twenty Years Late," *Variety*, May 16, 1975. As Maurice King would finally explain in this article, it was necessary to conceal Trumbo's authorship of *The Brave One* in order not to provoke the staunch anticommunist Howard Hughes from blocking distribution of the film through RKO, which he controlled.
259. In all, the case was emblematic: See Dalton Trumbo, *The Time of the Toad* (New York: Harper and Row, 1972).
261. "he walked around just looking at everything": Richard Quine in interview with Philippe Garnier for French television documentary, 1988.
261. "By September I shall probably be insanely homesick": John Fante to Joyce Fante, July 30, 1957. This passage is omitted from the version of this letter printed in *SL*,

p. 245. Also omitted is Fante's proposal that Joyce come to stay with him in Naples, a notion that ultimately proved impracticable.

262. "civilized, sophisticated": *SL*, p. 243.

262. Only the rich: See *SL*, p. 260.

262. "each with the face of the mother of God": *SL*, p. 243.

262. "the family man": Richard Quine in Philippe Garnier's 1988 interview.

262. "a fine old gentleman": *SL*, p. 256.

262. his stomach was going bad: On visiting an Italian physician Fante discovered that he had broken his nose when young, most likely while boxing. This information is omitted from the undated letter in *SL* on p. 258.

263. "Fante was shattered": Richard Quine in Philippe Garnier's 1988 interview. Just how good Fante's script was may be measured by the suggestion made by Bantam Books editorial director Saul David in a letter dated April 8, 1958, that Fante rewrite the story as a novel. Nothing ever came of this suggestion.

263. "[F]ailure is good": Denise Jacobson, "Writer John Fante Says He Never 'Felt Famous' until He Went to Italy for 'The Roses,' " *The Malibu Times*, n.d., summer 1958.

263. clippings from local newspaper sports sections: "Silky Annihilates Space and Derby Foes," *Los Angeles Times*, March 9, 1958; "Wild Comeback Spurs Ol' Archie to New Goals," *Los Angeles Mirror News*, December 11, 1958.

263. Fante teamed up with Harry Essex: *The Comeback*, cowritten by Essex and Fante, was registered with the WGA on May 23, 1958, purchased by Desilu for $2,000 on November 4, 1958, and produced by Quinn Martin for Desilu Playhouse, starring Dan Duryea.

264. "I have never met a person": Francis Ford Coppola, "Letter to the Reader," *Zoetrope* 1, no. 1 (Winter 1997): 11.

264. A partial listing of titles: All of these cowritten works are in Joyce Fante's files, which include documentation for several other Fante collaborations registered with the Writers Guild but no longer extant. Several of the Fante-Essex collaborations can be found in the Harry Essex Collection at the University of Wyoming's American Heritage Center. *Saint Anthony's Forty Blondes*, a fifty-one-page treatment by Fante and Carey McWilliams, can be found at the Arts Special Collection of UCLA's Charles E. Young Research Library.

264. *Thunder in the South*: Wayne's Batjac Productions purchased *Thunder in the South* on August 1, 1956.

265. This time it was 20th Century-Fox: John L. Scott, "Adler Signs Six Top Film Writers," *Los Angeles Times*, September 17, 1958. It was another lucrative season for Fante, with an extra $1,250 coming in when the film rights to his old story "The Dreamer" sold to Revue Productions.

265. "all eyes and ears": Carey McWilliams, diary entry for February 24, 1959. Carey McWilliams Collection, UCLA.

265. Dino DeLaurentiis was lobbying: In a letter to John Fante dated March 25, 1959, DeLaurentiis's American representative Ralph Serpe of Aurora Productions in New York conveyed DeLaurentiis's strong hope that Fante would come to Italy "to start immediately" on work that would "help establish himself in Italy."

265. "lost track of all time": *SL*, p. 262.

267. the story would remain unpublished: "The First Time I Saw Paris" first appeared in

SL, pp. 325–27. As he wrote this story Fante surely had in mind the glossy 1954 MGM melodrama *The Last Time I Saw Paris*, directed by Richard Brooks and starring Elizabeth Taylor and Van Johnson in an adaptation of F. Scott Fitzgerald's "Return to Babylon." Johnson plays a once-promising writer who has sold out and who subsequently loses the beautiful women in his life, both wife and daughter, because of his alcoholism. In "The First Time I Saw Paris," by contrast, Fante's alter-ego narrator drinks to forget his encounter with an old repulsive woman whom he compares to Notre Dame, and to whose mystery he is yet inexorably drawn back.

267. "quite a nice kid": *SL*, p. 264.

267. Zanuck opted to produce the play: The play was *The Dogs, or the Paris Play*. See Lee and Gifford, *Saroyan*, p. 266.

267. for dinner and a long walk: Carey McWilliams, diary entry for July 9, 1959. The Carey McWilliams Collection, UCLA.

268. "I never heard a harsh word": Interview with Edmund Morris, February 6, 1997.

269. Saul Bass's stunning credits sequence: The credits sequence is "a masterpiece of variable speed photography and optical work, featuring a sleek alley cat (Bass's own) wending its way through a concrete maze of pipes and iron fences, underscored by Elmer Bernstein's main title music." Willard Carroll, program notes to Columbia Pictures Diamond Jubilee Celebration, December 1, 1984. Margaret Herrick Library, Academy of Motion Picture Arts and Sciences.

269. a series based on Mark Twain's *Roughing It*: The title of the script adapted from *Roughing It* was *The Fabulous Feud*.

269. "Hated school, all the time": quoted in *Twentieth Century Authors: A Biographical Dictionary of American Literature*, ed. Stanley J. Kunitz and Howard Haycraft (New York: H. W. Wilson, 1942), p. 433.

269. "I don't know": I am grateful to Darrell Kastin for bringing this previously unpublished letter to my attention. The identity of the addressee, Mr. Hartley, is unknown.

271. a screenplay called *Black City*: This script was known alternately as *King of Poggioreale*. A copy of the script with the latter title, dated November 17, 1960 bears the names of both John Fante and Giuseppe Marotta as writers. Marotta was an Italian screenwriter who had written an earlier draft of *Citta Nera* or *Black City* which Fante had been hired to rewrite.

271. the martyr San Gennaro's blood: San Gennaro or Saint Januarius was the Bishop of Benevento. He was beheaded during the reign of the emperor Diocletian. See *SL*, p. 280.

272. "To hell with Marxian dogma": *SL*, p. 272.

272. "almost too perfect": *SL*, p. 273.

273. "where all the hookers hang out": John Fante in unpublished letter to William Saroyan, October 13, 1960. "In many ways [Nick] reminds me of you," Fante wrote Saroyan. "The first night he was here he found the Piazza Barberini where all the hookers hang out. He found a juke box with his favorite songs. He laughed and danced with the whores as they came in out of the rain, bought them coffee, and talked their language without knowing a word of Italian. Then he caught on with some Italian kids his age, began dating broads, and spread his activity all over Rome. He got more out of the town in a week than I have in ten."

273. Nick hightailed it out of Rome: In my interview with him at his Auburn, California, home on August 15, 1995, Nick Fante told me of going to the opera and enduring

the arranged date while he was in Rome with his father. He also talked of how his father had started him reading at a very early age with the same books that had fired his imagination, among others *The Brothers Karamozov, Crime and Punishment,* and *Hunger.* (He remembered reading *Wait Until Spring, Bandini* and *Ask the Dust* both before he was ten years old.) Fante mentioned that Nick was reading *Lolita* in part of a letter omitted from *SL,* p. 276. In a letter to his mother dated August 5, 1960, Nick mentioned visiting the Catacombs with his father.

273. dared "not grow optimistic": John Fante in a letter to Joyce Fante, omitted from the version published in *SL,* p. 275.

273. "grinding away": *SL,* p. 276.

273. Joyce, who tantalized him: "The Frederick's purchase intrigues me, even from 5000 miles." John Fante to Joyce Fante in part of a letter omitted from the version published in *SL,* p. 278.

273. "Goodnight my love": John Fante in a letter to Joyce Fante, omitted from the version published in *SL,* p. 277.

273. "a dash of the marvelous": John Fante to Joyce Fante, unpublished letter dated September 5, 1960.

273. "stirring letter": John Fante to Joyce Fante, unpublished letter dated September 5, 1960.

273. Soon he heard back: Fante mentions Falvey's intention to read the letter at mass in part of a letter dated September 22 omitted from the version published in *SL,* p. 281. Fante's letter to Falvey does not survive.

273. "The complexities of film writing today": *SL,* pp. 283–84.

274. "So we bend our necks": *SL,* p. 284.

274. Curtiz asked him to fix a scene: Curtiz's lavish *Francis of Assisi* was released in 1961, Fante receiving no credit for his admittedly minor contribution to the script.

274. "the color of Rome": *SL,* p. 271.

274. During these walks: "My left foot continues to give me trouble—no swelling but considerable pain if I walk too much." John Fante to Joyce Fante in part of a letter omitted from the version published in *SL,* p. 272.

274. "too heavy, too much oil": John Fante to Joyce Fante in part of a letter dated September 13, 1960, omitted from the version published in *SL,* p. 280.

274. purchased a .22 caliber automatic: Dichiarazione [Declaration], Armi Banchetti Sport di Banchetti Galliano, October 10, 1960.

CHAPTER 16

275. the gun was seized at Customs: Treasury Department Customs Form 6051, Receipt for Merchandise or Baggage Retained in Customs Custody No. 221207, October 21, 1960.

276. "We . . . want to tell him": John Fante in a November 17, 1960, letter to Teddy Wilcox, a friend of Joyce's from their days together at Stanford.

276. "in its own treacle": Kevin Thomas in the *Los Angeles Times,* April 1, 1963. Fante shared the screenplay credit on *My Six Loves,* which also featured David Janssen, with Joseph Calvelli and William Wood. Their screenplay was adapted from Peter V. K. Funk's novel of the same name, published in the March 1960 *Redbook.*

276. Fante hated everything about it: "I remember he went to the set one day . . . and he

came back in a rage. . . . 'Never fuckin' do that again.' " Interview with Nick Fante, August 15, 1995.

276. split the $25,000: Deal memo dated February 17, 1961.

277. "embarrassingly inept": Saturday Review, September 29, 1962; "ultimately touching": Los Angeles Times, November 4, 1962.

277. The comedy earned Fante $6,000: Revue Studios paid Fante $1,000 on January 15 and $5,000 on February 26 for Fante's untitled script. On September 27, 1962, the Writers Guild Arbitration Committee decided that Fante should be given story credit for "A Man for Mary," with credit for the teleplay going to George Tibbles.

277. a copy of Justine: Fante bought the DeSade volume on May 29 at Martindale's Bookshop in Santa Monica.

277. "pending projects" list: This list combines job prospects listed in two letters to Fante from agent Richard S. Harris, dated, respectively, December 20, 1962, and January 15, 1963.

278. While in New York Fante capitalized: See Carey McWilliams's diary entries for September 1, 8, 9, 11, 13, 15 and 17 of 1962. Carey McWilliams Collection, UCLA.

279. resulted in his firing: Fante was in New York from mid-August to mid-September of 1962 working for DeLaurentiis. In order to be paid for his services Fante had to file a grievance with the Writers Guild. The case was found in Fante's favor and he collected $3,000 on March 26, 1963.

279. "a very good man": Carey McWilliams, diary entry for June 3, 1963. Carey McWilliams Collection, UCLA.

280. "what would have happened": Larry Tajiri, "Novelist Fante Comes Home," Denver Post, n.d., summer 1963. The protagonist of early drafts of The Left-Handed Virgin is named Arturo Bandini. Fante changed the name in subsequent drafts to Dominic Molise. He also changed the title to 1933 Was a Bad Year, but he never finished writing the novel as he planned it. The version of the novel published in 1985 by Black Sparrow Press is faithful to Fante's latest draft. But a ten-page "Synopsis of What Follows" indicates that Fante intended to continue the story of Dom's flight from Colorado all the way to California. The projected novel would have included chapters on Dom's hitchhiking, freight-hopping trip west; his employment at the Toyo Fish Company on Terminal Island and his friendship with Filipino coworkers; his failed tryout as a pitcher with the Chicago Cubs at their spring training camp on Catalina Island; and his ultimate return to Colorado and reconciliation with his father.

280. The great sandstone edifice: Many of the stones remain of the 1908 church Nick Fante helped to build. They were used to construct the 1987 addition to the Episcopal church around the corner from Sacred Heart, their ecumenical usage commemorated in a plaque that reads, "This addition is built of the stone of the old Sacred Heart Church." My thanks to Monsignor Edward Madden, pastor of Sacred Heart, for leading me to see and touch these stones.

280. "without the poetic spontaneity": Pascal Covici to Max Wilkinson in a letter dated June 17, 1963. Wilkinson was briefly Fante's New York agent.

280. the story of a dreamy cannery worker: "Captain Al Sanchez," Goodson-Todman Production #4028 for The Richard Boone Show, property of Classic Films, Inc., MGM, October 2, 1963.

281. (His original contract): The contract was dated November 12, 1963. Special Collections, Margaret Herrick Library, Academy of Motion Picture Arts and Sciences.

281. "A timeless odyssey of boys": Los Angeles Times, July 8, 1966.

281. "John Fante's script": *Variety*, April 13, 1966.

282. not enough "new material": Kenneth N. Anglemire, Executive Vice President of Marquis Who's Who, Inc., to John Fante, March 6, 1963.

282. Frank Capra hired him back: Fante earned $7,500 for the Saint Joseph script *Father of the Son*, dated August 18, 1964; Father Ellwood E. Kieser, C.S.P., invited him: On March 10, 1965, Father Kieser sent Fante a confidential memorandum detailing the tax advantages of donating a script as a work of art to *Insight*, but Fante never wrote for the show.

282. bought the last twenty-four copies: For an additional $75 he had also purchased the plates and binding dyes, proof positive that *Full of Life*'s long and lucrative run was over. Joyce's check to Little, Brown for these items was dated September 11, 1962.

282. It would take five years: John Fante and Rudolph Borchert, *Bravo, Burro!* (New York: Hawthorn Books, 1970). Unlike all of Fante's other works, this novel has not been republished. Fante and Borchert collaborated on another film treatment entitled *Robinette*, registered with the Writers Guild on the same day as *Black Mountain*. Borchert would go on to a career as a versatile and prolific writer of episodic television, contributing to such shows as *The Rockford Files, Kojak, Police Woman*, and *The Night Stalker*.

283. an adaptation of the Marguerite Henry novel: Fante's contract for *King of the Wind*, signed July 22, 1965, was actually with the Munich firm of Bavaria Atelier Gesellschaft mbH, which was coproducing the project with King Brothers. The first draft of Fante's script was dated November 18, 1965.

283. Watts burned: The so-called Watts Riots raged in Los Angeles for several days during the middle of August 1965.

283. Joe Petracca had died: Petracca died of stomach cancer at age forty-nine on September 28, 1963.

283. a jangling new voice: See the postcard from Hunter S. Thompson to Carey McWilliams dated August 3, 1965, in the Carey McWilliams Collection, UCLA.

283. "I notice one thing": Dan Fante in a letter to John Fante dated September 23, 1965.

284. "We are all as well as can be expected": John Fante in part of a letter omitted from the version published in *SL*, p. 288.

284. one fight at the Cottage: Interview with William Asher, April 5, 1997.

284. "perilous and calamitous": Hearing Sahl's allegations, Fante wrote to McWilliams on October 10, 1966, to ask if they were true. McWilliams wrote back to Fante on October 17 saying that Sahl's story was "pure fantasy," blaming the misinformation on a story by conspiracy theorist Mark Lane that McWilliams had rejected when Lane submitted it to *The Nation*. On October 17 McWilliams also wrote to Sahl, requesting that he correct his mistake. Carey McWilliams Collection, UCLA.

285. an elegiac survey of Los Angeles: Carolyn See, "Will Excess Spoil the Hollywood Writer?" *Los Angeles Times West Magazine*, March 26, 1967, pp. 34–36.

286. "Screenwriting was easier": *My Dog Stupid* in WR, p. 55. Also in this volume is "The Orgy," a long story about a ten-year-old boy on a comically ill-fated mining expedition in the Colorado mountains with his drunkard father and his father's best friend and worst influence from the old country of the Abruzzi, the left-handed atheist bricklayer Frank Gagliano.

287. "I've done a little soul-searching": WR, pp. 50–51.

287. "To write one must love": WR, p. 109.

287. weekly-comedy-show magnate Sheldon Leonard: In a letter to Fante dated April 11, 1968, Leonard wrote that he was "sending *My Dog Stupid* on to higher channels."

287. "[I]t almost makes me weep": Elizabeth R. Otis to John Fante, March 4, 1968.

288. When Fante signed a contract: Fante's contract with American International was dated February 2, 1969. He submitted his script on March 4, an uncredited revision of an original by Norman Thaddeus Vane, who received screenplay credit for the 1969 film *Lola*, directed by Richard Donner and starring Charles Bronson.

288. Joyce was now fully immersed: Joyce's request to McWilliams for press credentials was dated May 3, 1971. On May 6 McWilliams sent her a letter of introduction entitling her to the usual journalistic courtesies as a writer on assignment for *The Nation*. Joyce interviewed a number of people for this project, including Dr. Israel Regardie, a protégé of the late Aleister Crowley, but no article ever resulted.

288. only gutted the story of all life: Fante and Essex were working on *Ask the Dust* in late 1969. Fante inscribed Essex's twenty-five-cent Bantam paperback of the novel thus: "For Harry—for invaluable service in assisting me on the screenplay of this celebrated work. Good luck, Harry! John Fante." On June 26, 1971, Essex responded to a letter from Fante, no longer extant, in which Fante evidently expressed a sense of guilt about their failure with *Ask the Dust*: "You mustn't blame or accuse yourself. . . . The treatment couldn't possibly have been the book as you first saw it. It *was* a cop-out. A commercial venture. A way to become part of the current market. A job, Johnny."

CHAPTER 17

291. "I never thought it would happen": John Fante to Carey McWilliams in a letter dated February 1, 1971. This part is omitted from the version published in *SL*, p. 288.

292. "My little black and white granddaughter": John Fante to Carey McWilliams in part of a letter omitted from the version published in *SL*, p. 289.

292. "to work trying to get my end": Peter Sellers to John Fante, September 29, 1971.

293. Towne and his then-wife: Interview with Julie Payne, July 19, 1997.

293. reappearing in new editions: By 1973 McWilliams's *North From Mexico*, *Prejudice* and *Southern California Country* and Bulosan's *America Is in the Heart* had all been republished and were gaining renewed attention, especially on university campuses nationwide.

293. "The [University of Washington Press] reprint": *SL*, p. 295.

293. "particularly interested in the immigrant experience": *SL*, p. 290.

293. "by all means"; "the new ethnicity": *SL*, p. 291.

293. "that *many* factors": *SL*, p. 293.

293. "for what it may be worth": *SL*, p. 291; "ate cold pie": p., 292.

294. "A curious fact about biographers": *SL*, p. 294.

294. "Indeed, . . . the whole romantic business": John Fante to Jay Martin, October 16, 1966. This letter is at the Huntington Library. I am indebted to Jay Martin—one of the first people I interviewed for this book—for sharing his recollections of interviewing John Fante. In attempting to demystify the Stanley Rose Bookshop for Martin, Fante may have had in mind the legend that had grown up as a result of such articles

as Budd Schulberg's "Saroyan: Ease and Unease on the Flying Trapeze" (*Esquire* October, 1960), as well as of comments by Saroyan himself in *Not Dying* (1963) and *Short Drive, Sweet Chariot* (1966). Saroyan would continue to remember Rose fondly in "Stanley Rose and the Unknown Writer" (*Westways*, August 1975) and *Sons Come and Go, Mothers Hang in Forever* (1976). See also Carey McWilliams's oral history at UCLA Special Collections (1978); Budd Schulberg's *Writers in America* (1983); Carolyn See's "When Sin Was Still Fun on Hollywood Boulevard" and Maurice Zolotow's "Larry Edmunds: The Boulevard's Greatest Lothario," both in *Los Angeles Magazine*, October 1977.

294. Fante took to raising garlic: This information is contained in a portion of a letter omitted from the version published in *SL*, p. 296.

295. "a cat like Carmen": John Fante and Leo Townsend, "The New World of Carmen Colombo" (also called "The Trouble with Carmen"), thirty-page treatment. In 1973 Roger Corman's New World Pictures paid $15,000 for this story, which was never made into a film.

295. "You said it one day": Harry Essex to John Fante, June 26, 1971.

295. Fante kept a holy card: A statue of Saint Teresa occurs as early as page 3 of *The Brotherhood of the Grape*, emblem of Mama Molise's "relentless Catholicism," which is itself announced on page 1.

295. At first Fante reported: See *SL*, p. 294.

295. "a tale revolving around my father": *SL*, p. 296.

295. Later still he would call it: See Ben Pleasants, "Stories of Irony from the Hand of John Fante," *Los Angeles Times Book Review*, July 8, 1979, p. 3.

296. "a study of the resources": Larry McMurtry, "John Fante's 'The Brotherhood of the Grape': A Small-Town Italian Family in Vivid Focus." *The Washington Post*, March 21, 1977, B7.

296. "Then a peculiar thing happened": *BG*, p. 119.

296. "The whole world had turned into a graveyard": *BG*, pp. 23–24.

297. "How could a man live without his father": *BG*, p. 136

297. "and you knew that somewhere": *BG*, p. 174.

297. "your book really changed my life": Robert Towne to Carey McWilliams, July 17, 1974. Carey McWilliams Collection, UCLA.

297. "two very powerful, very grumpy old men": In his introduction Towne also praised *Ask the Dust*, to which, he asserted, Nathanael West's great novel *The Day of the Locust* "suffered by comparison." *City* 9, no. 1 (July 6, 1975), pp. 34–35.

298. he had been so impressed: Interview with Dan Fante, September 21, 1995.

298. "Moneywise . . . something very dramatic": *SL*, p. 299.

298. the advice of his Bantam editor: Wendy Broad, an Associate Editor at Bantam, made this suggestion to Fante in a letter dated November 26, 1975.

298. one of his last whirlwind swings: Carey McWilliams, diary entries for November 10, 12, 15, 1975. Carey McWilliams Collection, UCLA.

299. The last story Fante would publish: "My Father's God," *Italian Americana* 2, no. 1 (Autumn 1975): 18–31. One year earlier, in the autumn of 1974, editor Ernest Falbo had sent Fante a complimentary copy of the journal's first issue, inscribing it "To John Fante, with warmest wishes from a longtime admirer."

299. "They weren't *my* sins": *WY*, p. 195.

300. "Suddenly my father laughed": *WY*, p. 198.

301. He watched his father get smaller: Interview with Jim Fante, March 8, 1996.
301. "[t]he compulsion to write": *SL*, p. 302.
302. Brian Moore's novella: The Irish novelist Brian Moore published *Catholics* in *New American Review* 15 (1972). See the Editors' Notes in this number for Alice Mayhew's thoughtful essay on the Second Vatican Council and the ecclesiastical and theological upheaval it provoked, inspiring Moore to write the story. Edited by Theodore Solotaroff, who would later publish Fante at Bantam, NAR ran for twenty-six numbers and showcased some of the best new writing of the sixties and seventies. A lapsed Catholic whose Catholic sensibilities colored virtually everything he ever wrote, Brian Moore "was regarded in international circles as Los Angeles' most important writer" at the time of his death in early 1999. See Tim Rutten, "Brian Moore, Noted Author, Dies at 77," *Los Angeles Times*, January 12, 1999, B1.
302. But the director was so consumed: Interview with Martin Sheen, June 19, 1997. For an inside view of the chaos surrounding the production of *Apocalypse Now*, see Fax Bahr and George Hickenlooper's fascinating 1991 documentary *Hearts of Darkness: A Filmmaker's Apocalypse*.
302. "to span every emotion": Carolyn See, "John Fante Births Another Novel about a Flawed Family," *Los Angeles Times Book Review*, April 3, 1977, p. 3.
302. "alternately full of cleansing laughter": *New York Times Book Review*, March 6, 1977.
302. "*The Brotherhood of the Grape* belies the myth": Larry McMurtry, "John Fante's 'The Brotherhood of the Grape': A Small-Town Italian Family in Vivid Focus," *Washington Post*, March 21, 1977.
303. "a delightful gentleman": Roscoe C. Webb, Jr., M.D., consultation report, June 24, 1977.
303. "The first great loss": *SL*, p. 302.
303. "for . . . I cry a lot these days"; "insufferably maudlin": *SL*, p. 303.
303. "absolute horror": *SL*, p. 304.
304. Fante was able to recognize: Diary entry for July 15, 1978. Carey McWilliams Collection, UCLA.
304. he received a letter informing him: Jack Ging, Chairman, Long Beach City College Hall of Fame, and John R. Fylpaa, Associated Student Body Advisor, to John Fante, September 14, 1978.
304. "Dear Sirs": John Fante, letter to Jack Ging and John R. Fylpaa, September 29, 1978.
306. "Dear John": Florence Carpenter to John Fante, November 30, 1978. The Kipling quotation is from his poem "If—." See *Rudyard Kipling's Verse* (Garden City, N.Y.: Doubleday & Co., 1940), p. 578.
307. the November issue of *Westways*: Frances Ring, then the editor of *Westways*, commissioned McWilliams to write this article. I am indebted to her for sending me a copy of her book *A Western Harvest: The Gatherings of an Editor* (Santa Barbara, Calif.: John Daniel and Company, 1991).
307. Towne had shown his true feelings: Towne's check to Fante for $44,500 was dated March 13, 1978.
308. a conscious homage to the two writers: See Stephen Cooper, "Madness and Writing in the Works of Hamsun, Fante and Bukowski," *Genre* 19 (1998): pp. 19–27.
308. fantasizing that he, Charles Bukowski: For accounts of Bukowski's life, see Neeli Cherkovski, *Bukowski: A Life* (South Royalton, Vt.: Steerforth Press, 1997); and Howard Sounes, *Locked in the Arms of a Crazy Life: A Biography of Charles Bukowski*

(Edinburgh: Rebel Inc, 1999). For a Marxist interpretation of the influences of Fante and Hamsun on Bukowski, see Russell Harrison, *Against the American Dream: Essays on Charles Bukowski* (Santa Rosa, Calif.: Black Sparrow Press, 1994).

308. "Who was your favorite author?": Charles Bukowski, *Women* (Santa Rosa, Calif.: Black Sparrow Press, 1978), p. 200.

309. This copy was sent to Martin: Interview with John Martin, February 6, 1998.

309. "Your French director": John Fante to Charles Bukowski, February 6, 1979.

309. When Fante received Bukowski's draft: Bukowski's letter to Fante enclosing his proposed preface and inviting suggestions for improvement was dated May 6, 1979.

310. "and there it was": Charles Bukowski, Preface to *Ask the Dust*, p. 6.

310. "running up and down the halls": See Charles Bukowski, "Remembering John Fante," *The New Haven Advocate*, February 27, 1989. In a videotaped supplement to the John Fante Conference held at California State University, Long Beach, May 4–6, 1995, Linda Bukowski mentioned to interviewer Gary Eisenberg hearing Weissmuller as well.

311. "baring teeth and snarling": Joyce Fante, medical log, September 1978.

311. Coppola had reestablished contact: Thomas E. Sternberg of Coppola's Omni Zoetrope Studios sent the script to Fante on August 2, 1979.

311. "in the big time": Charles Bukowski to John Fante, August 24, 1979.

312. "edited by the most renowned": *DBH*, p. 9.

312. "I now have a unique opportunity": Joyce Fante to Fran Stoffels, November 27, 1979.

312. a lightly fictionalized character: John Fante, interviews with Ben Pleasants, December 18, 1978, and July 20, 1979.

312. Fante assured one interviewer: John Fante, interview with Ben Pleasants, July 20, 1979.

312. "the reality of Bunker Hill": *DBH*, p. 85.

313. "Like a homing bird": *DBH*, p. 123.

313. "The overcoat felt warm": *DBH*, p. 134.

313. "that lobby that would last forever": *DBH*, p. 123.

313. "It was my kind of room": *DBH*, p. 146.

314. "for a man had to start someplace": *DBH*, p. 147. This discussion of the novel owes much to my article "John Fante's Eternal City" in *Los Angeles in Fiction*, ed. David Fine (Albuquerque: University of New Mexico Press, 1995), esp. pp. 94–95.

314. "I believe the one thing": Ben Pleasants, "Stories of Irony from the Hand of John Fante," *Los Angeles Times Book Review*, July 8, 1979, p. 3. Two years later Fante wrote to a distant relation in Philadelphia, "I am not bitter but I am discouraged." John Fante to Mary Rose Fante Cunningham, September 17, 1981.

314. "black comedy, scandalous": John Fante to Tom Sternberg, December 20, 1979.

314. "impotent period": Charles Bukowski to John Fante, December 2, 1979.

315. Tritia Toyota and Kelly Lange: See McWilliams's diary entries for September 6, and December 2, 1978.

315. Kay Mills: See McWilliams's diary entry for December 18, 1979. Carey McWilliams Collection, UCLA. See also Kay Mills, "California Revisited: The Education of Carey McWilliams," *Los Angeles Times*, February 3, 1980.

315. *Act of Violence*: Carey McWilliams, diary entry for November 10, 1979. Carey McWilliams Collection, UCLA.

315. Through it all he had been enduring: Carey McWilliams, diary entries for October 15 and November 30, 1979. Carey McWilliams Collection, UCLA.

315. told each other goodbye: See McWilliams's diary entry for December 24, 1979. Carey McWilliams Collection, UCLA. See also Carey McWilliams, "Return to Los Angeles," in Westways, September 1980, in which Carey gives a glowing account of his last meeting with Fante. For this same issue of Westways, Frances Ring excerpted the Sinclair Lewis scene from Dreams from Bunker Hill, running it alongside the McWilliams article.

315. Newspaper articles began to appear: Tom Christie, "The Great Los Angeles Novel," L.A. Weekly, December 28, 1979–January 3, 1980; Alva Svoboda, "The Consummate L.A. Novel," Santa Barbara News & Review, February 7, 1980; Wayne Warga, "A Reclamation of Bunker Hill," Los Angeles Times, March 5, 1980.

316. Letters began arriving: J. V. Cunningham to John Fante, February 5, 1980; Herman Cherry to John Fante, February 27, 1980; Marjorie Brown Shneidman to John Fante, March 5, 1980; Muriel D. Bradley to John Fante, March 7, 1980.

316. "obviously . . . is ducking me": John Fante to Tom Sternberg, February 28, 1980.

316. Wishing to keep the air clear: Thomas E. Sternberg to Michael Ovitz, March 3, 1980. Sternberg copied this letter to Fante.

316. Fante intimated: Tom Christie to John Fante, February 27, 1980.

317. Fante tried telling a joke: Linda Bukowski recounted this incident in a videotaped supplement to "John Fante: The First Conference," California State University, Long Beach, May 4–6, 1995.

318. the independent publisher's business: For insights into John Martin's success as an independent publisher, see "Publishing Rises in the West," Time, June 24, 1985, and "Penniless Poet to Laureate of Lowlife," U.S. News & World Report, January 9, 1989. (In the latter article Fante, still not yet a household name, is misidentified as "Joseph Fante.")

318. "I think that Ask the Dust is a major American novel": Joyce Fante to Teddy Wilcox, July 24, 1979.

318. the "worst result of blindness": John Fante to Mary Rose Fante Cunningham, September 17, 1981.

318. The letter was from his aged aunt: Dorothy Shearer to John Fante, September 20, 1981.

319. "the woman who brought all of this on": SL, pp. 308–9.

320. It was, he told one visitor: See Tom Christie, "Are You L.A. Literate?" Buzz 4, no. 5 (June/July, 1993).

320. Martin wanted to make sure: John Martin to Joyce Fante, March 17, 1982.

321. a thoughtful phone call from Towne: Interview with Dan Fante, September 21, 1995.

321. "So I went over there": Interview with A. I. Bezzerides, February 2, 1995, combined with Philippe Garnier's interview with A. I. Bezzerides for French television.

321. "I am afraid my copy is splashed with tears": Joyce Fante to John Martin, February 25, 1983.

322. Good morning, John Fante: Undated cassette recording from the files of Joyce Fante.

324. "There was an old man": See Thomas Byrom, Nonsense and Wonder: The Poems and Cartoons of Edward Lear (New York: E. P. Dutton, 1977), p. 91.

324. A priest was called: Interview with Nick Fante, August 15, 1995.

EPILOGUE

325. "I can say honestly": Paul C. Reinert, S.J., to Marcella D. Webster, May 26, 1983.

325. "He was a gritty warrior": John Martin to Joyce Fante, May 12, 1983.

325. "I had the privilege": Edmund Morris to Joyce Fante, May 22, 1983.

326. "Less than two weeks later": *L.A. Weekly*, May 20–26, 1983.

327. California State University, Long Beach: Shortly before he died Fante received a letter from poet Gerald Locklin. A professor of English at Cal State, Long Beach (CSULB), Locklin was writing Fante to thank him "for the pleasures afforded by your work" and to express the "hope [that] you'll be pleased to know that your books are used frequently in some of the classes here." Gerry Locklin to John Fante, January 11, 1983. A volume of essays, *John Fante: A Critical Gathering*, based on presentations made at the CSULB conference, will appear at about the same time as this biography.

327. Carey McWilliams's words: The Pershing Square inscription comes from pp. 375–76 of *Southern California Country*.

328. In 1984 Mayor Tom Bradley: Deane Dana made this proposal in a letter to the Honorable Tom Bradley, October 4, 1984.

328. "Los Angeles, give me some of you!": *AD*, p. 13.

328. the "father" of the Los Angeles novel: Tom Christie, "Fante's Inferno," *Buzz*, October 1995, p. 60; "the patron saint of . . . L.A. writing": Michael Tolkin, quoted in "L.A. Lit (Does It Exist?): A Symposium," *Los Angeles Times Book Review*, April 25, 1999, p. 8.

328. "saints can be the strangest of people": John Fante, "The First Time I Saw Paris," *SL*, p. 327.

329. in this article the screenwriter Robert Towne: Wayne Warga, "Writer Towne: Under the Smog, a Feel for the City," *Los Angeles Times Calendar*, August 18, 1974, p. 1 ff.

329. a note thanking me: Digby Diehl to author, June 12, 1975.

329. "Dear Steve": John Fante to author, May 7, 1975.

BIBLIOGRAPHY

Fante, John. *Ask the Dust.* New York: Stackpole Sons, 1939. Bantam paperback edition, 1954. Reprint, Santa Barbara: Black Sparrow Press, 1980.

———. *The Big Hunger: Stories 1932–1959.* Ed. Stephen Cooper. Santa Rosa: Black Sparrow Press, 2000.

Fante, John, and Rudolph Borchert. *Bravo, Burro!* Illustrated by Marilyn Hirsh. New York: Hawthorn Books, 1970.

———. *The Brotherhood of the Grape.* Boston: Houghton Mifflin, 1977. Reprint, Santa Rosa: Black Sparrow Press, 1988.

———. *Dago Red.* New York: The Viking Press, 1940.

———. *Dreams from Bunker Hill.* Santa Barbara: Black Sparrow Press, 1982.

———. *John Fante & H. L. Mencken: A Personal Correspondence 1930–1952.* Ed. Michael Moreau and consulting ed. Joyce Fante. Santa Rosa: Black Sparrow Press, 1989.

———. *John Fante: Selected Letters 1932–1981.* Ed. Seamus Cooney. Santa Rosa: Black Sparrow Press, 1991.

———. *Full of Life.* Boston: Little, Brown, 1952. Bantam paperback edition, 1953. Reprint, Santa Rosa: Black Sparrow Press, 1988.

———. *1933 Was a Bad Year.* Santa Barbara: Black Sparrow Press, 1991.

——. *Prologue to Ask the Dust*. Santa Rosa: Black Sparrow Press, 1990.
——. *The Road to Los Angeles*. Santa Barbara: Black Sparrow Press, 1985.
——. *Wait Until Spring, Bandini*. New York: Stackpole Sons, 1938. Reprint, Santa Barbara: Black Sparrow Press, 1983.
——. *West of Rome*. Santa Rosa: Black Sparrow Press, 1986.
——. *The Wine of Youth: Selected Stories*. Santa Barbara: Black Sparrow Press, 1983.

FILMOGRAPHY

Dinky. Warner Bros., 1935. Story by John Fante, Frank Fenton, and Samuel Gibson Brown.
East of the River. Warner Bros., 1940. Story by Fante and Ross B. Wills.
The Golden Fleecing. MGM, 1940. Story by Fante, Frank Fenton, and Lynn Root.
Youth Runs Wild. RKO Radio, 1940. Screenplay by Fante.
My Man and I. MGM, 1952. Screenplay by Fante and Jack Leonard.
Full of Life. Columbia, 1956. Adapted by Fante from his novel.
Jeanne Eagels. Columbia, 1957. Screenplay by Fante, Daniel Fuchs, and Sonya Levien.
A Walk on the Wild Side. Columbia, 1962. Adapted from Nelson Algren's novel by Fante and Edmund Morris.
The Reluctant Saint. Davis-Royal Films International, 1962. Screenplay by Fante and Joseph Petracca.
My Six Loves. Paramount, 1963. Screenplay by Fante, Joseph Calvelli, and William Wood.
Maya. MGM, 1966. Screenplay by Fante.
Something for a Lonely Man. Universal Television, 1968. Screenplay by Fante and Frank Fenton.

SELECTED SECONDARY BIBLIOGRAPHY

Collins, Richard. *John Fante: A Literary Portrait*. Forthcoming from Guernica Editions, 2000.
Cooper, Stephen. "John Fante's Eternal City." In *Los Angeles in Fiction*. Ed. David Fine. Albuquerque: University of New Mexico Press, 1995. 83–99.
——. "Madness and Writing in the Works of Hamsun, Fante and Bukowski." *Genre* 19 (1998): 19–27.
Cooper, Stephen, and David Fine, eds. *John Fante: A Critical Gathering*. Madison, N.J.: Fairleigh Dickinson University Press, 1999.
Donovan, Richard. "John Fante of Roseville." *San Francisco Chronicle: This World*, March 9, 1941, p. 13.
"Fante, John." In *Twentieth Century Authors*. Ed. Stanley J. Kunitz and Howard Haycraft. New York: H. W. Wilson Co., 1942. 433–34.
Fine, David. "Down and Out in Los Angeles: John Fante's *Ask the Dust*," *Californians* 9, no. 2 (September–October 1991): 48–51.
——. "John Fante." *Dictionary of Literary Biography* 130 (1993): 15–162.
Gardaphe, Fred L. "Breaking and Entering." *Forkroads* 1, no. 1 (Fall 1995): 4–14.

Gordon, Neil. "Realization and Recognition: The Art and Life of John Fante." *Boston Review* (October–November 1993): 24–29.

Kordich, Catherine J. *John Fante: His Novels and Novellas.* Forthcoming from Twayne Publishers, 2000.

Mullen, Michael. "John Fante: A Working Checklist." *Bulletin of Bibliography* 41 (1984): 38–41.

Pleasants, Ben. "Stories of Irony from the Hand of John Fante." *Los Angeles Times Book Review*, July 8, 1979, p. 3.

Shacochis, Bob. "Forgotten Son of the Lost Generation." *Vogue* (December 1987): 190 ff.

Spotnitz, Frank. "The Hottest Dead Man in Hollywood." *American Film* XIV, no. 9 (July–August 1989): 40–44, 54.

Ulin, David L. "Back from the Dust." *Los Angeles Times Book Review*, May 14, 1995, p. 9.

Wills, Ross B. "John Fante." *Common Ground* 1 (Spring 1941): 84–90.

ACKNOWLEDGMENTS

This book would not exist without the assistance of Joyce Smart Fante. From the beginning Mrs. Fante agreed with my insistence that a worthwhile biography of her late husband would seek the truth, whether or not the truth was flattering; and then she gave me much of my material and trusted me to make something of it. I have done my best. While I take responsibility for any errors of fact or mistakes in judgment, I am bound to credit Joyce Fante for her courage, honesty and generosity of heart in helping me tell the story right.

I gratefully acknowledge the Literary Trust of John T. Fante and the entire Fante family. Jim Fante, Vickie Fante Cohen, Dan Fante and the late Nick Fante were brave and generous in speaking with me about their father. Tom Fante provided invaluable insights into his brother John's life and the life of the Fante family.

I wish to thank Joyce Fante for permission to quote from John Fante's unpublished letters and manuscripts, as well as from her own unpublished poems, letters, and diaries; and John Martin of Black Sparrow Press for permission to quote from John Fante's published works.

For the encouragement of their early interest in this project I am indebted to Jay Martin, Ronald Gottesman, Gay Talese, Jonathan Galassi, Roger Straus and John Fowles. I am also happy to acknowledge my editor, Ethan Nosowsky, whose unfailing eye for the necessary and the sufficient helped shape and tone the book.

I owe much gratitude to Will Halm for his friendship and legal expertise.

Many members of my family, both immediate and extended and not all mentioned here, were indispensable in the making of this book. My parents, Paul and Betty Cooper, provided computer repairs, on-line research and, thanks to my mother's Dictaphone wizardry, nearly a thousand pages of interview transcriptions. My wife's parents, Sam and Lillian Stawisky, were equally constant in their support. My children, Daniel and Elizabeth, abided their father's long distraction with patience, grace and (usually) gentle good humor. More than anyone else I must thank my wife Janet for her mighty spirit of life and love. This book belongs to all of them.

Many others provided direct assistance, moral support and in some cases long-range inspiration. Special thanks to Dorothy Abrahamse, Joe Aidlin, Ronald Albert, Patricia Alémran, Tony Amodeo, Bob Andrew, Karen Andrew, Buckley and Grace Angell, Bill Armstrong, William Asher, Vera Austin, Libby Azevedo, Tanya Azores, Glenn Bach, Robert Barbera, Mary Baumgartner, Catherine Benamou, Jackson Benson, Jean F. Béranger, Scott Berg, Bill Berkholtz, Al Bezzerides, Jutta Birmele, Virginia Blaisdell, Brian Blanchfield, Rudolph Borchert, Ed Borowiec, Eddie Brandt, Hortense Brant, Leo Braudy, Lesley Brill, Cathy Brody, Charlotte Brown, the late Charles Bukowski, Linda Bukowski, Leonardo Buonomo, Knox Burger, Karen Burman, Mary Bucci Bush, Jamie Byng, the late Herb

Caen, Anne Caiger, Elisabeth Calamari, Darlene Campbell, the late Edward Campiglia, Peggy Campiglia, Frank Cannata, Becky Cape, Paul Capolungo, Maggie Carr, Noelle R. Carter, Larry Castagnola, Carlo Chiarenza, Tom Christie, Joe Cionni, Tom Clark, Barbara Cohen, Michael Cohen, Richard Collins, Ned Comstock, Seamus Cooney, Gino Cooper, Marsha Cooper, Francis Ford Coppola, Lucia Costa, Marty Covey, Ed Cray, Domenic Cretara, Tom Cullen, Jim Curtis, Scott Curtis, Markus Davids, Margaret Leslie Davis, Sally Ogle Davis, Emilie de Brigarde, Tony DeGravina, James J. Delaney, Dino DeLaurentiis, Gill Dennis, Dominique Deruddere, David Detweiler, John Dickson, Rene Diedrich, Gene L. Dinielli, Kathleen DiVito, the late Edward Dmytryk, Doug Domingo-Foraste, Clorinda Donato, Charles Donovan, Theo Douglas, Jeffrey S. Dunn, Doug Dutton, Lois and Robert Dwan, Carol Easton, Gary and Maria Eisenberg, Linda N. España-Maram, Bill Fagelson, John V. Fante, Mary and Dan Fante (Denver), Sharyn Fante, Thomas Fante (Weirton, West Virginia), Thomas Michael Fante, Frank Fata, René Féret, David Fine, Bob Finney, Noel Riley Fitch, Vincent Fitzpatrick, Stefan Foconi, Richard Ford, Kristie French, Della Minici Friedman, Jake Fuchs, Angelo Fusco, Christopher Fusco, Fred L. Gardaphe, Bobby Gardner, Scott Gardner, Philippe Garnier, Frank X. Gaspar, Peggy Gaughan, Dana Gioia, Sallee Gorce, Neil Gordon, Lucy Gray, Joe Grieco, Catherine Grimes, Dale Guerrero, George Guida, Joel Haertling, Oakley Hall, Judith Dwan Hallet, Evelyn Haralson, Russell Harrison, David M. Hays, Jennifer Heath, Joanne Hector, the late Don Heiney, Steve Hendrix, Jeffrey Herr, Zinaida (Sadie) Herrera, Grant Hier, Debbie Hildreth, Rust Hills, Dorothy Hinshaw, Ellenore Hittelman, Wade Hobgood, Elizabeth Hoffman, Norman N. Holland, Andrew Horton, Bob Houser, Wilma Hubbard, Lotte Inuk, James K. Jeffrey, Irene Jones, Thom Jones, Averil J. Kadis, Surya Kalsi, Darrell Kastin, Jack Keeley, Bernice Kert, Jascha Kessler, Marsha Kinder, Eileen Klink, Fred and Paulette Koehler, Kate Kordich, Patricia Kouba, Jon Krampner, Louise Krough, Brigitte J. Kueppers, Gavin Lambert, Helen Landgarten, Mark Laurila, Patrick Lee, Gary Leffew, Jack Lemmon, Beatrice "Honeybee" Lennartz, Randy Lewis, Paulino Lim, Mrs. Darrel Link, Gerald Locklin, Leif Lorentzon, Jan Louter, Mary Lou Luciano, Stefano Luconi, Suzanne Lummis, John Macias, Msgr. Edward Madden, Samuel Maio,

Gerald Mangan, Richard Manly, the late Father Vincent Martin, O.S.B., Carol Matthau, Robert Maxson, Greg McCarty, Dennis McDougal, Thomas McGuane, Louise Capolungo McLean, Sandy McMillan, Iris McWilliams, Wilson Carey McWilliams, Irene Meyer, Lee Ann Meyer, Billie Middleton, Jack Miles, Pete Miller, Kay Mills, Mr. and Mrs. Al Mirtoni, Ray Montalvo, Harle Montgomery, the late Brian Moore, Michael Moreau, Kirsten Moreno, Edmund Morris, Katharine M. Morsberger, Yetive Moss, Michael Mullen, the late Jim Murray, Louise Napolitano-Carmine, Bill Nericcio, Tom Nolan, Daniel Noyes, Frank Noyes, Msgr. James A. O'Callaghan, Tom Odell, Bill Oleson, Jane Osterhaudt, Cecilia Owen, Harry Parkin, John Payne, Julie Payne, David Peck, Tom Peters, Alfred Piccoli, Joe Piccoli, Catherine Pidancet, Adrienne Pilon, Ben Pleasants, Robert Polito, Kendra Poster, Micheal Pounds, Lawrence Clark Powell, Howard Prouty, Don and Diane Put, Donne Raffat, James Ragan, Clara Redmond, Cathy Reed, the Rev. Paul C. Reinert, S. J., Roger Reus, Frances Ring, Carl Rollyson, Leo Romero, Chris Rose, Mike Rose, Claudia Royal, Marilyn Sanders, John Sanford, Aram Saroyan, Bob Shacochis, Budd Schulberg, Roger Schultz, Bill Schwab, Ann Seaman, Jeff Seroy, Martin Sheen, Ernie Sjogren, Leslie Smith, Charlotte Smokler, Frank Spotnitz, Matt Sprinkel, Jim Stanley, Kevin Starr, Victoria Steele, Mark Stein, Francis J. Stoffels, the late Robert K. Straus, Mary Strobel, the late Richard Strobel, Lori Sudeck, Sheila Sullivan, Mark Sundeen, G. Thomas Tansell, Dace Taub, Sherry and Annette Terzian, Sister Louise Clare Tobin, B.V.M., Michael Tolkin, Benedetta Toto, Robert Towne, John Turturro, David L. Ulin, Gina Urbano, Linda Venis, Pasquale Verdicchio, David and Maria Viera, Peter Viertel, Diane Vipond, Cassandra Volpe, Diana Walti, Donald Weber, Steve Weinstein, Mrs. Paul L. Wilcox, Mark Wiley, John Williams, Joy Williams, William Wiser, the late Tom Wood, Paul Yamamoto, Jordan Young, Mohamed Zakariya, Richard D. Zanuck and Ray Zepeda.

I gratefully acknowledge the following institutions and their staffs for assisting me in my research:
Art Special Collections, Charles E. Young Research Library, UCLA; Bancroft Library, University of California at Berkeley; Boulder Public

Library; Carnegie Branch Library for Local History, Boulder Historical Society; Charles von der Ahe Library, Loyola Marymount Library; Cinema-Television Library, University of Southern California; Denver Public Library; Department of Special Collections, Charles E. Young Research Library, UCLA; Enoch Pratt Free Library of Baltimore; Family History Center, Church of Jesus Christ of Latter Day Saints, Los Angeles; Family History Center, Church of Jesus Christ of Latter Day Saints, Torrance, California; Huntington Library, San Marino, California; John Simon Guggenheim Memorial Foundation; Lilly Library, Indiana University; Los Angeles Maritime Museum; Los Angeles Public Library; Margaret Herrick Library, Academy of Motion Picture Arts and Sciences; Mayer Library, American Film Institute; National Archives and Records Administration, Pacific Region, Laguna Niguel, California; New York Public Library; Regional History Center, University of Southern California; Regis University, Alumni Relations; Roseville Historical Society; Roseville Public Library; Special Collections, California State University, Long Beach; UCLA Film and Television Archives; University of Colorado at Boulder, University Library Archives; University of Wyoming, American Heritage Center; Warner Bros. Archives, Doheny Library, University of Southern California; Wilmington Historical Society

INDEX